SECOND EDITION

The Concise Guide to Writing

Rise B. Axelrod
California State University, San Bernardino

Charles R. Cooper
University of California, San Diego

St. Martin's Press
New York

Editor: Jimmy Fleming
Development editor: Carla Kay Samodulski
Managing editor: Patricia Mansfield Phelan
Project editor: Nicholas Webb
Production supervisor: Scott Lavelle
Art director and cover design: Lucy Krikorian
Text design: EriBen Graphics

Library of Congress Catalog Card Number: 95-67053

For information, write:
St. Martin's Press, Inc.
175 Fifth Avenue
New York, NY 10010

ISBN: 0-312-11604-7

Acknowledgments

Ecology Action Centre, © Copyright 1995 The Ecology Action Centre, Halifax, Canada. (Design by Ronald S. Wood/artwork by Rob Hansen). Reprinted by permission.

Carnegie Mellon Lycos, the Lycos™ catalog of the Internet. Copyright © 1994, 1995 Carnegie Mellon University. All rights reserved. Reprinted by permission.

Acknowledgments and copyrights are continued at the back of the book on page 286, which constitutes an extension of the copyright page.

1996

SECOND
EDITION

The
Concise
Guide
to Writing

808.042
A 969
2 ed

Contents

157, 110

v

Guide to Writing

A Writer at Work

Reflecting on Your Writing 53

3   Explaining a Concept 54

Readings

Guide to Writing

5   Arguing a Position   120

A Writer at Work

6 *Proposing a Solution* 153

Readings

Guide to Writing

A Writer at Work

To the Instructor

T*he Concise Guide to Writing*, second edition, aims to show students how writing works and how written texts are shaped by the writing situations from which they arise. Through five essay assignment chapters, students experience three fundamentally different kinds of inquiry and composing: remembering events, explaining information, and convincing readers to take seriously one's judgments, positions, or proposals. Students see how these kinds of thinking and writing are important for them as college students, workers, and citizens. We also aim to show students that reading like a writer, planning essays systematically, getting critical comments on rough drafts, revising thoughtfully, and reflecting on their learning can improve their writing and confidence as writers. *The Concise Guide* challenges students, setting high standards for them with each essay they attempt and providing the support they need to achieve more than they imagined they could.

AN OVERVIEW OF THE BOOK

The Concise Guide to Writing has three sections:

Chapter 1 explains how writing works and what it contributes to thinking and learning. It also introduces students to the writing activities in the assignment chapters of Part One.

Part One   Chapters 2 through 6 present five different writing assignments: Remembering an Event, Explaining a Concept, Justifying an Evaluation, Arguing a Position, and Proposing a Solution. Instructors may choose among these chapters or teach them in any sequence that meets the needs of the course. The assignment chapters are arranged here to move students from writing about personal experience and observation to writing that calls for synthesis of information and for reasoned argument.

Each assignment chapter in Part One follows the same organizational plan.

- Several academic writing situations show students where they may encounter this kind of writing in their other courses.
- A For Group Inquiry activity gives students practice in the kind of writing under study in the chapter.
- A set of readings, including published writings as well as a student essay, each one accompanied by a critical apparatus, helps students explore the kind of writing.
- A summary details the purpose and audience and the basic features of the type of writing.

- A flexible Guide to Writing gives the chapter's writing assignment and escorts students through the composing process.
- A Writer at Work section shows how the student writer represented in the chapter's readings worked through some aspect of the writing process.
- A Reflecting on Your Writing activity encourages students to consider what they have learned while writing the essay.

Part Two   Chapters 7 through 11 look at various strategies for writing and research. Students learn how to use strategies for cueing readers, such as orienting statements, paragraphing, cohesive devices, and transitions. They also learn about strategies for writing to discover and develop ideas, for reading critically and evaluating arguments, for doing research both in the library and on the Internet, and for using and acknowledging sources.

NOTEWORTHY FEATURES

The Concise Guide to Writing contains several special features that contribute to the book's widespread acceptance. Chief among these are the practical Guides to Writing, the integration of reading and writing, the real-world kinds of writing assignments, and the promotion of collaborative work and group inquiry.

Practical Guides to Writing   In this book, we do not merely talk about the composing process; we also offer practical, flexible Guides to Writing that escort students through the entire composing process, from invention through revision and self-evaluation. Thus, this text is more than just a rhetoric for students to refer to occasionally. It is a guidebook that will help them to write. Commonsensical and easy to follow, the writing guides teach students to assess rhetorical situations, identify the kinds of information they need, ask probing questions and find answers, and organize their writing to achieve their purposes most effectively. The Guides to Writing also enable students to give and receive constructive advice for revising their drafts.

Systematic Integration of Reading and Writing   Because we see a close relationship between reading critically and writing well, *The Concise Guide to Writing* combines reading instruction with writing instruction. Each assignment chapter in Part One introduces one kind of writing, which students are led to consider both as readers and writers. The readings are each followed by a set of questions and commentary designed to make students aware of how they, as readers, understand and think critically about what others have written. At the same time, students become aware of the types of decisions all writers make. They are also challenged to apply these insights to their own writing as they imagine their prospective readers, set goals, and write and revise their drafts.

Real-World Kinds of Writing and Writing Situations   The writing assignments in Part One reflect the great diversity in the nonfiction being published in the United States today. Students gain a substantive introduction to the reading and writing of autobiography, explanation, and argument. Though we specify the type

of writing for each assignment, students are encouraged to choose their own subjects and designate their readers; they thereby establish a commitment to the
subjects they choose as well as learn the consequences of their choice for particular
readers. Students practice the various modes of writing—definition, classification,
illustration, narration, description, comparison and contrast—within the context
of purposeful real-world discourse.

Promotion of Collaboration and Group Inquiry   Each Part One assignment
chapter begins with a collaborative activity that invites students to rehearse the
kind of writing under study in the chapter. In addition, the readings in these
chapters are accompanied by questions for discussion designed to provoke
thoughtful group inquiry into the social and political dimensions of the reading.
Finally, the Guides to Writing include two specific collaborative activities that are
fundamental to good writing everywhere. The first, occurring near the end of the
invention stage, asks students to work in small groups to try out their writing
plans, to get advice from student readers on improving those plans and on how
best to approach their audiences, and to assess their interests in and commitments
to their chosen subjects. The second collaborative activity, Getting Critical Comments, gives students comprehensive and specific advice on how to revise their
classmates' drafts. Occurring at a crucial point in the writing process—just as
students are preparing to revise their own drafts—the activity also brings together
all that students have learned about the type of writing covered in the chapter.

NEW TO THIS EDITION

In this new edition of *The Concise Guide to Writing*, we have increased the emphasis
on academic writing assignments involving some form of argumentation, provided
students with more strategies for completing the assignments, and generally made
the book easier for students to use. Consequently, we have added new chapters
on justifying an evaluation, reading critically, conducting research in the library
and on the Internet, and using and acknowledging sources. A new critical thinking
activity—Reflecting on Your Writing—appears in each chapter in Part One. We
have also changed to a new spiral binding and included tips on using computers
on the inside front and back covers.

A New Chapter on Justifying an Evaluation   Chaper 4, "Justifying an Evaluation," teaches students how to evaluate a reading, movie, television program, or
some other subject. This kind of writing is not only enjoyable for students, but it
also teaches them how to think critically about their likes and dislikes and to
recognize that others may have different judgments. The chapter emphasizes that
in making an evaluation, writers use careful analysis to support their judgments.

A New Chapter on Reading Critically   Chapter 9, "Strategies for Reading Critically," presents several useful strategies for reading with a critical eye, including
outlining and summarizing, evaluating an argument, and reflecting on challenges
to one's beliefs and values. These critical reading strategies, which students can

use in their other courses as well, complement the attention given to critical reading in the writing assignment chapters and elsewhere in the book.

Two New Chapters on Research and Documentation   Chapter 10, "Strategies for Doing Research in the Library and on the Internet," provides comprehensive support for library and electronic research, while Chapter 11, "Strategies for Using and Acknowledging Sources," presents guidelines for integrating the results of that research into an essay. Chapter 11 also includes information on integrating quotations, paraphrasing and summarizing, and avoiding plagiarism, as well as on the MLA and APA styles of documentation.

A New Critical Thinking Activity   Each Part One assignment chapter concludes with a new activity, Reflecting on Your Writing. It encourages students to think critically about and reflect on what they learned from the writing assignment by focusing on how they identified and dealt with one specific problem encountered during the writing process.

A New Spiral Binding   The book's new spiral binding allows it to lie flat, making it easier for students to work with the Guides to Writing and other resources, whether they are on their own, in groups, or at the computer.

Tips on Using the Computer   The inside front and back covers offer useful tips for students working either in a writing lab, in a computerized classroom, or at their own computers at home.

USING THIS TEXT WITH OTHER RESOURCES

The Concise Guide to Writing, with its five major essay assignments, provides all that might be required in a first-year composition course. It could usefully be supplemented, however, by a handbook of usage and style, a composition reader, or a variety of trade books.

Instructors considering a rhetorically arranged reader would want to ensure that its readings and assignments align with those in *The Concise Guide.* One such reader is our own *Reading Critically, Writing Well,* fourth edition (St. Martin's Press). While both books are based on the same systematic approach to reading and writing, *The Concise Guide* offers more comprehensive support for composing than *Reading Critically.* Also available is *The Great American Bologna Festival,* second edition (St. Martin's Press), a collection of student essays written using our Guides to Writing. Instructors accustomed to assigning a thematic reader may find among its suggested writing assignments ones that match those in *The Concise Guide*'s five assignment chapters. An instructor considering trade books might choose an autobiography for students to read while working their way through the "Remembering an Event" chapter, and books on current social problems to read with the "Arguing a Position" and "Proposing a Solution" chapters. The *Instructor's Resource Manual* that accompanies this text contains teaching strategies, discussions of the readings, a chapter on general classroom techniques, and a selected bibliography in composition studies.

ACKNOWLEDGMENTS

Our debt grows year by year to those teachers and students who have used *The St. Martin's Guide to Writing*, on which *The Concise Guide* is based, and who have so generously encouraged and advised us.

The staff at St. Martin's Press continues to challenge and support us. We think they are remarkably creative, hardworking, and efficient. They have become a valued part of our professional lives. In particular, we thank Carla Samodulski, senior development editor at St. Martin's Press. A critical reader and strong writer herself, Carla has contributed creatively in many ways to this new edition. More important than her laudable thoroughness and efficiency have been her encouragement, collegiality, and problem solving. Every textbook writer would wish for an editor like Carla.

For this new edition of *The Concise Guide*, we also gratefully acknowledge the special contributions to Chapter 10 from Debora Person, University of Wyoming Law Library, and M. A. Syverson, University of Texas at Austin. Debora Person provided useful comments on the section on using the library. M. A. Syverson wrote the section on using the Internet to conduct research.

Many instructors from across the country have helped us to improve *The Concise Guide to Writing* by providing valuable feedback and commentary. For responding to a detailed questionnaire about the first edition, we thank James E. Anderson, University of Michigan at Flint; Frederick J. Antczak, University of Iowa; Kathryn N. Benzel, University of Nebraska at Kearney; Steven L. Berg, Kirtland Community College; Margaret Thompson Bieniek, New Hampshire College; Susan Brant, Humboldt State University; Donna M. Budani, University of Delaware; Ann Bukowski, Rochester Community College; Tracy D. Duckart, College of the Redwoods; Keith Fynaardt, Northern Illinois University; Patricia L. Geddes, Cypress College; Susan George, Northern Illinois University; Chandler Gilman, Lyndon State College; Cynthia Hagen, New Hampshire College; Pauline Harding, Hawkeye Community College; Mandy Harris, University of Minnesota, Twin Cities; Phyllis Hastings, Saginaw Valley State University; Kevin Heath, Cedarville College; Judith Hinman, College of the Redwoods; Robert Johnson, Midwestern State University; Pamela B. Kessler, College of the Redwoods; Suzanne M. Koons, Massachusetts Institute of Technology; Terry Lehr, SUNY at Brockport; John S. Lusk, St. Clair County Community College; Ann M. Lynch, College of the Redwoods; Robyn D. Lynn, Westmont College; Timothy F. McGinn, Oakland University; Kathryn Howd Machan, Ithaca College; Lynnea J. McHenry, Hawkeye Community College; Gordon E. Madson, Crafton Hills College; Salome C. Nnoromele, Cedarville College; Tami Phenix, University of Cincinnati; Carol Rainey, University of Cincinnati; Karen K. Reid, Midwestern State University; Maryanne Reigstad, Buffalo State College; Barbara C. Rhodes, Mohawk Valley Community College at Utica; David Rife, Lycoming College; Edwina Portelle Romero, New Mexico Highlands University; Robert E. Rubin, Wright State University; Karl Schnapp, Bridgewater State College; Carole Shaffer-Koros, Kean College; Becky Soglin, University of Iowa; Edward Spencer, Cedarville College; Diane Terezakis,

Pace University at Pleasantville; Darryl L. Tippens, Abilene Christian University; Nancy Vorkink, Community College of Denver; John Waite, Northern Illinois University; C. Dirk Wethington, Northern Illinois University; Ann Whelan, Rochester Community College; and Kenneth Womack, Northern Illinois University.

For carefully reviewing a draft of this second edition, we thank Susan George, Northern Illinois University; Judith A. Hinman, College of the Redwoods; Paul Kleinpoppen, Florida Community College; Lynnea McHenry, Hawkeye Community College; Joel Perkins, Indiana State University; Karen K. Reid, Midwestern State University; Karl Schnapp, Bridgewater State College; and Charlotte Smith, Virginia Polytechnic Institute and State University.

Charles acknowledges the inspiration and advice of the other writing member of his family, his daughter Susanna, associate editor for the McClatchy Newspaper Corporation and member of the editorial board at the *Sacramento Bee*. Susanna is an exemplary writer-in-the-world—informed, persistent, collaborative, personally courageous, and master of her genres. Rise wishes to thank her husband, Steven, for his enduring love, and to dedicate this edition with love to her mother Edna Borenstein, who always told her just to do the best she could—and had faith that she would.

Rise Axelrod
Charles Cooper

Introduction

Why is writing important? Is there a connection between writing and thinking? Can writing be learned? What does reading have to do with learning to write? How can I learn to write more effectively and efficiently? These are some of the questions you may be asking as you begin this writing course. Read on— for *The Concise Guide to Writing* offers some answers for these and other questions you may have.

WHY WRITING IS IMPORTANT

Writing has wide-ranging implications for the way we think and learn, as well as for our chances of success, our personal development, and our relations with other people.

Writing Influences the Way People Think

First, writing encourages us to be organized, logical, even creative in our thinking. Moreover, it urges us to ask questions, to look critically at what others have to say as well as what we ourselves think.

The grammatical and textual conventions of writing impose a certain kind of order on our thinking. To write comprehensible sentences and paragraphs, we need to put words in a certain order: follow subjects with verbs, coordinate parallel ideas, subordinate the particular to the general. And from different kinds of writing, we learn different ways of developing our thoughts: reflecting critically on our own behavior in autobiography; distinguishing fact from opinion in concept explanations; making judgments based on evidence and the dialectic between opposing points of view in position papers. Further, we learn to analyze and evaluate ideas and to synthesize what we learn from others and experience first-hand. In all these ways, writing fosters habits of critical inquiry.

> Writing keeps me from believing everything I read. —*Gloria Steinem*
>
> Those who are learning to compose and arrange their sentences with accuracy and order are learning, at the same time, to think with accuracy and order.
> —*Hugh Blair*

Writing Contributes to the Way We Learn

When we take notes in class or as we read, writing helps us sort information and highlight what is important. Taking notes helps us remember what we are learning and yields a written record to review later. Outlining or summarizing provides an overview of a new subject and also fosters close analysis of it. Annotating as we read, with underlining and marginal comments, involves us in conversation— even debate—with other writers. Thus, writing helps us learn effectively and think critically.

And because we as writers are always composing new meanings, writing helps us find and establish our own knowledge and ideas. It allows us to bring together and connect new and old ideas: as we discover and understand new concepts, writing helps us relate them to other ideas. Thus, writing helps us test, clarify, and extend our understanding of the world.

> I write to understand as much as to be understood. —*Elie Wiesel*
>
> The mere process of writing is one of the most powerful tools we have for clar- ifying our own thinking. I am never as clear about any matter as when I have just finished writing about it. —*James Van Allen*

Writing Promotes Success in College and on the Job

Because writing encourages us to think critically and helps us learn, it also makes a significant contribution to academic and professional success. Students whose writing is logically organized, well supported, and inventive usually do well in courses throughout the curriculum. Getting a job also depends partially on writing a persuasive application letter, and for many positions advancement requires fa- cility in writing memos, letters, reports, and proposals.

> The aim of school is to produce citizens who are able to communicate with each other, to defend points of view, and to criticize. . . . Writing is not just another subject. There is a symbiotic relationship between writing and thinking.
> —*Albert Shanker*

Writing Fosters Personal Development

Through writing, we learn to reflect deeply on our personal experience and ex- amine critically our most basic assumptions; thus, we come eventually to under- stand ourselves better. Moreover, becoming an author confers authority. It gives us the confidence to assert our own opinions, even in situations when others are likely to disagree.

> Writing is the act of saying *I*, of imposing oneself upon other people, of saying *listen to me, see it my way, change your mind.* —*Joan Didion*
>
> Writing has been for a long time my major tool for self-instruction and self- development. —*Toni Cade Bambara*

Writing Connects Us to the World

As writing contributes to the way we think, it also impels us to communicate our thoughts and feelings, to take part in the conversations around us. The impulse to write can be as urgent as the need to share an experience with a friend, to question an argument in a book, or to respond to a provocative comment in class discussion.

As writers, we speak out for many different reasons: to entertain, to let readers know what we think or how we feel, to influence readers' decisions, actions, or beliefs. We may even confront readers, presenting them with a critical view of their attitudes and behavior; in this sense, writing can be a powerful political tool, especially for those who are generally silenced or marginalized.

> Writing is a struggle against silence. —*Carlos Fuentes*
>
> Writing is a political instrument . . . a way to describe and control [your] circumstances. —*James Baldwin*

EXERCISE 1.1

Reflect on the role writing has played in your education and personal life. Maybe you can recall a time—writing for yourself or for a school assignment—when writing enabled you to think in a way that surprised you. What kind of writing were you doing and what did you discover? Or think of an occasion when you experienced great success with a school assignment. How did this come about and what did you achieve? Or perhaps once you urgently needed to communicate with someone—in anger, love, hope, jealousy, disagreement—and writing seemed the best way to do it. Describe this occasion. What brought it about, what did you say, and what was the response? Write a brief essay, giving specific examples of how writing has affected your life.

HOW WRITING IS LEARNED

Writing is important. But can it be learned? This is a crucial question because writing has for centuries been veiled in mystery. Many people think of writing as magical or the result of natural talent. They assume "real" writers can dash off a perfect draft in one sitting with minimal effort. They believe that if you don't write brilliantly from the start, you'll never learn to write well. However, research shows that these assumptions are wrong, writing can be learned: that in fact, while some people may seem to have a gift for writing, virtually anyone can learn to write confidently enough to handle the writing required in college and on the job.

> I believe in miracles in every area of life *except* writing. —*Isaac Bashevis Singer*
>
> Learning to write well takes time and much effort, but it can be done.
> —*Margaret Mead*

As you learn to write, you need to know three things:

- How written texts work
- How the writing process works
- How to think critically about your learning

These three kinds of learning are interdependent: your development as a writer depends on your knowing all three and understanding this interdependence. Written texts are not all alike. Because they differ, they require different writing processes to produce different kinds of written products. In this way, process and product are inextricably related, but in complex ways because the social situations calling for writing are so various. As you write in different situations, you need to reflect on what you are doing and learning. Such reflection reinforces and extends your learning.

How Written Texts Work

How a text works is a function of what it's for—its purpose and audience. Some texts—position papers, for example—try to convince readers to take the writer's point of view seriously. Other kinds of texts serve different purposes: an autobiographical essay conveys the significance of a particular event in the writer's life; a proposal urges readers to take certain actions to solve a problem; an explanation informs readers about something they don't know. Kinds of texts, then, can be categorized by their purposes and audiences. These categories are called writing *genres.*

Each genre has its own distinctive formal features and content. Autobiographical event essays, for example, are narrative in form and include descriptive detail and an indication of the event's significance. In contrast, proposals are argumentative in form, giving reasons why readers should adopt the proposed solution.

Although there's a lot of variation from one text to another within the same genre (no two autobiographies, for example, are exactly the same) texts in a genre nonetheless follow a general pattern. This textual patterning allows for a certain amount of predictability, without which communication would be difficult, if not impossible. Language—whether spoken or written—is a system of social interaction. Everyone who speaks the same language learns to recognize certain patterns—what particular words mean when used in different contexts, how words should be ordered to make sentences comprehensible, how sentences can be related to one another to make coherent paragraphs and essays, and so forth. These language patterns make communication possible.

To learn to read and write, we have to become familiar with the patterns or conventions of written texts. As readers, we develop expectations that enable us to anticipate where a text is going so that we can make sense of it as we read. Similarly, as writers we learn how to order and present our thoughts in language patterns that readers can recognize and follow. If you are writing a position paper, for example, you need to know that readers expect claims to be supported by relevant reasons and evidence.

Working within a genre does not mean, however, that writing must be formulaic or mechanical. Each genre has basic features but these are not a formula; rather, they provide broad frameworks within which writers are free to create. Most writers, in fact, find that working in a framework allows them to be more creative, not less. Some even blur the boundaries between genres, for example, by personalizing argument with autobiographical stories.

Change, as well as predictability, is built into the language system. Ultimately, what is considered proper or effective must reflect changing social contexts. New forms of expression or genres emerge, especially for those who have traditionally been silenced.

> To write as a complete Caribbean woman, or man for that matter, demands of us retracing the African part of ourselves. It means finding the art forms of our ancestors and speaking in the *patois* forbidden us. It means also, I think, mixing in the forms taught us by the oppressor, undermining his language and co-opting his style, and turning it to our purpose. —*Michelle Cliff*

How We Learn to Write Texts That Work

To learn the conventions of a particular genre, you need to read examples of the genre. At the same time, you should also practice writing in the genre.

> Read, read, read. . . . Just like a carpenter who works as an apprentice and studies the master. Read! —*William Faulkner*

Reading is crucial. As you read examples of a genre, you begin to recognize the predictable patterns as well as the possibilities for innovation. This knowledge is stored in memory and used both when you read and when you write in the genre.

Experienced writers read and learn from positive examples as well as negative ones. Sometimes, they focus on a particular problem—how to write realistic-sounding dialogue, for example. They don't look for answers in a single model, but sample many texts to see how different writers work with this feature of the genre. This is not imitation, but education. Like artists and craftspeople of all kinds, writers have always learned from other writers.

> I went back to the good nature books that I had read. And I analyzed them. I wrote outlines of whole books—outlines of chapters—so that I could see their structure. And I copied down their transitional sentences or their main sentences or their closing sentences or their lead sentences. I especially paid attention to how these writers made transitions between paragraphs and scenes.
>
> —*Annie Dillard*

EXERCISE 1.2

We've said that to learn to write in a particular genre, you need to read texts in that genre. To test this idea, make two lists: (1) list the genres you've read recently (such as explanations of how to do something, stories, autobiographies, reports of current events, opinion pieces, reviews evaluating something); and (2) list the genres you've written in and out of school. Based on your experience, does it help to have read something in the genre you are trying to write? Why, or why not?

How the Writing Process Works

Have you ever tried the dangerous method of writing? You begin by writing the first word of the introduction and write straight through to the last word of the conclusion. No planning or trying out ideas before writing; no adding, cutting, or revising as you write; no help from friends or teachers; no second drafts or second thoughts.

Desperate students, the night before a paper is due, may try the dangerous method. But it isn't a very effective way to write. All writers need to develop a process that will help them think critically about their subject and master the genre. They need to make writing a true process of discovery.

> I don't see writing as a communication of something already discovered, as "truths" already known. Rather, I see writing as a job of experiment. It's like any discovery job; you don't know what's going to happen until you try it.
> —*William Stafford*

Research on how writers write shows that the writing process is recursive, rather than linear. Instead of going from one word to the next, from introduction straight through to conclusion, the experience of writing is more like taking a path up a hill full of switchbacks, making you feel you're covering old ground when you're really rising to a new level.

Few writers begin with a complete understanding of their subject. Most use writing as a process of learning, recording ideas and information they've collected, exploring connections and implications, letting the writing lead them to greater understanding. As they develop their ideas and plan their draft, writers set goals for their writing: goals for the whole essay (to confront readers or inspire them, for example) and goals for particular passages (to make a sentence emphatic or include details in a paragraph). While writing, they often pause to reread what they've written to see whether they are satisfactorily fulfilling their goals. Rereading may lead to further invention and problem solving, to rewording or reorganizing, or even to reconsidering some goals. This continual shifting of attention is what makes the writing process recursive. Invention doesn't stop when drafting begins; it continues throughout the process. Most writers plan and revise their plans; they draft and revise their drafts; they write and read what they've written, then write some more. Even when they have a final draft, most writers reread it one more time—proofreading to edit for clarity, grammar, and spelling.

> You are always going back and forth between the outline and the writing, bringing them closer together, or just throwing out the outline and making a new one. —*Annie Dillard*

Experienced writers depend on the writing process to lead them to new ideas and insights. Many writers claim that they write in order to discover what they think.

> How do I know what I think until I see what I say. —*E. M. Forster*

Seasoned writers don't wait for inspiration. They work at their writing, knowing it takes time and perseverence. The hard work comes in thinking things out. Writers all have promising ideas, but until they've developed them in writing, they can't know if their ideas make sense or lead anywhere.

Don't think and then write it down. Think on paper. —*Harvey Kemelman*

Once immersed in invention—figuring out what they want to say about the subject, contemplating what readers already think about it, and so forth—most writers find that they continue the process even when away from their desks. Taking a walk, having a conversation, even dreaming can help the mind see connections or solve problems that had proved frustrating earlier.

I never quite know when I'm not writing. —*James Thurber*

Like most creative activities, writing is a form of problem solving. As they work on a draft, most writers continually discover and try to solve writing problems—how to bring a scene to life, how to handle objections, whether to begin with this point or that. The more writers know about the subject and genre, the better they can anticipate and solve problems. Experienced writers develop a repertoire of invention and writing strategies for solving problems they are likely to encounter. These are the tools of the trade.

Writing is probably like a scientist thinking about some scientific problem, or an engineer about an engineering problem. —*Doris Lessing*
You have to work problems out for yourself on paper. Put the stuff down and read it—to see if it works. —*Joyce Cary*

Although many writers do much of their work alone, writing does not have to be a solitary activity. Most writers share their ideas as well as their writing, actively seeking constructive critical comments from friends and colleagues. Playwrights, poets, and novelists attend writers' workshops, where other writers can read their drafts and offer suggestions for revising. Engineers, business executives, scientists, and government workers do much of their writing collaboratively, in teams.

For excellence, the presence of others is always required. —*Hannah Arendt*
I like working collaboratively from time to time. I like fusing ideas into one vision. I like seeing that vision come to life with other people who know exactly what it took to get there. —*Amy Tan*

EXERCISE 1.3

Writing is like jumping into a freezing lake and slowly coming to the surface.
—*A student*

To me, writing is a horseback ride into heaven and hell and back. I am grateful if I can crawl back alive. —*Thomas Sanchez*

How would you describe your own writing process? Think of a simile (*Writing is like* _____) or a metaphor (*Writing is* _____) that best expresses your view of writing. Compare your similes or metaphors with your classmates'. What do they suggest about your feelings toward writing?

How We Learn a Writing Process That Works

As a student learning to write, you need to develop a writing process that is flexible and yet provides structure, doesn't oversimplify the process but doesn't overwhelm you either, helps you learn about your subject and about writing the kind of essay you're attempting. What you need are the Guides to Writing in Part One of this book. These guides suggest what you need to think about for each different writing situation. The first few times you write in a new genre, you can rely on these guidelines. Until you've become familiar with the basic features and strategies of each genre, the guides provide a scaffolding to support your work.

When engaging in any new and complex activity—driving, playing an instrument, skiing, or writing—we have to learn procedures or routines. These basically break down the activity into a series of stages or steps. In learning to play tennis, for example, you can isolate lobbing from volleying, or work on your backhand or serve. Similarly, in writing about an autobiographical event, you might first recall what happened, then fill in details of the scene or reflect on the event's significance. At each point you focus your attention on one problem or issue at a time. Dividing the process in this way makes a complex writing task manageable without oversimplifying it.

> You know when you think about writing a book, you think it is overwhelming. But, actually, you break it down into tiny little tasks any moron could do.
>
> —*Annie Dillard*

EXERCISE 1.4

Describe how you normally write. How much time do you spend thinking and making notes before writing a draft? What kinds of things do you do to help with invention—read what others have written, talk with friends, do freewriting, cluster your ideas, or whatever? How many drafts do you usually write? Do you share your drafts with friends or teachers to get their critical comments? What do you do when you revise a draft—change the wording, rearrange parts, cut or add whole sections? Do you proofread for clarity, grammar, and spelling? If so, at what point in the process?

How to Think Critically about Your Learning

Research on learning makes it clear that thinking about your learning helps you remember what you've learned. It also helps you continue learning by bringing to mind what you've forgotten or didn't realize you knew.

Learning to write is like learning a foreign language. As young children, we are immersed in spoken language and acquire it naturally, almost effortlessly. In contrast, learning to write requires conscious effort. As beginners, we need to think about what we're doing—what verb tense to use, whether to use slang or more formal words, whether to concede a point or try to refute it, and so on.

As you practice different kinds, or genres, of writing, you will find that many of your decisions do not require conscious attention. You will be able to rely on strategies you know usually produce effective writing for you in that genre. But these strategies will not work in every case simply because every writing situation is unique. When you encounter a problem, you have to shift gears and deliberately seek a new way to solve the problem.

To find solutions, you have to bring to consciousness your knowledge of the genre and the writing process. Observations of writers at work show that experienced writers often reread what they have written to analyze and evaluate the approach they've taken to a writing problem. This reflection on what works and what does not helps writers anticipate and solve problems. It also helps them feel more competent and in charge of the process.

> Blot out, correct, insert, refine,
> Enlarge, diminish, interline,
> Be mindful, when invention fails,
> To scratch your head, and bite your nails. —*Jonathan Swift*

How We Learn from Our Writing Experiences

The exercises in this chapter are designed to help you begin thinking, writing, and talking with others about your writing experiences. As we've seen, such self-reflection is a key to learning to be a better writer. Each assignment chapter in Part One of this book concludes with the section Reflecting on Your Writing, which gives you an opportunity to look back and analyze your own problem-solving process.

> Always I think at the end, I see how the whole ought to have been written.
> —*Virginia Woolf*

> A writer is not so much someone who has something to say as he is someone who has found a process that will bring about new things he would not have thought of. —*William Stafford*

EXERCISE 1.5

What do you hope to learn in this course? Write a brief account of your strengths and weaknesses as a writer. What specific improvements do you hope to make in your writing—in the texts you produce as well as the process you use?

USING THIS BOOK

The book is divided into two major sections. *Part One* (Chapters 2–6) offers writing assignments for several important genres of nonfiction prose: autobiography, explanation, evaluation, position paper, and proposal. *Part Two* (Chapters 7–11) presents strategies for keeping readers oriented, for doing all-purpose invention, and for reading with a critical eye. It also provides guidelines for conducting research in the library and on the Internet and for acknowledging sources.

Each writing assignment chapter in Part One includes three readings in the genre under study so you can see how written texts of that kind work. Discussion of purpose and audience and a summary of the basic features and strategies of the genre precede the Guide to Writing, which leads you through the process of writing an essay of your own. Each chapter concludes with a Reflecting on Your Writing section to reinforce what you learned about writing in that genre.

The *readings* in Chapters 2–6, written by professional writers and college students, have been selected to reflect a wide range of topics and voices. By reading these selections with a critical eye, you will see the many different ways writers use the genres. Each selection is accompanied by questions and commentary to help you learn about how written texts in the genre work. Questions *for discussion* invite you to explore with other students the social dimensions of the reading; questions *for analysis* focus on key textual features and writing strategies; suggestions *for your own writing* offer topics you might write about; and the *commentary* points out additional features and strategies.

The *Guide to Writing* in each assignment chapter offers detailed guidelines for writing an essay in the genre presented, including help in invention and research, planning and drafting, getting critical comments, and revising and editing.

Invention and Research

Each Guide to Writing begins with invention activities designed to help you find a topic, discover what you already know about the topic, consider your purpose and audience, research the topic further to see what others have written about it, and develop your ideas.

Invention is not something you can skip. It is the basic ongoing preoccupation of all writing. As writers, we cannot choose *whether* to invent; we can only decide *how*.

Invention can be especially productive when it is systematic—and when it is written down. Not only does it focus your attention on your purpose and audience, but it also helps you identify and solve problems. Exploratory writing can free you for awhile from the responsibility of composing coherent and grammatical sentences and paragraphs and thus allow you to write more freely about your topic—turning writing into a mode of discovery.

Invention work may help you at several stages: while exploring your topic, while drafting, and while revising. The special advantage of the invention activities in each Part One chapter is that they focus on the issues of a particular genre of writing.

Use Writing to Explore Your Ideas

You can use invention writing to gather your thoughts and see where they lead. Simply try writing for five to ten minutes. The key to exploratory writing is to refrain from censoring yourself. Explore your ideas freely, letting one idea lead to another. Later you can reread what you've written and select the most promising ideas to develop.

Focus on One Issue at a Time

Explore your topic systematically by dividing it into its component parts and exploring them one at a time. For example, instead of trying to think of your whole argument, focus on one reason and the evidence you could use to support it, or focus on how you might refute one objection to your argument.

Give Your Ideas Time to Percolate

Begin the invention process well enough in advance of the deadline so that your thinking can develop fully. Spread your invention over several days, allowing your mind time to work on the topic.

Planning and Drafting

Once an initial period of invention is completed, you should review what you have learned about your topic and start to plan your essay. The Guides to Writing provide help—from setting goals to organizing ideas and information to achieve those goals. Planning requires you to put your ideas into a coherent, purposeful order appropriate to your readers; drafting challenges you to find the words that will be understandable and interesting for those readers. Invention continues as you draft, for you will make further discoveries about your topic as you work. But drafting requires you to shift your focus from generating new ideas and gathering further information to forging new and meaningful relations among your ideas and information. In Chapter 7, "Strategies for Cueing Readers," you will find strategies for guiding a reader through your writing. These orienting techniques help readers follow the logic and organization of an essay.

As you begin your first draft, you should try to keep in mind a number of helpful and practical points, many of which assist professional writers as they begin drafting.

Choose the Best Time and Place

You can write a draft any time and any place, as you probably already know. Writing gets done under the most surprising conditions. Drafting is likely to go smoothly, however, if you choose a time and place ideally suited for sustained and thoughtful work. The experience of writers (reported mainly in interviews) suggests that you need a place where you can concentrate for a few hours without repeated interruptions. Many writers find one place where they write best, and they return to that place whenever they have to write. Try to find such a place for yourself.

Make Revision Easy

Revision is easiest when you compose on a computer because you can add, delete, and move individual words or long passages without retyping. In fact, revising is so easy on a computer that you might possibly delete something you later want to use. To prevent this problem, simply save and number each version rather than typing over it. Then you can use windows to compare the different drafts or, if you prefer, print them out and compare them.

If you can't use a computer, make revision easier by writing on only one side of the page, leaving wide margins, and writing on every second or third line.

Set Reasonable Goals

Divide the task into manageable bits. A goal of completing a long essay may be so intimidating that it keeps you from starting. Aim instead for a small part of the essay—one section or paragraph—at a time.

Lower Your Expectations

Be satisfied with less-than-perfect writing. Remember, you are working on a draft that you will revise. Approach the draft as an experiment or an exercise. Try things out. Follow digressions. Later, you can always go back and cross out a sentence or a section. And do not be critical about your writing; save the criticism until you've gotten some distance from your draft.

Do Easy Parts First

Try not to agonize over the first sentence or paragraph. Just write. If you have trouble with the introduction, write an anecdote or example or assertion first, if that seems easier. If you have a lot of information, start with the part you understand best. If you get stuck at a difficult spot, skip over it and go on to an easier part. Just getting started can be difficult, but doing the simple parts first may ease this difficulty. If you put off getting started, your work will be rushed and late. Your ideas will not grow and change, and you will thus shut off your chances for important new insights about your topic. By starting late, you will increase your fear of writing; but by starting early with an easy part, you will find writing easier and more enjoyable. You will also do your best work.

Guess at Words, Spelling, Facts

If you cannot think of just the right word, or if you have forgotten an important fact, just keep on drafting. You can search out the fact or find the elusive word later. If you cannot remember how to spell a word, guess and keep going. Later, you can look it up in a dictionary. Inexperienced writers lose large amounts of time puzzling over a word or spelling or trying to recall a specific fact. Sometimes they become completely blocked.

Write Quickly

If you have reasonable goals, have not set your expectations too high, and are doing the easy parts first, then you should be able to draft quickly. Say what you want to say and move on. Review your notes, make a plan, and then put your notes aside. You can always refer to them later if you need an exact quote or fact. Now and then, of course, you will want to reread what you have written, but do not reread obsessively. Return to drafting new material as soon as possible. Avoid editing or revising during this stage. You need not have everything exactly right in the draft. If you want to delete a phrase or sentence, draw a line through it or use your word processor's strike-out function, in case you want to use the phrase or sentence later.

Take Short Breaks—and Reward Yourself!

Drafting can be hard work, and you may need to take a break to refresh yourself. But be careful not to wander off for too long or you may lose momentum. Set small goals and reward yourself regularly. That makes it easier to stay at the task of drafting.

Getting Critical Comments

After you have finished drafting your essay, you should make every effort to have it read by someone else. A critical reader's comments and advice often provide valuable information about improving your draft. Experienced writers very often seek advice from others.

To evaluate someone else's draft, you need to read with a critical eye. You must be both positive and skeptical—positive in that you try to identify what is workable and promising in the draft, skeptical in that you question the writer's assumptions and decisions. Each writing assignment chapter in Part One offers guidelines for getting critical comments on a draft. Here is some general advice on reading any draft critically.

Make a Record of Your Reading

While talking over your impressions of a draft may be pleasurable and useful, you can be most helpful to the writer by putting your ideas on paper. When you write down your comments and suggestions—either on the draft or on another piece of paper—you leave a record that can be used later when it is time to revise.

Read First for an Overall Impression

On first reading, try not to be distracted by errors of spelling, punctuation, or word choice. Look at big issues: a clear focus, a compelling presentation, forcefulness of argument, novelty and quality of ideas. What seems particularly good? What problems do you see? All you need to say is how the draft struck you initially: what you think it was trying to do and how well it did it. Write just a few sentences expressing your initial reaction.

Read Again to Analyze the Draft

This second reading focuses on individual parts of the draft, bringing to bear what you know about the genre and what you already know about the subject. In reading the draft at this level, you must shift your attention from one aspect of the essay to another. Consider how well the opening paragraphs introduce the essay and prepare you to understand and accept it. Attend to subtle shifts in tone as well as more obvious writing strategies.

As you analyze, you are evaluating as well as describing, but a critical reading should not be merely an occasion for criticizing the draft. A good critical reader helps a writer see how each part works and how all the parts work together. By describing what you see, you help the writer see the draft more objectively, a perspective that is necessary for thoughtful revising.

Offer Advice, but Do Not Rewrite

As a critical reader, you may be tempted to rewrite the draft—to change a word here, correct an error there, add your ideas everywhere. Resist the impulse. Your role is to read carefully, to point out what you think is or is not working, to make suggestions and ask questions. Leave the revising to the writer.

In turn, the writer has a responsibility to listen to your comments but is under no obligation to do as you suggest. Then why go to all the trouble, you might ask. There are at least two reasons. First, when you read someone else's writing critically, you learn more about writing—about the decisions writers make, how a thoughtful reader reads, and the constraints of particular kinds of writing. Second, you play an instrumental role in constructing a text. As a critical reader, you embody for the writer the abstraction called *audience*. By sharing your reaction and analysis with the writer, you complete the circuit of communication.

Revising

Even productive invention and smooth drafting rarely result in the essay a writer initially imagined. Experienced writers are not surprised or disappointed when this happens, however. They expect to revise a draft—unless an imminent deadline precludes revising. They know that revising will move them closer to the essay they really want to write. Reading their drafts thoughtfully and critically—and perhaps reflecting on critical readings by others—they see many opportunities for improvement. They may notice misspelled words or garbled sentences; most important, however, they discover ways to delete, move, rephrase, and add material in order to say what they want to say more clearly and thoughtfully.

View the Draft Objectively

To revise, you must read your draft objectively, to see if it actually says what you intended it to say. If you can, put the draft aside for a day or two. Getting critical comments from another reader can also help you to view the draft more objectively.

Reconsider Your Purpose and Audience

Ask yourself what you are trying to accomplish. Does your purpose still seem appropriate for these particular readers? How could you modify the essay to make it more effective? Consider each problem and possible solution in light of your overall writing strategy.

Revise in Stages

Do not try to do everything at once. Begin by looking at the whole and then move to an analysis of the parts. Focus initially on identifying problems; consider possible solutions only after you have a general understanding of how the draft fails to achieve its purpose.

Look at Big Problems First

Identify major problems that keep the draft from achieving its purpose. Does the essay have a clear focus, a compelling presentation, a consistent and appropriate tone? Are the ideas interesting and well developed? Does the essay have all the features that readers will expect?

Focus Next on Clarity and Coherence

Consider the beginning. How well does it prepare readers for the essay? Look at each section of the essay in turn. Do the paragraphs proceed in a logical order? Are there appropriate transitions to help readers follow from one point to the next? Are generalizations firmly and explicitly connected to specific details, examples, or supporting evidence?

Save Stylistic Changes and Grammatical Corrections for Last

Do not focus on word choice or sentence structure until you are generally satisfied with what you have written. Then carefully consider your style and diction. Focus primarily on key terms to be sure they are appropriate and well defined.

Editing

Once you have finished revising, you then want to edit carefully to make sure that every word, phrase, and sentence is clear and follows the rules and conventions of standard American English. Using nonstandard language and punctuation distracts readers and lessens your credibility as a writer.

Save editing until the end. Turn your attention to editing only *after* you have planned and worked out a revision. Too much editing too early in the writing process can limit, even block, invention and drafting.

Keep a List of Your Common Errors

Note the types of grammatical and spelling errors you discover in your own writing. Most likely you'll soon recognize error patterns, things to check for as you edit your work.

Begin Proofreading with the Last Sentence

To focus your attention on grammar and spelling, it may help to read backwards, beginning with the last sentence. Most writers get diverted thinking about what they are saying rather than how. Reading backwards makes it harder to pay attention to content, and thus easier to recognize writing problems.

Exchange Drafts with Another Student

Because it is usually easier to see errors in someone else's writing than in your own, you might consider trading essays with a classmate and proofreading one another's writing.

Reflecting on Your Own Writing

Each chapter in Part One concludes with an activity to help you think about what you learned studying the genre in that chapter. The activity asks you to analyze your writing process in order to see how you solved problems while writing that particular kind of essay.

If you are compiling a portfolio of your coursework to hand in at the end of the term, these reflections may help you write a descriptive or evaluative essay about your work in the course.

2 Remembering an Event

$\mathbf{W}$hy do people write autobiographical stories? Perhaps out of nostalgia for the past, but perhaps as well to make sense of the past. When we write about significant events in our lives, we come to know ourselves better, bringing into focus what's truly important to us and clarifying our beliefs and values. We also examine the forces—within ourselves and in our social structures—that have shaped our lives and perspectives.

In addition, writing about our lives for others to read—and reading about other people's lives—can help us better understand one another. Often, we can see in other people's autobiography reflections of our own lives. Yet we also are reminded of the differences among us: reading autobiography teaches us to celebrate individuality. It also shows us how the material conditions of our lives— whether we are rich or poor, male or female, black or white, young or old—may affect how we think of ourselves as well as how we're treated by others.

Writing about our lives for others to read is not the same as writing for yourself. As a writer, you must remember that autobiography is public, not private. While it invites self-disclosure, writing autobiography need not be confessional. You get to choose how you want to represent yourself, to decide what aspect of your life to write about, what side of yourself to reveal. Your choice depends on the rhetorical situation in which you are writing: who you expect to read your story (your audience) and what you want them to learn about you from it (your purpose). We obviously are *not* exactly the same in every situation, and don't necessarily want others to respond to us in the same way all the time. Based on our purpose in writing to a particular audience, we make choices on how to present ourselves, sometimes taking risks and at other times playing it safe.

Writing about personal experience involves fashioning a self in words much as a novelist constructs a character. As readers, we come to "know" the people we read about by the way they are described as well as by what they say and do.

As you work through this chapter, you will learn to present yourself purposefully by telling the story of your experience. You will learn to organize and pace the action to create dramatic tension; to describe scenes and people to make the story vivid and specific; to convey through words and images the event's significance to make the story meaningful.

Storytelling, you will discover, is an essential strategy in both academic and professional writing. Not only are some essays organized narratively like stories, but even essays organized topically often include the brief, "telling" stories we call anecdotes as illustrations for the main ideas.

WRITING IN YOUR OTHER COURSES

In college, you may well have occasion to write about some of your personal experiences for your courses. Consider, for example, the following typical assignments:

- *For a psychology course:* Erik Erikson observed that "young people . . . are sometimes preoccupied with what they appear to be in the eyes of others as compared with what they feel they are." Test this idea against your own adolescent experience. Recount a single event when you cared tremendously about what your peers thought of you. How did their judgment influence your behavior and your sense of self?

- *For a sociology course:* Case studies of victimization have shown that victims tend to become distrustful and socially isolated. If you have had the unfortunate experience of being a victim, write briefly about what happened and how it has affected your social interactions.

- *For a political science course:* Voter apathy is known to be a widespread problem, but not much is known about the origins of voting behavior. Recall the first time you became interested in an election, and tell about the incident in some detail. Looking back on the incident, what did it teach you about the origins of your own voting behavior?

- *For a linguistics course:* Many linguists argue that what is considered appropriate grammar and word choice varies from one context to another. Recall an occasion when you used language that others considered inappropriate or offensive. What did you say or write? How did you know your language had gone over prescribed boundaries? If you did it on purpose, explain why.

For Group Inquiry

Imagine that you have been asked to write about some childhood experience. Think of an event or incident that might "say something" about your life. It can be something startling, amusing, sad, exciting, whatever. The only requirement is for it to seem important to you now and for you to remember it well enough to tell about it.

Get together with two or three other students, and try out your stories on one another. You can be brief—three or four minutes for each will do. After each story is told, go around the group for each member to say something about what the incident told (or suggested) about its author. Does everyone "hear" the same thing?

Then, as a group, discuss the rhetorical situation of telling about a remembered event by considering the following points:

- Why did you choose the incident you did?
- How did the audience—that is, the group—affect your choice?
- What exactly did you want the others to learn from your story?
- Are you surprised by what they said they learned about you?

▪ What have you learned about telling stories purposefully by working in a group that you might not have learned by working alone?

Readings

Audre Lorde (1934–1992) wrote more than a dozen books of fiction and non-fiction. She's probably best known as a poet, but she was also an inspiring teacher and political activist.

This selection, from her autobiography *Zami: A New Spelling of My Name* (1982), recounts an event that occurred when Lorde was in the sixth grade at St. Catherine's School, where she was the only black student. Although she was born in New York, Lorde's parents were immigrants from the island of Grenada. Notice that Lorde uses some Grenadian dialect in recording her mother's speech, such as "what-the-france" (paragraph 5) and "among-you" (paragraph 7). As you read, think about why winning the election is so important to Lorde and why her mother tries to discourage her from running.

THE ELECTION
▪
Audre Lorde

In the spring of the sixth grade, Sister Blanche announced that we were going to hold elections for two class presidents, one boy and one girl. Anyone could run, she said, and we would vote on Friday of that week. The voting should be according to merit and effort and class spirit, she added, but the most important thing would be marks.

Of course, Ann Archdeacon was nominated immediately. She was not only the most popular girl in the school, she was the prettiest. Ilene Crimmons was also nominated, her blonde curls and favored status with the Monsignor guaranteed that.

I lent Jim Moriarty ten cents, stolen from my father's pocket at lunchtime, so Jim nominated me. A titter went through the class, but I ignored it. I was in seventh heaven. I knew I was the smartest girl in the class. I had to win.

That afternoon when my mother came home from the office, I told her about the election, and how I was going to run, and win. She was furious.

"What in hell are you doing getting yourself involved with so much foolishness? You don't have better sense in your head than that? What-the-france do you need with election? We send you to school to work, not to prance about with president-this election-that. Get down the rice, girl, and stop talking your foolishness." We started preparing the food.

"But I just might win, Mommy. Sister Blanche said it should go to the smartest girl in the class." I wanted her to see how important it was to me.

"Don't bother me with that nonsense. I don't want to hear any more about it. And don't come in here on Friday with a long face, and any 'I didn't win, Mommy,' because I don't want to hear that, either. Your father and I have enough trouble to keep among-you in school, never mind election.''

I dropped the subject.   8

The week was a very long and exciting one for me. The only way I   9
could get attention from my classmates in the sixth grade was by having
money, and thanks to carefully planned forays into my father's pants pockets every night that week, I made sure I had plenty. Every day at noon, I
dashed across the street, gobbled down whatever food my mother had left
for my lunch, and headed for the schoolyard. . . .

I knew better than to say another word to my mother about the presi-   10
dency, but that week was filled with fantasies of how I would break the
news to her on Friday when she came home.

"Oh, Mommy, by the way, can I stay later at school on Monday for a   11
presidents' meeting?'' Or "Mother, would you please sign this note saying
it is all right for me to accept the presidency?'' Or maybe even, "Mother,
could I have a little get-together here to celebrate the election?''

On Friday, I tied a ribbon around the steel barrette that held my unruly   12
mass of hair tightly at the nape of my neck. Elections were to be held in the
afternoon, and when I got home for lunch, for the first time in my life, I was
too excited to eat. I buried the can of Campbell's soup that my mother had
left out for me way behind the other cans in the pantry and hoped she had
not counted how many were left.

We filed out of the schoolyard and up the stairs to the sixth grade room.   13
The walls were still lined with bits of green from the recent St. Patrick's Day
decorations. Sister Blanche passed out little pieces of blank paper for our
ballots.

The first rude awakening came when she announced that the boy cho-   14
sen would be president, but the girl would only be vice-president. I thought
this was monstrously unfair. Why not the other way around? Since we could
not, as she explained, have two presidents, why not a girl president and a
boy vice-president? It doesn't really matter, I said to myself. I can live with
being vice-president.

I voted for myself. The ballots were collected and passed to the front   15
of the room and duly counted. James O'Connor won for the boys. Ann
Archdeacon won for the girls. Ilene Crimmons came in second. I got four
votes, one of which was mine. I was in shock. We all clapped for the
winners, and Ann Archdeacon turned around in her seat and smiled her
shit-eating smile at me. "Too bad you lost.'' I smiled back. I wanted to
break her face off.

I was too much my mother's daughter to let anyone think it mattered.   16
But I felt I had been destroyed. How could this have happened? I was the
smartest girl in the class. I had not been elected vice-president. It was as
simple as that. But something was escaping me. Something was terribly
wrong. It wasn't fair.

A sweet little girl named Helen Ramsey had decided it was her christian   17
duty to befriend me, and she had once lent me her sled during the winter.
She lived next to the church, and after school, that day, she invited me to
her house for a cup of cocoa. I ran away without answering, dashing across
the street and into the safety of my house. I ran up the stairs, my bookbag

banging against my legs. I pulled out the key pinned to my uniform pocket and unlocked the door to our apartment. The house was warm and dark and empty and quiet. I did not stop running until I got to my room at the front of the house, where I flung my books and my coat in a corner and collapsed upon my convertible couch-bed, shrieking with fury and disappointment. Finally, in the privacy of my room, I could shed the tears that had been burning my eyes for two hours, and I wept and wept.

I had wanted other things before that I had not gotten. So much so, that I had come to believe if I really wanted something badly enough, the very act of my wanting it was an assurance that I would not get it. Was this what had happened with the election? Had I wanted it too much? Was this what my mother was always talking about? Why she had been so angry? Because wanting meant I would not get? But somehow this felt different. This was the first time that I had wanted something so badly, the getting of which I was sure I could control. The election was supposed to have gone to the smartest girl in the class, and I was clearly the smartest. That was something I had done, on my own, that should have guaranteed me the election. The smartest, not the most popular. That was me. But it hadn't happened. My mother had been right. I hadn't won the election. My mother had been right.

This thought hurt me almost as much as the loss of the election, and when I felt it fully I shrieked with renewed vigor. I luxuriated in my grief in the empty house in a way I could never have done if anyone were home.

All the way up front and buried in my tears, kneeling with my face in the cushions of my couch, I did not hear the key in the lock, nor the main door open. The first thing I knew, there was my mother standing in the doorway of my room, a frown of concern in her voice.

"What happened, what happened? What's wrong with you? What's this racket going on here?"

I turned my wet face up to her from the couch. I wanted a little comfort in my pain, and getting up, I started moving toward her.

"I lost the election, Mommy," I cried, forgetting her warnings. "I'm the smartest girl in class, Sister Blanche says so, and they chose Ann Archdeacon instead!" The unfairness of it all flooded over me again and my voice cracked into fresh sobs.

Through my tears, I saw my mother's face stiffen with rage. Her eyebrows drew together as her hand came up, still holding her handbag. I stopped in my tracks as her first blow caught me full on the side of my head. My mother was no weakling, and I backed away, my ears ringing. The whole world seemed to be going insane. It was only then I remembered our earlier conversations.

"See, the bird forgets, but the trap doesn't! I warned you! What you think you doing coming into this house wailing about election? If I told you once I have told you a hundred times, don't chase yourself behind these people, haven't I? What kind of ninny raise up here to think those good-for-nothing white piss-jets would pass over some little jacabat girl to elect you anything?" Smack! "What did I say to you just now?" She cuffed me again, this time on my shoulders, as I huddled to escape her rain of furious blows, and the edges of her pocketbook.

"Sure enough, didn't I tell you not to come in here bringing down tears   26
over some worthless fool election?" Smack! "What the hell you think we
send you to school for?" Smack! "Don't run yourself behind other people's
business, you'll do better. Dry up, now, dry up!" Smack! She pulled me to
my feet from where I had sunk back onto the couch.

"Is cry you want to cry? I'll give you something hard to cry on!" And   27
she cuffed me again, this time more lightly. "Now get yourself up from
there and stop acting like some stupid fool, worrying yourself about these
people's business that doesn't concern you. Get-the-france out of here and
wipe up your face. Start acting like a human being!"

Pushing me ahead of her, my mother marched back through the parlor   28
and into the kitchen. "I come in here tired from the street and here you,
acting like the world is ending. I thought sure enough some terrible thing
happened to you, come to find out it's only election. Now help me put
away this foodstuff."

I was relieved to hear her tone mollify, as I wiped my eyes. But I still   29
gave her heavy hands a wide berth.

"It's just that it's not fair, Mother. That's all I was crying about," I said,   30
opening the brown paper bags on the table. To admit I had been hurt would
somehow put me in the wrong for feeling pain. "It wasn't the election I
cared about so much really, just that it was all so unfair."

"Fair, fair, what's fair, you think? Is fair you want, look in god's face."   31
My mother was busily dropping onions into the bin. She paused, and turning around, held my puffy face up, her hand beneath my chin. Her eyes so
sharp and furious before, now just looked tired and sad.

"Child, why you worry your head so much over fair or not fair? Just   32
do what is for you to do and let the rest take care of themselves." She
smoothed straggles of hair back from my face, and I felt the anger gone
from her fingers. "Look, you hair all mess-up behind from rolling around
with foolishness. Go wash your face and hands and come help me dress
this fish for supper."

For Discussion

As readers, we tend to look at stories from the perspective of our own experience
and our own time. The event portrayed in this selection took place more than
fifty years ago, just after World War II. What can you infer from this story about
the situation at that time for African Americans in America? Why does Lorde's
mother say at the end, "Fair, fair, what's fair, you think? Is fair you want, look in
god's face"? How does seeing the story in the context of the late 1940s lead you
to understand the mother's response?

For Analysis

1. Look closely at the way Lorde develops her narrative. It begins with the announcement of the election and ends a week later. How much space does she
devote to her electioneering during the week, to the election itself, and to what
happened afterward? Compare Lorde's narrative to Tobias Wolff's essay "On Being

a Real Westerner." Notice how their narratives compress time at some points, covering extended periods in a few sentences. Also notice that, at some points, they use several paragraphs to cover something that occurred in a relatively short time. What conclusions can you draw from this analysis about the ways these two writers represent time in their stories?

2. Reread paragraphs 15–19, in which Lorde shows us what she did after losing the election. Notice that at some point we see her as if she were on a movie screen, smiling back at Ann Archdeacon, for example, and running upstairs with her bookbag banging against her legs. In addition to dramatizing her actions, Lorde tells us what she was thinking. As you read, notice where she's showing action and where she's telling her thoughts. Bracket the passages where she's telling her thoughts so you can see more clearly the proportion of space Lorde devotes to each and how she intersperses telling with showing.

3. The most dramatic part of the story comes at the end when her mother discovers her crying. Reread these paragraphs, looking closely at the way Lorde makes them dramatic. Explain how you think she does it.

4. Relationships with parents often play an important role in autobiographical stories. Compare Lorde's relationship with her mother to the parent-child relationship in one of the other essays in this chapter: Wolff's relationship with his mother or Jean Brandt's relationship with her parents. Speculate about why, in writing about the event, each author also needed to write about the parent-child relationship. In each case, how does the relationship contribute to the event's significance?

For Your Own Writing

Can you think of a time when you had an emotional confrontation with another person? What was it about? Why do you think the emotions were so strong? If you were to write an autobiographical story about this event, how would you organize it? How would you decide how to present the confrontation? Would you dramatize it with direct dialogue? Would you paraphrase or summarize what was said?

Commentary

Lorde's story has a powerful impact on readers because feelings are expressed in raw language and action. You might wonder why Lorde chose to confront her readers in this way. To get some idea of Lorde's purpose, we might speculate about her assumptions, particularly about how her readers would likely react to the election results.

It's probable she assumed most readers would predict how the election was going to turn out. After all, there are only two alternatives: winning or losing. Think of stories like this that you've read or seen. Do they typically end with disappointment? Unless they have resulted from serious internal or physical struggle so that victory is a surprise, happy endings are often regarded as sappy.

There are also other, more important, reasons for readers to expect Lorde to lose the election. Most readers have had experiences in life that have led them to be cynical, or at least wary. We know that school elections very often are not decided on the basis of merit but on popularity. Therefore, we are not surprised when Ann Archdeacon wins; after all, we are told straight off, she "was not only the most popular girl in the school, she was the prettiest." Knowing also that the young Lorde is new at the school and has to bribe someone to nominate her makes the results that much more predictable. Furthermore, we might guess that Lorde's status as the only black student at the school would also affect the election results.

Assuming that Lorde wanted her readers to predict the election would be lost, how do you think she expected most of them to react? Some might share the young Lorde's point of view and be angered by the election results. But because the results are so predictable, many readers might be more likely to share the mother's point of view and wonder why the young Lorde put herself in a position where she would most likely be disappointed and hurt. For these readers, the mother's fury might echo their own frustration and sense of powerlessness at the injustice in society.

Lorde conveys this fury dramatically, using dialogue for most of this part of the story. Dialogue gives a narrative immediacy, vividness, and drama. For contrast, notice that Lorde begins the selection by paraphrasing Sister Blanche's announcement about the upcoming election instead of quoting directly. Lorde chooses to paraphrase, to use her own words, because there is little drama in the announcement. What the nun says is more important than how she says it. In portraying her mother's feelings and her own youthful reactions to them, however, Lorde must dramatize this significant part of her story by quoting directly. Paraphrasing or summarizing her mother's words would have created a very different impression.

Tobias Wolff is probably best known for his short stories and for a novel, *The Barracks Thief* (1984), for which he won the 1985 PEN/Faulkner award. "On Being a Real Westerner" comes from Wolff's autobiography, *This Boy's Life* (1989), which was made into a movie in 1993. Reflecting on his writing process, Wolff has said it is "part memory, part invention. I can no longer tell where one ends and the other begins. The very act of writing has transformed the original experience into another experience, more 'real' to me than what I started with."

The story Wolff tells here is based on an actual experience that occurred when he was ten years old. He and his mother had just moved west from Florida to Salt Lake City, followed by Roy, his divorced mother's boyfriend. "Roy was handsome," Wolff writes, "in the conventional way that appeals to boys. He had a tattoo. He'd been to war and kept a silence about it that was full of heroic implication." As you read, notice how Wolff's storytelling skills make this event come to life in the reader's imagination.

<table>
<tr><td>

ON BEING A REAL WESTERNER
■
Tobias Wolff

</td></tr>
</table>

Just after Easter Roy gave me the Winchester .22 rifle I'd learned to shoot with. It was a light, pump-action, beautifully balanced piece with a walnut stock black from all its oilings. Roy had carried it when he was a boy and it was still as good as new. Better than new. The action was silky from long use, and the wood of a quality no longer to be found. [1]

The gift did not come as a surprise. Roy was stingy, and slow to take a hint, but I'd put him under siege. I had my heart set on that rifle. A weapon was the first condition of self-sufficiency, and of being a real Westerner, and of all acceptable employment—trapping, riding herd, soldiering, law enforcement, and outlawry. I needed that rifle, for itself and for the way it completed me when I held it. [2]

My mother said I couldn't have it. Absolutely not. Roy took the rifle back but promised me he'd bring her around. He could not imagine anyone refusing him anything and treated the refusals he did encounter as perverse and insincere. Normally mute, he became at these times a relentless whiner. He would follow my mother from room to room, emitting one ceaseless note of complaint that was pitched perfectly to jelly her nerves and bring her to a state where she would agree to anything to make it stop. [3]

After a few days of this my mother caved in. She said I could have the rifle if, and only if, I promised never to take it out or even touch it except when she and Roy were with me. Okay, I said. Sure. Naturally. But even then she wasn't satisfied. She plain didn't like the fact of me owning a rifle. Roy said he had owned several rifles by the time he was my age, but this did not reassure her. She didn't think I could be trusted with it. Roy said now was the time to find out. [4]

For a week or so I kept my promises. But now that the weather had turned warm Roy was usually off somewhere and eventually, in the dead hours after school when I found myself alone in the apartment, I decided that there couldn't be any harm in taking the rifle out to clean it. Only to clean it, nothing more. I was sure it would be enough just to break it down, oil it, rub linseed into the stock, polish the octagonal barrel and then hold it up to the light to confirm the perfection of the bore. But it wasn't enough. From cleaning the rifle I went to marching around the apartment with it, and then to striking brave poses in front of the mirror. Roy had saved one of his army uniforms and I sometimes dressed up in this, together with martial-looking articles of hunting gear: fur trooper's hat, camouflage coat, boots that reached nearly to my knees. [5]

The camouflage coat made me feel like a sniper, and before long I began to act like one. I set up a nest on the couch by the front window. I drew the shades to darken the apartment, and took up my position. Nudging the shade aside with the rifle barrel, I followed people in my sights as they walked or drove along the street. At first I made shooting sounds—kyoo! kyoo! Then I started cocking the hammer and letting it snap down. [6]

Roy stored his ammunition in a metal box he kept hidden in the closet. As with everything else hidden in the apartment, I knew exactly where to find it. There was a layer of loose .22 rounds on the bottom of the box under shells of bigger caliber, dropped there by the handful the way men drop [7] pennies on their dressers at night. I took some and put them in a hiding place of my own. With these I started loading up the rifle. Hammer cocked, a round in the chamber, finger resting lightly on the trigger, I drew a bead on whoever walked by—women pushing strollers, children, garbage collectors laughing and calling to each other, anyone—and as they passed under my window I sometimes had to bite my lip to keep from laughing in the ecstasy of my power over them, and at their absurd and innocent belief that they were safe.

But over time the innocence I laughed at began to irritate me. It was a   8
peculiar kind of irritation. I saw it years later in men I served with, and felt it myself, when unarmed Vietnamese civilians talked back to us while we were herding them around. Power can be enjoyed only when it is recognized and feared. Fearlessness in those without power is maddening to those who have it.

One afternoon I pulled the trigger. I had been aiming at two old people,   9
a man and a woman, who walked so slowly that by the time they turned the corner at the bottom of the hill my little store of self-control was exhausted. I had to shoot. I looked up and down the street. It was empty. Nothing moved but a pair of squirrels chasing each other back and forth on the telephone wires. I followed one in my sight. Finally it stopped for a moment and I fired. The squirrel dropped straight into the road. I pulled back into the shadows and waited for something to happen, sure that someone must have heard the shot or seen the squirrel fall. But the sound that was so loud to me probably seemed to our neighbors no more than the bang of a cupboard slammed shut. After a while I sneaked a glance into the street. The squirrel hadn't moved. It looked like a scarf someone had dropped.

When my mother got home from work I told her there was a dead   10
squirrel in the street. Like me, she was an animal lover. She took a cellophane bag off a loaf of bread and we went outside and looked at the squirrel. "Poor little thing," she said. She stuck her hand in the wrapper and picked up the squirrel, then pulled the bag inside out away from her hand. We buried it behind our building under a cross made of popsicle sticks, and I blubbered the whole time.

I blubbered again in bed that night. At last I got out of bed and knelt   11
down and did an imitation of somebody praying, and then I did an imitation of somebody receiving divine reassurance and inspiration. I stopped crying. I smiled to myself and forced a feeling of warmth into my chest. Then I climbed back in bed and looked up at the ceiling with a blissful expression until I went to sleep.

For several days I stayed away from the apartment at times when I   12
knew I'd be alone there.

Though I avoided the apartment, I could not shake the idea that sooner   13
or later I would get the rifle out again. All my images of myself as I wished to be were images of myself armed. Because I did not know who I was, any image of myself, no matter how grotesque, had power over me. This much I understand now. But the man can give no help to the boy, not in this matter nor in those that follow. The boy moves always out of reach.

For Discussion

Consider what this story seems to be saying about identity and role playing. Why do you think Wolff takes so much delight in dressing up as a soldier? What connection do you see between his playing soldier and his desire to be a "real Westerner"?

Why do you think soldiers and cowboys are idealized masculine roles in our society? What qualities of character do they represent? What are the feminine roles our society values most? If possible, consider these questions together with two or three other students, preferably including both men and women in the group.

How do you feel about these gender-related roles? Do they embody ideals that you hold for yourself? Looking back at the essay, do you think Wolff calls these stereotypical roles into question or is basically uncritical of them?

For Analysis

1. What seems to be the significance of this story? What does Wolff learn from this particular incident? Where does he state the point most explicitly?

2. Successful narratives present a sequence of actions that build tension toward a high point or climax. To analyze this story's dramatic structure, first find the climax. Then, starting with the first paragraph, number each new step. What effect does this progression of steps have on you as a reader? Compare your response to that of your classmates. Did you all point to the same steps? If not, how can you account for the difference?

3. Look again at the opening paragraphs. What purpose do they serve? If the essay opened instead with part of the second sentence of paragraph 5 ("In the dead hours after school . . .), what would be lost or gained?

4. In paragraphs 7–13, Wolff describes his reactions at the time to what he was doing. Which of these remembered feelings and thoughts help you to understand what he was experiencing at the time? What impression do they give you of the young Wolff? Where do you see evidence of the adult writer's perspective? What does he seem to think about his younger self?

For Your Own Writing

Wolff describes experiencing what he calls the "ecstasy of my power" to inflict harm on others (paragraph 7). Can you recall any instances when you were in a position to exercise power over another person? What did you do? How did you feel? Think also of times when you were subject to someone else's power. How did you feel in that position? If you were to write about one of these instances, what ideas and feelings would you want to convey to your readers?

Commentary

"On Being a Real Westerner" illustrates two basic features of writing about re-membered events: a well-told story and an indication of its autobiographical significance. Good storytelling attracts readers' interest and makes them want to read on to find out what happened. Autobiographical significance gives a story its meaning. If a story doesn't interest us, we don't read it; if it doesn't have significance, we find it pointless.

Wolff's is a gripping story. One factor that makes it so dramatic is the topic. Putting a child together with a rifle immediately alerts readers to the possibility that something dreadful could happen. Thus the potential for suspense is great. But what makes the story so effective is Wolff's masterful use of two writing strategies: narration and description.

Good storytelling hinges on tension, usually on the reader's concern for the main character and anxiety about what will happen to him or her. If the tension slackens, if irrelevant details are introduced or the action meanders pointlessly, readers lose interest. Wolff instills tension in his narrative by pacing the action very carefully. He begins his story leisurely, summarizing his efforts to get Roy to give him the rifle and Roy's efforts to get Wolff's mother to let him have it. Once he gets the rifle, the pace picks up as the narrative moves with increasing speed from one incident to the next until finally the gun is fired and the squirrel drops.

Wolff uses another pacing technique when he gives a close-up of the action by showing concrete movements and gestures. In paragraph 7, for example, he builds suspense by focusing in on each minute action: "Hammer cocked, a round in the chamber, finger resting lightly on the trigger, I drew a bead on whoever walked by—women pushing strollers, children, garbage collectors laughing and calling to each other, anyone. . . ."

This specific narrative action also contributes to the vividness of the writing. Wolff uses it together with the descriptive techniques of naming, detailing, and comparing to help readers visualize key parts of the scene. He carefully names important objects and their parts. For instance, it's not just any gun, but a Winchester .22. He adds many details (italicized in our example) to further describe the rifle: "It was a *light, pump-action, beautifully balanced* piece with a *walnut* stock *black* from all its oilings." Finally, he uses comparison in the form of metaphor and simile to further enliven his description: "the action was silky," the dead squirrel "looked like a scarf someone had dropped."

In addition to holding our interest, a good story has a point: it has to lead somewhere. Wolff narrates a brief event from his childhood, but at the end of paragraph 7, as he watches innocent people passing by from his perch on the couch, he connects his experience to one that might be shared by others when he writes of "the ecstasy of my power" over the unsuspecting passersby. He reinforces the significance of his experience in paragraph 8, where he recalls experiencing the same feeling of irritation with innocent people years later when he served in Vietnam. He also recalls witnessing these feelings in "men I served with." This connection gives the event its significance. To be significant, an event need not be earthshaking. Wolff's childhood experience is significant because, years later, he comes to understand its meaning: "All my images of myself as I wished to be were images of myself armed. Because I did not know who I was, any image of myself, no matter how grotesque, had power over me. This much I understand now." Sometimes it takes a good deal of time and reflection before we gain insights into the past—another reason people write about remembered events. Writing gives us the opportunity to reflect on our experiences and, in hindsight, to figure out why they mean so much to us.

Jean Brandt wrote this essay as a first-year college student. In it she tells about something she did when she was thirteen. Reflecting on how she felt at the time, Brandt writes: "I was afraid, embarrassed, worried, mad." As you read, look for places where these tumultuous and contradictory remembered feelings are expressed.

> ### CALLING HOME
> ▪
> *Jean Brandt*

As we all piled into the car, I knew it was going to be a fabulous day. My grandmother was visiting for the holidays; and she and I, along with my older brother and sister, Louis and Susan, were setting off for a day of last-minute Christmas shopping. On the way to the mall, we sang Christmas carols, chattered, and laughed. With Christmas only two days away, we were caught up with holiday spirit. I felt lightheaded and full of joy. I loved shopping—especially at Christmas. 1

The shopping center was swarming with frantic last-minute shoppers like ourselves. We went first to the General Store, my favorite. It carried mostly knickknacks and other useless items that nobody needs but buys anyway. I was thirteen years old at the time, and things like buttons and calendars and posters would catch my fancy. This day was no different. The object of my desire was a seventy-five-cent Snoopy button. Snoopy was the latest. If you owned anything with the Peanuts on it, you were "in." But since I was supposed to be shopping for gifts for other people and not myself, I couldn't decide what to do. I went in search of my sister for her opinion. I pushed my way through throngs of people to the back of the store where I found Susan. I asked her if she thought I should buy the button. She said it was cute and if I wanted it to go ahead and buy it. 2

When I got back to the Snoopy section, I took one look at the lines at the cashiers and knew I didn't want to wait thirty minutes to buy an item worth less than one dollar. I walked back to the basket where I found the button and was about to drop it when suddenly, instead, I took a quick glance around, assured myself no one could see, and slipped the button into the pocket of my sweatshirt. I hesitated for a moment, but once the item was in my pocket, there was no turning back. I had never before stolen anything; but what was done was done. A few seconds later, my sister appeared and asked, "So, did you decide to buy the button?" 3

"No, I guess not." I hoped my voice didn't quaver. As we headed for the entrance, my heart began to race. I just had to get out of that store. Only a few more yards to go and I'd be safe. As we crossed the threshold, I heaved a sigh of relief. I was home free. I thought about how sly I had been and I felt proud of my accomplishment. 4

An unexpected tap on my shoulder startled me. I whirled around to 5
find a middle-aged man, dressed in street clothes, flashing some type of
badge and politely asking me to empty my pockets. Where did this man
come from? How did he know? I was so sure that no one had seen me! On
the verge of panicking, I told myself that all I had to do was give this man
his button back, say I was sorry, and go on my way. After all, it was only a
seventy-five-cent item.

Next thing I knew, he was talking about calling the police and having 6
me arrested and thrown in jail, as if he had just nabbed a professional thief
instead of a terrified kid. I couldn't believe what he was saying.

"Jean, what's going on?" 7

The sound of my sister's voice eased the pressure a bit. She always 8
managed to get me out of trouble. She would come through this time too.

"Excuse me. Are you a relative of this young girl?" 9

"Yes, I'm her sister. What's the problem?" 10

"Well, I just caught her shoplifting and I'm afraid I'll have to call the 11
police."

"What did she take?" 12

"This button." 13

"A button? You are having a thirteen-year-old arrested for stealing a 14
button?"

"I'm sorry, but she broke the law." 15

The man led us through the store and into an office, where we waited 16
for the police officers to arrive. Susan had found my grandmother and
brother, who, still shocked, didn't say a word. The thought of going to jail
terrified me, not because of jail itself, but because of the encounter with
my parents afterward. Not more than ten minutes later, two officers arrived
and placed me under arrest. They said that I was to be taken to the station
alone. Then, they handcuffed me and led me out of the store. I felt alone
and scared. I had counted on my sister being with me, but now I had to
muster up the courage to face this ordeal all by myself.

As the officers led me through the mall, I sensed a hundred pairs of 17
eyes staring at me. My face flushed and I broke out in a sweat. Now everyone knew I was a criminal. In their eyes I was a juvenile delinquent, and
thank God the cops were getting me off the streets. The worse part was
thinking my grandmother might be having the same thoughts. The humiliation at that moment was overwhelming. I felt like Hester Prynne being put
on public display for everyone to ridicule.

That short walk through the mall seemed to take hours. But once we 18
reached the squad car, time raced by. I was read my rights and questioned.
We were at the police station within minutes. Everything happened so fast
I didn't have a chance to feel remorse for my crime. Instead, I viewed what
was happening to me as if it were a movie. Being searched, although embarrassing, somehow seemed to be exciting. All the movies and television
programs I had seen were actually coming to life. This is what it was really
like. But why were criminals always portrayed as frightened and regretful?
I was having fun. I thought I had nothing to fear—until I was allowed my
one phone call. I was trembling as I dialed home. I didn't know what I was
going to say to my parents, especially my mother.

"Hi, Dad, this is Jean."   19
"We've been waiting for you to call."   20
"Did Susie tell you what happened?"   21
"Yeah, but we haven't told your mother. I think you should tell her   22
what you did and where you are."
"You mean she doesn't even know where I am?"   23
"No, I want you to explain it to her."   24
There was a pause as he called my mother to the phone. For the first   25
time that night, I was close to tears. I wished I had never stolen that stupid
pin. I wanted to give the phone to one of the officers because I was too
ashamed to tell my mother the truth, but I had no choice.
"Jean, where are you?"   26
"I'm, umm, in jail."   27
"Why? What for?"   28
"Shoplifting."   29
"On no, Jean. Why? Why did you do it?"   30
"I don't know. No reason. I just did it."   31
"I don't understand. What did you take? Why did you do it? You had   32
plenty of money with you."
"I know but I just did it. I can't explain why. Mom, I'm sorry."   33
"I'm afraid sorry isn't enough. I'm horribly disappointed in you."   34
Long after we got off the phone, while I sat in an empty jail cell, waiting   35
for my parents to pick me up, I could still distinctly hear the disappointment
and hurt in my mother's voice. I cried. The tears weren't for me but for her
and the pain I had put her through. I felt like a terrible human being. I would
rather have stayed in jail than confront my mom right then. I dreaded each
passing minute that brought our encounter closer. When the officer came
to release me, I hesitated, actually not wanting to leave. We went to the
front desk, where I had to sign a form to retrieve my belongings. I saw my
parents a few yards away and my heart raced. A large knot formed in my
stomach. I fought back the tears.
Not a word was spoken as we walked to the car. Slowly, I sank into   36
the back seat anticipating the scolding. Expecting harsh tones, I was relieved
to hear almost the opposite from my father.
"I'm not going to punish you and I'll tell you why. Although I think   37
what you did was wrong, I think what the police did was more wrong.
There's no excuse for locking a thirteen-year-old behind bars. That doesn't
mean I condone what you did, but I think you've been punished enough
already."
As I looked from my father's eyes to my mother's, I knew this ordeal   38
was over. Although it would never be forgotten, the incident was not mentioned again.

For Discussion

Brandt writes here about taking responsibility for her actions. Do you think she
ultimately accepts responsibility for what she has done, or does she transfer some
of the blame to others? If you have already read the essay by Tobias Wolff in this

chapter, you might compare his story to Brandt's. Both of them break social rules: she gets caught, whereas he gets away with it.

Discuss what society teaches us about breaking rules. Do some rules seem more bendable than others? Are some people treated differently than others for breaking the same rules? Why should accepting responsibility for what you have done change anything?

For Analysis

1. Reread Brandt's essay, this time paying special attention to the writer's use of dialogue. What do you learn about her from what she says and how she says it? What do you learn about her relationship with her parents?

2. Reread the essay again, looking for examples of the descriptive strategies of naming, detailing, and comparing. How well does Brandt use these strategies? Give at least one example of each as support for your evaluation.

3. The story begins and ends in a car, with the two car rides framing the story. Framing is a narrative device of echoing something from the beginning in the ending. What effect does this device have on your reading of the story?

4. The Writer at Work section on pages 47–53 includes some of Brandt's invention notes and her complete first draft. These materials show how her focus shifted gradually from the theft and subsequent arrest in her first draft to her emotional confrontation with her parents in the final revision. Read over these materials, and comment on the shift in focus. Why do you think Brandt decided to stress her confrontation with her parents? Why do you think she decided, against the advice of the student who commented on her draft, to cut the scenes in the police car and station? Notice, in particular, that she left out of the final version the vivid image of herself handcuffed to the table (see p. 52, paragraph 5).

For Your Own Writing

Can you think of a few occasions when you did something uncharacteristic? Perhaps you acted on impulse or took a chance you wouldn't ordinarily take. It doesn't have to be something reckless, dangerous, or illegal; it could be something quite harmless, even pleasant. Think of one such occasion you might like to write about. What would you want your readers to recognize about you on the basis of reading your story?

Commentary

By letting us see her commit a crime and be arrested for it, Brandt makes a rather personal self-disclosure in this autobiographical story. Although readers are always interested in candid personal revelation, autobiographers have to decide for themselves just how personal they want their story to be. Making this decision yourself is especially important when you are writing for class. You certainly shouldn't feel compelled to disclose something you don't want to disclose.

We can see in her Writer at Work materials some of Brandt's decision process. She indicates in her invention writing that she had always been too "ashamed to tell anyone" about this particular event (p. 49). She seems to decide to go ahead, in part, because she knows readers will recognize its significance. She also expects some readers to identify with her because they've done similar things. But her primary reason seems more personal. She finds that writing has helped her begin to come to terms with her many contradictory feelings about what she did and how she was treated. Without oversimplifying her feelings or fully understanding them, Brandt ultimately seems comfortable admitting what she did was wrong, while taking some pride in how she acted afterward.

As readers, we form our impressions of Brandt from what she does and from how she represents herself in her writing. Her revelation of remembered feelings and thoughts helps us see the experience from her point of view. We see, for example, the roller coaster of emotions she went through, her fear but also her exhilaration. She vividly conveys her panic at being caught, her terror at the prospect of going to jail, her feeling of being "alone and scared" on the way to the station, and her excitement when being searched.

While she claims in her invention writing no longer to feel angry at the manager or the police, she clearly satirizes the store manager. She portrays her experience with the police more ambiguously with an unusual emotional distance ("I viewed what happened to me as if it were a movie."), letting her father express righteous indignation instead of expressing it herself. She even omits from the final revision the first draft's disturbing image of her handcuffed to a table while being questioned by the police.

Perhaps the strongest emotions come out toward the end of the essay when she must confront her parents. Seeing herself reflected in their eyes seems to have been the most painful and memorable part of the experience. Maybe that is why she finally decided to write about this event: it gave her a way to replace that image with a more complex one that allows her to redeem some sense of pride.

Like Wolff's essay, Brandt's is an example of the way good storytellers build tension. Brandt's story has two climactic episodes—the arrest and the confrontation with her parents. (Some essays may have even more than two climactic episodes.)

Many writers rely on narrative time signals to pace the action. The most common methods are time markers, verb tense markers, and references to clock time. Time markers are words and phrases that locate an action at a particular point in time or that relate one point to another. Notice how Brandt uses time markers throughout her essay ("when," "next thing I knew," "long after"). Verb tense markers also play a role in presenting time in narrative. They indicate when the actions occur and whether they are complete or in progress. Finally, clock time signals the passage of time in a narrative. Most writers, including Brandt, use this valuable device sparingly. While Brandt describes the tense scene in the police station as seeming to take hours, she admits that the passage of time was actually quite short (with the officers arriving in only ten minutes, for instance).

PURPOSE AND AUDIENCE

Writers have various reasons for writing about their experiences. Reminiscing makes it possible to relive moments of pleasure and pain, but it also helps writers gain insight, to learn who they are now by examining who they used to be and the forces that shaped them. Reflecting on the past can lead to significant self-discovery.

Writing about personal experience is public, not private. The autobiographer writes to be read and is therefore as much concerned with self-presentation as with self-discovery. All writers want to influence the way readers think of them. They present themselves to readers in the way they want to be perceived. The rest they keep hidden, though readers may read between the lines.

We read about others' experiences for much the same reason that we write about our own—to learn about how we live our lives: the decisions we face, the delights we share, and the fate that awaits us all. Reading autobiography can validate our sense of ourselves, particularly when we see our own experience reflected in another's life. Reading about others' lives can also challenge our complacency and help us appreciate other points of view. Not only can autobiography lead us to greater self-awareness by validating or challenging us, it can also enlarge our sympathies by awakening our sense of humanity. When we read about others' lives, we are invited to empathize with another person's values and feelings and thus break the shell of our own isolation.

BASIC FEATURES OF ESSAYS ABOUT REMEMBERED EVENTS

Essays about remembered events share the following basic features.

A Well-Told Story

Writing about remembered events means first of all telling an interesting story: the writer makes us want to know what happens. Writers involve readers primarily by building suspense. In addition to telling a suspenseful story, good writers work to create tension in their narratives. *Tension* draws us into a story, making us nervous about what might happen. One moment we're distant observers, far from the action; the next, we're thrown right into it with the participants.

A Vivid Presentation of Scenes and People

Scenes and people play an important role in most writing about remembered events. Instead of giving a generalized impression, skillful writers actually re-create the scene and let us hear the people. By moving in close, a writer can name specific objects in a scene. For presenting important people, writers can give details of the person's appearance or show people in action. Writers also present people through dialogue, letting us infer from their own words what the people are like and how they feel about one another.

An Indication of the Significance

In essays about remembered events, we not only expect a well-told story with vivid details, but we also expect the story to have a point. Sometimes the event's meaning is merely implied; more often the meaning is stated explicitly. There are two ways a writer can communicate this significance: by *showing* that the event was important or by *telling* directly what it meant. Most writers do both.

Showing is the heartbeat of an essay about a remembered event, for the event must be dramatized if readers are to appreciate its importance and understand the writer's feelings about it. Telling also contributes mightily to a reader's understanding about the event's meaning and importance. Writers may tell us how they felt at the time, or how they feel now as they look back on the experience. Often they do both, recalling their past feelings and thoughts and reflecting on the past from their present perspective.

Telling is the main way writers interpret the event for readers, but skillful writers are careful not to append these reflections artificially, like a moral tagged on to a fable. They also try not to oversimplify or moralize, for most readers are skeptical of writing that is sentimental or self-serving. Readers don't expect autobiographers to reveal everything, but they do expect them to be truthful in what they do disclose. We may not be able to identify with Wolff's compulsive need for a gun, but we have to admire his openness. Similarly, while we may sympathize with Lorde's disappointment, we also recognize the reasons for her mother's anger.

Guide to Writing

▪ THE WRITING ASSIGNMENT

Write an essay about a significant event in your life. Choose an event that will engage readers and, at the same time, tell them something about you. Tell your story dramatically and vividly, giving a clear indication of its autobiographical significance.

INVENTION

The following invention activities are designed to help you choose an appropriate event, recall specific details, test your choice to be sure you can write about it successfully, and define its autobiographical significance.

Choosing an Event to Write About

Finding an event to write about requires some patience and reflection. Take time to sit quietly. Try to think of specific experiences you still remember well.

Listing Events

List some events you might write about, even if you already have a promising event in mind. Taking a few minutes now to list additional possibilities may help you decide whether your initial idea is the one to pursue, as well as give you backups if you need them later. One way to search your memory is to think in terms of categories. Use the following categories (and any others you can think of) to get started in your search.

- Any "first," such as when you first realized you had a special skill, ambition, or problem; when you first felt needed or rejected; when you first became aware of some kind of altruism or injustice
- Any painful memory: when you had to make a tough choice; when someone you admired let you down (or you let someone else down); when you struggled to learn or understand something
- Any occasion when things did not turn out as expected: when you expected to be praised but were criticized; when you were convinced you would fail but succeeded
- Any incident that challenged your basic values or beliefs
- Any humorous event, one you still laugh about, perhaps one that seemed awkward or embarrassing at the time
- Any event that shaped you in a particular way, making you independent, proud, insecure, fearful, courageous, or ambitious
- Any incident charged with strong emotions, such as love, fear, anger, embarrassment, guilt, frustration, hurt, pride, happiness, or joy
- Any incident that changed your relationship with a parent, spouse, or child

Focusing on key periods of time is another way to search your memory. Go back in five-year increments: one-to-five years ago, six-to-ten years ago, ten-to-fifteen, and so on. Try to recall an event from each period.

Choosing a Significant Event

Look over your list, and choose two or three promising events. These events can be common or unusual, humorous or serious, recent or distant, but consider them in light of the following questions:

- Will I be able to tell what happened from beginning to end?
- Can I recall specific details about the action, scene, and people?
- As a fragment of my life story, does this event reveal anything important about me?
- Will I feel comfortable writing about it?
- Will it arouse my readers' curiosity and interest?

Decide on one event to write about. Not everything needs to be clear to you at this point, but choose an event you feel drawn to explore further, one you expect will make a good story and lead you to insights about yourself.

Sketching the Story

Having chosen a promising event in your life, begin by making a rough sketch of the story. During the next few days, you'll recall many details to fill in your sketch. For now, write informally for about five minutes or so, as if you were telling a friend what happened. If it's easier, make an outline using brief phrases to indicate what you and others did.

Finally, reread your sketch or outline, and put an asterisk (*) next to the high point or climax, the point you think the story is building toward.

Describing the Scene

Stories take place in one or more specific places or scenes, some of which may be described in detail. For example, Brandt's story has many different scenes—the shopping center, the General Store, the manager's office, and the police station—most of which are described with just a few vivid images. To create vivid images, you need to name the *outstanding features* in the scene and identify their specific *sensory details*. You can also create *similes* and *metaphors*. The following activities calling upon the different senses will help you recall and describe the scene or scenes in which the event took place.

Sights

Imagine each important scene in your story as if it were in a photograph or a movie. Put yourself in the picture and list the objects you "see" as you look around or walk through the scene (excluding people for the moment). Then choose a few memorable objects and write for a few minutes about each, trying to recall specific visual details: size, shape, color, texture. Think also in terms of simile (as when Wolff describes the dead squirrel as looking "like a scarf someone had dropped") and metaphor (as when Brandt writes that "the shopping center was swarming with . . . shoppers").

Sounds

What sounds do you "hear" as you put yourself in the scene or scenes? Are there voices? animal sounds? horns honking? Is it quiet or noisy? Try simile and metaphor here too (remember Wolff comparing the sound of the rifle shot to "the bang of a cupboard slammed shut").

Smells, Tastes, Textures

As you picture each scene, what do you smell? Is there any element you can taste? Study some of the objects in your picture, and describe some of the textures or surfaces of anything you can touch. Are they soft or hard? smooth or rough? (Recall Wolff's description of the action of the rifle, "silky from long use.")

Dominant Impression

Now that you've imaginatively re-created the scene or scenes in which the event took place, write a sentence or two saying what dominant impression each scene should evoke. Should they seem homey? eerie? holiday-like? claustrophobic? Should every scene evoke the same mood?

Recalling Key People

Try to remember the significant people who played a role in the event—what they looked like, what they did, what they (or you) said.

Listing People

List all the people who played more than a casual role. You may have only one or two people to list, or you may have several.

Describing Key People

Choose one or two persons who made the event most significant for you. Take around five minutes to describe these people in writing—their appearance, their actions, and their significance in the event.

Re-Creating Conversations

Think about what was said: Can you recall any telling or unusual comments or choice of words? Do you remember any particular voices or accents? Try to reconstruct a conversation between one or more of these persons and yourself. (Don't worry about accuracy; try to catch the spirit of the exchange. Unless the conversation was recorded, dialogue is bound to be imagined to some extent.) Set it up as a dialogue, as Jean Brandt does on pages 47–48.

Finally, try to focus your thoughts about the key people in a sentence or two about your relationship with each of them and the role that each one played in the event.

Testing Your Choice

Pause now to be sure you've chosen an event you will be able to write about successfully by asking yourself these questions:

- Am I still interested in this event? Do I feel drawn to explore its significance in my life and to tell others about it?
- Have I been able to recall enough details to describe it vividly?
- Do I recall enough about other people who were involved with this event?

If you cannot answer these questions affirmatively and confidently, you may want to find a different event to write about. If so, return to your original list of events for other possible subjects.

You might find it useful to get together in a group with two or three other students and run your chosen events by one another. Assess the group members' interest in the event you wish to write about, and invite their advice about whether it sounds promising. Does it seem likely to lead to an essay they would care to read? Your purpose is to decide whether you have chosen a good event to write about and therefore whether you can proceed confidently to develop your essay.

Exploring the Significance

Following are some questions designed to help you better understand the meaning the event holds in your life.

Recalling Your Feelings at the Time

Try to remember your feelings during the event and immediately thereafter. Spend about ten minutes writing about your response, using the following questions to stimulate your memory:

- What was my first response to the event? What did I think? How did I feel? What did I do?
- How did I show my feelings?
- What did I want those present to think of me, and why?
- What did I think of myself at the time?
- Did I talk to anyone during or just after the event? What did I say?
- How long did these initial feelings last?
- What were the immediate consequences of the event for me personally?

Stop a moment to focus your thoughts. In two or three sentences try to articulate what your first response seems to disclose about the event's original importance.

Exploring Your Present Perspective

Next think about your present perspective on the event—your current feelings as well as any thoughts or insights you may have. Write for ten minutes about your present perspective, using these questions to get you started:

- Looking back, how do I feel about this event? Do I understand it differently now?
- What do my actions at the time of the event say about the kind of person I was then? In what ways am I different now? How would I respond to the same event if it occurred today?
- How would I summarize my current feelings? Are they settled, or do they still seem to be changing? Am I sure of my feelings about the event, or am I ambivalent?

In two or three sentences explain what your present perspective reveals about you or about the event's importance in your life.

Defining the Significance

In a sentence or two, state the significance of the event. What importance does it hold for you? What does it tell you about yourself? Then think about your readers and purpose. In another couple of sentences, explain why you've chosen to share this particular event. What, specifically, do you want your readers to think about you and the situation you were in?

PLANNING AND DRAFTING

The next activities are designed to help you use your invention writing to set goals, to organize your narrative, and to write a first draft.

Seeing What You Have

You have now done a lot of thinking and writing about elements basic to an essay about a remembered event: your feelings, the autobiographical significance, specific sensory details, dialogue. Before going any further, reread everything you've written so far to see what you have. As you read through your invention materials, be on the lookout for surprising details or new insights. Watch for meaningful patterns and relationships. Highlight promising material by underlining or by making notes in the margin. Guided by the questions that follow, you should now be able to decide whether you have enough material to write an essay and whether you understand the autobiographical significance well enough.

- Will I be able to tell an interesting—possibly amusing or dramatic—story about my experience?
- Do I have enough descriptive details to re-create the scene and people vividly? What will be the dominant impression of my description and how will it reinforce the event's significance?
- Does the event still seem significant to me? Will my readers also find it meaningful?

If you do not see interesting details, connections, or patterns in your invention writing, you are not likely to write a good draft. Starting over is no fun, but there is no sense in drafting a composition if you do not feel confident about your topic.

If your invention writing looks thin but promising, there are many ways to fill it out. For example, try reshaping the story, adding new scenes, recalling additional sensory details, thinking more about your own reactions to the event, elaborating on significant people, or developing the specific historical or cultural context in which it took place.

Setting Goals

Before starting to draft, you should set goals to guide further invention and planning. Some of these goals concern the piece as a whole, such as holding readers' interest with a compelling story, satisfying their curiosity by maintaining a good pace in the narrative, and framing the story in a satisfying way. Other goals have to do with smaller issues, such as including memorable sensory details, creating vivid images, and making dialogue sound like real conversation. You will make dozens of decisions—and solve dozens of problems—as you work your way through a draft; these decisions and solutions will be determined by the goals you set.

Following are some questions that can help you set goals before you start drafting. You may also want to return to them as you work, to help keep your goals in focus.

Your Readers

- What do I want my readers to think of me and my experience? If I want them to see the event from my point of view, should I show them how I felt at the time, as Lorde does? Should I tell them what I thought, as Wolff does? Do I want to show them how my perspective has changed, as Brandt does?
- If my readers are likely to have had similar experiences, how can I convey the uniqueness of my experience or its special importance in my life? Should I tell them more about my background or the particular context of the event? Should I give them a glimpse, as Wolff does, of its impact years later?
- If my readers are not likely to have had similar experiences, how can I help them understand what happened and appreciate its importance? Should I reveal the social implications, as Lorde does, or show the cultural influences acting on me, as Wolff does?
- If my readers may be alarmed by my disclosures or may judge me harshly, can I do anything to get them to see my point of view? Should I try to get them to question their own preconceptions, as Wolff does with his observations about the "ecstasy of power"? Should I present my experience without apology or explanation, as Brandt does? Should I try to get my readers to identify with my social situation, as Lorde does?

The Beginning

- How shall I begin? What can I do in the opening sentences that will capture my readers' interest? Should I begin with the main event, integrating essential background information as I tell the story, as Lorde does? Should I establish the setting and situation right away, as Brandt does? Should I first present myself, or should I provide the complete context for the event, as Wolff does? Or should I do something altogether different?

The Story

- What is the climax, or high point, of my story? For Wolff, it is shooting the squirrel.
- How can I build tension and suspense leading to the climax? Can I show specific narrative action, as Wolff does? Should I use dialogue, as Brandt and Lorde do?
- Should I tell the story chronologically? Would flashback or flashforward make the narrative more interesting?

- How can I use vivid descriptive detail to create a dominant impression that will reinforce the event's significance?

The Ending

- How should my essay end? Should I end with a reflection on the meaning of the experience, as Wolff does?
- If I want readers to think well of me, should I conclude with a philosophical statement, as Wolff does? Should I be satirical? Should I be self-critical and avoid smugness?
- If I want to leave readers with a sense of hope, can I find an image of harmony restored, as Lorde does, or an expression of optimism? If I want to underscore the event's continuing significance in my life, can I show that the conflict was never fully resolved, as Brandt does?
- Should I frame the essay by echoing something from the beginning to give readers at least a superficial sense of closure, as Brandt does by setting the last scene, like the first, in the family car?

Outlining

An essay about a remembered event should be above all a good story. The way you organize this story will depend on what happened, what significance it had for you, who your readers will be, and what impression you want to give them. As you draft and revise, you will discover the most appropriate organization for your story. For now, start to plan this organization by listing the main incidents in the order they took place. Then list them in the order in which you think they should be presented in your story.

Drafting

Start writing your essay, trying to maintain a focus on what took place in the event. Strive to paint a memorable picture of the scene and of any important people involved. Try also to describe the event in such a way as to say something about yourself and the event's significance in your life. If you feel stuck at any point in drafting the essay, try returning to the writing activities in the Invention section of this chapter. You may want to review the general planning and drafting advice given on pages 11–13.

GETTING CRITICAL COMMENTS

Now is the time to get a good critical reading. All writers find it helpful to have someone else read and comment on their drafts, and your instructor may schedule such a reading as part of your coursework. Otherwise, you can ask a classmate, friend, or family member to read it over. If your campus has a writing center, you might ask a tutor to comment on your draft. The guidelines in this section are designed to be used by *anyone*. (If you are unable to have someone else read your draft, turn ahead to the Revising and Editing section on pp. 44–47, which includes guidelines for reading your own draft with a critical eye.)

Your critical reader needs to know your intended audience and purpose. Briefly write out this information at the top of your draft:

Audience: Who are your readers?

Purpose: What do you want your readers to learn about you from reading about this event?

Reading with a Critical Eye

Reading a draft critically means reading it more than once, first to get a general impression and then to analyze its basic features.

Reading for a First Impression

Read first to enjoy the story and get a sense of its significance. As you read, try to notice any words or passages that contribute to your first impression, weak ones as well as strong ones.

After you've finished reading the draft, briefly give your impressions: How engaging is the story? Does the event seem truly significant? What in the draft do you think would especially interest the intended readers?

Reading to Analyze

Now reread the draft to focus on the basic features of writing about a remembered event. (See pp. 34–35 to review the basic features.)

Is the Story Told Well?

Identify the climax, and focus on how the narrative builds up to it. Note any places where the tension slackens and readers could lose interest in the outcome. Point to any sentences that seem boring or repetitious. Note any places where the story seems particularly vague or general.

Are Scenes and People Presented Vividly?

Indicate any scenes or people that seem nondescript or vague, that don't contribute to the dominant impression. Specify where dialogue rambles pointlessly, or where adding dialogue might help to dramatize a scene. Comment on the effectiveness of any similes or metaphors.

Is the Autobiographical Significance Clear?

Summarize the event's significance. What does it tell you about the author as an individual or about the cultural and economic forces that shaped the author's experience? Point to any places where the writer's remembered feelings and thoughts or present perspective could have been made clearer. Use an adjective or two (such as *thoughtful, self-deprecating, smug, sappy, vulnerable*) to describe your impression of the writer.

Is the Organization Effective?

Consider the *overall plan* for the essay, perhaps by outlining it briefly. Point to any places where the sequence of action isn't clear or where the narrative seems to meander pointlessly. Look to see if description or other information disrupts the flow of the narrative.

Look at the *beginning*. If it fails to draw you in or raises wrong expectations, say so. Point to another passage that might serve as a better opening.

Look at the *ending*. Indicate whether the resolution is too pat, overcomplicated, or unfocused. Point to any other passages that might work better as endings for the essay.

What Final Thoughts Do You Have?

What do you find most satisfying about this draft? Which parts of it need more work?

REVISING AND EDITING

This section will help you identify problems in your draft and revise and edit to solve them.

Identifying Problems

To identify problems in your draft, you need to read it objectively, analyze its basic features, and study any comments you've received from other readers.

Getting an Overview

Consider the draft as a whole, trying to see it objectively. It may help to do so in two steps:

1. *Reread.*   If at all possible, put the draft aside for a day or two before rereading it. When you do, start by reconsidering your purpose. Then read the draft straight through, trying to see it as your intended readers will.

2. *Outline.*   Make a scratch outline to get an overview of the essay's development. This outline can be sketchy—words and phrases instead of complete sentences— but it should identify the basic features as they appear.

Charting a Plan for Revision

You may want to make a double-columned chart to keep track of the problems you need to solve. In the left-hand column, list the basic features of writing about remembered events. As you analyze your draft and study any comments you've gotten from others, note the problems you want to solve in the right-hand column. Here is an example:

Basic Features	*Problems to Solve*
The story	
Scenes and people	
Autobiographical significance	
Organization	

Analyzing the Basic Features of Your Draft

Turn now to the questions for analyzing a draft on page 43. Using these questions as guidelines, identify problems in your draft. Note things to solve on your revision chart.

Studying Critical Comments

Review any comments you've received from other readers, and add to your chart any points that need attention. Try not to react defensively to these comments; by letting you see how others respond to your draft, the comments provide invaluable information about how you might improve it.

Solving the Problems

Having identified problems, you now need to figure out solutions and—most important of all—to carry them out. Basically, you have three ways of finding solutions: (1) review your invention and planning notes for additional information and ideas; (2) do further invention to answer questions you or your readers raised; and (3) look back at the readings in this chapter to see how other writers have solved similar problems.

Following are suggestions to get you started solving some of the problems common to writing about remembered events. For now, focus on solving those issues identified on your chart. Avoid tinkering with sentence-level problems at this time; that will come later when you edit.

The Story

- If the climax is hard to identify, look to find the high point of the narrative. Be sure the story has a climax, that it leads somewhere and doesn't just go on without a destination.
- If the tension slackens where it should build to the climax, try intensifying the pace—by adding specific details about movements and gestures, varying the sentence rhythm, or substituting lively quoted dialogue for summarized dialogue.
- If some sentences are repetitious, consider eliminating them or try varying them in terms of pattern and length. If they are all approximately the same length, try combining or shortening some to vary sentence rhythm.

Scenes and People

- If any scenes or people seem nondescript, try naming things more specifically and adding sensory details so that readers can see, touch, smell, taste, and hear aspects of the scene. Add similes and metaphors. Choose words that are concrete rather than abstract, specific rather than general.
- If any dialogue rambles pointlessly, liven it up with faster repartee or shorter, more pointed statements. Eliminate any unnecessary dialogue. Check the way it is introduced to see that it is not all in the form of "he said." Be more specific: "he cried out" or "she interrupted."

- If any description fails to contribute to the dominant impression, omit extraneous details or reconsider the impression you want to make.

Autobiographical Significance

- If the event's significance seems vague, look at the language you use to convey it. Ask yourself once again why the event stands out in your memory. What do you want readers to know about you from reading this essay?
- If the impression readers get of you is not the impression you want to make, look closely at the language you've used to express your feelings and thoughts. Consider whether you've projected a side of yourself you weren't aware of. If so, consider using this new insight to refocus what the story reveals about you.
- If your past or present feelings about the event do not come across clearly, review your invention writing or compose more expressive language—an image or metaphor perhaps—to show your feelings. Since feelings are often ambivalent and complicated, try to be expressive without oversimplifying.
- If readers don't appreciate the event's uniqueness or special importance in your life, consider giving them more insight into your background or cultural heritage. Consider whether you want to confront readers' complacency or provincialism with strong language or surprising revelations.

Organization

- If the story is hard to follow, restructure it so that the action unfolds clearly. Fill in any gaps. Eliminate unnecessary digressions.
- If description or other information disrupts the flow of the narrative, try integrating it more smoothly by adding transitions. If that doesn't help, consider taking it out or moving it.
- If the beginning is weak, see if there's a better place to start. Review the draft and your notes for an image, a bit of dialogue, or a remembered feeling that might catch readers' attention or arouse their curiosity.
- If the ending doesn't work, see if there's a better place to end—with a memorable image, perhaps, or a provocative assertion. Look to see if you can frame the essay by referring back to something in the beginning.

Editing and Proofreading

In working on your draft so far, you may have corrected some obvious errors, but grammar and style have not been a priority. Now is the time to check carefully for errors in usage, punctuation, and mechanics, as well as to consider matters of style. You may find that studying your draft in separate passes—first for paragraphs, then for sentences, and finally for words—will help you recognize problems.

Once you have edited your draft and produced a final copy, proofread it carefully to be sure there are no typos, misspellings, or other mistakes.

A Writer at Work

FROM INVENTION TO DRAFT TO REVISION

This section looks at the writing process that student writer Jean Brandt followed in composing her essay, "Calling Home." Here you will see some of her invention writing and her complete first draft, which you can then compare to the final draft printed on pages 29–31.

Invention

Brandt's invention produced about nine handwritten pages, but it took her only two hours, spread out over four days. Following is a selection of her invention writings. She begins by choosing an event and then recalling specific sensory details of the scene and the other people involved. She writes two dialogues, one with her sister Sue and the other with her father. Here is the one with her sister.

Re-Creating a Conversation

```
SUE: Jean, why did you do it?
ME: I don't know.  I guess I didn't want to wait in that
long line.  Sue, what am I going to tell Mom and Dad?
SUE: Don't worry about that yet; the detective might not
really call the police.
ME: I can't believe I was stupid enough to take it.
SUE: I know.  I've been there before.  Now when he comes
back try crying and act like you're really upset.  Tell
him how sorry you are and that it was the first time you
ever stole something but make sure you cry.  It got me
off the hook once.
ME: I don't think I can force myself to cry.  I'm not
really that upset.  I don't think the shock's worn off.
I'm more worried about Mom.
SUE: Who knows?  Maybe she won't have to find out.
ME: God, I hope not.  Hey, where's Louie and Grandma?
Grandma doesn't know about this, does she?
SUE: No, I sort of told Lou what was going on so he's
just taking Grandma around shopping.
ME: Isn't she wondering where we are?
SUE: I told him to tell her we would meet them in an hour.
ME: How am I ever going to face her?  Mom and Dad might
possibly understand or at least get over it, but Grandma?
This is gonna kill her.
```

```
SUE: Don't worry about that right now.  Here comes the
detective.  Now try to look like you're sorry.  Try to
cry.
```

This dialogue helps Brandt recall an important conversation with her sister. Dialogues are an especially useful form of invention for they enable writers to remember their feelings and thoughts.

Brandt writes this dialogue quickly, trying to capture the language of excited talk, keeping the exchanges brief. She includes a version of this dialogue in her second draft but excludes it from her revision. The dialogue with her father does not appear in any of her drafts. Even though she eventually decides to feature other completely different conversations, these invention dialogues enable her to evaluate how various conversations would work in her essay.

Next, we see her first attempts to bring the autobiographical significance of the event into focus as she explores her remembered feelings and present perspective:

```
Being arrested for shoplifting was significant because it
changed some of my basic attitudes.  Since that night
I've never again considered stealing anything.  This
event would reveal how my attitude toward the law and
other people has changed from disrespectful to very
respectful.
```

Brandt begins by stating tentatively that the importance of the event was the lesson it taught her. Reading this statement might lead us to expect a moralistic story of how someone learned something the hard way. As we look at the subsequent invention activities and watch the draft develop, however, we will see how her focus shifts to her relations with other people.

Recalling Remembered Feelings

```
    I was scared, humiliated, and confused.  I was terri-
fied when I realized what was happening.  I can still see
the manager and his badge and remember what I felt when
I knew who he was.  I just couldn't believe it.  I didn't
want to run.  I felt there wasn't anything I could do--I
was afraid, embarrassed, worried, mad that it happened.
I didn't show my feelings at all.  I tried to look very
calm on the outside, but inside I was extremely nervous.
The nervousness might have come through in my voice a
little.  I wanted the people around me to think I was
tough and that I could handle the situation.  I was
really disappointed with myself.  Getting arrested made
me realize how wrong my actions were.  I felt very
ashamed.  Afterward I had to talk to my father about it.
I didn't say much of anything except that I was wrong and
```

> I was sorry. The immediate consequence was being taken
> to jail and then later having to call my parents and tell
> them what happened. I hated to call my parents. That
> was the hardest part. I remember how much I dreaded
> that. My mom was really hurt.

Brandt's exploration of her first reaction is quite successful. Naming specific feelings, she focuses on the difference between what she felt and how she acted. She remembers her humiliation at being arrested as well as the terrible moment when she had to tell her parents. As we will see, this concern with her parents' reaction, more than her own humiliation, becomes the most important theme in her essay.

In exploring her first response to the event, Brandt writes quickly, jotting down memories as they come to mind. Next, she rereads this first exploration and attempts to state briefly what the incident really reveals about her:

> I think it reveals that I was not a hard-core criminal.
> I was trying to live up to Robin Files's (supposedly my
> best girlfriend) expectations, even though I actually
> knew that what I was doing was wrong.

After working on longer pieces of exploratory writing, stopping to focus her thoughts like this helps Brandt see the point of what she has just written. Specifically, it helps her to connect diverse invention writings to her main concern: discovering the autobiographical significance of the event. Thus she reflects on what her remembered feelings of the event reveal about the kind of person she was at the time: not a hard-core criminal. She identifies a friend, who will disappear from the writing after one brief mention. Next she looks at her present perspective on the event.

Exploring the Present Perspective

> At first I was ashamed to tell anyone that I had ar-
> rested. It was as if I couldn't admit it myself. Now
> I'm glad it happened, because who knows where I'd be now
> if I hadn't been caught. I still don't tell many people
> about it. Never before have I written about it. I think
> my response was appropriate. If I'd broken down and
> cried, it wouldn't have helped me any, so it's better
> that I reacted calmly. My actions and responses show
> that I was trying to be tough. I thought that that was
> the way to gain respectability. If I were to get ar-
> rested now (of course it wouldn't be for shoplifting), I
> think I'd react the same way because it doesn't do any
> good to get emotional. My current feelings are ones of
> appreciation. I feel lucky because I was set straight
> early. Now I can look back on it and laugh, but at the

> same time know how serious it was. I am emotionally dis-
> tant now because I can view the event objectively rather
> than subjectively. My feelings are settled now. I don't
> get upset thinking about it. I don't feel angry at the
> manager or the police. I think I was more upset about my
> parents than about what was happening to me. After the
> first part of it was over I mainly worried about what my
> parents would think.

Writing about her present perspective confirms for Brandt that she feels comfortable enough to write for class about this event. Having achieved some emotional
distance over time, she no longer feels humiliated or silenced by her embarrassment or her anger. Reassessing her reaction at the time, she is obviously pleased
to recall that she did not lose control and show her true feelings. Staying calm,
not getting emotional, looking tough—these are the personal qualities Brandt
wants others to see in her. Exploring her present perspective seems to have led to
a new, "respectable" self-image she can proudly display to her readers:

> My present perspective shows that I'm a reasonable per-
> son. I can admit when I'm wrong and accept the punish-
> ment that was due me. I find that I can be concerned
> about others even when I'm in trouble.

Next Brandt reflects on what she has written in order to articulate the autobiographical significance of the event.

Defining the Event's Autobiographical Significance

> The event was important because it entirely changed one
> aspect of my character. I will be disclosing that I was
> once a thief, and I think many of my readers will be
> able to identify with my story, even though they won't
> admit it.

After the first set of invention work, completed in about forty-five minutes on two
separate days, Brandt is confident she has chosen an event with personal significance. She knows what she will disclose about herself and feels comfortable about
doing it. In her brief focusing statements she begins by moralizing ("my attitude
. . . changed") and blaming others (Robin Files) but concludes by acknowledging
what she did. She is now prepared to disclose it to readers ("I was once a thief").
Also, she thinks readers will like her story because she suspects many of them will
recall doing something illegal and feeling guilty about it, even if they never got
caught.

The First Draft

The day after completing the invention writing, Brandt reviews her invention
materials and writes her first draft. It takes her about an hour. Her draft is hand-

written and contains few erasures or other changes, indicating that she writes steadily, probably letting the writing lead her where it will. She knows this will not be her only draft.

Before you read the first draft, reread the final draft, "Calling Home" (pp. 29–31). Then, as you read the first draft, consider what part it was to play in the total writing process.

It was two days before Christmas and my older sister   1
and brother, my grandmother, and I were rushing around
doing last-minute shopping. After going to a few stores
we decided to go to Lakewood Center shopping mall. It
was packed with other frantic shoppers like ourselves
from one end to the other. The first store we went to
(the first and last for me) was the General Store. The
General Store is your typical gift shop. It mainly has
the cutesy knick-knacks, posters, frames, and that sort.
The store is decorated to resemble an old-time western
general store but the appearance doesn't quite come off.

We were all browsing around and I saw a basket of but-   2
tons so I went to see what the different ones were. One
of the first ones I noticed was a Snoopy button. I'm not
sure what it said on it, something funny I'm sure and besides I was in love with anything Snoopy when I was 13.
I took it out of the basket and showed it to my sister
and she said, "Why don't you buy it?" I thought about it
but the lines at the cashiers were outrageous and I
didn't think it was worth it for a seventy-five-cent
item. Instead I figured just take it and I did. I
thought I was so sly about it. I casually slipped it
into my pocket and assumed I was home free since no one
pounced on me. Everyone was ready to leave this shop so
we made our way through the crowds to the entrance.

My grandmother and sister were ahead of my brother and   3
I. They were almost to the entrance of May Co. and we
were about 5 to 10 yards behind when I felt this tap on
my shoulder. I turned around already terror struck, and
this man was flashing some kind of badge in my face. It
happened so fast I didn't know what was going on. Louie
finally noticed I wasn't with him and came back for me.
Jack explained I was being arrested for shoplifting and
if my parents were here then Louie should go find them.
Louie ran to get Susie and told her about it but kept it
from Grandma. By the time Sue got back to the General
Store I was in the back office and Jack was calling the
police. I was a little scared but not really. It was

```
sort of exciting.  My sister was telling me to try and
cry but I couldn't.  About 20 minutes later two cops came
and handcuffed me, led me through the mall outside to the
police car.  I was kind of embarrassed when they took me
through the mall in front of all those people.
     When they got me in the car they began questioning me,      4
while driving me to the police station.  Questions just
to fill out the report--age, sex, address, color of eyes,
etc.
     Then when they were finished they began talking about        5
Jack and what a nuisance he was.  I gathered that Jack
had every single person who shoplifted, no matter what
their age, arrested.  The police were getting really fed
up with it because it was a nuisance for them to have to
come way out to the mall for something as petty as that.
To hear the police talk about my "crime" that way felt
good because it was like what I did wasn't really so bad.
It made me feel a bit relieved.  When we walked into the
station I remember the desk sergeant joking with the ar-
resting officers about "well we got another one of Jack's
hardened criminals."  Again, I felt my crime lacked any
seriousness at all. Next they handcuffed me to a table
and questioned me further and then I had to phone my mom.
That was the worst.  I never was so humiliated in my
life.  Hearing the disappointment in her voice was worse
punishment than the cops could ever give me.
```

This first draft establishes the main narrative line of events. About a third of it is devoted to the store manager, an emphasis that disappears by the final draft. What has prominence in the final draft—Brandt's feelings about telling her parents and her conversations with them—appears here only in a few lines at the very end. But its mention suggests its eventual importance, and we are reminded of its prominence in Brandt's invention writing.

Brandt writes a second draft for another student to read critically. In this draft, she includes dialogues with her sister and with the police officers. She also provides more information about her actions as she considered buying the Snoopy button and then decided to steal it instead. She includes visual details of the manager's office. This draft is not much different in emphasis from the first draft, however, still ending with a long section about the police officers and the station. The parents are mentioned only briefly at the end.

The student reader tells Brandt how much he likes her story and admires her frankness. However, he does not encourage her to develop the dramatic possibilities in calling her parents and meeting them afterward. In fact, he encourages her to keep the dialogue with the police officers about the manager and to include what the manager said to the police.

Brandt's revision shows that she does not take her critical reader's advice. She reduces the role of the police officers, eliminating the dialogue with them. She greatly expands the role of her parents: the last third of the paper is now focused on her remembered feelings about calling them and seeing them afterward. In dramatic importance the phone call home now equals the arrest. Remembering Brandt's earliest invention writings, we can see that she was headed toward this conclusion all along—but she needed invention, three drafts, a critical reading, and about a week to get there.

Reflecting on Your Writing

By this time, you've worked extensively in autobiography—reading it, talking about it, writing it. Now is a good time to think critically about what you've learned about this genre. Reflecting on your writing process will help you discover what you learned about solving problems you encountered writing about an event.

Begin by gathering your invention and planning notes, outlines, drafts, comments from other readers, revision plans, and final revision. Review these materials as you complete the following writing tasks.

- Identify *one* major problem you needed to solve as you wrote about a remembered event. Don't be concerned with sentence-level issues; concentrate on a problem unique to autobiographical writing. For example: Did you puzzle over how to present a particular scene or person? Was it difficult to structure the narrative so that it builds up to a climax? Did you find it hard (or uncomfortable) to convey the event's autobiographical significance?
- Determine how you came to recognize the problem. When did you first discover it? What called it to your attention? Did you notice it yourself, or did another reader point it out? Can you now see hints of it in your invention writing, your planning notes, or an earlier draft? If so, where specifically?
- Reflect next on how you went about solving the problem. Did you work on a particular passage, cut or add details, reorganize the essay? Did you reread one of the essays in the chapter to see how another writer handled similar material? Did you look back at the invention guidelines? Did you discuss the problem with another student, a tutor, or your instructor? If so, how did talking about it help, and how useful was the advice you got?
- Finally, write a page or so explaining the problem to your instructor, including how you discovered it, and how you tried to solve it. Be as specific as possible in reconstructing your efforts. Quote from your invention notes or early drafts, from readers' comments, from your revision plan, and from your final revision to show the various changes your writing underwent as you worked to solve the problem. If you're still uncertain about your solution, say so. The point is not to prove that you've solved the problem perfectly, but to show what you've learned about problem solving in the process of writing autobiography.

3 Explaining a Concept

Explanatory writing serves a limited but very important purpose: to inform readers. In general, it does not feature its writers' experiences or feelings, as autobiography does (see Chapter 2). Instead, successful explanatory writing confidently and efficiently presents information. This type of writing, required most every day in virtually every profession, may be based on firsthand observation, but it always moves beyond description of specific objects and events to explanation of general principles and patterns of behavior. Since it deals almost exclusively with established information, explanatory writing tends not to present an argument but to present information as if everyone assumes it were true. It does not aspire to be more than it is: a way for readers to find out about a particular subject. Much of what we find in newspapers, encyclopedias, instruction manuals, reference books, and research reports is explanatory writing.

This chapter focuses on one important kind of explanatory writing—explanations of concepts. The chapter readings explain the concepts "parthenogenesis," "contingent workers," and "schizophrenia." These concepts name processes and phenomena under study. Biologists, as you will see, use the concept "parthenogenesis" to identify the process of asexual reproduction observed among some animals and insects. Economists studying patterns in the work force use the concept "contingent workers" to describe the kind of workers, from chief executive officers to office assistants, who go from company to company to work on a specific project for a limited amount of time. Psychiatrists classify patients with certain symptoms as having the mental illness called "schizophrenia."

Every field of study has its concepts: physics has "entropy," "mass," and "fission"; literature has "irony," "romanticism," and "bildungsroman"; music has "harmony"; art has "perspective"; mathematics has "probability"; and so on. You can see from this brief list that concepts are central to the understanding of virtually every subject. Moreover, when you enter a new field, you're expected to learn a new set of concepts. That's why introductory courses and their textbooks teach a whole new vocabulary of technical terms and specialized jargon. When you read the opening chapter of this textbook, for example, you were introduced to many concepts important to the study of writing, such as "genre," "writing process," "invention," "revision," and "thinking critically."

Learning to explain a concept is especially important to you as a college student. It will help you read textbooks (which themselves exist to explain concepts);

it will prepare you to write a common type of exam and paper assignment; and it will acquaint you with the basic strategies common to all types of explanatory writing—definition, classification, comparision and contrast, cause and effect, and process narration.

WRITING IN YOUR OTHER COURSES

In your college courses you will frequently be asked to explain or apply concepts. Following are some typical assignments:

- *For a chemistry course:* In your own words, explain the "law of definite proportions" and show its importance to the field of chemistry.
- *For a government course:* Choose one emerging democracy in eastern Europe, research it, and report on its progress in establishing a democratic government. Consider carefully its present arrangements for "political parties," "majority rule," "minority rights," and "popular consent."
- *For an English course:* Many works of literature depict "scapegoat" figures. Select two written works and two films, and discuss how their authors and directors present the social conflicts that lead to the creation of scapegoats.

For Group Inquiry

Try explaining a concept you learned in school or at work to two or three other students. If you cannot think of an academic or work-related concept, you may choose a concept related to a hobby or an interest you have. For example, if you're a baseball fan, you could explain the concept of the "squeeze play"; if you're interested in computers, you could explain "hypertext"; if you know about music, you could explain "hip-hop"; or if you work out, you could explain "interval training."

Once you have chosen a concept, think about what others in the group are likely to know about it and how you can inform them about it in two or three minutes. Consider how you will define the concept and what other strategies you might use—description, comparison, and so on—to explain it in an interesting, memorable way. You might begin by indicating where you learned the concept and in what area of study or work it is usually used.

In turn, each group member should explain a concept. After each explanation, take turns telling the speaker one or two things you learned about the concept.

Once all group members have explained a concept, discuss what you learned from the experience of explaining a concept. Here are some discussion questions:

- What most surprised you about this activity?
- How did you decide which explanatory strategies to use?
- How did you decide what to include in your explanation and what to leave out?

Readings

David Quammen is both a novelist and a prolific science writer. His essays have been published in many magazines, including *Outside*, a nature magazine for which he writes a column called "Natural Acts." As you read this selection, first written for *Outside* and later published in *Natural Acts: A Sidelong View of Science and Nature* (1985), notice how Quammen engages readers' attention while presenting information about an important biological concept.

IS SEX NECESSARY?
▪
David Quammen

Birds do it, bees do it, goes the tune. But the songsters, as usual, would mislead us with drastic oversimplifications. The full truth happens to be more eccentrically nonlibidinous: Some- 1
times they *don't* do it, those very creatures, and get the same results anyway. Bees of all species, for instance, are notable to geneticists precisely for their ability to produce offspring while doing *without*. Likewise at least one variety of bird—the Beltsville Small White turkey, a domestic dinner-table model out of Beltsville, Maryland—has achieved scientific renown for a similar feat. What we are talking about here is celibate motherhood, procreation without copulation, a phenomenon that goes by the technical name *parthenogenesis*. Translated from the Greek roots: virgin birth.

And you don't have to be Catholic to believe in this one. 2

Miraculous as it may seem, parthenogenesis is actually rather common 3
throughout nature, practiced regularly or intermittently by at least some species within almost every group of animals except (for reasons still unknown) dragonflies and mammals. Reproduction by virgin females has been discovered among reptiles, birds, fishes, amphibians, crustaceans, mollusks, ticks, the jellyfish clan, flatworms, roundworms, segmented worms; and among insects (notwithstanding those unrelentingly sexy dragonflies) it is especially favored. The order Hymenoptera, including all bees and wasps, is uniformly parthenogenetic in the manner by which males are produced: Every male honeybee is born without any genetic contribution from a father. Among the beetles, there are thirty-five different forms of parthenogenetic weevil. The African weaver ant employs parthenogenesis, as do twenty-three species of fruit fly and at least one kind of roach. The gall midge *Miastor* is notorious for the exceptionally bizarre and grisly scenario that allows its fatherless young to see daylight: *Miastor* daughters cannibalize the mother from inside, with ruthless impatience, until her hollowed-out skin splits open like the door of an overcrowded nursery. But the foremost practitioners of virgin birth—their elaborate and versatile proficiency unmatched in the animal kingdom—are undoubtedly the aphids.

Now no sensible reader of even this can be expected, I realize, to care 4
faintly about aphid biology *qua* aphid biology. That's just asking too much. But there's a larger rationale for dragging you aphid-ward. The life cycle of

these little nebbishy sap-sucking insects, the very same that infest rose bushes and house plants, not only exemplifies *how* parthenogenetic reproduction is done; it also very clearly shows *why.*

First the biographical facts. A typical aphid, which feeds entirely on   5 plant juices tapped off from the vascular system of young leaves, spends winter dormant and protected, as an egg. The egg is attached near a bud site on the new growth of a poplar tree. In March, when the tree sap has begun to rise and the buds have begun to burgeon, an aphid hatchling appears, plugging its sharp snout (like a mosquito's) into the tree's tenderest plumbing. This solitary individual aphid will be, necessarily, a wingless female. If she is lucky, she will become sole founder of a vast aphid population. Having sucked enough poplar sap to reach maturity, she produces—by *live birth* now, and without benefit of a mate—daughters identical to herself. These wingless daughters also plug into the tree's flow of sap, and they also produce further wingless daughters, until sometime in late May, when that particular branch of that particular tree can support no more thirsty aphids. Suddenly there is a change: The next generation of daughters are born with wings. They fly off in search of a better situation.

One such aviatrix lands on an herbaceous plant—say a young climb-   6 ing bean in some human's garden—and the pattern repeats. She plugs into the sap ducts on the underside of a new leaf, commences feasting destructively, and delivers by parthenogenesis a great brood of wingless daughters. The daughters beget more daughters, those daughters beget still more, and so on, until the poor bean plant is encrusted with a solid mob of these fat little elbowing greedy sisters. Then again, neatly triggered by the crowded conditions, a generation of daughters are born with wings. Away they fly, looking for prospects, and one of them lights on, say, a sugar beet. (The switch from bean to beet is fine, because our species of typical aphid is not inordinately choosy.) The sugar beet before long is covered, sucked upon mercilessly, victimized by a horde of mothers and nieces and granddaughters. Still not a single male aphid has appeared anywhere in the chain.

The lurching from one plant to another continues; the alternation be-   7 tween wingless and winged daughters continues. But in September, with fresh tender plant growth increasingly hard to find, there is another change.

Flying daughters are born who have a different destiny: They wing back   8 to the poplar tree, where they give birth to a crop of wingless females that are unlike any so far. These latest girls know the meaning of sex! Meanwhile, at long last, the starving survivors back on that final bedraggled sugar beet have brought forth a generation of males. The males have wings. They take to the air in quest of poplar trees and first love. *Et voilà.* The mated females lay eggs that will wait out the winter near bud sites on that poplar tree, and the circle is thus completed. One single aphid hatchling—call her the *fundatrix*—in this way can give rise in the course of a year, from her own ovaries exclusively, to roughly a zillion aphids.

Well and good, you say. A zillion aphids. But what is the point of it?   9

The point, for aphids as for most other parthenogenetic animals, is (1)   10 exceptionally fast reproduction that allows (2) maximal exploitation of temporary resource abundance and unstable environmental conditions, while

(3) facilitating the successful colonization of unfamiliar habitats. In other words the aphid, like the gall midge and the weaver ant and the rest of their fellow parthenogens, is by its evolved character a galloping opportunist.

This is a term of science, not of abuse. Population ecologists make an illuminating distinction between what they label *equilibrium* and *opportunistic* species. According to William Birky and John Gilbert, from a paper in the journal *American Zoologist*: "Equilibrium species, exemplified by many vertebrates, maintain relatively constant population sizes, in part by being adapted to reproduce, at least slowly, in most of the environmental conditions which they meet. Opportunistic species, on the other hand, show extreme population fluctuations; they are adapted to reproduce only in a relatively narrow range of conditions, but make up for this by reproducing extremely rapidly in favorable circumstances. At least in some cases, opportunistic organisms can also be categorized as colonizing organisms." Birky and Gilbert also emphasize that "The potential for rapid reproduction is the essential evolutionary ticket for entry into the opportunistic life style." 11

And parthenogenesis, in turn, is the greatest time-saving gimmick in the history of animal reproduction. No hours or days are wasted while a female looks for a mate; no minutes lost to the act of mating itself. The female aphid attains sexual maturity and, bang, she becomes automatically pregnant. No waiting, no courtship, no fooling around. She delivers her brood of daughters, they grow to puberty and, zap, another generation immediately. If humans worked as fast, Jane Fonda today would be a great-grandmother. The time saved to parthenogenetic species may seem trivial, but it is not. It adds up dizzyingly: In the same time taken by a sexually reproducing insect to complete three generations for a total of 1,200 offspring, an aphid (assuming the *same* time required for each female to mature, and the *same* number of progeny in each litter), squandering no time on courtship or sex, will progress through six generations for an extended family of 318,000,000. 12

Even this isn't speedy enough for some restless opportunists. That matricidal gall midge *Miastor*, whose larvae feed on fleeting eruptions of fungus under the bark of trees, has developed a startling way to cut further time from the cycle of procreation. Far from waiting for a mate, *Miastor* does not even wait for maturity. When food is abundant, it is the *larva*, not the adult female fly, who is eaten alive from inside by her own daughters. And as those voracious daughters burst free of the husk that was their mother, each of them already contains further larval daughters taking shape ominously within its own ovaries. While the food lasts, while opportunity endures, no *Miastor* female can live to adulthood without dying of motherhood. 13

The implicit principle behind all this nonsexual reproduction, all this hurry, is simple: Don't argue with success. Don't tamper with a genetic blueprint that works. Unmated female aphids, and gall midges, pass on their own gene patterns virtually unaltered (except for the occasional mutation) to their daughters. Sexual reproduction, on the other hand, constitutes, by its essence, genetic tampering. The whole purpose of joining sperm with egg is to shuffle the genes of both parents and come up with a new combination that might perhaps be more advantageous. Give the kid something neither Mom nor Pop ever had. Parthenogenetic species, during their hur- 14

ried phases at least, dispense with this genetic shuffle. They stick stubbornly
to the gene pattern that seems to be working. They produce (with certain
complicated exceptions) natural clones of themselves.

But what they gain thereby in reproductive rate, in great explosions of   15
population, they give up in flexibility. They minimize their genetic options.
They lessen their chances of adapting to unforeseen changes of circum-
stance.

Which is why more than one biologist has drawn the same conclusion   16
as M. J. D. White: "Parthenogenetic forms seem to be frequently successful
in the particular ecological niche which they occupy, but sooner or later
the inherent disadvantages of their genetic system must be expected to lead
to a lack of adaptability, followed by eventual extinction, or perhaps in
some cases by a return to sexuality."

So it *is* necessary, at least intermittently (once a year, for the aphids,   17
whether they need it or not), this thing called sex. As of course you and I
knew it must be. Otherwise surely, by now, we mammals and dragonflies
would have come up with something more dignified.

For Discussion

We all have reason to care about developments in science, medicine, and health.
Surveys reveal, however, that few Americans leave school with much scientific
knowledge. Consequently, writers such as David Quammen play an important
role in explaining scientific concepts as well as medical and health findings to
newspaper and magazine readers. Discuss your own education in science. What
kinds of reading, lab activities, and teaching do you remember? How do you feel
as a student of science—competent, stimulated, bored, overwhelmed? How do
you keep up, if you do, with scientific developments—by reading newspaper
articles, by subscribing to a science magazine, by watching television programs
on science? How well do you understand what you're reading or seeing on television?

For Analysis

1. Analyze Quammen's plan for this essay by making a scratch outline. Given his
   purpose and readers, what advantages or disadvantages do you see in the way he
   organizes his information?

2. Consider ways Quammen helps readers follow his essay. What cues does he
   provide? Underline all the cueing devices you can find in his essay: forecasting
   statements, topic sentences, transitional words and phrases, summaries. How do
   these cues help to keep you, as one reader, oriented? Point to two or three especially effective cues. (For information about cueing, see Chapter 7.)

3. In paragraphs 5–10, Quammen explains the process of parthenogenesis among
   aphids. Look closely at these paragraphs, circling the time markers and verb tenses
   the writer uses to keep readers oriented as he explains a process that unfolds over
   seven months. How effectively does his narrative set out the order of events in
   this process?

4. To see how Quammen uses illustration, reread paragraphs 1 and 3 to find the examples. What purpose do you think these examples serve? Notice that he doesn't treat them all the same way. Whereas the second sentence in paragraph 3 simply lists eleven different kinds of animals, the remaining five sentences discuss at somewhat greater length several different kinds of insects. What advantages or disadvantages do you see in Quammen's using more than one example, and why do you think he treats them differently?

For Your Own Writing

What science concepts do you think you could, with a little reviewing, explain? Consider the science courses you've taken in the last year or two, and think of the concepts they covered. Choose one concept, and consider how you would go about writing an explanatory essay on it for a particular group of readers. The readers may already know something about the concept, or they may be totally unfamiliar with it.

Commentary

This reading illustrates the need to limit the scope of essays explaining concepts. Since Quammen cannot say everything that is known about parthenogenesis, he focuses on what is most important: defining the concept and explaining exactly how the process of parthenogenic reproduction works. In addition, he helps readers understand both the advantages of parthenogenesis and that these advantages make it far more common than they might have guessed.

Although most people read concept explanations because they need to know about a subject, Quammen goes to great lengths to interest readers in his topic. He gives his essay a provocative title, and he begins by quoting the familiar and humorous lyrics of a popular song—*"Birds do it, bees do it"*—and then immediately gives examples of bees and birds that *don't* always do it. At the end of the first paragraph, he defines parthenogenesis in human sexual terms (ones sure to be familiar to readers). He concludes by framing the essay in the same terms, appealing to readers' awareness of both the serious and the humorous aspects of sex. Another way Quammen maintains readers' interest is by using everyday language and images ("a solid mob of these fat little elbowing greedy sisters"). He occasionally addresses the reader directly ("dragging you aphid-ward," "well and good, you say") and makes a point of explaining insect parthenogenesis in human terms ("no waiting, no courtship, no fooling around"). Few writers try as hard or succeed as well as Quammen does in making his explanation interesting to readers.

Writers of concept explanation are careful about how they introduce and pace information. They avoid introducing too much information too soon or packing in so much information that readers lose interest. Quammen's first paragraph offers a lot of information. Before offering more information of this kind, however, he pauses (in paragraph 4) to address readers directly, acknowledging that they may not "care faintly about aphid biology," and explaining why the next paragraphs must detail the particular form of aphid parthenogenesis.

In paragraphs 5–8, Quammen uses process narration to explain the life cycle of the aphid. He pauses again, in paragraphs 9 and 10, to tell readers the point of the aphid example. The remainder of the essay continues this pattern of informing and pausing to explain why the information is important. You can see that Quammen recognizes and accommodates the limits on readers' tolerance for new information, especially on a subject about which they are not experts.

Janice Castro, a graduate of the University of California at Berkeley, is an associate editor at *Time*, where she writes about politics and business. Some of her major reports have addressed the high cost of medical care, drugs in the workplace, quality in American manufacturing, the state of the U.S. work force, and Japanese investment in the United States. In the following selection, originally published in *Time* in 1993, Castro discusses changes in the way American companies do business, changes that rely on part-time and free-lance workers. Castro uses the concept "contingent" workers to name both the phenomenon and the people it affects.

CONTINGENT WORKERS
■
Janice Castro

The corporation that is now the largest private employer in America does not have any smoke- stacks or conveyor belts or trucks. There is no clanging of metal on metal, no rivets or plastic or steel. In one sense, it does not make anything. But then again, it is in the business of making almost everything. 1

Manpower Inc., with 560,000 workers, is the world's largest temporary employment agency. Every morning, its people scatter into the offices and factories of America, seeking a day's work for a day's pay. As General Motors (367,000 workers), IBM (330,500) and other industrial giants struggle to survive by shrinking their payrolls, Manpower, based in Milwaukee, Wisconsin, is booming along with other purveyors of temporary workers, providing the hands and the brainpower that other companies are no longer willing to call their own. 2

Even as its economy continues to recover, the U.S. is increasingly becoming a nation of part-timers and free-lancers, of temps and independent contractors. This "disposable" work force is the most important trend in business today, and it is fundamentally changing the relationship between Americans and their jobs. For companies large and small, the phenomenon provides a way to remain globally competitive while avoiding the vagaries of market cycles and the growing burdens imposed by employment rules, antidiscrimination laws, health-care costs, and pension plans. But for workers, it can mean an end to the security and sense of significance that came from being a loyal employee. One by one, the tangible and intangible bonds that once defined work in America are giving way. 3

Every day, 1.5 million temps are dispatched from agencies like Kelly Services and Manpower—nearly three times as many as 10 years ago. But they are only the most visible part of America's enormous new temporary 4 work force. An additional 34 million people start their day as other types of "contingent" workers. Some are part-timers with some benefits. Others work by the hour, the day or the duration of a project, receiving only a paycheck without benefits of any kind. The rules of their employment vary widely and so do the attempts to label them. They are called short-timers, per-diem workers, leased employees, extra workers, supplementals, contractors—or in IBM's ironic computer-generated parlance, "the peripherals." They are what you might expect: secretaries, security guards, salesclerks, assembly-line workers, analysts and CAD/CAM designers. But these days they are also what you'd never expect: doctors, high school principals, lawyers, bank officers, X-ray technicians, biochemists, engineers, managers—even chief executives.

Already, one in every three U.S. workers has joined these shadow brigades carrying out America's business. Their ranks are growing so quickly that they are expected to outnumber permanent full-time workers by the end of this decade. Companies keep chipping away at costs, stripping away benefits or substituting contingent employees for full-time workers. This year alone, U.S. employers are expected to use such tactics to cut the nation's $2.6 billion payroll costs as much as $800 million. And there is no evidence to suggest that such corporate behavior will change with improvement in the economy.   5

No institution is immune to the contingent solution. Imagine the surprise of a Los Angeles woman, seriously injured in an auto accident, when she recently asked a radiology technician at the hospital about a procedure. "Don't ask me," he snapped. "I'm just a temp." In Appleton, Wisconsin, the Aid Association for Lutherans is using temps to keep track of $3.6 million in relief funds for victims of Hurricane Andrew. The State of Maine uses temps as bailiffs and financial investigators. IBM, once the citadel of American job security, has traded 10% of its staff for "peripherals" so far. Says IBM administrative manager Lillian Davis, in words that would have been unimaginable from a Fortune 500 executive 20 years ago: "Now that we have stepped over that line, we have decided to use these people wherever we can."   6

The number of people employed full time by Fortune 500 companies has shrunk from 19% of the work force two decades ago to less than 10% today. Almost overnight, companies are shedding a system of mutual obligations and expectations built up since the Great Depression, a tradition of labor that said performance was rewarded, loyalty was valued and workers were a vital part of the enterprises they served. In this chilly new world of global competition, they are often viewed merely as expenses. Long-term commitments of all kinds are anathema to the modern corporation. For the growing ranks of contingent workers, that means no more pensions, health insurance or paid vacations. No more promises or promotions or costly training programs. No more lawsuits for wrongful termination or other such hassles for the boss. Says Secretary of Labor Robert Reich: "These workers are outside the traditional system of worker-management relationships. As the contingent work force grows—as many people find themselves working part time for many different employers—the social contract is beginning to fray."   7

As the underpinnings of mutual commitment crumble, time-honored notions of fairness are cast aside for millions of workers. Working temp or part time often means being treated as a second-class citizen by both employers and permanent staff. Says Michelle Lane, a former temp in Los Angeles: "You're just a fixture, a borrowed thing that doesn't belong there." Being a short-timer also can mean doing hazardous work without essential training, or putting up with sexual and racial harassment. Placement officers report client requests for "blond bombshells" or people without accents. Says an agency counselor: "One client called and asked us not to send any black people, and we didn't. We do whatever the clients want, whether it's right or not." 8

Workers have little choice but to cope with such treatment since most new job openings are the labor equivalent of uncommitted relationships. More than 90% of the 365,000 jobs created by U.S. companies last month were part-time positions taken by people who want to work full time. "The fill-ins are always desperate for full-time jobs," says one corporate personnel officer. "They always ask." Richard Belous, chief economist for the National Planning Association in Washington, has studied the proliferation of tenuous jobs. "If there was a national fear index," he says, "it would be directly related to the growth of contingent work." 9

Once contingent workers appear in a company, they multiply rapidly, taking the places of permanent staff. Says Manpower chairman Mitchell Fromstein: "The U.S. is going from just-in-time manufacturing to just-in-time employment. The employer tells us, 'I want them delivered exactly when I want them, as many as I need, and when I don't need them, I don't want them here.'" Fromstein has built his business by meeting these demands. "Can I get people to work under these circumstances? Yeah. We're the ATMs of the job market." 10

In order to succeed in this new type of work, says Carvel Taylor, a Chicago industrial consultant, "you need to have an entrepreneurial spirit, definable skills and an ability to articulate and market them, but that is exactly what the bulk of the population holed up inside bureaucratic organizations doesn't have, and why they are scared to death." Already the temping phenomenon is producing two vastly different classes of untethered workers: the mercenary work force at the top of the skills ladder, who thrive; and the rest, many of whom, unable to attract fat contract fees, must struggle to survive. 11

The flexible life of a consultant or contract worker does indeed work well for a relatively small class of people like doctors, engineers, accountants and financial planners, who can expect to do well by providing highly compensated services to a variety of employers. David Hill, 65, a former chief information systems officer for General Motors, has joined with 17 other onetime auto-industry executives (median salary before leaving their jobs: $300,000) to form a top-of-the-line international consulting group. "In the future," says Hill, "loyalty and devotion are going to be not to a Hughes or Boeing or even an industry, but to a particular profession or skill. It takes a high level of education to succeed in such a free-flowing environment. We are going to be moving from job to job in the same way that migrant workers used to move from crop to crop." 12

Many professionals like the freedom of such a life. John Andrews, 42, 13
a Los Angeles antitrust attorney, remembers working seven weeks without
a day off as a young lawyer. He prefers temping at law firms. Says he:
"There's no security anymore. Partnerships fold up overnight. Besides, I
never had a rat-race mentality, and being a lawyer is the ultimate rat-race
job. I like to travel. My car is paid for. I don't own a house. I'm not into
mowing grass."

But most American workers do better with the comfort and security of 14
a stable job. Sheldon Joseph was a Chicago advertising executive until he
was laid off in 1989. Now he temps for $10 an hour in a community job-
training program. Says the 56-year-old Joseph: "I was used to working in
the corporate environment and giving my total loyalty to the company. I
feel like Rip Van Winkle. You wake up and the world is all changed. The
message from industry is, 'We don't want your loyalty. We want your work.'
What happened to the dream?"

Employers defend their new labor practices as plain and simple sur- 15
vival tactics. American companies are evolving from huge, mass-production
manufacturers that once dominated markets to a new species of hub-and-
network enterprises built for flexibility in a brutally competitive world. The
buzz phrase at many companies is "accordion management"—the ability
to expand or contract one's work force virtually at will to suit business
conditions.

Boardroom discussions now focus on what are called "core compe- 16
tencies"—those operations at the heart of a business—and on how to shed
the rest of the functions to subcontractors or nonstaff workers. Managers
divide their employees into a permanent cadre of "core workers," which
keeps on shrinking, and the contingent workers, who can be brought in at
a moment's notice. Most large employers are not even certain at any given
time how many of these helpers are working for them—nor do they usually
care. Says a manager: "We don't count them. They're not here long enough
to matter." Some analysts wonder whether America's celebrated rise in
productivity per worker (2.8% last year) is all it seems to be, since so many
of those invisible hands are not being counted. So profound is the change
that the word *core* has evolved a new meaning, as in "she's core," meaning
that she is important and distinctive because she is not part of the contingent
work force.

Indeed, managers these days can hire virtually any kind of temp they 17
want. Need an extra lawyer or paralegal for a week or so? Try Lawsmiths
in San Francisco or Project Professionals in Santa Monica, California. Need
a loan officer? Bank Temps in Denver can help. Engineers? Sysdyne outside
Minneapolis, Minnesota. CAD/CAM operators? You don't even need to buy
the equipment: in Oakland, California, Western Temporary Services has its
own CAD/CAM business, serving such clients as the U.S. Navy, the Air
Force, Chevron, Exxon and United Technologies. Doctors and nurses? A
firm called Interim in Fort Lauderdale, Florida, can provide them anywhere
in the country. Need to rent a tough boss to clean up a bad situation? Call
IMCOR, a Connecticut-based firm that boasts a roster of senior executives

expert at turnarounds. Says IMCOR chairman John Thompson: "Services like ours are going to continue to flourish when businesses change so rapidly that it's in no one's interest to make commitments. Moving on to the next place where you're needed is going to be the way it is. We will all be free-lancers."

For now, most citizens will have to scramble to adapt to the new age 18 of the disposable worker. Says Robert Schaen, a former comptroller of Chicago-based Ameritech who now runs his own children's publishing business: "The days of the mammoth corporations are coming to an end. People are going to have to create their own lives, their own careers and their own successes. Some people may go kicking and screaming into the new world, but there is only one message there: You're now in business for yourself."

For Discussion

Janice Castro reports on a surprising change in the employment conditions of American workers. As recently as ten to fifteen years ago, most workers held full-time jobs with health care coverage, paid vacations, and pension plans. Many had virtual job security, continuing on the same job for thirty or forty years, until retirement. Now one-third of American workers are contingent, and Castro predicts that they will outnumber permanent, full-time workers by the year 2000. What might this change mean for you personally? Do you consider this a setback or an opportunity?

For Analysis

1. Although Castro provides a lot of information about the concept of the contingent worker, she selects the information carefully from all that is available to her. What questions about contingent workers do you think she is trying to answer for her readers?

2. Writers of essays explaining concepts nearly always must create their own definitions for the central concept and other key terms. In paragraph 4, Castro tentatively defines "contingent workers." How does she go about constructing this definition? What is included in it? How satisfactory do you find this initial definition of the concept?

3. In explaining a concept, writers often use the strategy of comparing and contrasting. Where does Castro use this strategy and for what purpose? Compare her use of comparison and contrast to David Quammen's in his essay earlier in the chapter.

4. For readers to accept a writer's explanation of a concept, they must believe the writer is an expert on the subject. Review both the Quammen and Castro essays, listing qualities that make them seem authoritative and trustworthy, as well as qualities that make you doubt their expertise. How successful are they in winning your confidence?

For Your Own Writing

Consider writing about the contingent worker concept but with a focus different from Castro's. For example, you could focus on the debate between labor and business over contingent work (sorting out the issues and reporting what you learn, but not taking a side yourself), the history of contingent or part-time work in America, or changes brought about in the lives of those who have had to give up full-time jobs and take up contingent work. Or you could write about some other concept central to current discussions of work, such as career path, glass ceiling, burnout, networking, mentoring, management styles, or collective bargaining.

Commentary

Castro makes good use of a variety of sources. As a business reporter, she has access to published materials and computer data sources that provide the many facts and statistics she includes about corporations and employment trends. Since she has written about contingent workers and related topics before, she has developed a store of information. In addition, she apparently interviewed fourteen people for this new report, and it may be that some of her facts and statistics come from these interviews. Following her magazine's convention for citing sources, she names her interviewees but does not identify other sources of information, perhaps because she knows her readers will accept the information as well established. Apparently, *Time* assumes that readers will accept Castro's statistics about American business just as they accept baseball scores and weather reports.

Castro's role is much like your role in writing an essay for this chapter: relying on a variety of authoritative sources, you, too, will explain a concept to readers who know less about it than you do. However, you will need to cite your sources more precisely and fully than Castro does because complete citation of sources is expected in all academic writing by students and professors. Student writer Veronica Murayama's essay (later in this chapter) as well as Chapter 11 provide guidance in using and acknowledging sources.

Writers face special challenges in planning and organizing essays that explain concepts. First, they gather a lot of information about a concept. Then they must find a way to explain the concept that will interest and inform their readers. Finally, writers must organize the information so that readers can understand it without too much uncertainty or frustration.

Let's consider Castro's plan. Here is a scratch outline of her essay, with paragraph numbers indicated parenthetically:

Ironic opening: Manpower Inc. employs more than GM. (1–2)

Increase in part-time and free-lance employment represents a fundamental change. (3)

The concept of contingent workers is defined. (4)

The number of contingents is growing and not likely to decline when the economy improves. (5)

All kinds of institutions and businesses are relying on contingents. (6)

Mutual obligations between employer and employee are being shed. (7)

Contingents are second-class citizens. (8, 9)

Demand for contingents is increasing. (10)

Some contingents find success. (11–13)

But most Americans still prefer a secure job. (14)

Employers have a number of arguments for relying on contingents. (15)

Employers distinguish sharply between core and contingent employees. (16)

Some contingents are highly specialized. (17)

Workers will have to adapt to this change. (18)

At the beginning, Castro contextualizes and defines the concept (paragraphs 1–4). She then reports on the nature of contingent work (5–10) and its mixed impact on employees (11–14). Finally, she presents employers' views (15–17) and concludes with a new way for contingent workers to see themselves—as being in business for themselves (18). Most readers will find this plan easy to follow.

Finally, special kinds of sentence structures enable writers to present information effectively. For example, Castro relies on appositives and parenthetical explanations that efficiently combine into one sentence information that might otherwise require two sentences:

> "IBM, *once the citadel of American job security*, has traded 10% of its staff for 'peripherals' so far." (paragraph 6)
>
> "Says Michelle Lane, *a former temp in Los Angeles*: 'You're just a fixture, a borrowed thing that doesn't belong there.' " (8)
>
> "As General Motors (*367,000 workers*), IBM (*330,500*), and other industrial giants struggle to survive. . . ." (2)

Further efficiency can be gained in explanatory writing by combining information into series or lists:

> ". . . avoiding the vagaries of market cycles and the growing burden imposed by *employment rules, antidiscrimination laws, health-care costs, and pension plans*." (paragraph 3)
>
> "They are called *short-timers, per-diem workers, leased employees, extra workers, supplementals, contractors*—or in IBM's ironic computer-generated parlance, '*the peripherals*.' " (4)
>
> "They are what you might expect: *secretaries, security guards, salesclerks, assembly-line workers, analysts, and CAD/CAM designers*." (4)

Items in a series or list must be grammatically parallel. Lists can be introduced by a colon, as in the last example above.

Veronica Murayama wrote this essay as a first-year college student. In it she defines a psychiatric concept, the debilitating mental illness called schizophrenia. Since this illness has been exhaustively studied and so much has been written about it, Murayama had to find a manageable focus for her essay. As you read, consider how she made this choice. Notice, too, how she seeks to engage your interest in the concept.

SCHIZOPHRENIA: WHAT IT
LOOKS LIKE, HOW IT FEELS
■
Veronica Murayama

Some mental illnesses, like depression, are more   1
common than schizophrenia, but few are more
severe. A schizophrenic has delusions and hallucinations, behaves in bizarre ways, talks in-
coherently, expresses little feeling or else feel-
ings inappropriate to the situation, and is incapable of normal social
interactions. Because these symptoms are so severe, about half the hospitalized mentally ill in America are schizophrenics. Only 1 percent of Americans (between 2 and 3 million) are schizophrenic, and yet they occupy
about one-fourth of the available beds in our hospitals ("Schizophrenic,"
1987, p. 1533). Up to 40 percent of the homeless may be schizophrenic
(King, 1989, p. 97).

Schizophrenia has been recognized for centuries, and as early as the   2
seventeenth century its main symptoms, course of development, and outcome were described. The term "schizophrenia," first used in 1908, refers
to the disconnection or splitting of the mind that seems basic to all the
various forms of the disease. It strikes both men and women, usually during
adolescence or early adulthood, and is found all over the world. Treatment
may include chemotherapy, electroconvulsive therapy, psychotherapy, and
counseling. Hospitalization is ordinarily required, but usually not for more
than a few months. It seems that about a third of patients recover completely
and the rest can eventually have "a reasonable life adjustment," but some
effect of the illness nearly always remains, most commonly lack of feeling
and reduced drive or ambition ("Schizophrenic," 1987, pp. 1533, 1537–
1539). Schizophrenia hits adolescents especially hard, and the effect on
their families can be disastrous.

Though much is known about schizophrenia and treatment is reason-   3
ably effective, specialists still argue about its causes. For example, various
researchers blame an unsatisfactory family life in which one or both parents
suffer from some form of mental illness (Lidz, 1973), some combination
of genetic inheritance and family life ("Schizophrenic," 1987, p. 1534;
"Schizophrenia," 1987, p. 192), or "an early developmental neuropatho-
logical process" that results in reduced size of certain brain areas (Suddath,
Cristison, Torrey, Casanova, & Weinberger, 1990, p. 793). What is known
and agreed on, however, is what schizophrenia looks like to an observer
and what it feels like to a sufferer, and these are what I want to focus on in
this essay. I have always believed that when people have knowledge about
any type of human suffering, they are more likely to be sympathetic with
the sufferer. Schizophrenic symptoms are not attractive, but they are easy
to understand. The medical manuals classify them approximately as fol-

lows: bizarre delusions, prominent hallucinations, confusion about identity, unconnected speech, inappropriate affect, disturbances in psychomotor behavior, impaired interpersonal functioning, and reduced drive.

Schizophrenics themselves experience the disease to a large extent as delusional thinking. For example, one woman said, "If I see a phone, I can talk on it without picking it up, immediately, anywhere in the world. But I don't abuse it. I'm authorized by AT&T. In the Yukon. And RCA" (Shane, 1987). It is common for schizophrenics to have delusions that they are being persecuted—that people are spying on them, spreading false stories about them, or planning to harm them. Events, objects, or people may be given special threatening significance, as when a patient believes a television commentator is making fun of him. Other delusions are very likely: "the belief or experience that one's thoughts, as they occur, are broadcast from one's head to the external world so that others can hear them; that thoughts that are not one's own are inserted into one's mind; that thoughts have been removed from one's head; or that one's feelings, impulses, thoughts, or actions are not one's own, but are imposed by some external force" ("Schizophrenia," 1987, p. 188). Sometimes delusions are grandiose, as when a patient thinks that he is the Messiah and will save the world or that she is the center of a conspiracy. A woman patient wrote, "I want a revolution, a great uprising to spread over the entire world and overthrow the whole social order. . . . Not for the love of adventure! No, no! Call it unsatisfied urge to action, if you like, indomitable ambition" (cited in Lidz, 1973, p. 134).

Related to delusions are hallucinations, which are very common in schizophrenics. Usually they hear voices coming from inside or outside the head, making insulting remarks, commenting on behavior, or giving commands that can sometimes be dangerous to others. Sometimes they hear sounds like humming, whistling, or machinery.

These false ideas and imaginary sensations leave schizophrenics confused about their identities. Feeling ruled by forces outside themselves, they lack normal feelings of individuality and uniqueness. One patient wrote, "I look at my arms and they aren't mine. They move without my direction. Somebody else moves them. . . . I have no control. I don't live in me. The outside and I are all the same" (cited in Mendel, 1974, p. 111).

Besides revealing their delusions and hallucinations, schizophrenics' speech is often rambling and unconnected. It may shift rapidly from one topic to another that is seemingly completely unrelated or only loosely related, and the speaker does not show any awareness of the lack of connection. One patient, a man, said, "I have always believed in the good of mankind but I know I am not a woman because I have an Adam's apple" ("Schizophrenic," 1987). Sometimes the topics are so unrelated that the patient's speech becomes incoherent and incomprehensible. Even when it is connected, schizophrenic speech can sometimes contain very little information because it is vague, abstract, or repetitive.

Schizophrenics also present themselves in recognizable ways, referred to as "inappropriate affect." Their voices are often monotonous and their faces expressionless. They may express little if any emotion, and their emotional responses do not seem varied. On the other hand, their responses

may seem completely inappropriate to the situation, or there may be un-
predictable outbursts of anger.

Another visible feature of schizophrenia is disturbed psychomotor be-   9
havior. The most severely ill may move around very little or sit rigidly and
resist being moved. Here is what one patient felt: "When I was acting so
stiff and wasn't talking I had the feeling that if I moved the whole world
might collapse. . . . I don't know why, but I seemed like I was the center of
everything and everything depended on my not moving" (cited in Mendel,
1974, p. 108). Patients may take up strange postures or engage in rocking
or pacing. At the other extreme, they may move excitedly and apparently
purposelessly. Unfortunately, violent behavior is possible as well. One
manual points out that "grotesque violence, with self-mutilation (often of
sexual organs) or murderous attacks, may occur. Matricide [killing one's
mother], the rarest form of murder, is most often perpetrated by schizophrenics, as is filicide [killing one's brother or sister]. . . . The risk of suicide
is increased in all stages of schizophrenic illness" ("Schizophrenic," 1987,
p. 1535). One woman patient wrote, "Death is the greatest happiness in
life, if not the only one. Without hope of the end, life would be unendur-
able" (cited in Mendel, 1974, p. 137).

Even if violence does not occur, it is not surprising that the speech and   10
behavioral symptoms I have described are almost invariably accompanied
by—and contribute to—impaired interpersonal functioning. Once schizophrenics become obsessed with delusions, hallucinations, and illogical
ideas, they are often too distracted and centered on themselves to interact
with other people. Such patients are notable for their emotional detachment
even from family members or friends they were previously close to. They
also withdraw from all other social interactions, dropping out of school or
leaving jobs. They simply cannot face the outside world. Some schizophrenics behave quite differently, however, at least during some phases of
the illness. They "cling to other people, intrude upon strangers, and fail to
recognize that excessive closeness makes people uncomfortable and likely
to pull away" ("Schizophrenia," 1987, p. 189).

Along with social impairment comes loss of drive or ambition. Schizo-   11
phrenics typically have difficulty in initiating actions, making decisions, or
following through with plans, and their work and other responsibilities often
suffer severely as a result.

It is important to know that doctors, counselors, and psychoanalysts   12
do not easily label someone schizophrenic. They do not do so unless many
of the symptoms I have described are present and unmistakable. Since depression has some of the same symptoms as schizophrenia and the treatment of the two is quite different, doctors have to be especially careful not
to confuse them. We have come a long way from the time when schizophrenics were considered dangerous lunatics and were locked away without treatment, sometimes for life. Doctors now recognize the illness and
can counsel both patients and families and prescribe drugs that have proven
effective. The problem today is that so many of the homeless are believed
to be schizophrenic, and it seems unlikely that many of them ever receive
treatment.

References

King, K. (1989, November). Lost brother. *Life*, 94–98.

Lidz, T. (1973). *The origin and treatment of schizophrenic disorders*. New York: Basic.

Mendel, W. M. (1974). A phenomenological theory of schizophrenia. In A. Burton, J. Lopez-Ibor, & W. M. Mendel (Eds.), *Schizophrenia as a life style* (pp. 106–155). New York: Springer.

Schizophrenia. (1987). *Diagnostic and statistical manual of mental disorders* (3rd ed.) (pp. 187–198). Washington, DC: American Psychiatric Association.

Schizophrenic disorders. (1987). *The Merck manual of diagnosis and therapy* (15th ed.) (pp. 1532–1539). Rahway, NJ: Merck and Company.

Shane, S. (1987, July 28). Relatives bear demoralizing task of patient care. [Baltimore] *Sun*, p. 14.

Suddath, R. L., Cristison, G. W., Torrey, E. F., Casanova, M. F., & Weinberger, D. R. (1990). Anatomical abnormalities in the brains of monozygotic twins discordant for schizophrenia. *The New England Journal of Medicine, 322*, 791–793.

For Discussion

Veronica Murayama's essay demonstrates that schizophrenia is a diagnosable medical problem. It is only one of many mental illnesses, perhaps the most widespread being depression, which afflicts 15 percent of Americans. People with mental illness need help because their suffering is acute and the costs to their families and to society are great, yet mental health funds are often the first to be cut in times of budget constraints. How would you explain the neglect of mental health resources? What community resources for the mentally ill are you aware of?

For Analysis

1. How, in paragraph 1, does Murayama seek to engage readers' interest in her topic? Compare her strategy with Quammen's and Castro's. In what ways do their beginnings seem appropriate or inappropriate for their subjects?

2. How does Murayama frame her essay? (Framing means referring at the end to something mentioned at the beginning.) Compare her use of framing with Quammen's. What advantages do you see in framing an explanatory essay?

3. Do you find Murayama's organizing strategies logical and easy to follow? Support your answer with specific examples from the essay.

4. Turn to pages 86–89 to see how Murayama surveyed sources and found a focus for her essay. In that Writer at Work section, you will find a list of the sources for paragraph 9. With the help of the Commentary that follows, analyze the relation between paragraph 9 and the list of sources. What conclusions can you reach about Murayama's use of sources? Notice where she quotes, paraphrases, or summarizes. How might you have used the sources differently?

For Your Own Writing

Consider writing an essay that would help you learn about another type of mental illness, such as hypochondriasis, mood disorders, bipolarism, phobic behaviors, or autism. The two manuals Murayama cites catalog many such illnesses. You would also want to look for current research and popular articles on your topic.

Commentary

Assuming her audience knows little about schizophrenia, Murayama tries to give readers some reasons to learn about the illness. Her first sentence acknowledges that readers may be more familiar with other more common types of mental illness such as depression. She then implies why it is important to learn about schizophrenia: because it is one of the most "severe" mental diseases. To illustrate what she means by "severe," Murayama briefly lists some of the common symptoms of schizophrenia and indicates the disproportionate number of people who need to be hospitalized for the illness.

By mentioning in the last sentence of paragraph 1 that up to 40 percent of homeless people may suffer from schizophrenia, she implies yet another, more immediate reason for readers to learn about the illness: they may actually witness many of the symptoms when they encounter homeless people on the street. This reason tells us that Murayama wants not only to inform readers about schizophrenia but also to affect how they regard the homeless. She indicates this secondary, but no less important, purpose for explaining the concept in paragraph 3, where she refers to her belief that "knowledge about . . . human suffering" can make people "more likely to be sympathetic with the sufferer."

In paragraph 3, Murayama forecasts the plan of her essay. A forecast identifies the main topics or ideas in an essay, usually in the sequence in which they will be discussed. The list of schizophrenic symptoms Murayama gives lays out her topics and their sequence; it also identifies the key terms she will rely on throughout the essay. Readers seeking information benefit from such an obvious cue because it enables them to predict what is coming.

It is also worth noting some of the ways Murayama incorporates quoted material into her own sentences. In some cases, she uses a dialogue cue, such as *he said*, or *she wrote*:

> One patient, *a man, said,* "I have always believed in the good of mankind. . . ." (paragraph 7)
>
> One *woman patient wrote,* "Death is the greatest happiness in life. . . ." (9)

In other cases, she uses a colon to introduce dialogue:

> Here is what one patient felt: "When I was acting so stiff and wasn't talking. . . ." (9)

She also uses a noun clause with *that*:

> One manual points out *that* "grotesque violence . . . may occur." (9)

(For more on quoting sources, see pp. 255–63.)

PURPOSE AND AUDIENCE

Though it often seeks to engage readers' interests, explanatory writing gives prominence to the facts about its subject. It aims at readers' intellects rather than their imaginations, determined to instruct rather than entertain or argue.

To set out to teach readers about a concept is no small undertaking. To succeed, you must know the concept so well that you can explain it simply, without jargon or other confusing language. You must be authoritative without showing off or talking down. You must also estimate what your readers already know about the concept in order to decide which information will be truly new to them. You want to define unfamiliar words and pace the information carefully so that your readers are neither bored nor overwhelmed.

This assignment requires a willingness to cast yourself in the role of expert that may not come naturally to you in this stage of your development as a writer. Students are most often asked to explain things in writing to readers who know more than they do—their instructors. When you plan and draft this essay, however, you will be aiming at readers who know less—maybe much less—than you do about the concept you will explain. Like Quammen and Castro, you could write for a general audience of adults who regularly read a newspaper and subscribe to a few magazines. Even though some of them may be widely educated, you can readily and confidently assume the role of expert after a couple of hours of research. Your purpose may be to deepen your readers' understanding of a concept they may already be familiar with. You could also write for upper-elementary or secondary-school students, introducing them to an unfamiliar concept, or to your classmates, demonstrating to them that a concept in an academic discipline they find forbidding can actually be made not only understandable but also interesting. Even if your instructor asks you to consider your reader to be him or her alone, you can assume your instructor is willing to be informed about nearly any concept you choose, except for concepts central to his or her academic specialty.

You've spent many years in school reading explanations of concepts: your textbooks in every subject have been full of concept explanations. Now, instead of receiving these explanations, you'll be delivering one. To succeed, you'll have to accept your role of expert. Your readers expect you to be authoritative and well informed; they expect that you have limited the focus of your explanation but that you haven't excluded anything essential to their understanding.

BASIC FEATURES OF EXPLANATORY ESSAYS

Essays explaining concepts display the following basic features.

A Well-Focused Concept

The primary purpose for explaining a concept is to inform readers, but writers of explanatory essays cannot possibly hope to say everything there is to say about a concept, nor would they want to. Instead, they must make choices about what to include, what to emphasize, and what to omit. Most writers focus on one aspect of the concept.

An Appeal to Readers' Interests

Most people read explanations of concepts for work or study. Consequently, they don't expect the writing to entertain them, but simply to inform them. Yet explanations that make clear the concept's importance and that keep the reader awake with lively writing and vivid detail are usually appreciated. The essays in this chapter show some of the ways writers try to appeal to readers—for example, by using humor and unaffected, everyday language; by giving readers reasons for learning about the concept; by showing how the concept might apply personally to them.

A Logical Plan

Since concept explanations present information that is new to readers and can therefore be hard to understand, writers need to develop a plan that presents new material bit by bit in a logical order. The most effective explanations are carefully organized and give readers all the obvious cues they need, such as forecasting statements, topic sentences, transitions, and summaries. In addition, the writer may try to frame the essay for readers by relating the end to the beginning. Good writers never forget that their readers need clear signals. Because writers already know the information and are aware of how the essay is organized, it can be difficult for them to see the essay the way someone reading it for the first time would. That is precisely how it should be seen, however, to be sure that the essay includes all the cues the reader will need.

Clear Definitions

Essays explaining concepts depend on clear definitions. In order to relate information clearly, a writer must be sensitive to readers' knowledge; any terms that are likely to be unfamiliar or misunderstood must be explicitly defined.

Careful Use of Sources

Explaining concepts nearly always draws on information from many different sources. Writers often draw on their own experience and observation, but they almost always do additional research into what others have to say about their subject. Referring to sources, particularly to expert ones, always lends authority to an explanation.

How writers treat sources depends on the writing situation. Certain formal situations, such as college assignments or scholarly papers, have prescribed rules for citing and documenting sources. Students and scholars are expected to cite their sources formally because their readers judge their writing in part by what they've read and how they've used their reading. On more informal writing occasions—newspaper and magazine articles, for example—readers do not expect writers to include page references or publishing information, but they do expect them to identify their sources in some way; this is often done casually within the text of the article.

Sources should be used with the greatest care. Since you nearly always find more sources on a concept than you can use, you must evaluate them carefully, choosing those that are the most reputable and current and that provide the best support for the point you want to make about the concept. (For more on reading sources with a critical eye, see pp. 252–54.)

Experienced writers make judicious decisions about when to paraphrase, summarize, or quote their sources. (Summary conveys only the gist, while paraphrase rewords but retains much of the detail.) They take special care to integrate quotations smoothly into their own texts, deliberately varying the way they do it. (For more on using sources, see Chapter 11.)

USING WRITING STRATEGIES

Many writing strategies are useful for presenting information. The strategies a writer uses are determined by the way he or she focuses the essay and the kind of information available to work with. Following are some of the writing strategies that are particularly useful in explaining concepts.

Classification

One way of presenting information is to sort it into groups and discuss them one by one. Murayama, for example, uses the classification of schizophrenic symptoms found in medical manuals as a way of organizing her description of the disease. She lists the symptoms at the end of paragraph 3 and then discusses each one in turn.

Process Narration

Process narration typically explains how something is done or how to do it. Many concepts involve processes that unfold over time, such as the geologic scale, or over both time and space, such as bird migration, which could be illustrated by telling a story of a typical bird's migration between Canada and Mexico. Process narration involves some of the basic storytelling strategies covered in Chapter 2: narrative time signals, sentence rhythm, summarizing action, and transitions showing temporal relationship. For example, Quammen narrates the life cycle of the aphid, a temporal process unfolding over about seven months. Throughout, he gives us time signals—"in March," "in late May," "suddenly there is a change," "in September," "meanwhile, at long last."

Comparison and Contrast

The comparison-contrast strategy is especially useful for explaining concepts because it helps readers to understand something new by showing how it is similar to or different from things they already know. Every essayist in this chapter makes use of comparison-contrast. Quammen compares the benefits of asexual and sexual reproduction, and Murayama contrasts schizophrenics who withdraw from others with those who cling and intrude. Castro contrasts Manpower Inc. and General Motors, as well as core and contingent workers.

Cause and Effect

Still another useful strategy for explaining a concept is to report its causes or effects, as Quammen does by explaining the effects on the aphid population of parthenogenisis. Castro describes throughout her essay the effects of contingent employment on workers and the workplace.

Note that most explanatory essays either report established causes or effects or report others' speculated causes or effects as if they were established facts. They usually do not speculate about possible causes or effects.

Guide to Writing

▪ THE WRITING ASSIGNMENT

Write an essay that explains a concept. Choose a concept that interests you and that you want to study further. Consider carefully what your readers already know about it and how your essay might add to what they know.

INVENTION AND RESEARCH

The following guidelines will help you find a concept, understand it fully, select a focus appropriate for your readers, test your choice, and devise strategies for presenting what you've discovered in a way that will be truly informative for your particular readers.

Finding a Concept

Even if you already have a concept in mind, completing the following activities will help you to be certain of your choice.

Listing Concepts

List as many concepts as you can. The longer your list, the more likely you are to find just the right concept to write about. And should your first choice not work out, you will have a ready list of alternatives. Include concepts you already know something about as well as some you know only slightly and would like to research further. Consider the concepts suggested in For Your Own Writing on pages 60, 66, and 72.

Your courses provide many concepts you will want to consider. Following are typical concepts from several academic and other subjects. Your class notes or textbooks will suggest many others.

- *Literature:* hero, antihero, picaresque, the absurd, pastoral, realism
- *Philosophy:* existentialism, nihilism, logical positivism, determinism
- *Business management:* autonomous work group, quality circle, cybernetic control system, management by objectives, zero-based budgeting
- *Psychology:* Hawthorne effect, assimilation/accommodation, social cognition, moratorium, intelligence, divergent/convergent thinking, operant conditioning, short-term memory, tip-of-the-tongue phenomenon
- *Government:* majority rule, minority rights, federalism, popular consent, exclusionary rule, political party, political machine, interest group, political action committee, one person/one vote
- *Biology:* photosynthesis, morphogenesis, ecosystem, electron transport, plasmolysis, phagocytosis, homozygosity, diffusion
- *Art:* cubism, Dadaism, surrealism, expressionism
- *Math:* Mobius transformation, boundedness, null space, eigenvalue, factoring, Rolle's theorem, continuity, derivative, indefinite integral
- *Physical sciences:* matter, mass, weight, energy, gravity, atomic theory, law of definite proportions, osmotic pressure, first law of thermodynamics, entropy
- *Public health:* alcoholism, winter depression, contraception, lead poisoning, prenatal care
- *Environmental studies:* acid rain, recycling, ozone depletion, toxic waste, endangered species
- *Sports:* squeeze play, hit and run (baseball); power play (hockey); nickel defense, wishbone offense (football); serve and volley offense (tennis); setup (volleyball); pick and roll, inside game (basketball)
- *Personal finance:* mortgage, budget, insurance, deduction, revolving credit
- *Law:* tort, contract, plaintiff, defendant, liability, reasonable doubt
- *Sociology:* norm, deviance, role conflict, ethnocentrism, class, social stratification, conflict theory, functionalist theory

Choosing a Concept

Now look over your list and select one concept to explore. Pick a concept that interests you, one you feel eager to learn more about. Consider also whether it might interest others. You may know very little about the concept now, but the guidelines that follow will help you research it and understand it fully.

Researching the Concept

Discovering What You Already Know

Start with what you know. Take a few minutes to write out whatever you know about the concept you have chosen and why you find it interesting and worth knowing about. Write quickly, without planning or organizing. Feel free to write in phrases or lists as well as in sentences. You might also want to make drawings or charts. Ask questions.

Gathering Information

Check any materials you already have at hand that explain your concept. If you are considering a concept from one of your academic courses, you will find explanatory material in your textbook or lecture notes.

To acquire a comprehensive, up-to-date understanding of your concept and to write authoritatively about it, you may also need to know how experts besides your textbook writer and instructor define and illustrate the concept. To find this information, you may need to locate relevant articles or books in the library, search for resources or make inquiries on the Internet, or consult experts on campus or in the community. Chapter 10 recommends a search strategy and specific sources for researching your concept.

As you get a better understanding of the concept and decide which aspect of it you will focus your essay on, you may need to do additional research to get answers to specific questions.

If you can, it's a good idea to make photocopies or print out information you download from CD-ROMs or the Internet. If you must rely on notes, be sure to copy the language exactly, mistakes and all, so that later you can quote sources accurately.

Since you don't know what information you will ultimately use, keep a careful record of the author, title, publication date, and page numbers for all the source material you gather. Check with your instructor about whether you should follow the Modern Language Association (MLA) or American Psychological Association (APA) style of acknowledging sources. In this chapter, the Murayama essay follows the APA style. (For MLA and APA guidelines, see Chapter 11.)

Focusing the Concept

Once you have done some research on your concept, you need to choose a way to focus your essay. Since more is known about most concepts than you can include in an essay, and since concepts can be approached from so many perspectives (for example, history, definition, significance), you must limit your explanation. Doing so will help you avoid a common problem: trying to explain superficially and hurriedly everything that is known about a concept.

Because the focus must reflect both your special interest in the concept and what you think is likely to be your readers' knowledge of and interest in it, you will need to explore both your own interest and your readers' potential interest in the concept.

Exploring Your Own Interests

To consider which aspect of the concept most interests you, review what you know about the concept. As you review this information, make a list of different topics or different ways you could approach the concept, skipping a few lines after each item on the list. Murayama, for example, might have listed the history of schizophrenia, different treatments and their effectiveness, its possible causes, different kinds of schizophrenia, as well as its various symptoms.

Under each item in your list, indicate whether you know enough to begin writing about that aspect of the concept, what additional questions you would need to answer, and what's important or interesting to you about that particular aspect.

Analyzing Your Readers

To decide what aspect of the concept to focus on, you also need to think about who your prospective readers are likely to be and to speculate about their knowledge of and interest in the concept. Even if you are writing only for your instructor, you should give some thought to what he or she knows and thinks about the concept.

Take about five minutes to analyze your readers in writing. The following questions are designed to help you with your analysis:

- Who are my readers and what are they likely to know about this concept?
- What, if anything, might they know about the field of study in which this concept is usually used?
- What could I point out that would be useful for them to know about this concept, perhaps something that could relate to their life or work?
- What connections could I make between this concept and others that my readers are likely to be familiar with?

Choosing a Focus

With your interests and your readers' interests in mind, choose an aspect of your concept on which to focus and write a sentence justifying its appropriateness.

Testing Your Choice

Pause now to test whether you have chosen a workable concept and focused it appropriately. As painful as it may be to consider, starting fresh with a new concept would be better than continuing with an unworkable one. The following questions can help you test your choice:

- Do I understand my concept well enough to explain it?
- Have I discovered a focus for writing about this concept?
- Have I located enough information for an essay with such a focus?
- Do I see possibilities for engaging my readers' interest in this aspect of my subject?

If you cannot answer all of these questions affirmatively, you should consider refocusing your subject or selecting another concept to write about.

For Group Inquiry

At this point it might be a good idea to get some response to your subject. Work in a group with two or three other students. One by one, announce your concepts and intended readers, and then briefly explain the concept and the aspect of it you plan to focus on. Ask the group members whether your plan sounds interesting for your intended readers. Get them to help you speculate about what these readers are likely to know about your concept, and what new information about it might be especially interesting and informative for them.

Considering Explanatory Strategies

Before you move on to plan and draft your essay, consider some possible ways of presenting the concept. Following are some questions that can help you determine which writing strategies might prove useful. Answer each one with a sentence or two.

- What term is used to name the concept, and what does it mean? (definition)
- How is this concept like or unlike related concepts? (comparison and contrast)
- How can an explanation of this concept be divided into parts? (classification)
- How does this concept happen, or how do you do it? (process narration)
- What are its known causes or effects? (cause and effect)

PLANNING AND DRAFTING

Here are some guidelines to help you get the most out of your invention notes, to determine specific goals for your essay, and to write a first draft.

Seeing What You Have

Reread everything you have written so far. This is a critically important time for reflection and evaluation. Before beginning the actual draft, you must decide whether your subject is worthwhile and whether you have sufficient information for a successful essay.

It may help, as you read, to annotate your invention writings. Look for details that will help you explain the concept so that your readers can grasp it. Underline or circle key words, phrases, or sentences; make marginal notes. Your goal here is to identify the important elements in what you have written so far.

Be realistic. If at this point your notes do not look promising, you may want to refocus your concept or select a different concept to write about. If your notes seem thin but promising, you should do further research to find more information before continuing.

Setting Goals

Successful writers are always looking beyond the next sentence to larger goals. Indeed, the next sentence is easier to write if you keep larger goals in mind. The following questions can help you set these goals. Consider each one now and then return to them as necessary while you write.

Your Readers

- How can I build on my readers' knowledge?
- What new information can I present to them?
- How can I organize my essay so that my readers can follow it easily?
- What tone would be most appropriate? Would an informal tone like Quammen's or a formal one like Murayama's be more appropriate?

The Beginning

- How shall I begin? Should I open with a provocative quotation, as Quammen does? Should I begin with a general statement about the concept, as Murayama does? With a surprising or ironical fact as Castro does? With a question?
- How can I best forecast the plan my explanation will follow? Should I offer a detailed forecast? Or is a brief description sufficient?

Writing Strategies

- What terms do I need to define? Can I rely on brief sentence definitions or will I need to write extended definitions?
- How can I categorize the information?
- What examples can I use to make the explanation more concrete?
- What comparisons or contrasts would help readers understand the information?
- Do I need to explain any processes or known causes or effects?

The Ending

- Should I relate the ending to the beginning, as Quammen does, so as to frame the essay?
- Can I find an emphatic or memorable quote with which to end the essay, as Castro does?

Outlining

Give some thought now to organization. Many writers find it helpful to outline their material before actually beginning to write. Whatever outlining you do before you begin drafting, consider it only tentative. Never be a slave to an outline. As you draft, you will usually see some ways to improve on your original plan. Be ready to revise your outline, to shift parts around, to drop or add parts. Consider the following questions as you plan:

- Which writing strategies should I use to present the information?
- What order will best serve my purpose?
- What kinds of transitions can I use between the different strategies or parts of the essay?

Drafting

Begin drafting your essay, keeping your main point in mind. Remember also the needs and expectations of your readers; organize and define and explain with them in mind. Work to increase their understanding of your concept. You may want to review the drafting advice on pages 11–13.

GETTING CRITICAL COMMENTS

Now is the time to get a good critical reading. All writers find it helpful to have someone else read and comment on their drafts, and your instructor may schedule such a reading as part of your coursework. If not, you can ask a classmate, friend, or family member to read it over. If your campus has a writing center, you might ask a tutor to read and comment on your draft. The guidelines that follow are designed to be used by *anyone* reviewing an explanatory essay. (If you are unable to have someone else read your draft, turn ahead to the Revising and Editing section on pp. 84–86, which gives guidelines for reading your own draft with a critical eye.)

In order to provide focused, helpful comments, your critical reader must know your intended audience and purpose. Briefly write out this information at the top of your draft:

Audience: Who are your readers?

Purpose: What do you want to tell your readers about the concept?

Reading with a Critical Eye

Reading a draft critically means reading it more than once, first to get a general impression and then to analyze its basic features.

Reading for a First Impression

Read first to get a sense of the concept. Then briefly give your impressions. Is the concept well focused and clearly explained? Did you find the essay informative and easy to follow? What in the draft do you think would especially interest the intended readers?

Reading to Analyze

Now reread the draft to focus on the basic features of explanatory essays. (See pp. 73–75 to review the basic features.)

Is the Concept Clearly Explained and Focused?

Restate, in one sentence, what you now understand the concept to mean. Indicate any confusion or uncertainty you have about its meaning. Given the concept, does the focus seem appropriate, too broad, or too narrow? Can you think of another more interesting aspect of the concept on which to focus the explanation?

Is the Content Appropriate for Its Intended Readers?

Does it tell them all they are likely to want to know about this concept? Can you suggest additional information that should be included? What questions about the concept that readers are likely to have are not answered? Point to any information that seems superfluous or too predictable.

Is the Organization Effective?

Look at the way the essay is organized, outlining it briefly. Is the information logically divided? If not, suggest a better way to divide it. Also consider the order— can you suggest a better way of sequencing the information?

Look at the *beginning*. Will it pull intended readers into the essay and make them want to continue? Does it adequately forecast the direction of the essay? If possible, suggest a better way to begin.

Find the obvious *transitions* in the draft. Are they helpful? If not, try to improve one or two of them. Look for additional places where transitions would be helpful.

Look at the *ending*. Is it effective? Does it frame the essay by referring back to something at the beginning? Should it? If you can, suggest a better way to end.

Are Definitions Clear?

Examine the definitions. Are any likely to be unclear to readers? Point out any other terms that may need to be defined for the intended readers.

Are Writing Strategies Appropriately Used?

Besides definition, what writing strategies are used and how effective are they? Examine each recognizable use of process narration, comparison and contrast, cause and effect, or classification, and identify any that seem unclear, incomplete, or otherwise ineffective. If you can, suggest ways to improve these and point to any other places where another strategy would enable readers to comprehend the concept more fully.

Are Sources Carefully Used?

If sources have been used, begin by reviewing the list of sources cited. Given the purpose, readers, and focus of the essay, does the list seem balanced and are the selections appropriate? Try to suggest concerns or questions readers knowledgeable about the concept might raise. Then consider the use of sources within the text of the essay. Should there be more (or fewer) source citations? Where? Are there places where summary or paraphrase would be preferable to quoted material or vice versa? Note any places where quoted material is awkwardly inserted into the text and recommend ways to smooth them out.

What Final Thoughts Do You Have?

Which part needs the most work? What do you think the intended readers will find most informative or memorable? What did you like best about the essay?

REVISING AND EDITING

This section will help you identify problems in your draft and revise and edit to solve them.

Identifying Problems

To identify problems in your draft, you need to get an overview of it, analyze its basic features, and study any comments you've received from other readers.

Getting an Overview

First consider the draft as a whole, trying to see it objectively. It may help to do so in two steps:

1. *Reread.*   If possible, put the draft aside for a day or two before rereading it. When you go back to it, start by reconsidering your audience and purpose. Then read the draft straight through, trying to see it as your intended readers will.

2. *Outline.*   Make a scratch outline to get an overview of the essay's development. This outline can be sketchy—words and phrases instead of complete sentences— but it should identify the main ideas as they appear.

Charting a Plan for Revision

You may want to make a double-columned chart like the following one to identify the problems you need to solve. In the left-hand column, list the basic features and strategies of concept explanation, skipping several lines between each. As you analyze your draft and study any comments you've gotten from others, note the problems you want to solve in the right-hand column.

Basic Features	*Problems to Solve*
Concept focus	
Appeal to readers	
Organization	
Definitions	
Writing strategies	
Sources	

Analyzing the Basic Features of Your Draft

Turn now to the questions for analyzing a draft on pages 82–83. Using these as guidelines, reread the draft yourself to identify problems and note them on the chart you've made under "Problems to Solve."

Studying Critical Comments

Review any comments you've received from other readers, and add to your chart any other points that need attention. Try not to react defensively to these comments; by letting you see how others respond to your draft, the comments provide invaluable information about how you might improve it.

Solving the Problems

Having identified problems, you now need to figure out solutions and to carry them out. Basically, you have three ways of finding solutions: (1) review your invention and planning notes and sources for additional information and ideas; (2) do further invention or research to answer questions your readers raised; and (3) look back at the readings in this chapter to see how other writers have solved similar problems.

Following are suggestions to get you started solving some of the problems common to explanatory essays. For now, focus on solving those issues identified on your chart. Avoid tinkering with sentence-level problems; that will come later when you edit.

The Focus

- If the focus is too broad, consider limiting it further so you can treat the concept in more depth. If readers were uninterested in the aspect you focused on, consider focusing on some other aspect of the concept.
- If the focus is too narrow, you may have isolated too minor an aspect. Go back to your invention and look for other larger or more significant aspects.

Appeal to Readers

- If you think readers will have unanswered questions, review your invention writing and sources for further information to satisfy your readers' needs or answer their concerns and questions.
- If any of the content seems superfluous, eliminate it.
- If the content seems predictable, search for novel or surprising information to add.

Organization

- If the essay does not unfold logically and smoothly, reorganize it so that it is easy to follow. Try constructing an alternative outline. Add transitions or summaries to help keep readers on track.
- If the beginning is weak, try making your focus and point obvious immediately, forecasting the plan of your essay, or opening with an unusual piece of information that would catch readers' interest.
- If the ending is inconclusive, consider restating your point there or moving important information to the end. Try summarizing highlights of the essay or framing it by referring back to something in the beginning. Or you might reflect on the future of the concept or assert its usefulness.

Definitions

- If your concept is not clearly defined, add a concise definition early in your essay, or consider adding a brief midpoint or concluding summary that defines the concept. Remove any information that may blur readers' understanding of the concept.
- If other key terms are inadequately defined, supply clear definitions, searching your sources or checking a dictionary if necessary.

Writing Strategies

- If the content seems thin or the definition of the concept blurred, consider whether any other writing strategies would improve the presentation.
- Try comparing or contrasting the concept with a related one, preferably one more familiar to readers.
- Consider ways to classify the information that would make it easier to understand or provide an interesting perspective on the topic.
- Try explaining its known causes or effects.
- See whether adding examples enlivens or clarifies your explanation.
- Tell more about how the concept works.

Use of Sources

- If sources are inadequate, return to the library or the Internet to find additional ones. Consider dropping weak or less reliable sources. Ensure that your sources cover the aspect on which you focus in a comprehensive, balanced way.
- If you rely too much on quoting, summarizing, or paraphrasing, change some of your quotations to summaries or paraphrases, or vice versa.
- If quoted material is not smoothly integrated into your own text, revise to make it so.
- If there are discrepancies in your in-text citations or list of sources, check citation styles in Chapter 11. Be sure all of the citations exactly follow the style you are using.

Editing and Proofreading

In working on your draft so far, you may have corrected some obvious errors, but grammar and style have not been a priority. Now is the time to check carefully for errors in usage, punctuation, and mechanics, as well as to consider matters of style. You may find that studying your draft in separate passes—first for paragraphs, then for sentences, and finally for words—will help you to recognize any problems.

Once you have edited your draft and produced a final copy, proofread it carefully to be sure there are no typos, misspellings, or other mistakes.

A Writer at Work

USING SOURCES

This section describes how student writer Veronica Murayama searched for sources and integrated them into one part of her essay on schizophrenia, which appears on pages 68–71.

Finding Sources

Following directions in the Invention and Research section of this chapter, Murayama went to the library to see what she could find on schizophrenia. She wanted a quick orientation to the concept so that she could decide on a focus for her essay and for further research. This initial search led her right away to two books and four current articles:

Schizophrenia as a Life Style, 1974

The Origin and Treatment of Schizophrenic Disorders, 1973

"Drug Gains FDA Approval," *Science News*

"Drugs among Young Schizophrenics," *Science News*

"Seeking Source of Schizophrenia," *USA Today*

"Relatives Bear Demoralizing Task of Patient Care," [Baltimore] *Sun*

She read the articles, skimmed the books, and then talked to a reference librarian. When Murayama explained the assignment—emphasizing her need for an overview—and showed the materials she had already collected, the librarian recommended that she check two basic references on mental illness. The first book is relied on by medical doctors, the second by psychiatrists and other mental health counselors:

The Merck Manual of Diagnosis and Therapy

Diagnostic and Statistical Manual of Mental Disorders

After reading closely the materials on schizophrenia in these two sources, she decided that given the information in all her sources she had enough material on these topics:

the history of the description and treatment of schizophrenia

its effects on families of schizophrenics

the current debate about its causes

the current preferred treatment of it

current research on it

its symptoms

She was drawn both to the debate about causes and to symptoms, but when she discussed these alternatives with a small group in her writing class, she recognized that the others, like herself before she began her research, knew so little about schizophrenia that they would be most engaged and informed by a description of the illness itself—what it looks like to a therapist diagnosing it and what it feels like to a patient experiencing it.

When Murayama met with her instructor, he pointed out that she should seek out recent reports in a respected medical journal such as the *New England Journal of Medicine*. In that journal she found the research report demonstrating that certain areas of schizophrenics' brains appear to be smaller than the same areas in brains of those not suffering from the illness. This interesting research finding appears as one clause in paragraph 3 of her essay.

Now she returned to the library and reread the sources that provided information about the symptoms of schizophrenia. The basic information she needed was in the two reference manuals. Her quotes from patients came mainly from one of the books, *Schizophrenia as a Life Style.* She did not use or cite the *Science News* and *USA Today* articles.

Murayama's search for sources was far from comprehensive, but it was certainly adequate for a brief essay. She wisely stopped searching when she felt she had the information she needed. It turned out that she used only a small part of her information on symptoms.

Integrating Sources

Two paragraphs from Murayama's essay illustrate a sound strategy for integrating sources into your essay, relying on them fully—as you nearly always must do in explanatory writing—and yet making them your own. Here are paragraphs 10 and 11 from Murayama's essay (the sentences are numbered for ease of reference):

> (1) Even if violence does not occur, it is not surprising that the speech and behavioral symptoms I have described are almost always accompanied by—and contribute to—impaired interpersonal functioning. (2) Once schizophrenics become obsessed with delusions, hallucinations, and illogical ideas, they are often too distracted and centered on themselves to interact with other people. (3) Such patients are notable for their emotional detachment even from family members or friends they were previously close to. (4) They also withdraw from all other social interactions, dropping out of school or leaving jobs. (5) They simply cannot face the outside world. (6) Some schizophrenics behave quite differently, however, at least during some phases of the illness. (7) They "cling to other people, intrude upon strangers, and fail to recognize that excessive closeness makes other people uncomfortable and likely to pull away" ("Schizophrenia," 1987, p. 189).
>
> (8) Along with social impairment comes loss of drive or ambition. (9) Schizophrenics typically have difficulty in initiating actions, making decisions, or following through with plans, and their work and other responsibilities often suffer severely as a result.

All of the information in these paragraphs comes from the following brief sections of the *Diagnostic and Statistical Manual of Mental Disorders.*

> *Volition.* The characteristic disturbances in volition are most readily observed in the residual phase. There is nearly always some disturbance in self-initiated, goal-directed activity, which may grossly impair work or other role functioning. This may take the form of inadequate interest, drive, or ability to follow a course of action to its logical conclusion. Marked ambivalence regarding alternative courses of action can lead to near-cessation of goal-directed activity.

Impaired interpersonal functioning and relationship to the external world. Difficulty in interpersonal relationships is almost invariably present. Often this takes the form of social withdrawal and emotional detachment. When the person is severely preoccupied with egocentric and illogical ideas and fantasies and distorts or excludes the external world, the condition has been referred to as "autism." Some with the disorder, during a phase of the illness, cling to other people, intrude upon strangers, and fail to recognize that excessive closeness makes other people uncomfortable and likely to pull away.

Comparing the source and Murayama's paragraphs 10–11, we can see that her first sentence introduces the name of the symptom, which she borrows in part from the symptom name in the source. Sentence 2 paraphrases the source. Sentences 3–5 are her own elaborations of the material in the source, basically giving concrete examples of the more abstract discussion in the original source. Sentence 6 again paraphrases the source. Then, finally, she quotes the source. Following the quotation, in sentences 8 and 9 she summarizes the information in the source paragraph labeled *Volition.*

After Murayama researched and wrote her essay, a new fourth edition of the *Diagnostic and Statistical Manual of Mental Disorders* was published. If you are curious, you might like to look up the current edition to see what changes have been made and then to revise Murayama's paragraphs 10 and 11 to reflect these changes.

Reflecting on Your Writing

At this point, you have considerable experience with essays explaining concepts—reading them, talking about them, even writing one of your own. Now is a good time to consider what you've learned about this genre. Reflecting on your own writing process will help you discover what you've learned about solving problems you encountered in explaining a concept.

Begin by gathering your invention and planning notes, drafts, critical comments from classmates and your instructor, revision notes and plans, and final revision. Review these materials as you complete the following writing tasks.

- Identify *one* writing problem you needed to solve as you worked to explain the concept in your essay. Don't be concerned with sentence-level problems; concentrate instead on a problem unique to developing a concept explanation. For example: Did you puzzle over how to focus your explanation? Did you worry about how to appeal to your readers' interests, identify and define the terms your readers would need explained, or clearly forecast the main ideas without boring readers? Did you have trouble integrating sources smoothly?

- How did you recognize the writing problem? When did you first discover it? What called it to your attention? If you didn't become aware of the problem until someone else pointed it out to you, can you now see hints of it in your invention writings? If so, where specifically? How did you respond when you first recognized the problem?

- How did you go about solving the problem? Did you work on the wording of a particular passage, cut or add information, move paragraphs or sentences around, add transitions or forecasting statements, use any different writing strategies? Did you reread one of the essays in this chapter to see how another writer handled the problem or look back at the invention suggestions? If you talked about the writing problem with another student, a tutor, or your instructor, did talking about it help? How useful was the advice you got?

- Finally, write a page or so telling your instructor about the problem, how you discovered it, and how you tried to solve it. Be as specific as possible in reconstructing your efforts, quoting from your invention, your draft, others' critical comments, your revision plan, and your revised essay to show the various changes your writing underwent as you tried to solve the problem. If you're still uncertain about your solution, say so. The point is not to prove that you've solved the problem perfectly, but to show what you've learned about problem solving in the process of explaining a concept.

4 *Justifying an Evaluation*

We all make judgments. Many times each day we make evaluations, usually spontaneously, in response to events, people, things. In everyday conversation we often share our evaluations. Rarely do we think out a reasoned, detailed argument for our evaluations, although we constantly give reasons for our opinions in a casual way. By contrast, we expect judgments stated in writing to be authoritative and persuasive, with a planned, coherent, reasoned argument. We expect that the writer will use appropriate standards of evaluation, and that the judgment will be supported with reasons and evidence.

If your college has a system of student course evaluations, you will regularly evaluate your instructors. On the job, you will be evaluated and may eventually evaluate others for promotions, awards, or new jobs. You may also be asked to evaluate various plans and proposals, and your success at these important writing tasks may in large part determine your career success. In a more fundamental way, studying and writing evaluations contributes to your intellectual development, teaching you to define the standards for any judgments you are called upon to make and then to develop a reasoned argument with evidence to support your evaluation.

Your purpose in writing evaluations is to convince readers that you have made an informed judgment. You may want to convince them that a particular movie is worth seeing, a research report seriously flawed, a product brilliantly innovative, an applicant for a position not the person to hire. In these and innumerable other writing situations in college and on the job, you must establish your authority and credibility in order to win the trust of your readers. You do that essentially by basing your judgment on sound reasoning and solid evidence. This evidence comes from a thorough analysis of your subject, an analysis that ensures a detailed and comprehensive understanding.

WRITING IN YOUR OTHER COURSES

Evaluation is basic to thinking and learning—and thus to writing. It underlies all types of argument, forming with cause-and-effect analysis the basic building blocks of argument. As a college student, you may be asked to evaluate books, artwork, scientific discoveries, or current events, as these typical assignments suggest:

- *For a film studies course*: Of the genres we've studied this semester, I've selected action films as the basis for your final exam. In the library, at either 2:00 or 8:00 p.m. on December 6, you can view *The Sugarland Express* (Steven Spielberg, 1974). You may want to see the film twice. Take notes to prepare for the following essay exam: explain how the film belongs to the action genre and evaluate it as an example of the genre, comparing it to other action films screened and discussed in class.
- *For an astronomy course*: Which of two theories—the big bang theory or the pulsating universe theory—better explains the origin of the universe?
- *For a political science course*: Evaluate the two major presidential candidates' performances during one of their scheduled televised debates. If possible, record the debate so that you can analyze it closely and quote the candidates directly. Make a file of newspaper and magazine clippings on the debate, along with reports of polls taken before and after it. Take notes on the post-debate television commentary. Use this material to support your judgment of who won the debate.
- *For a twentieth-century American history course*: Review one of several published studies of the Vietnam War. Your review should describe the approach taken in the book and evaluate both the accuracy of its facts and the quality of its interpretation.

For Group Inquiry

Assume that you have been asked to review some form of popular entertainment. Get together with two or three other students and choose a type of entertainment you all know fairly well: country-western music, horror movies, music videos, magic acts, or any other kind of entertainment. Then discuss what standards should be used in reviewing this type of entertainment. For example, the standards for reviewing a movie might include the movie's entertainment value (if it's a comedy, is it funny?), the quality of its ideas (if it's about relationships, is it insightful?), and its technical qualities (such as acting, direction, cinematography). See if you can agree on the two or three most important standards; if you disagree, consider how you would refute (argue against) the standards with which you disagree. Then reflect on what you have learned about the role of such standards in making evaluations:

- Which standards did you agree about readily, and which created disagreement in the group?
- How can you account for these differences?
- Where do you suppose your standards came from?
- How do you think experts decide on theirs?

Readings

David **Ansen** wrote the following review of a controversial 1989 movie, *Do the Right Thing*, for *Newsweek* magazine. Along with other magazines and television talk shows, *Newsweek* ran special features on the movie and its producer-director-writer, Spike Lee.

If you have not seen *Do the Right Thing* or do not remember it, you might want to rent the video, but knowing the movie is not essential, since reviews are written primarily for readers who are trying to decide whether to see particular films. As you read this review, consider whether you would decide to see *Do the Right Thing* on the basis of what Ansen says about it.

**SEARING, NERVY, AND
VERY HONEST**

▪

David Ansen

Somewhere near the midpoint in Spike Lee's *Do the Right Thing*—as the summer heat in Bedford-Stuyvesant reaches the boiling point—there occurs an astonishing outpouring of racial invective, five short soliloquies of ethnic slurs directed straight at the camera. A black man insults Italians. An Italian defames blacks. A Puerto Rican castigates Koreans. A white cop rips into Puerto Ricans. A Korean slanders Jews. At which point Lee cuts to the neighborhood radio deejay, Mister Señor Love Daddy, screaming into his mike "Time Out!" . . .   1

Nigger, dago, kike, spic. There they are, America's dirtiest words, hurled across the screen in Lee's nervy, complex, unsettling movie. The sequence makes you catch your breath, but you also laugh as you laughed when Lenny Bruce or Richard Pryor touched a raw nerve of publicly unspoken experience. And Lee's rude comic impulse is the same as theirs: unless we air these noxious fumes, and acknowledge just how dire the racial situation has become, this great unmelted pot might well explode.   2

When white filmmakers deal with race (from Stanley Kramer's *The Defiant Ones* to Alan Parker's *Mississippi Burning*), no matter how fine their intentions, they tend to speak in inflated, self-righteous tones, and they always come down to Hollywood's favorite dialectic, bad guys versus good guys. They allow the audience to sit comfortably on the side of the angels. In *Do the Right Thing*, Lee blows away the pieties and the easy answers. He prefers abrasion and ambiguity to comfort and tidiness. As a black filmmaker, he's too close to the subject—and too much the artist—to oversimplify the issues. The beauty of *Do the Right Thing* is that all the characters, from the broadest cartoons to the most developed, are given their humanity and their due.   3

At the end of the story there is violence, police brutality, a riot. Sal's pizzeria, a white-run business that has existed peacefully in the black community for 25 years, suddenly becomes the target of pent-up rage. The owner, Sal (Danny Aiello, who's never been better), is no ogre—he's a sympathetic figure, a peacemaker who's arguably an unconscious racist.   4

His son Pino (John Turturro), on the other hand, is blatantly antiblack, the closest to a villain the movie gets. Lee isn't saying the violence is inevitable, or even just. But we see how it comes to pass, a combination of heat, irritation, insensitivity, stubbornness and centuries of systematic oppression.

Lee trusts his audience: he doesn't need to stack the deck. You can   5
feel he's working out his own ambivalence on screen. His rich portrait of the Bed-Stuy community is both affectionate and critical. Take the character of Buggin' Out (Giancarlo Esposito). He's the most militant black in the movie, but Lee shows his rage as misplaced and foolish. His attempt to boycott Sal's because there are no pictures of blacks on the walls—only Italian-Americans—is greeted by most with derision. When Mother Sister (Ruby Dee), the block's wise old watchdog, sees Sal's go up in flames we're startled by her exhilaration at the violence. But moments later she's wailing in despair at the destruction. It's one of the movie's points that we are all nursing wildly contradictory impulses: our heads and hearts aren't always in sync. This is no cop-out, it's unusually honest reporting.

Do the Right Thing is a kind of compacted epic played out in jazzy,   6
dissonant scenes that dance in and out of realism. Lee's deliberately dis-cordant style didn't jell in *School Daze*, an ambitious but turgid look at the divisions in a black college. Here the clashing styles add up and pay off. You leave this movie stunned, challenged and drained. To accuse Lee of irresponsibility—of inciting violence—is to be blind to the movie he has made. The two quotes that end the film—Martin Luther King's eloquent antiviolent testament and Malcolm X's acknowledgment that violence in self-defense may be necessary—are the logical culmination of Lee's method. There can be no simple, tidy closure. Not now. Not yet. Lee's conscience-pricking movie is bracing and necessary: it's the funkiest and most informed view of racism an American filmmaker has given us.

For Discussion

Ansen refers to the two quotations that appear at the end of *Do the Right Thing*: the first, by Martin Luther King, Jr., asserts that violence is always to be avoided, whereas the second, by Malcolm X, counters that violence may sometimes be necessary. Reflecting on your own experience, consider whether violence is ever justifiable. Can you recall an occasion when you used violence or were tempted to? What did you think the use or the show of force would accomplish in this particular situation? What alternatives did you have? In general, why do you think people resort to violence? In what ways does American culture encourage or dis-courage violence?

For Analysis

1. At the beginning of this chapter, we make the following assertions about writing that evaluates. Consider whether each of these assertions is true of Ansen's review:

    ▪ It makes a judgment.
    ▪ It tries to convince readers that the judgment is reasonable.

- It bases its judgment on standards appropriate to its subject.
- It strives to show that it fully understands its subject.
- It gives reasons for its judgment.
- It supports its reasons with evidence.

2. Ansen uses the writing strategy of comparing and contrasting at two points in the essay. Find these passages. Which of the two strategies—comparison or contrast—is being used in each case? What does each accomplish in this essay?

3. In paragraph 6 Ansen refers to an objection by some that *Do the Right Thing* may incite people to violence. On what grounds does he refute this criticism? In your view, how effective is his refutation? What advantages or disadvantages do you see in placing this refutation in the last paragraph?

4. To influence readers' decisions about whether to see a movie, the reviewer needs to gain readers' confidence. Has Ansen won your confidence? If so, how? If not, why not?

For Your Own Writing

If you were to review a movie, which one would you choose? What would be your basic judgment of this movie? What reasons would you give to convince your readers to support your judgment? Are there any criticisms of the movie that you would need to respond to in your review? If so, how would you handle them?

Commentary

Ansen's essay is typical of most movie reviews in that it primarily addresses readers who have only heard about the movie and are trying to decide whether to see it. These readers want to know whether the film is worth their time and money. Ansen answers this question for *Do the Right Thing* with a thumbs up, but he knows that a good review must do more than simply assert a judgment. It must also give reasons for that judgment and cite evidence from the movie to support these reasons.

A scratch outline will help us understand his argumentative strategy:

a shockingly frank scene from the movie, immediately illustrating Ansen's title (paragraph 1)

response to this scene, interpretation of it (2)

Lee's refusal to oversimplify (3)

final scene and its key characters (4)

point of the final scene (4)

Lee's trust in his audience to tolerate ambivalence and contradiction (5)

comparison to Lee's previous film (6)

refutation of the objection that Lee is irresponsible, explicit judgment of the film (6)

Ansen's title—"Searing, Nervy, and Very Honest"—lets us know immediately what he thinks about the film. This judgment is echoed in paragraph 2 in slightly different terms: "nervy, complex, unsettling." Although Ansen doesn't state explicitly, "I like this film," readers can readily see that he is praising *Do the Right Thing* and on what grounds.

His reasons for admiring the film center on the way it represents the current racial situation in America. Ansen argues that Spike Lee departs from the safe route that most other filmmakers have taken when dealing with issues of racial tension. Instead of oversimplifying the situation, he says, Lee portrays relations between blacks and whites in all their disturbing complexity. Rather than leaving viewers feeling complacent and self-satisfied, Lee challenges them to reflect on their own values and actions.

Because Ansen knows that most moviegoers won't like being challenged, he must convince his readers that *Do the Right Thing* unsettles viewers for a good reason, and that they should admire Lee for being "nervy" and "honest." This is the essence of his argumentative strategy. Ansen carries through this strategy by trying to convince his readers that "honest reporting" is especially important in this case, airing the "noxious fumes" of racial hatred and thus helping readers to realize "how dire the racial situation has become." He even goes so far as to suggest that this film might possibly help to prevent an explosion of violence.

The idea that a movie attempting to portray reality should do so honestly, without oversimplifying or giving easy answers to the difficult questions it poses, is Ansen's primary basis for judging the film. Writers do not always have to justify the basis for their judgments, as Ansen does here. If they think their judgment will not be readily understood or accepted by readers, however, they must develop an argumentative strategy like Ansen's that establishes the basis for their judgment.

Finally, Ansen offers evidence from the movie to support his argument. In arguing that *Do the Right Thing* doesn't oversimplify, for example, he shows that Sal is portrayed sympathetically, even though he's "arguably an unconscious racist," while the militant Buggin' Out is shown to be "foolish." And to illustrate the film's "nerviness," he summarizes a sequence of scenes in which members of different ethnic groups mouth ethnic slurs.

Concrete details and examples drawn from the movie give a review credibility, helping readers both to understand and to accept the writer's argument. They also give readers a taste of the movie so that they can make their own judgments about whether it seems interesting and worth seeing. To achieve this degree of specificity, the reviewer probably has to see the film more than once and almost certainly has to take notes during or immediately after it. When you plan your own evaluation essay, make sure that you will have the opportunity to do this kind of intensive note-taking, whether you review a film or some other subject.

Barbara Ehrenreich is the author of several books, including a critique of the 1980s, *The Worst Years of Our Lives: Irreverent Notes from a Decade of Greed* (1990), and a study of the middle class, *Fear of Falling* (1989). Her essays appear regularly in the *American Scholar*, the *Atlantic*, and the *New Republic*, where this selection originally appeared in April 1990. In it she reviews the television situation comedy *Roseanne*. As you read, notice how the writer includes numerous specific details and examples from different episodes of the show as evidence to support her evaluation.

THE WRETCHED OF THE HEARTH
▪
Barbara Ehrenreich

Roseanne the sitcom, which was inspired by Barr[1] the standup comic, is a radical departure simply for featuring blue-collar Americans— and for depicting them as something other than half-witted greasers and low-life louts. The   1
working class does not usually get much of a role in the American entertainment spectacle. In the seventies mumbling, muscular blue-collar males (*Rocky, The Deer Hunter, Saturday Night Fever*) enjoyed a brief modishness on the screen, while Archie Bunker, the consummate blue-collar bigot, raved away on the tube. But even these grossly stereotyped images vanished in the eighties, as the spectacle narrowed in on the brie-and-chardonnay class. Other than *Roseanne*, I can find only one sitcom that deals consistently with the sub-yuppie condition: *Married . . . with Children*, a relentlessly nasty portrayal of a shoe salesman and his cognitively disabled family members. There may even be others, but sociological zeal has not sufficed to get me past the opening sequences of *Major Dad, Full House* or *Doogie Howser*.

Not that *Roseanne* is free of class stereotyping. The Connors must bear   2
part of the psychic burden imposed on all working-class people by their economic and occupational betters. . . . They indulge in a manic physicality that would be unthinkable among the more controlled and genteel Huxtables. They maintain a traditional, low-fiber diet of white bread and macaroni. They are not above a fart joke.

Still, in *Roseanne* I am willing to forgive the stereotypes as markers   3
designed to remind us of where we are: in the home of a construction worker and his minimum-wage wife. Without the reminders, we might not be aware of how thoroughly the deeper prejudices of the professional class are being challenged. Roseanne's fictional husband Dan (played by the irresistibly cuddly John Goodman) drinks domestic beer and dedicates Sundays to football; but far from being a Bunkeresque boor, he looks to this feminist like the fabled "sensitive man" we have all been pining for. He treats his rotund wife like a sex goddess. He picks up on small cues signaling emotional distress. He helps with homework. And when Roseanne works overtime, he cooks, cleans, and rides herd on the kids without any of the piteous whining we have come to expect from upscale males in their rare, and lavishly documented, encounters with soiled Pampers.

Roseanne Connor has her own way of defying the stereotypes. Variously employed as a fast-food operative, a factory worker, a bartender, and a telephone salesperson, her real dream is to be a writer. When her twelve-   4

---

[1]Barr was Roseanne's surname when the show was first broadcast.

year-old daughter Darlene (brilliantly played by Sara Gilbert) balks at a poetry-writing assignment, Roseanne gives her a little talking-to involving Sylvia Plath:[2] "She inspired quite a few women, including *moi*." In another episode, a middle-aged friend thanks Roseanne for inspiring her to dump her chauvinist husband and go to college. We have come a long way from the dithering, cowering Edith Bunker.

Most of the time the Connors do the usual sitcom things. They have   5 the little domestic misunderstandings that can be patched up in twenty-four minutes with wisecracks and a round of hugs. But *Roseanne* carries working-class verisimilitude into a new and previously taboo dimension—the workplace. In the world of employment, Roseanne knows exactly where she stands: "All the good power jobs are taken. Vanna turns the letters. Leona's got hotels. Margaret's running England. . . . 'Course she's not doing a very good job. . . ."[3]

The class conflict continues on other fronts. In one episode, Roseanne   6 arrives late for an appointment with Darlene's history teacher, because she has been forced to work overtime at Wellman. The teacher, who is leaning against her desk stretching her quadriceps when Roseanne arrives, wants to postpone the appointment because she has a date to play squash. When Roseanne insists, the teacher tells her that Darlene has been barking in class, "like a dog." This she follows with some psychobabble—on emotional problems and dysfunctional families—that would leave most mothers, whatever their social class, clutched with guilt. Not Roseanne, who calmly informs the yuppie snit that, in the Connor household, everybody barks like dogs.

It is Barr's narrow-eyed cynicism about the family, even more than her   7 class consciousness, that gives *Roseanne* its special frisson. Archie Bunker got our attention by telling us that we (blacks, Jews, "ethnics," WASPS, etc.) don't really like each other. Barr's message is that even within the family we don't much like each other. We love each other (who else do we have?); but The Family, with its impacted emotions, its lopsided division of labor, and its ancient system of age-graded humiliations, just doesn't work. Or rather, it doesn't work unless the contradictions are smoothed out with irony and the hostilities are periodically blown off as humor. Coming from mom, rather than from a jaded teenager or a bystander dad, this is scary news indeed. . . .

On the one hand, she presents the family as a zone of intimacy and   8 support, well worth defending against the forces of capitalism, which drive both mothers and fathers out of the home, scratching around for paychecks. On the other hand, the family is hardly a haven, especially of its grown-up females. It is marred from within by—among other things—the patriarchal division of leisure, which makes dad and the kids the "consumers" of mom's cooking, cleaning, nurturing, and (increasingly) her earnings. Mom's

[2]American poet and novelist (1932–1963).

[3]Vanna White is a television quiz show personality. Leona Helmsley is a Manhattan hotel owner sent to prison in 1991 for income tax evasion. Margaret Thatcher was prime minister of England from 1979 to 1990.

job is to keep the whole thing together—to see that the mortgage payments are made, to fend off the viperish teenagers, to find the missing green sock— but mom is no longer interested in being a human sacrifice on the altar of "pro-family values." She's been down to the feminist bookstore; she's been reading Sylvia Plath.

This is a bleak and radical vision. Not given to didacticism, Barr offers   9 no programmatic ways out. Surely, we are led to conclude, pay equity would help, along with child care, and so on. But Barr leaves us hankering for a quality of change that goes beyond mere reform: for a world in which even the lowliest among us—the hash-slinger, the sock-finder, the factory hand—will be recognized as the poet she truly is.

For Discussion

Some people consider America a classless country, but Barbara Ehrenreich sees definite class divisions within our society. She specifically identifies a working or blue-collar class and a professional or yuppie class. How difficult do you think it is for people to move from a lower class into a higher class? In other words, to what extent is the American Dream really possible? If you think moving up the social ladder is largely a myth, why do so many people continue to believe in it? Do you ever feel you want to move up? Do you have a plan for doing so?

For Analysis

1. What is Ehrenreich's judgment of *Roseanne*? Find the passage that you think is the most explicit statement of her thesis. On what basis does she make this judgment? (For more on thesis statements, see pp. 189–90.)

2. Skim the essay, noting where Ehrenreich relates *Roseanne* to other television programs and films. What part does comparison and contrast play in the writer's overall argumentative strategy?

3. In providing evidence from the television sitcom, Ehrenreich refers both to specific episodes and to elements that occur throughout the television series. Skim her essay, marking references to specific episodes with a line in the margin and general references to the series with a double line. Where she evaluates the series as a whole, why do you think she refers to specific episodes? What does each kind of reference contribute to her review?

4. Ehrenreich has some fun with this essay. Reread it, noting passages where her writing seems especially witty. How does her use of humor influence your willingness to accept her judgment?

For Your Own Writing

Ehrenreich evaluates a television series, not just a single program. If you were assigned to evaluate some type of series—such as the *Star Wars* or *Die Hard* movies, Rembrandt's or Van Gogh's self-portraits, P. D. James's mysteries, or a television series—what would you choose? Whatever you were to choose, you would need to examine closely several items in the series, taking notes for evidence to support your judgment.

Commentary

A great temptation for writers evaluating a subject they feel strongly about is to give it unqualified praise or blame. Few things, however, are all good or all bad, and readers are likely to see such a characterization as either/or thinking—a logical fallacy, or error in reasoning, that weakens an argument partly by undermining the writer's credibility. Ehrenreich is enthusiastic about *Roseanne* but tempers her praise in paragraph 2, where she points out that the program is not "free of class stereotyping."

Also notable is the way Ehrenreich makes her writing readable by careful use of topic sentences. A topic sentence announces the topic of the paragraph it introduces, but it may also connect the paragraph to the preceding one. Paragraph 2, for example, begins with a sentence that refers explicitly to class stereotyping, the central idea of the first paragraph. The opening sentence of paragraph 7 makes a similarly helpful connection, summarizing the central point of the first six paragraphs and identifying the main topic of the next few paragraphs. (For more on strategies for achieving coherence, see pp. 199–202.)

Two stylistic features of the essay also deserve mention: the use of the colon and repetition of sentence openings. Ehrenreich uses the colon for a variety of purposes. Sometimes it introduces an example: "Other than *Roseanne*, I can find only one sitcom that deals consistently with the sub-yuppie condition: *Married . . . with Children . . .*" (paragraph 1). At other times the colon specifies or defines: "Still, in *Roseanne* I am willing to forgive the stereotypes as markers designed to remind us of where we are: in the home of a construction worker and his minimum-wage wife" (paragraph 3). And at still other times the colon introduces a quotation: "*Roseanne* gives her a little talking-to involving Sylvia Plath: 'She inspired quite a few women, including *moi*'" (paragraph 4).

Ehrenreich repeats sentence openings to strengthen the bonds between sentences, to create a pleasing rhythm, and to emphasize the material that is repeated. The last three sentences in paragraph 2, for example, open with a "*they* + verb" construction. In paragraph 3, Ehrenreich uses a "*he* + verb" pattern in three consecutive sentences but then varies it by beginning the next sentence with a prepositional phrase followed by the expected pattern.

Kevin Stewart wrote this essay for a first-year college composition course. It evaluates Tobias Wolff's remembered event essay, "On Being a Real Westerner," in Chapter 2 of this book and reveals Stewart's reasons for valuing it. As you read, notice how Stewart provides evidence to support his argument both by citing many details from the selection and by relating his personal experience.

<table>
<tr><td>

**AN EVALUATION OF
TOBIAS WOLFF'S "ON
BEING A REAL WESTERNER"**

▪

Kevin Stewart

</td><td>

Tobias Wolff's "On Being a Real Westerner"   1
was a pleasure to read, and the story's tension
built quickly. On rereading, I had time to admire
Wolff's strategies of narrative action and detail-
ing of the scene and people. On reflection, I was
able to relate the story to my personal experi-

</td></tr>
</table>

ence, and to appreciate the way Wolff expressed the significance of the
event for his life.

This selection is unquestionably a "good read." It is not a simple story,   2
because it reveals a lot and shows a range of emotions, but it is very easy
to read. In the opening paragraph Wolff describes how he got a rifle from
his stepfather Roy over the objections of his mother. Once we get to the
main event in paragraph 5, the story moves quickly. The young Wolff's
dressing up in combat and hunting gear and following people in the rifle
sights of the unloaded gun seem harmless and even comical, but my response to the story changes abruptly at the beginning of paragraph 7 with
the mention of live ammunition: "Roy stored his ammunition in a metal
box he kept hidden in the closet." The tension and the possibility for disaster
increase in paragraph 8, with mention of Wolff's irritation, and then become nearly unbearable with the opening of paragraph 9, "One afternoon
I pulled the trigger," an action that the next sentence immediately suggests
will be directed at one of the two elderly people Wolff says he is aiming at
on the street. We must bear this suspense until the elderly people round a
corner and the boy gets the two squirrels in the rifle sights. That offers some
relief from the tension, but in the back of my mind I kept thinking that maybe
this is the beginning of a shooting spree in which several people will be
killed.

While the tension contributes powerfully to my engagement with the   3
story, the careful focus of the scene and action also contributes. The scene
is the apartment and specifically the living room, including what the boy
can see of the street from the window. Wolff doesn't digress to describe the
view or to tell us what people are wearing or whether the squirrels are gray
or brown or black. Instead, Wolff keeps the focus on his actions and feelings. Only once does Wolff break the forward movement, and that is in
paragraph 8, where he reflects briefly on the connection of this childhood
event to his experience years later in the Vietnam War.

Still another thing that adds to my interest in the story and increases   4
the tension for me as a reader is the narrative action, Wolff's specific movements and gestures and those of other actors in the scene that help me
imagine what is going on. As I've said, some of the boy's actions seem
comical and some seem terrifying. For example, he marches around the
apartment, "striking brave poses in front of the mirror" and sets up a "nest"
on the couch, assuming his "position," like a sniper in a Sarajevo apartment
building. Then, ominously, we see him "nudging the shade aside" and
"cocking the hammer and letting it snap down." In the climactic paragraph
9, we learn that he is "aiming at two old people" who "walked so slowly."
We see the squirrels "chasing each other back and forth on the telephone

wires." Wolff tells us he fired, and the squirrel "dropped straight into the road." These specific actions greatly increase my interest in the story because they each give me a strong visual image, almost as real to me as the memory of observing actions like these or seeing a film of them.

Besides enjoying this selection as a "good read," I admire the way it   5
details objects and participants in the scene. The first paragraph provides examples by naming objects and detailing them. The objects of attention are the rifle (or "piece"), its action, and its stock. The rifle is detailed as follows: "light, pump-action, beautifully balanced," "better than new." The action is detailed as "silky from long use," and the stock as "walnut," "black from all its oilings," "the wood of a quality no longer to be found." These details help me understand Wolff's intense interest in the rifle, his deep desire to own it, and his great pleasure in having it for himself. In paragraph 5, the details provide a different impression, a comic or perhaps even pathetic one, based on the boy's attempts to dress up like a real Westerner. Wolff goes beyond mentioning that he dressed up in hunting gear to provide specific details: "fur trooper's hat, camouflage coat, boots that reached nearly to my knees."

Another reason I especially liked the story was that it reminded me of   6
the few times I hunted with a weapon. One fall when I was thirteen, my uncle took me twice to hunt doves. He lent me one of his small-gauge shotguns, and we walked along ranch roads looking for doves. In nearly treeless western Oklahoma, doves perch on telephone or electrical lines. Practicing good sportsmanship, we would shoot only when they flew. I never killed a dove because they were so fast. They would leave a line at top speed within a second and would be out of range usually before I could aim and fire. I never hit anything in many tries, but my uncle managed to kill two or three doves both times we went out. Except for frustration over my bad aim and timing, I really enjoyed the two hunting trips, and the doves tasted delicious when my aunt baked them. But I never asked to go again, and I never owned a shotgun. When I was ten, though, I did make a kill with my own weapon. Like most of my friends, I owned a BB gun. I bought it with money saved from earnings from my newspaper route. We shot at cans, as well as lizards, horned toads, and birds. We rarely killed or injured any of these creatures, but one time when I was on my own, pinging discarded cans and watching for toads and birds, I spotted a yellow and black oriole. I shot at it without even aiming carefully. To my surprise, it fell out of the mesquite tree, like Wolff's squirrel dropping from the telephone line. I remember the feelings of guilt and regret I experienced when I picked up this bird. I had noticed orioles migrating through our town, but I had never seen one up close. It was larger and more beautiful than I had imagined. I buried it and never told anyone about it, but I thought about it many times afterward and never forgot the emotion I felt.

Finally, I liked Wolff's recollection of this boyhood event because the   7
significance was easy to grasp. I know that significance can be implied, but I prefer that the writer actually state the significance of the event. Wolff declares the significance of the event at the beginning and end, framing the story, as well as in the middle. At the beginning he makes clear why, from his adult perspective, the rifle was important to him as a boy: "[I]t com-

pleted me when I held it." He also says, "A weapon was the first condition
. . . of being a real Westerner," and he very much wanted to be that sort of
person. At the end, he returns to this idea of what the rifle did for him. He
says that he could only imagine himself armed because "any image of
myself, no matter how grotesque, had power over me." He makes the point
that these are not insights he had at the time of the event but reflections
from his present perspective as an adult. It's not surprising that these powerful images of himself with a rifle would remind Wolff of his later experiences in Vietnam. In paragraph 8, Wolff reflects on the dangers and limits
of power: "Power can be enjoyed only when it is recognized and feared.
Fearlessness in those without power is maddening to those who have it."
Wolff seems to conclude that the power that comes from carrying a gun is
fragile, uncertain, and temporary.

I haven't yet read much autobiography, but it's hard for me to imagine   8
a more successful story of a remembered event than Wolff's. We get a
dramatic engaging story filled with many vivid details. Probably anyone
who has ever fired a pistol, rifle, or shotgun can relate some personal experience to that of Wolff's. We know that the event is significant in Wolff's
life because he tells us so, but beyond that we recognize that the event
reveals something important about the images and myths that attract young
American men. Wolff seems to have gained insights into who he was, who
he became in Vietnam, and who he is now. Yet he stops short of moralizing,
and he doesn't allow sentimentality to creep into his remembered feelings
and present perspective.

For Discussion

Kevin Stewart suggests that writing about personal experience should avoid sentimentality—expression of trite or predictable feeling or excessive, indulgent expression of feeling. Think about a time when you've related personal experiences
to people you've known well. Think also about personal experiences you've especially enjoyed hearing other people tell. What part do remembered and present
feelings play in those stories? Consider also the kinds of movies, television dramas,
and novels you enjoy. Do these feature or avoid obvious emotions or overstated
expression of feelings? From these reflections, what can you conclude about the
role of expressed emotion or feeling in everyday stories and popular culture?

For Analysis

1. Notice in the opening paragraph that Stewart forecasts his reasoning and his plan.
    Make a scratch outline of the essay and check to confirm that each reason men-
    tioned in Stewart's introduction is in fact argued in the essay and in just the
    sequence Stewart forecasts. Also notice whether any other writers in this chapter
    use forecasting in the opening paragraph. What advantages or disadvantages do
    you see in forecasting an evaluation? (For more on forecasting, see pp. 190–91.)

2. Stewart uses different types of reasons to justify his evaluation. Categorize the
    reasons by type, and identify each type with a brief phrase. Do you find any type

inappropriate? If so, why? Do you find one type more convincing than another? If so, explain briefly.

3. Stewart gives readers cues to each stage of his essay. To examine his cues, underline the first sentence in each paragraph, beginning with paragraph 2. Notice first which cues signal a new reason and which signal further parts of the argument for the same reason. Then examine each cue, noticing whether it refers to what has come before, what is to come next, or both. Pick two or three paragraph transition cues that seem particularly effective to you and explain how they do their work. (For more on transitional cues, see pp. 202–4.)

4. Review paragraphs 3, 5, and 6, underlining each piece of evidence from the Wolff selection. Then, given Stewart's purpose in each of these paragraphs, decide which one is the most effectively argued. What about the amount, type, and appropriateness of the evidence encouraged you to single out this paragraph as the one that contains the best argument?

For Your Own Writing

Like Stewart, you may write an evaluation of one of the essays in Part One of this book. While Stewart evaluates an autobiographical essay, you might prefer to evaluate how well an essay explains a concept (Chapter 3), or how logically an essay makes its argument (Chapters 5 and 6). To review possible bases for your evaluation, you would want to reread carefully the Commentary following the reading you choose as well as the Purpose and Audience and Basic Features sections that follow it. The Guide to Writing in this chapter provides further help with this writing task.

Commentary

Encouraged to evaluate a reading in any Part One chapter for which his class had written an essay, Stewart readily chose Chapter 2, "Remembering Events," because he believed he had written his best essay for that chapter. Since the selection from Tobias Wolff's autobiography was easily his favorite reading, he was drawn to finding out more about why he liked it so much in order to make a case for readers that it is an outstanding example of its genre.

Stewart felt he was in a particularly authoritative position to evaluate Wolff's piece: he had not only read the other selections in the chapter, broadening his understanding of writing about a remembered event, but had also written such an essay, giving him an insider's view of how the genre works. Moreover, he had written about and discussed the Reflecting on Your Writing activity at the end of the chapter.

To review and consolidate what he had learned, Stewart reread the four selections in the chapter, the Commentaries following each, and the Basic Features discussion. He was not constrained by the Commentary following the Wolff selection; in fact, he went well beyond it. Nor did he attempt to evaluate the selection from all possible perspectives offered by the resources in the chapter. Rather, he justified his evaluation with reasons particularly appropriate for the Wolff selection: engagement with a well-told story, detailing of objects and participants in the scene, relation to personal experience, and explicit statement of significance.

In his essay, Stewart does not compare or contrast the Wolff selection with others in the chapter because his writing situation did not invite it. The selections are meant to illustrate various approaches and strategies for writing a readable, memorable remembered event essay. Therefore, Stewart could not plausibly argue that the Wolff selection is the "best" in the chapter. Instead, he argues that it is an outstanding example of its genre, giving appropriate reasons to support his judgment.

PURPOSE AND AUDIENCE

When you evaluate something, you seek to influence readers' judgments and possibly their actions. Your primary aim is to convince readers that your judgment is well informed and reasonable, and therefore that they can feel confident in making decisions based on it. Good readers don't simply accept reviewers' judgments, however, especially on subjects of importance. More likely, they read reviews to learn more about a subject so that they can make an informed choice themselves. Consequently, most readers care less about the forcefulness with which you assert your judgment than about the reasons and evidence you cite to support it.

Effective writers develop an argumentative strategy designed for their particular readers. Your argumentative strategy determines every writing decision you make, from what you reveal about the subject to the way you construct your argument—which reasons you use, whether you justify the basis for your reasoning, how much and what kinds of evidence you cite.

You may want to acknowledge directly your readers' knowledge of the subject, perhaps revealing that you understand how they might judge it differently. You might even let readers know that you have anticipated their objections to your argument. In responding to objections, reservations, or different judgments, you could agree to disagree on certain points but seek to find common ground for judgment on other points.

BASIC FEATURES OF EVALUATION ESSAYS

Evaluation essays generally include the following basic features.

A Clearly Defined Subject

The subject being evaluated should be clearly identified, usually with some description. In general, evaluations provide only enough information to give readers a context for the judgment. Movie and book reviews may include more information than other kinds of evaluations because reviewers assume readers will be unfamiliar with the subject and are reading, in part, to learn more about it.

A Clear, Balanced Judgment

Evaluation essays are focused around a judgment—an assertion that something is good or bad or that it is better or worse than something else of the same kind or group. This judgment is the thesis, or main point, of the essay. Usually the judgment is clearly stated in various ways throughout the essay and reasserted at the end. Although readers expect a definitive judgment, they also appreciate a balanced one that acknowledges both good and bad points of the subject.

A Convincing Evaluative Argument

An evaluation cannot merely state its judgment but must also argue for it. To be convincing, an evaluative argument must give reasons for the judgment. In addition, writers of evaluations must support their judgments with evidence. The selections in this chapter rely primarily on textual evidence—describing, quoting, paraphrasing, and summarizing aspects of the movie, television program, or essay. Other kinds of evidence include facts, statistics, expert testimony, and personal anecdote. Sometimes reviewers anticipate and respond to readers' objections or questions. They may accommodate these objections by making concessions to readers or by refuting their objections.

Pointed Comparisons

Comparisons are not a requirement of evaluative writing, but they are often useful. One good way to assess something, after all, is to set it next to another of its kind. To evaluate a movie, for example, you would naturally judge it relative to other movies of the same kind. You would compare it to other movies, looking at similarities; or you would contrast it, looking at differences.

Guide to Writing

▪ THE WRITING ASSIGNMENT

Choose a subject to evaluate. Write an essay assessing your subject addressed to a particular group of readers, giving them all of the background information, reasons, and evidence they will need to accept your evaluation. Your principal aim is to convince these readers that your judgment of this subject is informed and reasonable.

INVENTION AND RESEARCH

At this point you need to choose a subject, evaluate it closely, analyze your readers, develop an argument to support your evaluation, and test your choice.

Choosing a Subject

You may already have something in mind to evaluate. Even so, consider some other possibilities to be sure you make the best choice.

Listing Possible Subjects

List anything you would be interested in evaluating, trying to think of at least one subject in each of the following categories.

- *Media*: a television program, magazine, or newspaper
- *Arts*: a movie, recording, performance, or work of art
- *Written works*: a poem, short story, novel, essay, or reading from this book
- *Education*: a school, program, teacher, textbook, or computer software program
- *Government*: a government department or official, a proposed or existing law, or a candidate for public office
- *Campus*: a class, department, library, or sports team
- *Leisure*: an amusement park, museum, restaurant, resort, national or state park, or scenic highway

Making a Choice

Review your list, looking for a subject that you could evaluate with authority— something you already know well or could examine closely. Consider whether you know the standards by which people ordinarily evaluate something of this kind. Then choose the subject that seems most promising.

Exploring Your Subject

Before going any further, you need to make a tentative judgment and to ascertain what you already know about the subject and what additional information you may need.

Considering Your Present Judgment

Although your opinion about your subject may change as you think and write about it in more detail, for now, set down your current opinion as clearly as you can. In a sentence or two, simply state your judgment. Don't explain why you're making this judgment; just say what it is.

Considering What You Think and Know about Your Subject

Write for around ten minutes about your feelings and knowledge about your subject, considering these questions for guidance:

- How certain am I of my judgment? Do I have any doubts? Why do I feel the way I do?
- Do I like (or dislike) everything about my subject, or only certain parts?
- Are there any similar things I should consider (other restaurants or movies, for example)?

- Is there anything I will need to do right away in order to evaluate this subject authoritatively? If I need to do research, how can I get the information I need?

Analyzing Your Readers

You want to convince particular readers to consider your evaluation seriously, perhaps even to take some action as a result—to see a certain television series, for instance, or take a specific class. Consequently, you must analyze these readers carefully, considering what they are likely to know and think about your subject. Take ten minutes to analyze your readers in writing. Use these questions to stimulate your analysis:

- Who are my readers? What values and attitudes do we share that might enable me to gain their trust?
- What are they likely to know and think about my subject?
- What other subjects of the same type might they be familiar with? How are they likely to judge these other subjects?
- What about my judgment might surprise them? On what basis might they disagree with me?

Developing an Argumentative Strategy

Once you have some sense of who your readers will be, you can begin to think about your argumentative strategy. Basically, an argumentative strategy is a plan for accomplishing a particular purpose with specific readers. For an evaluation, your purpose is to convince your readers to accept your judgment about the subject; your argumentative strategy is to present reasons for your judgment and to show evidence to support those reasons. The reasons you give must be appropriate to the subject and selected with your readers' sensibilities in mind.

It might help, in working out your argumentative strategy, to keep track of your reasons and evidence on a chart. Simply divide a piece of paper into two vertical columns, labeling the first *Reasons* and the second *Evidence*. Putting all your material on such a chart will help you see at a glance where your argument is strong and where you need to give it more thought or collect more evidence.

List the Reasons for Your Judgment

Consider the reasons for your judgment: Why do you like or dislike the film or restaurant or whatever you are evaluating? To identify your reasons, try completing the following statement:

_____ is a good/bad _____ because _____.

Kevin Stewart, for example, might have begun to state his reasons for liking Tobias Wolff's essay as follows:

"On Being a Real Westerner" is a good essay because the author builds tension skillfully.

Put down all the reasons you can think of for your judgment about your subject, and then look over your list to decide which reasons would be the most convincing for your particular readers. Imagine you were evaluating the Walt Disney hotel designed by Michael Graves, for instance. If your readers were professional architects, you would probably look for architectural reasons: that it is the most architecturally distinctive hotel at Walt Disney World, for instance. If, however, your readers were school children, you'd surely focus on some other reasons: that it is the only hotel filled with familiar Disney characters, perhaps.

Finding Evidence

After you have listed as many reasons as you can, look to find evidence to illustrate each reason. Evidence comes in many forms: descriptive details, quotations, statistics, authoritative testimony, anything that supports a reason. Most, if not all, evidence in evaluations of the type you will write comes from the thing being evaluated. For that reason, it is important for you to examine your subject closely even if you are already quite familiar with it—resee the movie, revisit the restaurant, reread the novel. As you do so, enter evidence next to the relevant reason in your reasons-and-evidence chart. Evidence for the architectural distinctiveness of Michael Graves's Disney hotel might be that other well-respected architects have praised it; for the hotel's featuring Disney characters everywhere, that it has Mickey Mouse doorknobs and Dumbo lampposts. You will probably find that the amount of evidence you can show for each reason will vary. Some reasons will have only one piece of evidence, while others may have many.

Justifying Your Reasons.   If your readers are likely to be surprised by some of your reasons, to object to any of them, or to expect you to use reasons other than the ones you've chosen, you will need to justify your choice of reasons. Consider your reasons individually and as a set. Begin by writing about each one, explaining why it is appropriate for evaluating this kind of subject. Then write about the set, explaining why you've chosen to use these reasons and not others that readers might expect you to use.

Drawing Comparisons.   It is a good idea to get some sense of how your subject compares to others of the same type or category. Doing this will help you recognize strengths and weaknesses in your subject, and may lead you to material you can use in your essay. Comparing *Roseanne* with *Married . . . with Children* helps Ehrenreich make the point that *Roseanne* offers a more complex portrait of a working-class family than do other situation comedies with blue-collar protagonists.

Testing Your Choice

Pause now to decide whether you have the makings of a convincing evaluative argument. Ask yourself the following questions:

- Do I know enough about my subject to evaluate it fully?

▪ Do I care enough about this subject to want to convince readers to accept my opinion about it?

▪ Are my reasons for thinking what I do about my subject strong ones? Are they reasons that will appeal to my readers?

▪ Do I have adequate evidence to convince readers that my reasons have a basis? Will I be able to check out my subject closely again if I need additional evidence?

For Group Inquiry

At this point it might be helpful to get some response to your subject. Work in a group with two or three other students. Announce your subject and intended readers, state your judgment, and give the reasons for your judgment. Then ask the group members whether these seem to be convincing reasons. Can they suggest any other reasons that might strengthen your argument? This kind of feedback can help you determine whether your reasoning is likely to impress readers as strong justification for your judgment.

PLANNING AND DRAFTING

The following guidelines will help you review your invention writings to see what you have so far, to establish goals for your evaluation, and to make a tentative outline to guide you as you draft.

Seeing What You Have

By now you have done considerable thinking and writing about your evaluation. You have explored many aspects of your subject, analyzed your readers, and developed an argumentative strategy. Take some time now to reread your invention notes thoughtfully, highlighting anything you think you will be able to use in the draft and noting connections between ideas. Also keep an eye out for problems you may have overlooked earlier, and consider how you might deal with them. For example, look for places where your evidence is thin or contradictory or where your reasoning is weak.

Setting Goals

Before you begin drafting, think seriously about the overall goals of your evaluation. Having clear goals will make the draft not only easier to write but almost surely more focused as well, and therefore more convincing.

Following are some questions designed to help you focus on what exactly you want to accomplish with this evaluation. You may find it useful to return to them while you are drafting.

Your Readers

- What do I want my readers to think about the subject as a result of reading my essay? Do I want to show them how the piece I am evaluating succeeds, as all of the writers in this chapter do, or how it fails?
- Should I assume, as Ansen does, that my readers are likely to have read other evaluations of the subject? Or should I assume that I am introducing readers to it?
- How can I gain my readers' trust? Should I show them how familiar I am with comparable subjects? Should I indicate any special knowledge I have?
- What tone should I take? Should I be witty like Ehrenreich, serious like Ansen and Stewart, or enthusiastic?

Presentation of the Subject

- Should I place the subject historically, as Ehrenreich tries to do?
- If the subject has a plot, how much of it should I tell?
- How can I capture the flavor of my subject? Can I cite notable details, as Ansen and Stewart do, or refer to some typical incidents, as Ehrenreich does?

Your Evaluative Argument

- How should I state my judgment? Should I make it a comparative judgment, as Ansen does? Should I put it up front, as Stewart does, or wait a bit, like Ansen, until I've provided a context?
- How can I show that my judgment is fair and well balanced? Can I refer to specific weaknesses without taking away from the larger strengths, as Ehrenreich does?
- How can I support my reasons? Can I find textual evidence to quote or paraphrase, as Stewart does? Can I call upon authorities?
- What facts, statistics, or other evidence could I use?

The Beginning and the Ending

- Should I open by stating my judgment, as Ehrenreich and Stewart do? By describing the subject, as Ansen does? By comparing my subject with one more familiar to readers?
- How should I conclude? Should I try to frame the essay by echoing something from the opening, or from another part of the essay, as Ehrenreich does? Should I conclude by restating my judgment, as Ansen does?

Outlining

Evaluations may be organized in various ways. The important thing is to include all essential parts: a presentation of the subject, a judgment of some kind, and reasons and evidence to support the judgment. In addition, you want to arrange your reasons in some logical order: from most obvious to least obvious, most general to most technical, least convincing to most convincing, least important to most important.

For readers already familiar with the topic, your outline might look like this:

presentation of the subject

judgment

    reason 1

      evidence

    reason 2

      evidence

    reason 3

      evidence, with a comparison

consideration of an opposing judgment

conclusion

For readers unfamiliar with the topic, you need to begin with a description of your subject, including perhaps some background discussion and definition of terms.

There are many other possible organizations. Whichever you choose, remember that an outline should serve only as a guide. It can help you organize your invention materials and provide a sense of direction as you start drafting, but you should feel free to depart from it if you see a better way of developing your argumentative strategy.

Drafting

Before you begin to draft your evaluation, reread all your notes and, if possible, take a last look at your subject. If you are evaluating a published work (such as a poem, story, or novel), reread it. If you are writing about a movie, see it again. Your subject must be completely fresh in your mind.

Start drafting, focusing on your readers and how you can convince them to share your judgment of the subject. If you run into trouble, reconsider each element in your evaluation. Perhaps you should think of better reasons or add more evidence to support the reasons you give. You may need to take another look at your criteria. If you really get stuck, turn back to the invention activities in this chapter to see if you can fill out your material. You might also want to review the general advice about drafting on pages 11–13.

GETTING CRITICAL COMMENTS

Now is the time to get a good critical reading. All writers find it helpful to have someone else read their drafts and give them critical comments. Your instructor may arrange such a reading as part of your coursework; if not, you can ask a classmate, friend, or family member to read your draft. If your college has a writing center, you might ask a tutor to read and comment on your draft. Following are guidelines designed to be used by *anyone* reviewing an evaluation essay. (If you cannot get someone else to read your draft, turn to the Revising and Editing section on pp. 114–116, which includes guidelines for reading your own draft with a critical eye.)

In order to provide helpful comments, your critical reader must know your intended audience and purpose. Briefly write out this information at the top of your draft:

Audience: Who are your readers?

Purpose: What do you want your readers to think about your subject from reading this essay?

Reading with a Critical Eye

Reading a draft critically means reading it more than once, first to get a general impression and then to analyze its basic features.

Reading for a First Impression

Read first to understand the essay's judgment. As you read, try to notice any words or passages that contribute, either favorably or unfavorably, to your first impression. After you've finished reading the draft, briefly write down your impressions. What is the essay's judgment? How convincing do you think the argument will be for the intended readers?

Reading to Analyze

Now reread the draft, this time focusing on the basic features of evaluation essays. (See pp. 105–6 to review the basic features.)

Is the Subject Clearly Presented?

Check to see how the subject is described. Is there anything else that intended readers might be curious about or might need to know? Point to any details that seem unnecessary or redundant.

Is the Judgment Clear and Balanced?

Is the judgment about the subject stated explicitly enough? Is it clear? Check to see that there is a balanced appraisal, acknowledging how the subject succeeds as well as fails.

Is the Argument Convincing?

Do the reasons given for the judgment seem relevant? Is sufficient evidence given for each reason? Is the argument convincing?

Are Any Comparisons Pointed and Appropriate?

Look at any comparisons or contrasts between the subject and other things of the same kind. What do they contribute to the evaluation? Are there too many comparisons? Are there places where comparisons might be added?

Is the Organization Effective?

Note any places where the essay seems disorganized or confusing. Are there topic sentences at the beginning of paragraphs? Would adding others make the essay easier to read? Consider whether any reasons ought to be reordered.

Look at the *beginning*. Is it engaging? If not, can you see any other passages in the draft that might be more interesting? Does it provide sufficient background information?

Look at the *ending*. Does it leave you thinking about the subject? Point to any passage elsewhere in the draft that might work as a conclusion.

What Final Thoughts Do You Have?

What is the strongest part of the argument? What is the weakest part, most in need of further work?

REVISING AND EDITING

This section will help you identify problems in your draft and revise and edit to solve them.

Identifying Problems

To identify problems in your draft, you need to read it objectively, analyze its basic features, and study any comments you've gotten from other readers.

Getting an Overview

Consider the draft as a whole, trying to judge it objectively. It may help to do so in two steps:

1. *Reread.*   If possible, put the draft aside for a day or two before rereading it. When you do, start by reconsidering your audience and purpose. Then read the draft straight through, trying to see it as your intended readers will.

2. *Outline.*   Make a scratch outline to get an overview of the essay's development. This outline can be sketchy—words and phrases instead of complete sentences— but it should identify the basic features as they appear.

Charting a Plan for Revision

You may want to use a double-columned chart to keep track of the problems you need to solve. In the left-hand column, list the basic features of evaluative writing. In the right-hand column, note the problems you want to solve. Here is an example:

Basic Features	*Problems to Solve*
Subject	
Judgment	
Argument	
Comparisons	
Organization	

Analyzing the Basic Features of Your Draft

Turn now to the questions for analyzing a draft on pages 113–14. Using these questions as guidelines, identify problems in your draft. Note anything you need to solve on your revision chart.

Studying Critical Comments

Review any comments you've received from other readers, and add to your chart any points that need attention. Try not to react defensively to these comments; by letting you see how others respond to your draft, the comments provide invaluable information about how you might improve it.

Solving the Problems

Having identified problems, you now need to figure out solutions and to carry them out. Basically, you have three ways of finding solutions: (1) review your invention and planning notes for information and ideas to add to the draft; (2) do further invention and research to answer questions your readers raised; and (3) look back at the readings in this chapter to see how other writers have solved similar problems.

Following are suggestions to get you started on solving some of the problems common to evaluative writing. For now, focus on solving those issues identified on your chart. Try not to worry about sentence-level problems at this time; that will come later when you edit.

Subject

- If the subject is not clear, name it explicitly and describe it in specific detail. Try to anticipate and answer your intended readers' questions.
- If the subject is presented in too much detail, cut extraneous and repetitive details. If your subject has a plot, try to sketch it without telling the whole story.

Judgment

- If the judgment is vague or ambiguous, restate it so that there can be no confusion about your evaluation.
- If the judgment seems too one-sided, try balancing your praise or criticism. Note something worth praising or a possible weakness.

Argument

- If any reasons seem inappropriate or vague, try to clarify them. Review your invention writing, looking for material to strengthen your reasons. Or you may need to explore your reasons further. Consider whether any of the reasons should be combined or separated.
- If the evidence is thin, review your invention writing and reexamine the subject for additional evidence.

Comparisons

- If any comparisons or contrasts seem pointless or inappropriate, eliminate them.
- If there are too many comparisons, consider dropping some.
- If you don't compare or contrast your subject with anything else, try to do so and see whether it strengthens your argument.

Organization

- If the essay seems disorganized or confusing, you may need to add transitions, summaries, or topic sentences. You may also need to do some major restructuring, such as moving your presentation of the subject or reordering your reasons.
- If the beginning is weak, see if there's a better place to start. Review your notes for an interesting quotation, image, or scene to open with.
- If the ending doesn't work, see if you can frame the essay by echoing a point made earlier.

Editing and Proofreading

In working on your draft so far, you may have corrected some obvious errors, but grammar and style have not been a priority. Now is the time to find and correct any errors in mechanics, usage, punctuation, and spelling, as well as to consider matters of style. You may find that studying your draft in separate passes—first for paragraphs, then for sentences, and finally for words—will help you recognize problems.

Once you have edited your draft and produced the final copy, proofread it carefully, making any final corrections before turning it in.

A Writer at Work

LISTING REASONS AND FINDING EVIDENCE

An evaluation essay succeeds only if there are plausible reasons to support the judgment and evidence to support the reasons. These features are the heart of the argument. In this chapter, the Guide to Writing invited you to list reasons and collect evidence. Both activities stem from an intimate knowledge of the subject being evaluated. Reasons come from answering the question, "Why do I like (or dislike) this subject?" Evidence comes from closely analyzing the subject to find specific material that supports each reason.

This section shows how student writer Kevin Stewart listed reasons and collected evidence for his essay, "An Evaluation of Tobias Wolff's 'On Being a Real Westerner,'" which appears on pages 101–3. Here are Stewart's invention notes listing reasons and evidence:

Reasons	*Evidence*
I just liked reading it--it was a "good read."	Tension and suspense--dressing up in combat and hunting gear; loading the rifle; aiming at the elderly people; killing the squirrel
	Focus of the scene and action--scene doesn't move from the living room except for a brief reflection on the Vietnam War
	Narrative action is comical and terrifying--"striking brave poses in front of the mirror"; "nudging the shade aside"; "cocking the hammer and letting it snap down"; "aiming at two old people"; squirrels "chasing each other back and forth on the telephone wires"
I admired the details about objects and people.	Rifle--"light, pump action;" "better than new"
	Action--"silky from long use"
	Stock--"walnut"; "black from its oilings"
	Hunting gear--"fur trooper's hat, camouflage coat, boots that reached nearly to my knees" and looking pathetic
It reminded me of when I went dove hunting with my uncle and of the time I shot an oriole with my BB gun.	
I liked the way Wolff made the significance explicit.	"A weapon was the first condition . . . of being a real Westerner"; "any image of myself, no matter how grotesque, had power over me"; "Power can be enjoyed only when it is recognized and feared"; no real power from carrying a gun

Effective invention notes enabled Stewart to discover whether he really had an argument, whether he could come up with several plausible reasons to explain his judgment of Wolff's essay as a fine example of autobiographical writing, and whether there was evidence in that essay to support his reasoning. After discussing his reasons-and-evidence chart with other students, Stewart felt he had a plausible argument to support his judgment of Wolff's essay. In that group discussion, he also tried out brief versions of the two personal stories—one about dove hunting with his uncle and the other about shooting an oriole with his BB gun—and found that he could recall enough details to write effective narratives of both events.

By comparing Stewart's completed essay with his invention notes, you can see that the notes did not predict every detail that made its way into the essay. Once Stewart began drafting the essay, and as he continued to reread Wolff's story, he discovered additional evidence for his essay.

Reflecting on Your Writing

Now that you've read and discussed several evaluation essays as well as written one such essay yourself, you're in a good position to think critically about what you've learned. Reflecting on your own writing process will help you discover what you learned about solving problems you encountered in making an evaluation.

Begin by gathering your invention and planning notes, drafts and critical comments, revision plan, and final revision. Review these materials as you complete the following writing tasks.

- Identify *one* significant writing problem you encountered while writing the essay. Don't be concerned with sentence-level problems; focus on a problem specific to writing an evaluation. For example: Did you have trouble deciding how much information to include in presenting your subject? Did your initial judgment come across as vague or as too one-sided? Was it difficult to come up with clear reasons for your judgment or enough evidence to support those reasons?
- How did you first recognize this problem? Was it, for example, when you were thinking about how to state your judgment, trying to decide on your argumentative strategy, determining your organizational plan, or getting critical comments on a draft? What called the problem to your attention? Looking back, do you see signs of it in your early invention work? If so, where specifically?
- Reflect on how you attempted to solve the problem. If it arose during invention, did you go back to look at your subject again (rereading an essay, for example, or rewatching a movie)? Did you look for other related subjects with which to compare the subject of your evaluation? If it arose during drafting, did you do

further invention to solve the problem—listing more reasons for your judgment, for example? Did you rethink your presentation of the subject? If you noticed the problem as you were revising, did you reword, reorganize, add new material, or simply cut the part that was problematic? Did you review your invention notes or return again to your subject for further evidence to support your judgment?

▪ Finally, write a page or so explaining to your instructor what the problem was, how you discovered it, and how you went about solving it. Be specific by quoting from your invention writing and drafts, others' critical comments, your own revision plan, and your final revision. Show the various changes your writing and thinking underwent. If you're still uncertain about your solution, say so. The point is not to prove that you've solved the problem perfectly, but to show what you've learned about problem solving in the process of writing an evaluation.

5 *Arguing a Position*

When you take a position, your aim is not primarily to express yourself (as in Chapter 2) or to inform readers (as in Chapter 3), but to justify your views (as in Chapter 4). Your primary aim in this chapter is to persuade readers to adopt your position. Or when persuasion is not possible—when fundamental interests and values are irreconcilable—you make the best possible case for your position and assertively refute objections.

Although we may feel very strongly about our opinions, there is seldom a simple right or wrong answer in controversies. Opinions depend to some extent on facts, but they also depend on less objective factors such as values and principles. To be convincing, an argument must not only present logical reasons backed by solid evidence; it must also be based on shared values and assumptions.

Writing a persuasive position paper is intellectually challenging. It requires you to look critically at your own thinking and to understand others' points of view. You must separate opinion from fact, reason logically, marshal supporting evidence, and recognize the values and beliefs underlying your own and others' opinions.

The most convincing arguments, you will see, appeal to readers in several ways. They appeal to logic by making a sound, well-reasoned, and well-supported argument. They appeal to emotion by helping the reader understand the writer's concerns about the issue. They appeal to the reader's ethical sense by establishing the writer's credibility and by basing the argument on a common set of values and principles.

As citizens in a democracy, we have a special duty to inform ourselves about current issues, to weigh thoughtfully the pros and cons of these issues, and to participate in the public debate over them. Some current issues we might be expected to take a position on include whether explicit sex education and condom distribution to prevent AIDS should take place in public schools, whether taxes should be raised to build more housing for the homeless, whether experiments on animals should be banned. In your future occupations, you may have many occasions to take a position. Educators, for example, may argue over admissions standards and course requirements; business executives debate marketing strategies and investment decisions; health care providers argue over treatment options and hospital policies.

WRITING IN YOUR OTHER COURSES

In your college courses, you will frequently be asked to take positions and support them with appropriate evidence. Consider, for instance, these typical assignments:

- *For an American history course:* Does the Monroe Doctrine justify the American invasion of Panama under President Bush and the occupation of Haiti under President Clinton?
- *For an economics course:* David M. Gordon claims in "Class and the Economics of Crime" that "ghetto crime is committed by people responding quite reasonably to the structure of economic opportunities available to them." Write an essay agreeing or disagreeing with this statement.
- *For a sociology course:* "Organized crime is inevitable as long as drug use is illegal." Drawing on course readings, agree or disagree with this position.
- *For a health sciences course:* Summarize the debate over aerial malathion spraying to control the Mediterranean fruit fly and take a position, arguing for or against it. Make clear your reasons for taking one side or the other.

For Group Inquiry

Get together with another student, and choose an issue that has at least two clearly opposing positions. You don't have to be an authority on the issue, but you should be familiar with some of the arguments that are usually raised on each side. Then decide which of you will argue which side. The side you take doesn't have to be the one you prefer; in fact, taking the opposing position can help you think through your own position.

Spend five minutes alone considering the various reasons you could put forth in support of your position. Choose the single best reason and develop a brief argument to convince your partner why this reason should change his or her mind. Make notes about what you plan to say.

Then debate the issue. For each side, follow three steps: one person argues for his or her best reason, the other person attempts to refute (argue against) that reason, and finally the first person responds to the refutation. You will likely need no more than five minutes for each side.

After the debate, spend some time discussing this argument process by considering the following questions:

- On what basis did you each choose the reason you put forth?
- Knowing now how it can be refuted, would you still choose the same reason? Would you argue for it any differently?
- How did your partner's refutation or argument alter your view of the issue? Your understanding of your partner's view?

Readings

Suzan Shown Harjo is president and executive director of the Morning Star Foundation, trustee of the National Museum of the American Indian, and former executive director of the National Congress of American Indians. A poet and an advocate for Native Americans, she writes here about an issue that affects her personally as a Native American of Cheyenne and Creek heritage. "Last Rites for Indian Dead" first appeared in the *Los Angeles Times* on September 16, 1989.

Before reading the essay, recollect what you know about the way Native Americans have been treated historically. As you read, notice how Harjo reminds readers of this historical context. How does it influence your responsiveness to her argument?

**LAST RITES
FOR INDIAN DEAD**
■
Suzan Shown Harjo

What if museums, universities and government agencies could put your dead relatives on display or keep them in boxes to be cut up and otherwise studied? What if you believed that the spirits of the dead could not rest until their human remains were placed in a sacred area? 1

The ordinary American would say there ought to be a law—and there is, for ordinary Americans. The problem for American Indians is that there are too many laws of the kind that make us the archeological property of the United States and too few of the kind that protect us from such insults. 2

Some of my own Cheyenne relatives' skulls are in the Smithsonian Institution today, along with those of at least 4,500 other Indian people who were violated in the 1800s by the U.S. Army for an "Indian Crania Study." It wasn't enough that these unarmed Cheyenne people were mowed down by the cavalry at the infamous Sand Creek massacre; many were decapitated and their heads shipped to Washington as freight. (The Army Medical Museum's collection is now in the Smithsonian.) Some had been exhumed only hours after being buried. Imagine their grieving families' reaction on finding their loved ones disinterred and headless. 3

Some targets of the Army's study were killed in noncombat situations and beheaded immediately. The officer's account of the decapitation of the Apache chief Mangas Coloradas in 1863 shows the pseudoscientific nature of the exercise. "I weighed the brain and measured the skull," the good doctor wrote, "and found that while the skull was smaller, the brain was larger than that of Daniel Webster." 4

These journal accounts exist in excruciating detail, yet missing are any records of overall comparisons, conclusions or final reports of the Army study. Since it is unlike the Army not to leave a paper trail, one must wonder about the motive for its collection. 5

The total Indian body count in the Smithsonian collection is more than 19,000, and it is not the largest in the country. It is not inconceivable that the 1.5 million of us living today are outnumbered by our dead stored in 6

museums, educational institutions, federal agencies, state historical socie-
ties and private collections. The Indian people are further dehumanized by
being exhibited alongside the mastodons and dinosaurs and other extinct
creatures.

Where we have buried our dead in peace, more often than not the sites   7
have been desecrated. For more than 200 years, relic-hunting has been a
popular pursuit. Lately, the market in Indian artifacts has brought this ab-
horrent activity to a fever pitch in some areas. And when scavengers come
upon Indian burial sites, everything found becomes fair game, including
sacred burial offerings, teeth and skeletal remains.

One unusually well-publicized example of Indian grave desecration   8
occurred [in 1987] in a western Kentucky field known as Slack Farm, the
site of an Indian village five centuries ago. Ten men—one with a business
card stating "Have Shovel, Will Travel"—paid the landowner $10,000 to
lease digging rights between planting seasons. They dug extensively on the
40-acre farm, rummaging through an estimated 650 graves, collecting burial goods, tools and ceremonial items. Skeletons were strewn about like
litter.

What motivates people to do something like this? Financial gain is the   9
first answer. Indian relic-collecting has become a multimillion-dollar industry. The price tag on a bead necklace can easily top $1,000; rare pieces
fetch tens of thousands.

And it is not just collectors of the macabre who pay for skeletal re-   10
mains. Scientists say that these deceased Indians are needed for research
that someday could benefit the health and welfare of living Indians. But just
how many dead Indians must they examine? Nineteen thousand?

There is doubt as to whether permanent curation of our dead really   11
benefits Indians. Dr. Emery A. Johnson, former assistant Surgeon General,
recently observed, "I am not aware of any current medical diagnostic or
treatment procedure that has been derived from research on such skeletal
remains. Nor am I aware of any during the 34 years that I have been involved in American Indian . . . health care."

Indian remains are still being collected for racial biological studies.   12
While the intentions may be honorable, the ethics of using human remains
this way without the full consent of relatives must be questioned.

Some relief for Indian people has come on the state level. Almost half   13
of the states, including California, have passed laws protecting Indian burial
sites and restricting the sale of Indian bones, burial offerings and other sacred items. Rep. Charles E. Bennett (D-Fla.) and Sen. John McCain (R-Ariz.)
have introduced bills that are a good start in invoking the federal government's protection. However, no legislation has attacked the problem
head-on by imposing stiff penalties at the marketplace, or by changing laws
that make dead Indians the nation's property.

Some universities—notably Stanford, Nebraska, Minnesota and Seat-   14
tle—have returned, or agreed to return, Indian human remains; it is fitting
that institutions of higher education should lead the way.

Congress is now deciding what to do with the government's extensive   15
collection of Indian human remains and associated funerary objects. The
secretary of the Smithsonian, Robert McC. Adams, has been valiantly at-

tempting to apply modern ethics to yesterday's excesses. This week, he announced that the Smithsonian would conduct an inventory and return all Indian skeletal remains that could be identified with specific tribes or living kin.

But there remains a reluctance generally among collectors of Indian remains to take action of a scope that would have a quantitative impact and a healing quality. If they will not act on their own—and it is highly unlikely that they will—then Congress must act.   16

The country must recognize that the bodies of dead American Indian people are not artifacts to be bought and sold as collector's items. It is not appropriate to store tens of thousands of our ancestors for possible future research. They are our family. They deserve to be returned to their sacred burial grounds and given a chance to rest.   17

The plunder of our people's graves has gone on too long. Let us rebury our dead and remove this shameful past from America's future.   18

For Discussion

In noting that the secretary of the Smithsonian has attempted "to apply modern ethics to yesterday's excesses," Harjo implies that a society shares a common set of values, which may change over time. Consider her assumptions. In the nineteenth century, what were Americans' attitudes toward the Native American and other racial or ethnic minorities? How are our attitudes today similar or different?

For Analysis

1. The essay begins by posing two questions. As a reader, how do you react to being asked these questions? How do you think Harjo wants you to react? Do you think her strategy is a good way to begin a position paper? Why, or why not?

2. To get a sense of how Harjo's argument is organized, make a scratch outline. Given her readers and purpose, what advantages or disadvantages do you see in Harjo's organization?

3. What evidence does Harjo offer to support her claim that collecting Native American bodies in the past was pointless, if not also malicious, and that keeping them today is unjustified? How convincing do you find this part of her argument (paragraphs 3–5 and 10–12)?

4. Why do you think Harjo includes paragraphs 13–15? How do they support her argument?

For Your Own Writing

Think of an issue about which you feel strongly, and identify your position. What arguments would you make to convince readers to agree with you? What role, if any, should your feelings play in the argument?

Commentary

Word choice is important in all writing, but it plays a crucial role in a position paper, especially when the issue is highly emotional and the writer seeks to make readers aware of an injustice and inspire them to take action to remedy the situation. Harjo argues rationally by supporting her statements with evidence. But she also consciously chooses words that express her outrage. She attempts to move us through her use of vivid images, challenge us with rhetorical questions, startle us with horrifying statistics, and upset our assumption that things have changed with a surprising statement by a respected authority. Such appeals to emotion are no substitute for appeals to reason, but they can support and strengthen a logical, well-supported argument.

A good example of how Harjo uses vivid language to move readers is the metaphor "mowed down," which emphasizes the helplessness of the "unarmed Cheyenne people" during the Sand Creek massacre (paragraph 3). Another example is her description of a relic hunter "rummaging through" graves in a Kentucky field and leaving skeletons "strewn about like litter" (paragraph 8). These images express her feelings indirectly. She expresses them more directly when she calls laws that make Native American remains "archeological property" an insult (paragraph 2).

Harjo uses rhetorical questions in her attempt to establish a common bond of shared values and beliefs with readers. She opens her essay with two rhetorical questions and includes two others in paragraphs 9 and 10. Although writers generally know how most readers would normally answer such questions, they often supply the answers anyway, as Harjo does, to emphasize the point.

In addition to these emotional appeals, Harjo cites statistics and authorities as evidence to support her argument. It is worth noting that she uses the evidence not only to substantiate her claim but also to sustain our outrage. We cannot avoid asking ourselves whether as many as 4,500 skulls were really needed for a "crania study." Similarly, we may be startled by the number of Native American skeletons still kept in museums and in private collections. The idea that they might outnumber the 1.5 million living Native Americans is likely to astound most readers. To refute the government's argument that these remains are needed for scientific research, Harjo quotes an authority, a former government official with no personal stake in the controversy. His words carry a lot of weight because they indicate that things have not really changed in the last hundred years.

Donella H. Meadows is a professor of environmental studies at Dartmouth College and the author of several books, including *The Global Citizen* (1991) and *Beyond the Limits: Confronting Global Collapse, Envisioning a Sustainable Future* (1992). This selection first appeared in the *Los Angeles Times* on February 12, 1993. In it Meadows addresses the question of whether radio and television talk shows foster democracy. The issue came to the fore during the 1992 presidential campaign, after Ross Perot launched his candidacy on *Larry King Live* and promised, if elected, to hold "electronic town meetings" to debate solutions for the nation's problems. (The town meeting is a New England institution dating from colonial times.)

Before reading the essay, reflect on the talk shows you have seen on television or heard on radio, such as those moderated by Rush Limbaugh, Oprah Winfrey, or G. Gordon Liddy. Do you usually think of these shows as contributing to the national debate on important issues? Why, or why not? Following the federal building bombing in Oklahoma City in April 1995, President Clinton blamed some talk-radio programs for inflaming the antigovernment hatred that apparently motivated the suspected bombers. In what ways might talk shows foster and/or disrupt public debate?

**RUSH AND LARRY,
COAST TO COAST:
THIS IS NOT DEMOCRACY
IN ACTION**
▪
Donella H. Meadows

I'm a talk-show junkie. I'd rather listen to real folks stumbling to express their own thoughts than to polished puppets reading what others have written. I tune into Larry, Rush and the folks who call in, to keep myself awake, chuckling, thinking and every now and then yelling in outrage.   1

One item of talk I hear is about the power of talk shows. They are restoring democracy, it is said, to a nation that has concentrated too much power within one narrow East Coast Beltway. Just by venting our opinions into a national satellite feed, you and I can scuttle a congressional pay raise, elevate a wise-cracking Texan to a presidential candidacy or bring down a potential attorney general because she hired an illegal alien.[1]   2

We don't need Ross Perot to create an electronic town meeting, they say. It's already going on, coast-to-coast, on multiple channels, 24 hours a day.   3

Now, much as I like the talk shows, I'm also from New England, and I can say that there's a big difference between the Rush Limbaugh show and a town meeting. And much as I like town meetings, they are not as effectively democratic as they could be.   4

One problem with both call-in shows and town meetings is that they're not representative. Only those who take the trouble, and don't have to go to work, and aren't busy with the kids can participate. Even within that set, the loudest mouths and most made-up minds dominate the air time. At town meetings, you can see the shy folks, the ones who have trouble sounding off in public, leaning against the back wall or bending over their knitting. On talk radio, those people are invisible, but they're there. It's a mistake to think that the blowhards who call in speak for the nation.   5

A second problem is that, as we know well from town meetings, the power isn't with the people, it's with the moderator. He or she establishes the rules, decides who to call on, changes the subject, cuts people off. In talk radio, there is only one rule: Break for the commercial on time.   6

Some call-in moderators are neutral and courteous. Then there's Rush Limbaugh, who is funny and pompous and a scapegoater and hatemonger.   7

---

[1]Washington, DC, is the area within the "East Coast Beltway"; Ross Perot is the "wise-cracking Texan"; and Zoë Baird is the "potential attorney general" whose candidacy was withdrawn when it was discovered that she had hired an illegal alien to care for her children.

His popularity could cause you to draw some terrible conclusions about the state of mind of the American people. It helps to remember that Bill Cosby is popular, too. I heard an interview the other day with a psychologist who was hired by Cosby to go over each script to be sure it contained no "put-down" humor—no joke made at the expense of any person or group. Limbaugh's show is pure put-down humor.

The purpose of the commercial media is not to foster democracy, of   8 course; it's to entertain in order to attract attention in order to sell. Therefore, talk shows have a fast pace. They flip from topic to topic. There is time to spout off, but no time for serious debate. Talk shows can only transmit knee-jerk responses to hot-button items. They can deal with Zoë Baird's child-care arrangements, but they seem uninterested in Ron Brown's links to corporations and foreign governments. They have plenty to say about gays in the military, but they can't fathom Yugoslavia. They get exercised about Congress bouncing checks worth a few thousand dollars, while billions of dollars slide away into the S&L disaster.[2]

The talk shows not only miss the biggest, most profound issues; they   9 can be breeding grounds for careening falsehoods. One man tells Larry King that a cellular phone gave his wife brain cancer, causing a national panic before there's a shred of evidence. Rush Limbaugh pronounces the greenhouse effect a fiction made up by commie-pinko environmentalists, and decades of good science are swept away.

Even if everyone could participate, even if the moderators were fair   10 and responsible, even if the pace were deliberate enough to have a real conversation, there would be a final problem with democracy by talk radio. We are not very good at talking to one another. We are better at coming back with one-liners than at listening with open minds. We have few public role models showing us how to demand and judge evidence, how to weigh conflicting opinions, how to deal with uncertainty and complication.

What I hear every day on talk radio is America's lack of education—   11 and I don't mean lack of college degrees. I mean lack of the basic art of democracy, the ability to seek the great truths that can come only by synthesizing the small truths possessed by each of us.

The world is richly varied and wildly complicated. Each person ex-   12 periences only a piece of it. To make any sense of the world, to make the right decisions as a nation, we need many points of view—east and west, rich and poor, male and female, liberal and conservative, urban and rural, black and white, yes, even straight and gay. Democracy wins out over any government dominated by just one point of view, because only democracy has at least the potential of seeing the world complete and whole.

That's why talk shows and town meetings are good things. They will   13 be even better when they let all voices be heard with respect, with inquiry, and with dedication to finding the truth, rather than ridiculing the opposition.

[2]Zoë Baird is the candidate for attorney general referred to earlier, while Ron Brown is a former head of the Democratic party and the current secretary of commerce. Gays in the military, the war in Yugoslavia, Congress bouncing checks, and the S&L (savings and loan) problem were all newsworthy events at the time the article was written. [editors' note]

For Discussion

In paragraph 10, Meadows makes a series of assertions about Americans: "We are not very good at talking to one another. We are better at coming back with one-liners than at listening with open minds. We have few public role models showing us how to demand and judge evidence, how to weigh conflicting opinions, how to deal with uncertainty and complication."

Recall the last occasion when you argued with someone over a controversial issue. What was the issue? How do you think Meadows would describe the argument—as basically an exchange of one-liners or as an open-minded exchange of views? How would you describe it?

Do you agree with Meadows's assumption that we should listen to one another with open minds? What if you think the other person's position is morally objectionable?

For Analysis

1. Notice, in the opening paragraph, that Meadows describes herself as a "talk-show junkie." Skim the essay, noting in the margin other places where Meadows represents herself to readers. What adjectives would best describe the image of Meadows you get from reading this essay? How does this image affect your willingness to be convinced by her argument?

2. Meadows, like most writers of position papers, tries to convince readers by using logic. In paragraphs 4–5, for example, she argues that talk shows are "not as effectively democratic as they could be" because, like town meetings, they are not "representative." She assumes that for something to be considered democratic, it must be representative. To examine the logic of her argument, ask yourself the following questions: First, do you agree that if something is not representative, it cannot be considered democratic? Second, do you agree that call-in talk shows are not representative? Third, if you accept the first assumption as well as the second, then must you also accept Meadows's conclusion that talk shows are not democratic? Why, or why not?

3. In paragraph 3, Meadows reports a common belief that the electronic town meeting already exists in the form of the talk show. Then, she spends three paragraphs comparing town meetings and talk shows. Why do you think she uses the strategy of comparison and contrast to try to make her argument more convincing? How convincing do you find this part of her argument?

4. The primary kind of evidence Meadows uses to support her argument is example. Skim the essay and put brackets around each example; then, explain briefly how these examples contribute to her argument.

For Your Own Writing

Consider any other controversial issues you can think of that involve the media—television, radio, film, music video, or recording. For example, should individuals be able to sell videotapes they've copied from commercial broadcasts? Should prime-time television programs be permitted to show nudity? Should movies that represent conflict between different nationalities or American ethnic groups be monitored to prevent stereotyping? Should store owners be prohibited from selling "R-rated" recordings to people under eighteen?

Select one issue on which you have a position. What assumptions have led you to choose this position? How might you, like Meadows, construct an argument based on some of your assumptions? Which of your assumptions do you think readers who take an opposing position might respond to positively?

Commentary

Writers taking a position on a controversial issue develop an argumentative strategy based on what they assume readers already think and feel about the issue as well as on what they want readers to think and feel. Meadows assumes that her readers are misinformed about the value of talk shows. Her aim is to set them right. She wants to convince readers that talk shows neither substitute for nor foster democratic debate. She also wants to educate readers about what she calls "the basic art of democracy."

Meadows's argumentative strategy, then, is to counterargue or refute the position that talk shows are "restoring democracy." The following scratch outline shows how refutation organizes the essay:

identifies herself as liking talk shows (paragraph 1)

reports the opposing position: talk shows are "restoring democracy" (2–3)

states her own position: talk shows are "not as effectively democratic as they could be" (4)

reason 1: "they're not representative" (5)

reason 2: they give moderators the power; "power isn't with the people" as it should be in a democracy (6–7)

reason 3: because their purpose is to entertain and sell products, they allow "no time for serious debate" and therefore breed falsehood (8–10)

reason 4: participants "lack the basic art of democracy" (10–12)

restates her position: talk shows would be better if they practiced the art of democracy (13)

Notice that Meadows begins her refutation by trying to establish her credibility with readers as someone who likes talk shows. Using such phrases as *it is said* and *they say*, Meadows indicates that the position she's refuting is popular. In paragraph 4, she makes her disagreement explicit by assertively stating her position, or claim, which is also the thesis of her essay. Then she systematically gives reasons (in paragraphs 5–12) why the popular opinion is wrong, and concludes by restating her own position. (For more about thesis statements, see pp. 189–91.)

Her plan is simple and straightforward. Because she wants to make it easy for readers to follow her argument, Meadows provides clear cues and transitions. For example, the word *Now* (paragraph 4) signals her disagreement with the popular

view, and the phrases *One problem* and *A second problem* announce her first two
reasons in paragraphs 5–6. She doesn't go on in this vein, presumably because
she doesn't want to bore readers by numbering every point, but she does provide
a summary of her points at the beginning of paragraph 10: "Even if everyone could
participate, even if the moderators were fair and responsible, even if the pace were
deliberate enough to have a real conversation, there would be a final problem with
democracy by talk radio. We are not very good at talking to one another." This
summary also serves as a transition to her last and most important point about
the art of democracy. (For more on cues and transitions, see pp. 202–4.)

Meadows concludes by defining the art of democracy, as she sees it. *Democracy*
is the key term in this debate. Readers' acceptance or rejection of Meadows's
argument depends largely on what they think is appropriate democratic debate.
Meadows argues that talking loudly, having one's mind already made up, scape-
goating, hatemongering, putting others down, spouting off, giving knee-jerk responses, and so on, do not foster democracy. Instead, she argues that democracy
requires a different set of behaviors, such as listening with an open mind, demanding and judging evidence, dealing with uncertainty and complication, seeking the great truths by synthesizing the partial truths. If she can convince readers
to accept her definition of what is and is not democratic speech, Meadows assumes
they will also accept her position on talk shows.

Jessica Statsky wrote the following essay about children's competitive sports for
a first-year college composition course. Before reading, recall your own experiences as an elementary school child playing competitive sports, either in or out
of school. If you weren't actively involved yourself, did you know anyone who
was? Looking back, do you think that winning was unduly emphasized? What
value was placed on having a good time? On learning to get along with others?
On developing athletic skills and confidence?

> **CHILDREN NEED TO PLAY,
> NOT COMPETE**
> ■
> *Jessica Statsky*

Over the past three decades organized sports for   1
children have increased dramatically in the
United States. And though many adults regard
Little League Baseball and Peewee Football as
a basic part of childhood, the games are not al-
ways joyous ones. When overzealous parents and coaches impose adult
standards on children's sports, the result can be activities that are neither
satisfying nor beneficial to children.

I'm concerned about all organized sports activities for children be-   2
tween the ages of six and twelve. The damage I see results from noncontact
as well as contact sports, from sports organized locally as well as those
organized nationally. Highly organized competitive sports such as Peewee
Football and Little League Baseball are too often played to adult standards,
which are developmentally inappropriate for children and can be both

physically and psychologically harmful. Furthermore, because they eliminate many children from organized sports before they are ready to compete, they are actually counterproductive for developing either future players or fans. Finally, because they emphasize competition and winning, they unfortunately provide occasions for some parents and coaches to place their own fantasies and needs ahead of children's welfare.

One readily understandable danger of overly competitive sports is that 3 they entice children into physical actions that are bad for growing bodies. For example, a twelve-year-old trying to throw a curve ball may put abnormal strain on developing arm and shoulder muscles, sometimes resulting in lifelong injuries (Koppett 294). Contact sports such as football can be even more hazardous. Thomas Tutko, a psychology professor at San Jose State University and coauthor of the book *Winning is Everything and Other American Myths*, said: "I am strongly opposed to young kids playing tackle football. It is not the right stage of development for them to be taught to crash into other kids. Kids under the age of fourteen are not by nature physical. Their main concern is self-preservation. They don't want to meet head on and slam into each other. But tackle football absolutely requires that they try to hit each other as hard as they can. And it is too traumatic for kids" (qtd. in Tosches A1).

As Tutko indicates, even when children are not injured, fear of being 4 hurt detracts from their enjoyment of the sport. One mother of an eight-year-old Peewee Football player explained, "The kids get so scared. They get hit once and they don't want anything to do with football anymore. They'll sit on the bench and pretend their leg hurts . . . " (qtd. in Tosches A32). Some children are driven to even more desperate measures. For example, in one Peewee Football game a reporter watched the following scene as a player took himself out of the game:

> "Coach, my tummy hurts. I can't play," he said. The coach told the player to get back onto the field. "There's nothing wrong with your stomach," he said. When the coach turned his head the seven-year-old stuck a finger down his throat and made himself vomit. When the coach turned back, the boy pointed to the ground and told him, "Yes there is, coach. See?" (Tosches A1)

Besides physical hazards and anxieties, competitive sports pose psy- 5 chological dangers for children. Martin Rablovsky, a former sports editor for the *New York Times*, said that in all his years of watching young children play organized sports, he noticed very few of them smiling. "I've seen children enjoying a spontaneous pre-practice scrimmage become somber and serious when the coach's whistle blows," Rablovsky said. "The spirit of play suddenly disappears, and sport becomes joblike" (qtd. in Coakley 94). The primary goal of a professional athlete—winning—is not appropriate for children. Their goals should be having fun, learning, and being with friends. Although winning does add to the fun, too many adults lose sight of what matters and make winning the most important goal. Several studies have shown that when children are asked whether they would rather be warming the bench on a winning team or playing regularly on a losing team, about 90 percent choose the latter (Smith, Smith, and Smoll 11).

Winning and losing may be an inevitable part of adult life, but they   6
should not be part of childhood. Too much competition too early in life
can affect a child's development. Children are easily influenced, and when
they sense that their competence and worth are based on their ability to
live up to their parents' and coaches' high expectations—and on their ability to win—they can become discouraged and depressed. According to Dr.
Glyn C. Roberts, a professor of kinesiology at the Institute of Child Behavior
and Development at the University of Illinois, 80 to 90 percent of children
who play competitive sports at a young age drop out by sixteen (Kutner).

This statistic illustrates another reason I oppose competitive sports for   7
children: because they are so highly selective, very few children get to
participate. Far too soon a few children are singled out for their athletic
promise, while many others, who may be on the verge of developing the
necessary strength and ability, are screened out and discouraged from trying
out again. Like adults, children fear failure, and so even those with good
physical skills may stay away because they lack self-confidence. Consequently, teams lose many promising players who with some encouragement
and experience might have become stars. The problem is that many parent-
sponsored, out-of-school programs give more importance to having a winning team than to developing children's physical skills and self-esteem.

Indeed, it is no secret that too often scorekeeping, league standings,   8
and the drive to win bring out the worst in adults who are more absorbed
in living out their own fantasies than in enhancing the quality of the experience for children (Smith, Smith, and Smoll 9). Recent newspaper articles
on children's sports contain plenty of horror stories. *Los Angeles Times*
reporter Rich Tosches, for example, tells the story of a brawl among seventy-
five parents following a Peewee Football game. As a result of the brawl,
which began when a parent from one team confronted a player from the
other team, the teams are now thinking of hiring security guards for future
games. Another example is provided by a *Times* editorial about a Little
League manager who intimidated the opposing team by setting fire to one
of their team's jerseys on the pitching mound before the game began. As
the editorial writer commented, the manager showed his young team that
"intimidation could substitute for playing well" ("Bad News").

Although not all parents or coaches behave so inappropriately, the   9
seriousness of the problem is illustrated by the fact that Adelphi University
in Garden City, New York, offers a sports psychology workshop for Little
League coaches, designed to balance their "animal instincts" with educational theory in hopes of reducing the "screaming and hollering," in the
words of Harold Weisman, manager of sixteen Little Leagues in New York
City. In a three-and-one-half hour Sunday morning workshop, coaches
learn how to make practices more fun, treat injuries, deal with irate parents,
and be "more sensitive to their young players' fears, emotional frailties, and
need for recognition" (Schmitt). Little League is to be credited with recognizing the need for such workshops.

Some parents would no doubt argue that children can't start too soon   10
preparing to live in a competitive free-market economy. After all, secondary
schools and colleges require students to compete for grades, and college
admission is extremely competitive. And it is perfectly obvious how im-

portant competitive skills are in finding a job. Yet the ability to cooperate is also important for success in life. Before children are psychologically ready for competition, maybe we should emphasize cooperation and individual performance in team sports rather than winning.

Many people are ready for such an emphasis. In 1988 one New York   11
Little League official who had attended the Adelphi workshop tried to ban scoring from six-to-eight-year-olds' games—but parents wouldn't support him (Schmitt). An innovative children's sports program in New York City, City-Sports-for-Kids, emphasizes fitness, self-esteem, and sportsmanship. In this program's basketball games, every member on a team plays at least two of six eight-minute periods. The basket is seven feet from the floor, rather than ten feet, and a player can score a point just by hitting the rim (Bloch). I believe this kind of local program should replace overly competitive programs such as Peewee Football and Little League Baseball.

Authorities have clearly documented the excesses and dangers of many   12
competitive sports programs for children. It would seem that few children benefit from these programs and that those who do would benefit even more from programs emphasizing fitness, cooperation, sportsmanship, and individual performance. Thirteen- and fourteen-year-olds may be eager for competition, but few younger children are. These younger children deserve sports programs designed specifically for *their* needs and abilities.

Works Cited

"The Bad News Pyromaniacs?" Editorial. *Los Angeles Times* 16 June 1990: B6.

Bloch, Gordon B. "Thrill of Victory Is Secondary to Fun." *New York Times* 2 Apr. 1990, late ed.: C12.

Coakley, Jay J. *Sport in Society: Issues and Controversies.* St. Louis: Mosby, 1982.

Koppett, Leonard. *Sports Illusion, Sports Reality.* New York: Houghton, 1981.

Kutner, Lawrence. "Athletics, through a Child's Eyes." *New York Times* 23 Mar. 1989, late ed.: C8.

Schmitt, Eric. "Psychologists Take Seat on Little League Bench." *New York Times* 14 Mar. 1989, late ed.: B2.

Smith, Nathan, Ronald Smith, and Frank Smoll. *Kidsports: A Survival Guide for Parents.* New York: Addison-Wesley, 1983.

Tosches, Rich. "Peewee Football: Is It Time to Blow the Whistle?" *Los Angeles Times* 3 Dec. 1988: A1+.

For Discussion

Statsky makes the point that competition is highly valued in our culture, whereas cooperation tends to be downplayed. In what ways does our society encourage competition? Does the educational system, in your experience, encourage one more than the other? Which of the two seems to be valued most highly in advertising, television, and movies? Who do you think benefits most from this cultural preference? Who loses?

For Analysis

1. Make a scratch outline of Statsky's argument. Then evaluate her organization. Put brackets around the cueing devices—statements forecasting what is to come, summaries of what has just been said, topic sentences, and transitions—she uses to help readers stay on track. (For discussion and illustration of these cueing devices, see Chapter 7.) Point to any places where you lose track or get confused.

2. Statsky's argumentative strategy includes showing that she and her readers share the same values. Point to a passage where you feel she is trying to build a bridge of shared values between herself and her readers. How does this appeal affect your response to this passage and to the whole essay?

3. Skim the essay, noting each time Statsky quotes an authority. What do you think is the cumulative effect of quoting so many different people? Choose the quotation that you find most effective, and explain why.

4. Reread the conclusion. What is Statsky trying to accomplish by ending the essay this way? How well do you think her conclusion works?

5. Read the Writer at Work discussion on pages 149–51. Notice in the analysis of purpose and audience how Statsky describes the readers she intends to address and her proposed argumentative strategy. Review the final essay to see whether she kept to this plan or modified it in some way.

For Your Own Writing

Make a list of issues related to childhood and adolescence. (For example: Should elementary and secondary schools be on a year-round schedule? Should children have the right to "divorce" their parents? Should adolescents who commit serious crimes be tried as adults?) Then choose an issue that you think you could write about. What position would you take? Why?

Commentary

Writers of position papers must be especially careful not to define the issue too broadly or to overstate their position. Statsky defines her issue by identifying several parameters, such as age, geography, school affiliation, and type of sport. She restricts the subject by both age and school affiliation, limiting it to children between the ages of six and twelve (paragraph 2) and to "parent-sponsored out-of-school" sports (paragraph 7). However, she also allows for sports organized nationally as well as locally and for all kinds of sports, noncontact as well as contact. Finally, to ensure that her readers know the kind of organized, competitive team sports she's talking about, Statsky gives two familiar examples: Peewee Football and Little League Baseball.

Statsky also qualifies her thesis by avoiding absolute or unconditional language. In the opening paragraph, for example, she softens her assertion: "These games are *not always* joyous ones." Similarly, in the next sentence, instead of saying "the result is" she allows for other possibilities by saying "the result *can be*." Such minor adjustments in word choice can have an important effect on readers. Here they make Statsky's position seem reasonable, without making her seem indecisive. Indeed, Statsky presents her argument confidently and assertively.

In paragraph 10, Statsky successfully counterargues an anticipated objection from her readers. From her own observations and from the reading she has done, she knows that some parents believe their children cannot start too soon learning how to survive "in a competitive free-market economy." Without insulting these parents, she successfully refutes this objection to her own position. She reiterates that children are not psychologically ready for competitive sports (a point she made in paragraphs 5–7) and argues that learning to cooperate is as important to success as learning to compete. She goes even further to suggest that team sports should emphasize cooperation. Knowing that parents who oppose her views likely have not considered such a possibility, she gives an example in paragraph 11 of noncompetitive City-Sports-for-Kids in New York City. She concludes this paragraph by firmly asserting her view: "I believe this kind of local program should replace overly competitive programs such as Peewee Football and Little League Baseball."

Counterargument is nearly always a part of taking a position on an issue. Meadows, for example, counterargues the idea that talk shows are "restoring democracy." Harjo refutes the argument that Native American remains are needed for research. Counterargument directly acknowledges your readers' objections, questions, and reservations about your argument and confronts the fact that some readers may or will hold opposing views. You increase your authority by counterarguing and therefore improve your chances of having your argument taken seriously by those who disagree with you. The Guide to Writing in this chapter will help you counterargue readers' objections and opposing views.

PURPOSE AND AUDIENCE

In writing a paper that takes a position on a controversial issue, you may have a variety of purposes. First and foremost, you aim to express your opinion. But you do more than simply state what you think; you also present an argument explaining and justifying your point of view. Although position papers are nearly always written for others to read, writing can also lead you to clarify your own thinking. Anticipating others' views—accepting the points you consider well taken and refuting those with which you disagree—helps you develop your understanding of the issue and confidence in your own point of view.

In addition to expressing an opinion, most position papers are intended to influence other people's thinking on important issues. Assuming that logical argument will prevail over prejudice, you try to change readers' minds by presenting compelling reasons supported by solid evidence, and by pointing out flaws in others' reasoning. You seek common ground in shared interests, values, and principles. You may show that you are reasonable by moderating your own views and urging others to compromise as well, in order to reach a consensus of opinion.

When agreement seems beyond reach, however, it is highly unlikely that you will be able to change readers' minds with a single essay, no matter how well written it is. Most writers addressing an audience so opposed to their position are satisfied if they can simply win their readers' respect for their different point of view. Often, however, all that can be done is to sharpen the differences. Position papers written in these circumstances tend to be more contentious than compromising.

Purpose and audience are thus closely linked when you write a position paper. In defining your purpose and developing an effective argumentative strategy, you need also to define your readers clearly: where they stand on the issue (whether they oppose your position, are undecided, or basically agree with you) and how they think about the issue (whether they see it as a moral issue, an issue of civil liberties, or an issue that affects them personally).

BASIC FEATURES OF POSITION PAPERS

Position papers generally share the following basic features.

A Well-Defined Issue

Position papers deal with controversial issues, matters on which reasonable people disagree. The issue may arise from a particular occasion or be part of an ongoing debate. In either case, the writer must clearly explain the issue, taking into account how familiar readers are likely to be with it.

In addition to establishing that the issue exists, the writer needs to define it for the writing purpose. Defining an issue means saying what kind of issue it is. Sometimes, defining the issue also involves marking its boundaries. Jessica Statsky, for example, limits her discussion of organized team sports to those sponsored by parents outside school for children of certain ages.

A Clear Position

In addition to defining the issue, a position paper should also clearly indicate the writer's position on the issue. Writers may qualify their claims to accommodate strong objections, but they should avoid vagueness and indecision.

Very often writers declare their position in a thesis statement early in the essay. The advantage of this strategy is that it lets the audience know right away where the writer stands. The thesis may instead appear later in the essay, however. Postponing the thesis is particularly appropriate when the writer wants to weigh the pros and cons before announcing his or her position. (For more about the thesis statement, see pp. 189–91.)

A Convincing Argument

A position paper cannot merely assert a writer's views. To convince readers, writers must provide sound reasoning and solid evidence in support of their claims. They must also anticipate opposing views and either accommodate or refute them.

Sound Reasoning and Solid Evidence

To be sure that readers will be able to follow an argument, the main points supporting a claim should not only be stated clearly but also explained and fully developed. A writer can cite various kinds of evidence in support of a position, including anecdotes, authorities, and statistics. Anecdotes are used to bolster and to illustrate an argument. Testimony from authorities—people especially knowledgeable about the issue—also enhances the credibility of an argument. Writers can also make good use of statistics. (For guidance on finding published and electronic sources, see Chapter 11.)

Anticipation of Readers' Concerns

In addition to presenting reasons and evidence, a writer also needs to acknowledge opposing points of view in order to accommodate or refute them. Accommodating an opposing view basically involves admitting that it has validity and qualifying one's own view to account for it. Views that strike the writer as wrong, on the other hand, should be refuted. Refuting an opposing argument means trying to show *how* it is wrong, not merely stating *that* it is wrong.

An Appropriate Tone

Position papers often concern highly controversial issues about which writers—and readers—feel very strongly. The challenge for writers, therefore, is to find a tone that adequately expresses their feelings without shutting down communication altogether. Ideally, writers gain readers' confidence and respect both by the way they reason and by the language they use.

Guide to Writing

▪ THE WRITING ASSIGNMENT

Write a position paper on a controversial issue. Present the issue to readers, take a position, and develop a reasoned argument in support of your position.

INVENTION AND RESEARCH

At this point you need to choose and explore an issue, consider your purpose and audience, formulate your thesis, test your choice, develop your reasoning, and anticipate readers' concerns.

Choosing an Issue

Writing a position paper offers an opportunity to think deeply about an important issue. Following are some activities that can help you choose a promising issue and that may suggest ways to begin thinking about it.

Listing Issues

Begin by making a list of issues you might want to write about. Put them in the form of questions, like the following examples. Make the list as long as you can. Include both issues on which you already have ideas and ones you do not know much about but would like to explore further.

- Should drug testing be allowed in sports and industry?
- Should the primary purpose of a college education be job preparation?
- Should parents of teenagers have to give permission for their children to get contraceptives or abortions?
- Should schools attempt to teach spiritual and moral values?
- Should undercover police officers be permitted to pose as high school students in order to identify sellers and users of drugs?
- Should extended training in music performance or art making (drawing, painting, sculpting) be required of all high school or college students?
- Should college admission be based solely on academic achievement?
- Should colleges provide day-care or night-care services for students taking classes?
- Should the recording industry be required to provide warning labels on recordings that contain violent or sexually explicit lyrics?
- Should fathers have an equal chance of gaining custody of their children after a divorce?
- Since fraternity hazing practices have caused injuries and even deaths, should fraternities be banned from college campuses?
- Should women serve in combat positions in the military?
- Should public schools require students to perform community service as a condition of graduation?

Choosing an Intriguing Issue

Select an issue from your list that seems especially interesting, one that you would like to know more about. It should be an issue about which people disagree.

Your choice may be influenced by whether you have time for research or whether your instructor requires it. For example, you would have to research affirmative action programs fairly extensively before you could adequately define a position and argue it well. Issues that have been debated for years and written about repeatedly make excellent topics for extended research projects. Other issues, such as whether warning labels should be put on potentially offensive recordings, may be approached more confidently from personal experience and limited research. Still other topics may be more suitable if your time is limited or your instructor wants you to argue a position without doing research, topics such as separate college organizations for African American, Asian, and Latino students or special academic assistance for athletes. One possibility is to write about an issue currently affecting your community or college. You could define and explore fully issues like these with classmates or friends; and, with care, you could identify a wide range of opposing arguments.

Exploring the Issue

To understand the issue and the rhetorical situation, you need to define the issue, determine whether to do research, and decide on your position.

Defining the Issue

To begin thinking about the issue, write for about five minutes explaining how you understand it. If you feel strongly about the issue, briefly state why, but don't present your argument at this time. Focus on defining what you think the issue is. Who cares about it, and why? How does the issue affect different people? What's at stake? What kind of issue is it—personal, political, economic, environmental, moral? Describe its features, scope, and history.

Doing Research

If you do not know very much about the issue or the various views on it, do some research before continuing. You can gather information by talking to others or by reading what others have written.

If you do not have time for research and lack confidence in your knowledge of the issue, you should consider another subject, one about which you are better informed. Return to your list of possible issues and start over again.

Deciding on a Tentative Position

State the position you now take on the issue. This is a tentative position, liable to change as you develop your ideas and learn more about the issue.

Considering Your Purpose and Audience

Now that you've taken a tentative position, you are ready to consider your purpose and audience. Write for a few minutes, identifying your readers and clarifying your purpose. You can usually place your readers in one of the following categories: (1) those who agree with you but know very little about the issue and have given little thought to arguing a position, (2) those who agree with you and know something about the issue but need to have you confirm for them that the position you share is indeed reasonable, (3) those who incline toward disagreeing with you and resist your argument even though they know little about the issue, and (4) those who oppose your position strongly. The particular issue you have chosen might lead you to address a particular group of local readers, knowledgeable, specialist readers, or general readers such as typical newspaper readers. It can be helpful to tentatively identify a possible publisher for your position paper—a group or community newsletter, a campus or community newspaper, a national magazine or journal. As you write, consider the following questions:

- Who will be my readers?
- What do I expect my readers to know about the issue?
- What do I expect my readers to think and feel about the issue?
- What basic values or assumptions about this and related issues do we share?
- What fundamental differences in worldview and experience keep us from agreeing?
- What kind of argument are they most likely to find convincing?
- What is my purpose in addressing these readers? How do I hope to influence them?

Stating Your Thesis

Write a sentence or two stating your thesis. Choose your words carefully. Try to make your position clear and assertive, stated neither too timidly nor bombastically.

You will have ample opportunity to revise your thesis as you learn more about the issue and develop your argument. Stating it now, though tentatively, will help you focus the rest of your invention and planning.

Testing Your Choice

This is a good time to evaluate whether you should proceed with this particular issue. To make your decision, ask yourself the following questions:

- Does this topic really interest me? Have I begun to understand the issue and to formulate my own view?
- Do I now know enough about the issue to plan and write my essay, or can I learn what I need to know in the time I have remaining?
- Is the topic manageable within my time and space limits?
- Do I have a good sense of how others view this issue and how I might address my readers' concerns?

As you explore the issue further and develop your argument, you will want to reconsider these questions. If at any point you decide that you cannot answer them affirmatively, you may want to choose a different issue.

Developing Your Reasoning

To construct a convincing argument, you need to list reasons for your position, choose the strongest ones, and develop them fully.

Listing Reasons

Write down every plausible reason you could give to convince readers that *your* position on this issue should be taken seriously. It might help to think of your reasons as *because* or *that* clauses attached to your thesis statement. For example, "My position is X because . . . " or "A reason I believe X is that: . . . "

Choosing the Strongest Reasons

Review your list with your readers in mind. Put a check by the reasons that would carry the most weight with them and are most important to you. If none of your reasons seems very strong, you might need to reconsider your position, do some more research, or even pick another topic.

Developing Your Best Reasons

Take your strongest reasons and write for five minutes on each one, explaining it and providing evidence to support it. You may discover that you need some specific information. Do not stop to locate it now; just make a note about what you need and continue writing. If you decide not to include some of these reasons, you may not need the information after all. Later, before drafting or when revising, you will be able to follow up and locate any information you still need.

For Group Inquiry

At this point in your invention work, you will find it helpful to get together with two or three other students to try out your argument and to get their advice. Present your arguments to each other in turn: define your issue and describe your readers briefly and then summarize your argument, focusing on the reasons for your position. Help each other think of further reasons and support for the reasons. Also, anticipating your next revision task, think of objections readers might have to each argument.

Anticipating Readers' Concerns

Now you need to anticipate readers' concerns and decide which ones you will accommodate and which you will refute. For an example, see how Jessica Statsky anticipates her readers' concerns on pages 149–51.

Listing Opposing Arguments

Begin by listing all the opposing arguments and objections to your argument you can think of. You will almost certainly have discovered some in researching the issue and talking with others about your plans.

Accommodating Readers' Concerns

Review your list of opposing arguments and objections to your argument, and decide which of them you think you should change your argument to accommodate. Write a few sentences for each one, indicating how you will have to qualify your thesis or change your argument. Also, briefly explain why you are conceding this point.

Refuting Readers' Objections

Review the list to find opposing arguments and objections to your argument that you can refute. Choose one, and write for five minutes trying out a refutation. Try to explain why you do not find the objection convincing. It may seem irrelevant, only partially true, or not true at all. It may seem fallacious: a "straw man" or "*ad hominem*" argument, for example. (See pp. 222–27 for more on logical fallacies.) Or it may simply be based on a totally different and irreconcilable set of assumptions about the rights and responsibilities of individuals and society, for example.

If you need to check facts or find some other information, make a note to do so later. It will be most efficient at this point simply to list the points you need to check and to save the research until later.

Restating Your Thesis

Now that you have developed your argument, you may want to reformulate your thesis. Consider whether you should change your language to qualify or limit your claim.

PLANNING AND DRAFTING

Take some time now to review your invention notes and see what you have, to set goals for your essay, to prepare an outline, and to draft your position paper.

Seeing What You Have

If you completed all of the invention work, you have accumulated several pages of notes. Review these carefully to see what you might use in your draft. Mark passages that seem especially promising, that show conviction, have vivid writing, contain pointed examples, demonstrate strong reasoning.

If your invention notes are skimpy, you may not have given enough thought to the issue or know enough at this time to write a convincing essay about it. You have several alternatives. You can do more invention and research. You can go on to write a draft, hoping that you will get more ideas as you write. Or you can go back and choose a new topic.

Setting Goals

Experienced writers set overall goals for themselves before drafting their essays. They decide what they will try to achieve and how they will go about it. To help you set realistic goals, consider the following questions now. You may also find it helpful to return to some of these questions as you outline and draft your essay.

Your Purpose and Audience

- What can I realistically hope to accomplish by addressing these particular readers? Are they deeply committed to their opinions? Should I try, as Meadows does, to make readers see that their view is mistaken?
- Can I address readers' special concerns, acknowledge the legitimacy of their feelings, or define the issue in terms that appeal to common values and assumptions? Shall I appeal, as Harjo does, to readers' sense of moral outrage? Can I demonstrate, as Meadows does, that I am aware of the civic issues involved?

- Can I draw on any common experiences that relate to this issue? Could I share my own experience, as Meadows does?

The Beginning

- How can I engage readers' attention immediately? Should I use a rhetorical question, as Harjo does, or a surprising example, a personal anecdote, or startling statistics to draw readers into the argument?
- How much do I need to explain about the controversy and what terms do I need to define before proceeding with my argument? Should I summarize both sides? Should I limit the issue, as Statsky does?

Your Argument

- If I have more than one reason, how should I order the reasons? From strongest to weakest? From most to least predictable? From simplest to most complex? Can I sequence them logically, so that one leads inevitably to the next?
- Which objections to my argument and opposing arguments should I mention, if any? Shall I acknowledge and refute them all, as Meadows does? Shall I focus, as Statsky does, on two? What would I gain from conceding something? What would I lose?

The Ending

- How can I conclude my argument effectively? Should I repeat my thesis, as Statsky does? Shall I look to the future, as Meadows does, or urge readers to take action, as Harjo does?
- Can I end on a note of agreement by reminding readers of the common concerns and values we share?

Outlining

Some position papers include everything—an extended definition of the issue, an elaborate argument with multiple reasons and evidence, and several opposing arguments, some of which are accommodated and others refuted. Your essay may not be so complicated, but you will still have to decide how to arrange the different parts. Once you have considered strategies for beginning and ending your essay and determined how you might order your reasons, consider the organization carefully and prepare a tentative outline.

Here is how Statsky organized her position paper on children's competitive sports:

identifies issue, states thesis, and gives reasons

explains and supports reason 1—competing at too early an age is developmentally inappropriate and may be harmful physically

explains and supports reason 2—competing at too early an age also may be harmful psychologically

refutes opposing argument—that children need to learn to live in a competitive world—by arguing that childhood is just the training period, not the real thing explains and supports reason 3—because competitive sports are so selective, very few children participate and reap the potential benefits

explains and supports reason 4—parents and coaches sometimes use children's sports to act out their own fantasies in ways harmful to the children

refutes opposing argument—that children need to learn to live in a competitive world—by arguing that cooperation ought to be emphasized because it is as important to society as is competition

concludes by reasserting the position and framing the essay

However you choose to arrange your essay, making an outline before drafting will help you to get started. An outline presents a route, neither the only one nor necessarily the best, but one that will get you going in the right direction.

Drafting

With an outline and goals as your guide, begin drafting your essay. As you draft, keep in mind your purpose in addressing your particular readers.

Use your outline to guide your drafting, but do not worry if you diverge from your original plan. Writing sometimes has a logic of its own that carries the writer along. As you pick up momentum, you may leave the outline behind. If you get stuck, refer to it again. You might want to review the general advice on drafting on pages 11–13.

GETTING CRITICAL COMMENTS

Now is the time for your draft to get a good critical reading. All writers find it helpful to have someone else read and comment on their drafts. Your instructor may arrange such a reading as part of your coursework; otherwise, you can ask a classmate, friend, or family member to read it over. If your school has a writing center, you might ask a tutor to read and comment on your draft. The guidelines in this section are designed to be used by *anyone* reviewing a position paper. (If you are unable to have someone else review your draft, turn ahead to the Revising and Editing section on pp. 146–49 for help reading your own draft with a critical eye.)

In order to provide focused, helpful comments, your critical reader must know your intended purpose and audience. Briefly write out this information at the top of your draft.

Audience: To whom are you directing your argument? What do you assume they already know and think about this issue?

Purpose: What effect can you reasonably expect your argument to have on these particular readers?

Reading with a Critical Eye

Reading a draft critically means reading it more than once, first to get a general impression and then to analyze its basic features.

Reading for a First Impression

Read the essay through quickly to get a sense of its argument. Then, write a few
sentences describing your initial reaction. Did you understand the writer's position? Indicate whether the argument bolstered your own opinion, made you reconsider or defend your own position, or made you think seriously about the issue
for the first time. What did you find most convincing in the essay? Least convincing?

Reading to Analyze

Read now to evaluate the argument, focusing on the basic features of position
papers. (See pp. 136–37 to review the basic features.)

Is the Issue Well-Defined?

Check to see how the issue is defined. Indicate if there is enough information
to understand the issue and why it is important. What questions still need to be
answered? Determine whether the issue, as it is stated, is even arguable. For example, does it seem to be a question of fact or is it basically a matter of faith—
and therefore not worth arguing?

Is the Thesis Clear?

Find the clearest statement of the thesis, and write it down or underline it.
Given the writer's description of audience and purpose, how appropriate are the
terms of the thesis? Indicate if you think the thesis should be qualified.

Is the Argument Supported by Convincing Reasons and Evidence?

Find the reasons given to support the thesis, and number them in the margin:
Reason 1, Reason 2, and so on. Then consider each reason in turn, looking at how
it is explained and supported. Point to any reasons that need to be explained more
clearly or supported more convincingly. Have any important reasons been left out
or any weak ones overemphasized? Note any supporting evidence that seems weak
as well as places where more evidence is needed.

Look for faulty reasoning. Note any sweeping generalizations (broad statements asserted without support). Indicate whether the issue has been oversimplified or whether either/or reasoning (unfairly limiting the argument to only two
alternatives) has been used. (See Chapter 9 for more on logical fallacies and faulty
reasoning.)

How Are Objections and Opposing Arguments Handled?

Look for places where other positions on this issue are mentioned, and specifically where objections are acknowledged and opposing arguments entertained.
Note any areas of potential agreement that could be emphasized and any concessions that need to be made. Check for any attempts to refute arguments, and
suggest, if you can, how the refutations could be strengthened.

Again, look for faulty reasoning. Point out any personal attacks on opponents
rather than on their reasoning. Have only the weakest objections or opposing
arguments been acknowledged, thus misrepresenting the opposition?

Is the Tone Appropriate?

What words would you use to describe the tone of this essay—bitter or sarcastic, for example? Given the writer's description of purpose and audience, how appropriate does this tone seem to you? Point to places in the essay where you could suggest word changes that might make the tone more effective.

Is the Organization Effective?

Look at the *beginning* and *ending* to evaluate their effectiveness and, if necessary, suggest how they might be made stronger. In particular, note whether the beginning gives a preview of the argument or whether one is needed. Review the sequence in which the reasons and any opposing arguments are presented to see if they should be reordered. Check to see if any evidence is misplaced. Point to effective uses of transitions, summaries, and topic sentences and places where they could be added.

What Final Thoughts Do You Have?

What is the strongest part of the argument? What is the weakest part, most in need of further work?

REVISING AND EDITING

This section will help you identify problems in your draft and revise and edit to solve the problems.

Identifying Problems

To discover problems in your draft, you need to read it objectively, analyze its basic features, and study any comments you've received from other readers.

Getting an Overview

Consider the draft as a whole, trying to see it objectively. It may help to do so in two steps:

1. *Reread.*   If at all possible, put the draft aside for a day or two before rereading it. When you do, start by reconsidering your purpose. Then read the draft straight through, trying to see it as your intended readers will.

2. *Outline.*   Quickly outline the draft to see where the issue is defined, the position is stated, each reason is explained and supported, and any opposing arguments are refuted.

Charting a Plan for Revision

You may want to use a double-columned chart to keep track of the work you need to do as you revise. In the left-hand column, list the basic features of position papers. As you analyze your draft and study any comments from other readers, use the right-hand column for noting the problems to solve. Here is an example:

Basic Features

Definition of the issue

Thesis statement

Reasons and evidence

Counterarguments

Tone

Organization

Problems to Solve

Analyzing the Basic Features of Your Draft

Turn now to the questions for analyzing a draft on pages 145–46. Following these guidelines, note the specific problems you need to solve on your revision chart.

Studying Critical Comments

Review any comments you've gotten from other readers, and add to your chart any that you intend to act on. Try not to react defensively to these comments; by letting you see how other readers respond to your draft, the comments provide invaluable information about how you might improve it.

Solving the Problems

Having identified problems in your draft, you now need to figure out solutions and—most important of all—to carry them out. Three possible means of finding solutions are to (1) review your invention and planning notes for information and ideas to add to the draft, (2) do further invention and research to answer questions your readers raised, and (3) look back at the readings in this chapter to see how other writers have solved similar problems. Following are some suggestions on how you might respond to some of the problems common to writing position papers.

Definition of the Issue

- If the essay does not provide enough information about the issue for a reader to understand it, add more. Consider adding examples, quoting authorities, or simply explaining the issue further.
- If the issue might strike readers as unimportant, state explicitly why you think it is important and why, in your view, they should think so too. Try to provide an anecdote that would demonstrate its importance.

Thesis Statement

- If readers might not find or recognize your thesis, you may need to rewrite your thesis statement to make it clearer. If your thesis is implied but not directly expressed, consider stating it explicitly so as to avoid misunderstanding.
- If your thesis is not appropriately qualified to account for exceptions or strong objections to your argument, modify it by limiting its scope.

Reasons and Evidence

- If readers might have difficulty identifying your reasons, announce them more explicitly.
- If any reason seems vague or weak, either delete it or explain it more fully. Consider telling an anecdote or using comparison and contrast to show how this reason relates to the others.
- If your evidence seems weak or scanty, review your invention notes or do more research to gather additional facts, statistics, or testimony from authorities.
- If you use any sweeping generalizations, try to be more specific and to support your assertions with evidence and examples.
- If you have oversimplified the argument—for example, by using either/or reasoning—add some qualifying language that shows you are aware of the issue's true complexity.

Counterarguing

- If you can make any concessions to opposing views, consider doing so. Try to find common ground with readers by acknowledging the legitimacy of their concerns. Show readers where you share their values, interests, and assumptions.
- If your attempt to refute an objection seems unconvincing, try to strengthen it. Avoid attacking your opponents. Instead, provide solid evidence—respected authorities, facts and statistics from reputable sources—to convince readers that you can argue credibly.
- If you have ignored strong opposing arguments, take account of them. If you cannot plausibly refute them, you might have to acknowledge their legitimacy.

Tone

- If the tone seems inappropriate, consider altering your language. Think more about your feelings, purpose, and audience. You may need to express strong feelings about the issue more directly or indicate why you feel as you do. If you expect readers to dismiss your concerns, you might try a more combative or confrontational style—forcefully refuting their arguments. If you want to build a bridge of shared concerns, consider personalizing your writing by using "I" or a personal anecdote.

Organization

- If the beginning seems weak or dull, consider opening with a striking anecdote or surprising quotation.
- If readers might have trouble following your argument, consider adding a brief forecast of your main points at the beginning of your essay. (See Chapter 7 for advice about cueing readers so they can follow your argument.)
- If the reasons and refutations are not logically arranged, reorder them. Consider announcing each reason and refutation more explicitly.
- If any evidence does not closely follow the point it is intended to support, move it.

■ If the ending seems weak or vague, search your invention notes for a strong quotation or add language that will reach out to readers.

Editing and Proofreading

In working on your draft so far, you may have corrected some obvious errors, but grammar and style have not been a priority. Now is the time to edit it carefully to correct any errors in mechanics, usage, and punctuation, as well as to consider matters of style. You may find that studying your draft in separate passes—first for paragraphs, then for sentences, and finally for words—will help you recognize problems.

After you have produced the final copy, be sure to proofread it carefully and make corrections before handing it in.

A Writer at Work

ANTICIPATING READERS' CONCERNS

Student writer Jessica Statsky, whose essay appears on pages 130–33, sought to anticipate her readers' concerns. She felt that many readers would either be undecided about whether children should participate in competitive sports or would strongly support such participation. First, she listed opposing arguments and decided tentatively which to accommodate and which to refute. Then, in order to begin thinking seriously about this important part of her argument, she tried out brief accommodations and refutations. (See pages 150–51 for the invention activities she completed.)

Listing Opposing Arguments

Statsky listed the following opposing arguments and likely objections to her position:

```
--competition teaches children how to succeed in later
  life

--children who are allowed to feel the thrill of winning
  experience a boost of self-esteem

--allows children to prove to themselves and others their
  capabilities

--gives children an incentive to excel
```

```
--children need not be strained and damaged physically in
   competitive sports if research is done to determine
   their limits at different ages and care is taken to ob-
   serve their limits
```

This list appears to pose serious challenges to Statsky's argument, but she benefits considerably by facing up to her readers' objections before she drafts her essay. By preparing this list, she gains insight into how she must support her own argument in light of these predictable objections, and she can begin thinking about which objections she might accommodate and which she must refute. She gains authority because she can demonstrate in her essay a good understanding of opposing positions. Consequently, her readers—those who agree, are undecided, or oppose—will find her argument more plausible.

Accommodating Readers' Concerns

Looking over her list of opposing arguments, Statsky decided that she could accommodate readers by conceding that competitive sports can sometimes be fun for children—at least for those who win. Following are her invention notes:

```
   It is true that children do sometimes enjoy getting
prizes and being recognized as winners in competitions
adults set up for them. I remember feeling very excited
when our sixth-grade relay team won a race at our
school's sports day. And I felt really good when I would
occasionally win the candy bar for being the last one
standing in classroom spelling contests. But when I think
about these events, it's the activity itself I remember
as the main fun, not the winning. I think I can concede
that winning is exciting to 6-12 year olds, while arguing
that it's not as important as adults think. I hope this
will win me some friends among readers who are undecided
about my position.
```

In Statsky's revised essay, this accommodation appears in paragraph 5 as the sentence beginning "Although winning does add to the fun. . . ."

Refuting Readers' Objections

Statsky recognized that she must attempt to refute the other objections in her list. She chose one and tried out the following refutation:

```
   It irritates me that adults are so eager to make first
and second graders go into training for getting and keep-
ing jobs as adults. I don't see why the pressures on
adults need to be put on children. Anyway, both my par-
ents tell me that in their jobs cooperation and teamwork
```

```
are the keys to success. You can't get ahead unless
you're effective in working with others. Maybe we should
be training children and even high school and college
students in the skills necessary for cooperation, rather
than competition. Sports and physical activity are impor-
tant for children, but elementary schools should empha-
size achievement rather than competition--race against
the clock rather than against each other. Rewards could
be given for gains in speed or strength instead of for
defeating somebody in a competition.
```

The major benefit of this brief invention activity was to alert Statsky to the importance of learning more about the effects of competition on children, as well as about the possibilities for more cooperative physical activities and programs. You can see from her revised essay that refuting the benefits of competition is a theme that runs through her entire essay.

While this invention activity did not produce sentences she could use in her draft, it advanced her a giant step in thinking about her readers and purpose and brought an early, productive focus to her library research on competition in children's sports.

Reflecting on Your Writing

Now that you've read and discussed several essays arguing a position and written one of your own, it's a good time to think critically about what you've learned. Reflecting on your own writing process will help you discover what you learned about solving problems you encountered in writing a position paper.

Begin by gathering your invention and planning notes, drafts and critical comments, revision plan, and final revision. Review these materials as you complete the following writing tasks.

- Identify *one* writing problem you encountered as you worked on the essay. Don't be concerned with general writing problems; focus on a problem that specifically involves planning and writing a position paper. For example: Did you puzzle over how to convince your readers that the issue is important? Did you have trouble asserting your position forcefully while acknowledging other points of view? Was it difficult to refute any objection readers might raise?
- At what stage in the process did you first recognize the problem? Was it, for example, when you were thinking about your readers' attitudes, trying to decide how to sequence your ideas, or getting critical comments on a draft? What called the problem to your attention? If you didn't become aware of it until rather late

in the process, can you now see hints of it in your invention writings or early drafting? If so, where specifically?

- Reflect on how you tried to solve the problem. Did you reword, reorganize, or simply cut the part that was problematic? Did you reread your invention writing? Did you need to do more invention or research? Did you seek advice from a classmate or your instructor?

- Finally, write a page or so explaining to your instructor what the problem was, how you discovered it, and how you went about solving it. Be specific by quoting from your invention writing and drafts, others' critical comments, your own revision plan, and your final revision. Show the various changes your writing and thinking underwent. If you're still uncertain about your solution, say so. The point is not to prove that you've solved the problem perfectly, but to show what you've learned about problem solving in the process of arguing a position.

6 Proposing a Solution

Proposals serve an important role in a democracy, informing citizens about problems affecting their well-being and suggesting actions that could be taken to remedy these problems. People write proposals every day in business, government, education, and the professions. Proposals are a basic ingredient of the world's work.

As a special form of argument, proposals have much in common with position papers, described in Chapter 5. Both present a subject and take a definite stand on it. Both give reasons and evidence and acknowledge readers' likely objections or concerns. Proposals, however, go further: they urge readers to support a particular policy or take specific action. They argue for a proposed solution to a problem, succeeding or failing by the strength of that argument.

In most disciplines and professions, problem solving is a basic way of thinking. For example, scientists use the scientific method, a systematic form of problem solving; political scientists and sociologists propose solutions to troubling political and social problems; engineers regularly employ problem-solving techniques in building bridges, automobiles, and computers; attorneys find legal precedents to solve their clients' problems; teachers continually make decisions about how to help students with learning problems; counselors devote themselves to helping clients solve personal problems; business owners or managers daily solve problems large and small.

Problem solving depends on a questioning attitude. In addition, it demands imagination and creativity. To solve a problem, you need to see it anew, to look at it from new angles and in new contexts.

Since a proposal tries to convince readers that its way of defining and solving the problem makes sense, proposal writers must be sensitive to readers' needs and expectations. As you plan and draft a proposal, you will want to determine whether your readers are aware of the problem and whether they recognize its seriousness, and you will want to consider their views of any other solutions. Knowing what your readers know—their assumptions and biases, the kinds of arguments likely to appeal to them—is a central part of proposal writing.

Writing in Your Other Courses

College students find occasions both in class and at work to propose solutions to problems. Following are some examples of typical college assignments calling for problem-solving skills:

▪ *For an economics class:* The *maquiladora* industry along the U.S.–Mexican border provides foreign exchange for Mexico and low-paying jobs for half a million Mexicans, as well as profits for American manufacturers. Yet this innovative binational arrangement has created serious problems on the Mexican side of the border: inadequate housing, health care, and public services; on-the-job injuries; and environmental damage. Study one of these problems, research it, and propose a solution. Address your proposal to the mayor of Nogales, Tijuana, or Juarez.

▪ *For a business class:* Take the case of a corporation wishing to install a workstation network but unwilling as yet to give up its mainframe computers. Propose a solution to this problem. Research the possibilities of mainframe-workstation integration, explain the problem carefully, and argue convincingly for your solution. Address your proposal to the CEO of the corporation.

▪ *For a biology class:* Apply the principle of circadian rhythm to the problem of jet lag. Explain circadian rhythm, define jet lag in light of it, and speculate about how knowledge of circadian rhythm might help reduce the effects of jet lag. It might help to think of yourself as writing an article for the travel section of a newspaper.

For Group Inquiry

You can readily experience the complexities and possibilities involved in proposing solutions by thinking through a specific problem and trying to come up with a feasible proposal. With two or three other students, form a group and select someone to take notes during your discussion.

▪ First, identify two or three problems within your college or community, and select one that you all recognize and agree needs to be solved.

▪ Next, consider possible solutions to this problem, and identify one solution that you can all support.

▪ Finally, determine which individual or group has the authority to take action on your proposed solution and how you would go about convincing this audience that (1) the problem is serious and must be solved and (2) your proposed solution is feasible and should be supported. Consider carefully what questions this audience might have about your proposal and what objections might be raised.

As a group, reflect on your efforts at proposing a solution to a problem. What surprised or pleased you? What difficulties did you encounter?

Readings

William L. Kibler holds degrees from the University of Florida and Texas A & M University, where he is presently associate director of the Department of Student Affairs. His many publications on academic integrity include a 1987 coauthored book, *Academic Integrity and Student Development: Legal Issues and Policy Perspectives.* The following proposal appeared in the *Chronicle of Higher Education* (11 November 1992), a weekly source of news and opinion read primarily by college administrators and faculty. Kibler's proposal is based on his belief that cheating in college is not simply misbehavior to be punished when students are caught at it; rather, it is a larger moral problem to be addressed by the whole campus in terms of students' personal integrity.

Though Kibler aims his essay at administrators and faculty, he also envisions a central role for students in promoting academic integrity. As you read, notice the role he assigns students, as well as the proposed consequences for students caught cheating. Would Kibler's proposal reduce cheating?

CHEATING: INSTITUTIONS NEED A COMPREHENSIVE PLAN FOR PROMOTING ACADEMIC INTEGRITY ▪ *William L. Kibler*

Research suggests that students on most, if not all, campuses cheat on their course work and tests. Donald McCabe, associate professor of management at Rutgers University, recently conducted a survey in which 67 percent of the students responding, who attended 31 highly selective colleges and universities, admitted to cheating in college. It is difficult to document whether the problem is increasing, but most experts agree that it is a serious issue affecting all segments of higher education. 1

Cheating, of course, is not a new problem, either in higher education or in society at large. But part of the reason that cheating remains a problem in colleges and universities may be that institutions are treating it as a behavioral aberration rather than as a moral issue. When cheating is discovered, most institutions address only the misbehavior, without requiring the student to confront the moral issues involved in deciding to cheat to achieve a goal. By failing to address those underlying issues, colleges are missing the chance to discuss the importance of integrity. 2

College administrators seem unsure about how to approach the problem. I discovered last year, after conducting a national study of nearly 200 colleges and universities, that on many campuses little is being done to prevent or deal effectively with cheating. Following is a summary of some of the disturbing results of the research: 3

- *Unavailability of data.* Nearly one-half of the institutions surveyed could not report the number of cases of cheating handled on their campuses over the previous three academic years, because they had not kept track.
- *Lack of honor codes.* Only 27 percent of the institutions had honor codes. Fewer than half of those institutions had implemented the elements to make them "working honor codes," such as requiring students to sign a pledge stating they would not cheat, mandating that students report offenders, and administering unproctored exams. When many institutions abandoned their honor codes because of concerns about their effectiveness, they also abandoned the chance to offer a communitywide statement on the importance of integrity and why dishonesty would not be tolerated.
- *Inadequate involvement of faculty members and students.* Only two-thirds of the institutions reported that their faculty members were involved in

developing and enforcing standards, and only one-third said that any students were involved.

- *Lack of coordination.* Two-thirds of the institutions reported that no office or person was responsible for coordinating efforts to prevent cheating or to promote academic integrity.
- *Lack of training.* Fewer than half of the institutions offered any kind of training to faculty members or teaching assistants on how to deal with academic dishonesty. Almost 70 percent of the people responsible for determining sanctions for cheating had no training in student development, making it unlikely that the developmental level of the student—such as his or her decision-making skills or ability to relate moral reasoning and behavior—were considered or that sanctions such as a required educational seminar were used.
- *Lack of educational programs.* Only 3 percent (just six institutions) required students who were caught cheating to participate in some educational program designed to help them reconsider their behavior. The most prevalent sanctions were just to fail the student on the assignment or in the course.

Unfortunately, there is no quick fix, no single or simple solution to the problem of student cheating. Adopting an honor code and widely publicizing it is not enough. Institutions must adopt a comprehensive approach involving the entire institution—students, faculty members, and administrators.   4

The solution I propose, based on my recent research, is built on the concept that the most effective way to prevent cheating is to actively promote academic integrity, while at the same time effectively confronting those who do cheat. Confronting cheating should include sanctions that respond to the behavior as well as educational programs or seminars that address developmental issues.   5

The first step is for institutions to establish an ethos that promotes academic integrity, one that defines it and holds it up as something to be revered. Such an ethos can be created with the help of an honor code, code of conduct, or other strong, clear statements about what the institution expects from its students, exactly how cheaters will be punished, and why cheating actually hurts, rather than helps, students. Students must understand that integrity is valuable and that if their grades are not based on honest accomplishment, they may mislead employers and others. If they also cheat in their careers and are discovered, they could damage any professional reputation they've developed.   6

After setting out its standards, the institution then must use all the tools it has to communicate its position on academic integrity and its intention not to tolerate dishonesty: direct correspondence to faculty members and students; mandated discussions about cheating during orientation meetings for students and faculty members, as well as during individual classes at the beginning of semesters; printed material such as handbooks; and the campus news media.   7

Faculty members are the most critical element in insuring the success of any campuswide effort to promote academic integrity. They should reflect, communicate, and enforce the institution's values. They also should   8 be involved in developing and implementing whatever system the institution creates; their participation will give them a sense of personal commitment to, and ownership of, the system.

Many faculty members refuse to address the problem of academic dishonesty, feeling the rules are too complicated and the procedures for enforcing them too time-consuming. Others try to minimize the problem for fear that it may reflect badly on their ability to teach. Young faculty members, in particular, may ignore cheating because it might reveal that they lack the skills or experience to avert it. Still others do not like to report cheating because they do not want to be branded as "zealots" or "troublemakers" by colleagues or students. The institution must help train faculty members in ways to prevent cheating and in how to create a classroom atmosphere in which honesty is clearly the expected standard.   9

It also is essential that students be involved in developing and carrying out systems to promote academic integrity. Failure to involve students creates an "us versus them" atmosphere, which tends to promote cheating. Students can serve on honor or disciplinary boards and on review committees that assess how well an institution's process for assuring academic integrity is working.   10

Finally, an institution must coordinate its efforts to insure that all the elements of its system are implemented. One office should be responsible for monitoring relevant data, assessing the effectiveness of policies and procedures, coordinating communication efforts, and coordinating training programs on academic dishonesty and ways to prevent it.   11

Besides acting to create an ethos of academic integrity, institutions must develop policies that deal effectively with students who still choose to cheat. Those policies should include: 12

- Appropriate sanctions. These might include a notation concerning academic dishonesty on a transcript, required counseling, and required attendance at a class or seminar on academic integrity.
- A required educational program for offenders. Such a program should include discussion of what cheating is and why it is unacceptable. It should also include education in moral development, to help students understand the relationship between moral reasoning and behavior. By using discussions, case studies, and role-playing exercises, students can be helped in responding to ethical dilemmas. Finally, the program or seminar should include training in academic skills to help students gain confidence in their abilities to succeed in the classroom without cheating.
- Testing policies that emphasize prevention of cheating. These could include procedures that protect the security of tests before they are administered, proctoring services, assigned seating and use of different versions of the same test during exams, and guidelines for making writing assignments that limit opportunities for plagiarism.
- Methods of reporting cheating that are unintimidating—for example, that allow the person reporting cheating to remain anonymous.

Faculty members and administrators can no longer ignore their responsibilities to promote academic integrity. They must help students develop the values they need to deal effectively with the moral and ethical dilemmas facing them. Clearly communicating an institution's expectations   13 for academic honesty is an important way to foster students' development. Frequent discussions about integrity provide the opportunity for academics to communicate the value they place on integrity relative to other values such as achievement and competition. When cheating does occur, campus procedures should make students confront the ethical implications of their behavior, expose them to discussion of moral reasoning, and help them understand that effective learning depends on honesty, respect, rigor, and fairness.

For Discussion

Kibler assumes that students cheat in college because they either don't know the rules or don't respect them. For him, cheating is a moral issue, a simple question of right and wrong: students cheat because they lack moral integrity or because they have not reached a stage of moral development to recognize that cheating represents such a lack of integrity. Kibler does acknowledge, however, that certain teaching practices may contribute to the problem. Do you think any of the following factors may also contribute to cheating in college: large class sizes; the way courses are organized, exams given, and papers assigned; the way teachers teach— the kind of inspiration and enthusiasm they offer students and the kind of help they give with challenging assignments?

Discuss how your teachers might make it less tempting or easy to cheat. Consider also whether a clearly established and strictly enforced honor code would discourage cheating.

For Analysis

1. At the beginning of this chapter we make the following assertions about writing that proposes solutions. Consider whether each of these assertions is true of Kibler's proposal essay.

    ▪ A proposal analyzes a problem and takes a definite stand on it.
    ▪ It strives to see the problem in new ways, looking at it from new angles and in new contexts.
    ▪ It gives reasons for readers to support the proposed solution.
    ▪ It anticipates that readers may prefer solutions other than the one being proposed.
    ▪ It anticipates readers' questions and reservations about the solution being proposed.

2. Reread paragraphs 1–3 to see how Kibler presents the problem. What resources and strategies does he use to demonstrate that the problem exists and that it is serious?

3. Though Kibler names the problem "cheating," he never defines it. Given his readers, do you think this is a weakness in his presentation of the problem? In your opinion, what does cheating involve?

4. In arguing for his solution, beginning at paragraph 5, Kibler is careful to help his readers follow his argument from one point to the next. Look at the first sentences

in paragraphs 5–13, and underline the word or phrase that connects each paragraph explicitly to the one before it. What cues does Kibler employ to keep readers on track? (For more on cues, see Chapter 7.)

5. Writers proposing solutions to problems usually try to anticipate readers' questions, objections, and reservations. Kibler does so briefly in paragraph 9. What specific objections does he anticipate? Does he seem sympathetic or dismissive toward faculty concerns?

For Your Own Writing

Consider writing about a problem on your college campus or in your community. List two or three problems you would like to see solved, and then focus on one of them in order to consider what would be involved in writing about it. To whom would you address your proposal to solve this problem, hoping this individual or group would take your proposed solution seriously and even lead the effort to implement it? Consider how you would present the problem and describe your solution. What reasons would you give to support your solution? How would you anticipate readers' questions, reservations, or outright objections?

Commentary

Think of essays proposing solutions as having two basic parts: presenting a problem and proposing a solution for it. A scratch outline of Kibler's essay reveals this basic two-part plan:

Problem (paragraphs 1–3)

cheating widespread; considered a serious issue (1)

colleges fail to treat cheating as a moral problem (2)

little is being done to stop cheating—colleges usually don't know how much cheating is going on; few schools have honor codes; faculty and students are uninvolved; no coordinated effort, no training for faculty, and no programs for students caught cheating exist (3)

Solution (paragraphs 4–13)

a comprehensive approach to cheating is required (4)

promote academic integrity, punish cheating (5)

establish an ethos (6)

communicate the position on academic integrity (7)

get faculty involved, offer training (8, 9)

get students involved (10)

coordinate all efforts (11)

develop policies to reduce cheating and deal with cheaters—sanctions, programs, test security, methods for reporting cheating (12)

recap (13)

This scratch outline also helps us understand Kibler's argumentative strategy. He begins by demonstrating the seriousness of the problem: 67 percent of students cheat, and no college is immune; colleges seem confused about the problem and unsure of what to do. It is easy to imagine that with this opening strategy, Kibler would get the attention of conscientious college administrators. From the beginning he tries to redefine the problem as moral, not behavioral. The success of his argument for his solution depends on his readers' willingness to accept this redefinition. Here he takes a big risk. And he takes another risk in announcing that the problem has "no quick fix," that it will require a comprehensive, campuswide effort to implement his proposed solution. Even the faculty will have to become involved. Since some busy administrators prefer quick fixes and shrink from attempting to divert faculty from their teaching and research, they might just stop reading at this point. We can assume that Kibler believes they will keep reading, though, because of the way he has redefined the problem—as a moral problem rooted in the issue of academic integrity. What president or dean would not wish for greater academic integrity at his or her college?

Kibler is then extremely careful to reassure readers that a complex campuswide effort can be achieved with a step-by-step approach. First, the college must establish an "ethos that promotes academic integrity." (*Ethos* refers to a widely held belief, in this case that cheating is immoral.) Then, certain faculty and students must devise an honor code and educate everyone about it, and a coordinator must ensure that everything works as planned. Finally, policies must be announced that explain the consequences for students who violate the campus ethos and honor code.

The key to his argumentative strategy seems to be devoting considerable space—well over half the essay—to explaining how his demanding solution may be implemented. In order not to be viewed as only a complainer or moralizer and lose credibility with his readers, he must show authoritatively the pragmatic actions that can be undertaken to reduce cheating.

The writer's authority is further enhanced by the fact that he has not only read the research on this problem but has also conducted research himself, surveying two hundred colleges. You, too, may find that research is essential to the success of your proposal. For example, if you propose a solution to a college or community problem, you may need to interview several people to learn more about the problem and to discover what questions or reservations they have about your proposed solution. Interviewing people involved makes sense: you want them to accept your definiton of the problem, approve your solution, and work energetically to see that it is implemented.

Adam Paul Weisman wrote this article in 1987 for the *New Republic*, a national news and opinion magazine. It proposes a solution to the problem of teenage pregnancy. As you read, ask yourself how Weisman's admission that his solution is not original—that it has already been tried—affects your reaction to it.

BIRTH CONTROL IN THE SCHOOLS ∎ *Adam Paul Weisman*

Should contraceptives be distributed to teen-   1
agers in public schools? A research panel of the
National Academy of Sciences spent two years
studying adolescent pregnancy in America, and
decided they should. Its 1986 report, *Risking the
Future*, prompted a new wave of angry debate about how to reduce the
high rate of teenage pregnancy in the United States.

No one disputes the severity of the problem. Teen pregnancy ruins   2
young lives and perpetuates a tragic cycle of poverty. According to the Alan
Guttmacher Institute, the rate of pregnancy among American women aged
15 to 19 was almost 10 percent in 1981. That far outstrips the next closest
industrialized nation, England, where the rate is less than 5 percent. Guttmacher estimates that more than 80 percent of teenage pregnancies in the
United States are unintended and unwanted. Every year about four in 100
women aged 15 to 19 have an abortion. But those looking for ways to
reduce these statistics have divided into two distinct camps: one favoring
contraception, the other, sexual abstinence.

The contraception advocates point out that a majority of teenagers   3
have already rejected abstinence. In 1986, 57 percent of 17-year-olds [said]
they have had sex. This camp believes that schools, as a central location
in young peoples' lives, are a good place to make contraceptives available.
Three recent studies (by the National Academy of Sciences, the Guttmacher
Institute, and the Children's Defense Fund) have taken this view, while also
calling for programs geared toward postponing adolescent sexual involvement and including parents in school sex education classes.

The abstinence advocates believe the answer lies in inculcating values   4
based on a clear understanding that sex is simply wrong for teenagers. They
say that moral lessons are best taught by parents in the home, but that
schools should continue the job by teaching a chaste morality. Secretary of
Education William Bennett[1] has been the most outspoken proponent of this
view. Exposing students to "mechanical" means of pregnancy prevention,
he says, encourages "children who do not have sexual intimacy on their
minds to . . . be mindful of it."

Bennett concedes that "birth control clinics in schools may prevent   5
some births." And indeed, whatever the drawbacks, the contraception advocates have one strong advantage in this debate: their approach works.
The only rigorous study of a pregnancy prevention program for urban teenagers was conducted in Baltimore from 1982 to 1983 by researchers from
Johns Hopkins Medical School. The Hopkins-run birth-control clinic, located across the street from one school and nearby another, reduced the
pregnancy rate in the schools it served by 30 percent while pregnancy rates
in control schools soared 58 percent.

"Why did this program work?" asks Dr. Laurie Zabin, the program's   6
director, in her report on the experiment. "Access to high-quality, free services was probably crucial to its success. Professional counseling, education, and open communications were, no doubt, also important. All these
factors appear to have created an atmosphere that allowed teenagers to

---

[1]William Bennett was Secretary of Education during most of the Reagan administration.

translate their attitude into constructive preventive behavior." And what of those students who were virgins? According to Zabin, that group of girls (not very large) delayed initiation of sexual activity an average of seven months longer than those in the control groups, strong evidence that awareness of contraception is not directly linked to promiscuity.

But the existing school-based clinics that distribute or arrange for birth   7
control are not just rooms plastered with Planned Parenthood posters where contraceptives are handed out. They are full-service health clinics that came into existence to provide young people with comprehensive health care. Public health officials, including many who have doubts about distributing contraceptives in schools, agree that in many places, particularly the inner city, health care for adolescents is inadequate. The school-based clinic, like the school lunch program, seeks to make all students healthy enough to get the most out of education.

This is not to say that school-based clinics don't do a lot in the way of   8
contraception. According to Douglas Kirby, director of research for the Center for Population Options, a group that advocates and monitors school-based clinics, 15 percent to 20 percent of visits to clinics are for family planning. The majority are for general health care. Twenty-eight percent of • the clinics actually dispense contraceptives or other prescription drugs. About half of the clinics write prescriptions that are filled off-campus; the rest diagnose and counsel teens before making referrals to outside health agencies.

The clinics also seem to help reduce unintended pregnancies. In St.   9
Paul 33 percent of girls made use of the clinic's contraceptive services, and birth rates dropped by 50 percent. Thanks to the clinic's counseling, four out of five of the girls who did have children stayed in school, and only 1.4 percent of them had another pregnancy before graduation. Nationally, about 17 percent of teenage mothers become pregnant again within a year.

Bennett argues that distributing birth control is "not what school is for,"   10
and that doing so represents "an abdication of moral authority." Many educators have similar concerns. They fear that communities and government are trying to dump another social problem—like drug counseling and AIDS education—on the schools when they could better be handled in the home. Diane Ravitch, an adjunct professor of history and education at Teachers College in New York, says, "Schools are increasingly being pushed to be social service centers, and they don't do that well."

Yet clearly schools do more than teach students the three R's. Schools   11
are where many teenagers learn to drive, weld, and cook. And numerous surveys reveal that over 80 percent of parents think it is a proper place for their children to learn about sex. Dr. Stephen Joseph, health commissioner for New York City, explains that if it weren't for the involvement of schools, the United States never could have achieved 100 percent immunization rates, a worthy goal that "wasn't perceived as the role of the school either at that time."

If the pressing health crisis were non-sexual in nature—tuberculosis,   12
for example—it's hard to believe that educators such as Bennett wouldn't be the first to volunteer schools as a locus for a solution. And of course, if the problem of teen pregnancy is one that the schools shouldn't be expected

to deal with, that would exclude any program of anti-sex indoctrination as well as the distribution of contraceptives. Putting such indoctrination into the curriculum is, arguably, more intrusive on the schools' basic function than the existence of a birth control or general health clinic. Bennett's speeches rule out the very real possibility that schools could prosecute a moral agenda and *also* support a clinic.

Despite the success of Zabin's off-campus model, there is a good rea- 13 son school-based clinics receive such wide support in the health services community: teenagers are notoriously lazy. As Cheryl Hayes, director of the NAS study explains, "If teenagers have to wait in the rain for a bus to take them to a clinic, there is a good chance they will never make it to the clinic." If the goal is providing health care and family planning services to teenagers, it is unlikely that anything will work as well as locating those services where most teenagers are: at school.

Of course the real question that excites people isn't whether teenagers 14 should get birth control at school, but whether they should get it at all. There is no hard evidence linking exposure to contraception with promiscuity, and it is unlikely any teenager who watches prime-time television is less than "mindful" (as Bennett puts it) of sexual intimacy. Although Bennett has dismissed the recommendations of *Risking the Future* as "stupid," the opponents of making contraception available to teenagers have yet to offer an effective alternative. As for the "parental authority" that birth control availability is said to undermine, a 1986 Planned Parenthood survey of 1,000 teenagers revealed that 31 percent of parents discuss neither sex nor birth control with their children. The failure of parental authority is manifest in the almost 900,000 unintended teenage pregnancies in 1983. *Risking the Future* only makes that failure painfully clear.

For Discussion

How do you react to Weisman's proposal that school-based health clinics be permitted to distribute birth-control information and contraceptives? Do you think it is appropriate for schools to play such a role? What advantages or dangers do you see?

For Analysis

1. How does Weisman set the stage for his argument in the title and the first two paragraphs? What advantages or disadvantages do you see in his opening? Compare Weisman's opening paragraphs to the two opening paragraphs in Kibler's essay. What can you conclude about strategies for opening essays proposing solutions to problems?

2. Weisman at first appears to be a neutral reporter rather than an advocate for a particular solution. Is this tone maintained consistently throughout the essay? Point to passages where the same tone is evident or where a different tone emerges. How does the neutral reporter's tone serve Weisman's overall argumentative strategy?

3. In paragraph 5, Weisman cites the example of the Johns Hopkins University birth-control clinic. How does he use this example to support his argument? How effective is the example?

4. To get a better idea of Weisman's overall argumentative strategy, make a scratch outline of his essay. What advantages do you see in his plan?

5. How does Weisman present the advantages of his solution to increase their appeal to supporters of the abstinence solution? What common values and concerns does he call upon?

For Your Own Writing

Teenagers are part of the problem in this proposal, but they can also play positive roles in solving social problems. For example, high school students can refurbish playgrounds and parks or teach illiterate adults to read. Think of a problem that teenagers might be able to help solve. If you were to propose a solution to this problem, how would you explain the problem? How would you go about convincing a group of teenagers that they should participate?

Commentary

Weisman's essay illustrates a strategy that is often important in proposals: acknowledging an alternative solution, evaluating that alternative, and then refuting it.

After establishing the problem, Weisman introduces the two solutions that have been proposed: encouraging teenagers to abstain from sexual activity and providing birth-control information to them. To demonstrate his fairness, Weisman presents the abstinence solution objectively, even sympathetically. He accepts the legitimacy of this proposed solution and objects only on the grounds that it does not work.

The fact that Weisman's proposed solution does appear more effective is the cornerstone of his argument. He uses Secretary Bennett's own words to argue that the contraception solution works in at least some cases, then cites the Johns Hopkins study as the centerpiece of his argument. Furthermore, by noting that birth-control counseling "delayed initiation of sexual activity" for some of the teenagers, he makes a forceful appeal to those in favor of abstinence.

Not only does Weisman support his solution with reasons and evidence, but he also anticipates and refutes a major objection to it. This objection, that schools should not be used to solve social and moral problems, he refutes in two ways. First, he reasons that the problem of teenage pregnancy is a health crisis and that there is ample precedent for dealing with such problems through the schools. This argument appeals to humanitarian concerns, but is unlikely to convince those who consider teenage pregnancy a moral issue. To those readers, he offers a second argument: if birth-control information is excluded from the schools, then "any program of anti-sex indoctrination" must also be excluded. In other words, the argument against school-based birth-control clinics could also be made against teaching sexual abstinence. Both are forms of sex education.

Weisman's argumentative strategy in this proposal is to show that he understands and respects the values of those who advocate an alternative solution and that he shares their desire to remedy the problem. He appeals to them on practical grounds, arguing that his solution will get the job done.

Patrick O'Malley wrote the following essay while he was a first-year college student. In it, he proposes that college professors give students frequent brief examinations in addition to the usual midterm and final exams. After discussing with his instructor his unusual rhetorical situation—a student advising professors—he decided to revise the essay into the form of an open letter to professors on his campus, a letter that might appear in the campus newspaper.

O'Malley's essay may strike you as unusually authoritative. This air of authority is due in large part to what O'Malley learned about the possibilities and problems of frequent exams as he interviewed two professors (his writing instructor and the writing program director) and talked with several students. As you read, notice particularly how he anticipates professors' likely objections to his proposals and their preferred solutions to the problem he identifies.

MORE TESTING,
MORE LEARNING
■
Patrick O'Malley

It's late at night. The final's tomorrow. You got   1
a C on the midterm, so this one will make or
break you. Will it be like the midterm? Did you
study enough? Did you study the right things?
It's too late to drop the course. So what happens
if you fail? No time to worry about that now—you've got a ton of notes to
go over.

Although this last-minute anxiety about midterm and final exams is   2
only too familiar to most college students, many professors may not realize
how such major, infrequent, high-stakes exams work against the best interests of students both psychologically and intellectually. They cause unnecessary amounts of stress, placing too much importance on one or two days
in the students' entire term, judging ability on a single or dual performance.
They don't encourage frequent study, and they fail to inspire students' best
performance. If professors gave additional brief exams at frequent intervals,
students would be spurred to study more regularly, learn more, worry less,
and perform better on midterms, finals, and other papers and projects.

Ideally, a professor would give an in-class test or quiz after each unit,   3
chapter, or focus of study, depending on the type of class and course material. A physics class might require a test on concepts after every chapter
covered, while a history class could necessitate quizzes covering certain
time periods or major events. These exams should be given weekly, or at
least twice monthly. Whenever possible, they should consist of two or three
essay questions rather than many multiple-choice or short-answer questions. To preserve class time for lecture and discussion, exams should take
no more than 15 or 20 minutes.

The main reason professors should give frequent exams is that when 4
they do, and when they provide feedback to students on how well they are
doing, students learn more in the course and perform better on major exams, projects, and papers. It makes sense that in a challenging course containing a great deal of material, students will learn more of it and put it to
better use if they have to apply or "practice" it frequently on exams, which
also helps them find out how much they are learning and what they need
to go over again. A recent Harvard study notes students' "strong preference
for frequent evaluation in a course." Harvard students feel they learn least
in courses that have "only a midterm and a final exam, with no other personal evaluation." They believe they learn most in courses with "many
opportunities to see how they are doing" (Light, 1990, p. 32). In a review
of a number of studies of student learning, Frederiksen (1984) reports that
students who take weekly quizzes achieve higher scores on final exams
than students who take only a midterm exam and that testing increases
retention of material tested.

Another, closely related argument in favor of multiple exams is that 5
they encourage students to improve their study habits. Greater frequency
in test taking means greater frequency in studying for tests. Students prone
to cramming will be required—or at least strongly motivated—to open their
textbooks and notebooks more often, making them less likely to resort to
long, kamikaze nights of studying for major exams. Since there is so much
to be learned in the typical course, it makes sense that frequent, careful
study and review are highly beneficial. But students need motivation to
study regularly, and nothing works like an exam. If students had frequent
exams in all their courses, they would have to schedule study time each
week and gradually would develop a habit of frequent study. It might be
argued that students are adults who have to learn how to manage their own
lives, but learning history or physics is more complicated than learning to
drive a car or balance a checkbook. Students need coaching and practice
in learning. The right way to learn new material needs to become a habit,
and I believe that frequent exams are key to developing good habits of study
and learning. The Harvard study concludes that "tying regular evaluation
to good course organization enables students to plan their work more than
a few days in advance. If quizzes and homework are scheduled on specific
days, students plan their work to capitalize on them" (Light, 1990, p. 33).

By encouraging regular study habits, frequent exams would also 6
decrease anxiety by reducing the procrastination that produces anxiety.
Students would benefit psychologically if they were not subjected to the
emotional ups and downs caused by major exams, when after being
virtually worry-free for weeks they are suddenly ready to check into the
psychiatric ward. Researchers at the University of Vermont found a strong
relationship between procrastination, anxiety, and achievement. Students
who regularly put off studying for exams had continuing high anxiety and
lower grades than students who procrastinated less. The researchers found
that even "low" procrastinators did not study regularly and recommended
that professors give frequent assignments and exams to reduce procrastination and increase achievement (Rothblum, Solomon, & Murakami, 1986,
pp. 393, 394).

Research supports my proposed solution to the problems I have described. Common sense as well as my experience and that of many of my friends support it. Why, then, do so few professors give frequent brief exams? Some believe that such exams take up too much of the limited class time available to cover the material in the course. Most courses meet 150 minutes a week—three times a week for 50 minutes each time. A 20-minute weekly exam might take 30 minutes to administer, and that is one-fifth of each week's class time. From the student's perspective, however, this time is well spent. Better learning and greater confidence about the course seem a good tradeoff for another 30 minutes of lecture. Moreover, time lost to lecturing or discussion could easily be made up in students' learning on their own through careful regular study for the weekly exams. If weekly exams still seem too time-consuming to some professors, their frequency could be reduced to every other week or their length to 5 or 10 minutes. In courses where multiple-choice exams are appropriate, several questions take only a few minutes to answer.

Another objection professors have to frequent exams is that they take too much time to read and grade. In a 20-minute essay exam a well-prepared student can easily write two pages. A relatively small class of 30 students might then produce 60 pages, no small amount of material to read each week. A large class of 100 or more students would produce an insurmountable pile of material. There are a number of responses to this objection. Again, professors could give exams every other week or make them very short. Instead of reading them closely they could skim them quickly to see whether students understand an idea or can apply it to an unfamiliar problem; and instead of numerical or letter grades they could give a plus, check, or minus. Exams could be collected and responded to only every third or fourth week. Professors who have readers or teaching assistants could rely on them to grade or check exams. And the scantron machine is always available for instant grading of multiple-choice exams. Finally, frequent exams could be given *in place of* a midterm exam or out-of-class essay assignment.

Since frequent exams seem to some professors to create too many problems, however, it is reasonable to consider alternative ways to achieve the same goals. One alternative solution is to implement a program that would improve study skills. While such a program might teach students how to study for exams, it cannot prevent procrastination or reduce "large test anxiety" by a substantial amount. One research team studying anxiety and test performance found that study skills training was "not effective in reducing anxiety or improving performance" (Dendato & Diener, 1986, p. 134). This team, which also reviewed other research that reached the same conclusion, did find that a combination of "cognitive/relaxation therapy" and study skills training was effective. This possible solution seems complicated, however, not to mention time-consuming and expensive. It seems much easier and more effective to change the cause of the bad habit rather than treat the habit itself. That is, it would make more sense to solve the problem at its root: the method of learning and evaluation.

Still another solution might be to provide frequent study questions for students to answer. These would no doubt be helpful in focusing students' time studying, but students would probably not actually write out the answers unless they were required to. To get students to complete the questions in a timely way, professors would have to collect and check the answers. In that case, however, they might as well devote the time to grading an exam. Even if it asks the same questions, a scheduled exam is preferable to a set of study questions because it takes far less time to write in class, compared to the time students would devote to responding to questions at home. In-class exams also ensure that each student produces his or her own work.

Another possible solution would be to help students prepare for mid-   11
term and final exams by providing sets of questions from which the exam questions will be selected or announcing possible exam topics at the beginning of the course. This solution would have the advantage of reducing students' anxiety about learning every fact in the textbook, and it would clarify the course goals, but it would not motivate students to study carefully each new unit, concept, or text chapter in the course. I see this as a way of complementing frequent exams, not as substituting for them.

From the evidence and from my talks with professors and students, I   12
see frequent, brief in-class exams as the only way to improve students' study habits and learning, reducing their anxiety and procrastination, and increase their satisfaction with college. These exams are not a panacea, but only more parking spaces and a winning football team would do as much to improve college life. Professors can't do much about parking or football, but they can give more frequent exams. Campus administrators should get behind this effort, and professors should get together to consider giving exams more frequently. It would make a difference.

References

Dendato, K. M., & Diener, D. (1986). Effectiveness of cognitive/relaxation therapy and study-skills training in reducing self-reported anxiety and improving the academic performance of text-anxious students. *Journal of Counseling Psychology, 33,* 131–135.

Frederiksen, N. (1984). The real test bias: Influences of testing on teaching and learning. *American Psychologist, 39,* 193–202.

Light, R. J. (1990). *Explorations with students and faculty about teaching, learning, and student life.* Cambridge, MA: Harvard University Graduate School of Education and Kennedy School of Government.

Rothblum, E. D., Solomon, L., & Murakami, J. (1986). Affective, cognitive, and behavioral differences between high and low procrastinators. *Journal of Counseling Psychology, 33,* 387–394.

For Discussion

O'Malley advocates frequent brief exams as a solution to the problems of midterm and final exam anxiety, poor study habits, and disappointing exam performance. What do you think of his proposal in light of your own experience? Which of your high school or college courses have included frequent exams? Did they offer the benefits O'Malley claims? Did you learn more because of them? Did courses without frequent exams produce the problems he identifies?

For Analysis

1. Reread paragraph 3 carefully to discover how O'Malley defines and qualifies the solution. Underline key words and phrases that indicate what kind of exams he advocates. For his purpose and readers, does he adequately qualify the solution? Does anything seem unnecessary? Should anything be added? Does each key term hold up usefully throughout the essay?

2. In paragraph 2, how does O'Malley forecast the plan of his essay? Does the forecast predict the order of main parts? What else, if anything, might he have included in the forecast? (For a discussion of forecasting statements, see pp. 190–91.)

3. Reread paragraphs 4–6 and underline the most direct statements of the reasons O'Malley gives in support of his proposal. Why do you think he makes these reasons so easy to notice? What role do they play in the proposal?

4. Compare how O'Malley and Weisman acknowledge alternative solutions and establish shared values with their readers. What role do these two strategies play in the overall argumentative strategy of each writer's essay? How successfully does each writer manage the two strategies?

5. Turn to the Writer at Work discussion on pages 185–87. Compare the last paragraph in the section of O'Malley's draft with paragraph 4 in his revision, and list specific changes he made from draft to revision. Knowing his purpose and readers, what advantages do you see in his changes?

For Your Own Writing

Much of what happens in high school and college is predictable and conventional. Examples of conventional practices that have changed very little over the years are exams, group instruction, graduation ceremonies, required courses, and lower admission requirements for athletes. Think of additional examples of established practices in high school or college; then select one that you believe needs to be improved or refined in some way. What changes would you propose? What individual or group might be convinced to take action on your proposal for improvement? What questions or objections should you anticipate? How could you discover whether others have previously proposed improvements in the practice you are concerned with? Who might you interview to learn more about the practice and the likelihood of changing it?

Commentary

O'Malley's essay demonstrates the importance of taking readers seriously. Not only did he interview both those who would carry out his proposal (professors) and those who would benefit from it (students), but he also featured in his essay what he had learned in these interviews. Paragraphs 7–11 directly acknowledge pro-

fessors' objections, their questions, and the alternative solutions they would probably prefer. If at all possible, it is good to interview possible readers and thus to
find out their likely objections, questions, and preferred solutions.

O'Malley's plan is also worth noting:

opening: a scenario to introduce the problem

presentation of the problem and introduction of the solution

details of the solution

reason 1: to support the solution: improved learning and performance

reason 2: improved study habits

reason 3: decreased procrastination and anxiety

accommodate objection 1: class time is limited

accommodate objection 2: too much work

refute alternative solution 1: offer study skills training

refute alternative solution 2: provide study questions

accommodate alternative solution 3: provide sample exam questions

closing: reiterate the proposed solution and advise briefly about first steps in
implementing it

The essay follows an appropriate order for O'Malley's purpose and readers. It is
especially easy to follow because of the explicit cues given to readers: forecasts
(previews of what comes next), paragraph breaks, transitions, and summaries.
Most important, the plan is logical and convincing. It is not the only possible
plan—the alternative solutions might have been acknowledged before O'Malley
argues for his solution, for example—but it is a very effective plan. This orderly
plan was developed over several days of invention, drafting, and revising.

PURPOSE AND AUDIENCE

More than any other kind of writing, proposals depend on the writer to anticipate
readers' needs and concerns—because most proposals are calls to action. They
attempt not only to convince readers but also to inspire them, to persuade them
to support or to put into effect the proposed solution. What your particular readers
know about the problem and what they are capable of doing to solve it determine
how you should address them.

Readers of proposals are often unaware of the problem. In this case, your task
is clear: present them with facts that will convince them of its existence. These
facts may include statistics, testimony from witnesses or experts, and examples.
You can also speculate about the cause of the problem and describe its ill effects.

Sometimes readers recognize the existence of a problem but fail to take it
seriously. When this is so, you may need to connect the problem closely to readers'
own concerns. For instance, you might show how much they have in common
with those directly affected by it, or how it affects them indirectly. However you

appeal to readers, you must do more than alert them to the problem; you must also make them care about it. You want to touch readers emotionally as well as intellectually.

At other times, readers concerned about the problem may assume that someone else is taking care of it and that they need not become personally involved. Faced with this situation, you might want to demonstrate that those they thought were taking care of the problem have failed. Another assumption readers might make is that a solution they supported in the past has already solved the problem. You might point out that the original solution has proved unworkable or that new solutions have become available through changed circumstances or improved technology. Your aim is to rekindle these readers' interest in the problem.

Perhaps the most satisfying proposals are addressed to those who can take immediate action to remedy the problem. Your chances of writing such a proposal are good if you choose a problem faced by a group to which you belong. You not only have a firsthand understanding of the problem but also have a good idea what solution other members of the group will support. (You might informally survey some of them before you submit your proposal in order to test your definition of the problem and your proposed solution.) When you address readers who are in a position to take action, you obviously want to assure them that it is wise to do so. You must demonstrate that the solution is feasible—that it can be implemented and that it will work.

BASIC FEATURES OF PROPOSAL PAPERS

Effective proposals share certain predictable features.

A Well-Defined Problem

A proposal is written to offer a solution to a problem. Before presenting the solution, a proposal writer must be sure that readers know what the problem is. All the writers in this chapter state the problem explicitly. Stating the problem is not enough, however; the writer also has to establish that the problem indeed exists and is serious enough to need solving. Sometimes a writer can assume that readers will recognize the problem. At other times, readers may not be aware of the problem and will need to be convinced that it deserves their attention.

In addition to stating the problem and establishing its existence and seriousness, a proposal writer may need to analyze the problem, exploring its causes, consequences, and history as well as past efforts of dealing with it. This information not only helps readers better understand the problem but may also provide grounds for the proposed solution.

A Proposed Solution

Once the problem is established, the writer must present and argue for a particular solution. Announcing the solution is the thesis of the proposal.

A Convincing Argument

The main purpose of a proposal is to convince readers that the writer's solution is the best way of solving the problem. Proposals argue for their solutions by trying to demonstrate all of the following:

The proposed solution will solve the problem.

It is a feasible way of solving the problem and can be easily implemented.

It stands up against anticipated objections or reservations.

It is better than alternative solutions.

A Reasonable Tone

Regardless of the proposal or the argument made on its behalf, proposal writers must adopt a reasonable tone. The objective is to advance an argument without "having" an argument. That is, writers should avoid taking an adversarial or quarrelsome stance with their readers. The aim is to bridge any gap that may exist between writer and readers, not to widen it.

Writers can build such a bridge of shared concerns by showing respect for their readers and treating their concerns seriously. Writers discuss anticipated objections and reservations as an attempt to lay to rest any doubts readers may have. They consider alternative solutions as a way of showing they have explored every possibility in order to find the best possible solution. Most important, they do not attack those raising objections or offering other solutions by questioning their intelligence or goodwill.

Guide to Writing

▪ THE WRITING ASSIGNMENT

Write an essay proposing a solution to a problem. Choose a problem faced by a community or group to which you belong, and address your proposal to one or more members of the group or to an outsider who might help solve the problem.

INVENTION AND RESEARCH

As you prepare to write your proposal, you will need to choose a problem you can write about, analyze and define the problem, identify your prospective readers, find a tentative solution, defend your solution, test your choice, develop reasons for adopting your proposal, and consider alternative solutions.

Choosing a Problem

One possible problem you could write about may come to mind immediately. Even so, you will want to think about various problems before settling on a topic. The following exercise is a good way to get started.

Considering Problems in Various Communities

Divide a piece of paper into two columns. In the left-hand column list all communities, groups, or organizations to which you belong. Include as many communities as possible: college, neighborhood, hometown, cultural or ethnic groups. Also include groups you participate in: sports, musical, work, religious, political, support, hobby, and so on. In the right-hand column list any problems that exist within each group. Here's how such a chart might begin:

Community	*Problem*
Your college	poor advising or orientation
	shortage of practice rooms in music building
	no financial aid for part-time students
	lack of facilities for handicapped students
	lack of enough sections of required courses
	classes scheduled so that working students or students with children find it difficult to take courses
Your neighborhood	need for traffic light at dangerous intersection
	unsupervised children getting into trouble
	"megastores" driving away small business
	lack of safe places for children to play

Choose one problem from your list that you consider especially important. It should be one that seems solvable (though you need not know the exact solution now) and that concerns others in the group or community. It should also be a problem you can explore in detail and are willing to discuss in writing.

Proposing to solve a problem in a group or community to which you belong gives you one inestimably important advantage: you can write as an expert, an insider. You know about the history of the problem, have felt the urgency to solve it, and perhaps have already thought of possible solutions. Equally important, you know precisely to whom to address the proposal, and you can interview others in the group to get their views of the problem and to understand how they might resist your solution. You are in a position of knowledge and authority—from which comes confident, convincing writing. Local problems are not at all unimportant just because they lack national scope.

Should you want to propose a solution for a large national social problem, concentrate on one with which you have direct experience and for which you can suggest a detailed plan of action. Even better, focus on unique local aspects of the problem. For example, if you would like to propose a solution to the lack of affordable child care for children of college students or working parents, you have a great advantage if you are a parent who has experienced the frustration of finding professional, affordable child care. Moreover, it may well be that even though such a problem is national in scope, it can *only* be solved campus by campus, business by business, neighborhood by neighborhood.

Analyzing and Defining the Problem

You need now to analyze the problem carefully and then try to define it. Keep in mind that you will have to demonstrate to readers that the problem exists and is serious, and that you have a more than casual understanding of its causes and consequences. If you find that you cannot do so, you will want to select some other problem to write about.

Analyzing

Start analyzing the problem by writing a few sentences in response to these questions:

- Does the problem really exist? How can I tell?
- What caused this problem? Can I identify any immediate causes? Any deeper causes? Is the problem caused by a flaw in the system, a lack of resources, individual misconduct or incompetence? How can I tell?
- What is the history of the problem?
- What are the bad effects of the problem? How is it hurting members of the community or group? What goals of the group are endangered by the existence of this problem? Does it raise any moral or ethical questions?
- Who in the community or group is affected by the problem? Be as specific as possible: Who is seriously affected? Minimally affected? Unaffected? Does anyone benefit from its existence?
- What similar problems exist in this same community or group? How can I distinguish my problem from these?

Defining

Write a definition of the problem, being as specific as possible. Identify who or what seems responsible for it, and give one recent example.

Identifying Your Readers

Whom do you wish to address—everyone in the community or group, a committee, an individual, an outsider? You want to address the person or group who can take action to implement the solution you propose. In a few sentences, describe your readers, stating your reason for directing your proposal to them. Then take ten minutes to write about these readers:

- How informed are my readers likely to be about the problem? Have they shown any awareness of it?
- Why would this problem be important to them? Why would they care about solving it?
- Have they supported any other proposals to solve the problem? If so, what do their proposals have in common with mine?
- Do they ally themselves with any group that might cause them to favor or reject my proposal? Do we share any values or attitudes that could bring us together to solve the problem?
- How have they responded to other problems? Do their past reactions suggest anything about how they may respond to my proposal?

Finding a Tentative Solution

Solving problems takes time. Apparent solutions often turn out to be impossible. After all, a solution has to be both workable and acceptable to the community or group involved. Consequently, you should strive to come up with several possible solutions whose advantages and disadvantages can be weighed. Keep in mind that the most imaginative solutions sometimes occur only after you've struggled with a number of other possibilities.

Look back at the way you defined the problem and described your readers. Then, with these factors in mind, list as many possible solutions as you can think of. For ideas, reflect on the following problem-solving questions:

- What solutions to this problem have already been tried?
- What solutions have been proposed for related problems? Might they solve this problem as well?
- Is a solution required that would disband or change the community or group in some way?
- What solution might eliminate some of the causes of the problem?
- What solution would eliminate any of the bad effects of the problem?
- Maybe the problem is too big to be solved all at once. Try dividing it into several parts. What solutions might solve these parts?
- If a series of solutions is required, which should come first? Second?
- What solution would ultimately solve the problem?
- What might be a daring solution? What would be the most conservative solution, acceptable to nearly everyone in the community or group?

Give yourself enough time to let your ideas percolate, continuing to add to your list of possible solutions and to consider the advantages and disadvantages of each one in light of your prospective readers. If possible, discuss your solutions with members of the community or group who can help you consider advantages and disadvantages of the possible solutions.

Choosing the Most Promising Solution

In a sentence or two, state what you would consider the best possible way of solving the problem.

Determining Specific Steps

Write down the steps necessary to carry out your solution. This list will provide an early test of whether your solution can, in fact, be implemented.

Defending Your Solution

Proposals have to be feasible—that is, they must be both reasonable and practical. Imagine that one of your readers opposes your proposed solution and confronts you with the following statements. Write several sentences refuting each one.

- It won't really solve the problem.
- I'm comfortable with things as they are.
- We can't afford it.
- It will take too long.
- People won't do it.
- Too few people will benefit.
- I don't even see how to get started on your solution.
- It's already been tried, with unsatisfactory results.
- You're making this proposal because it will benefit you personally.

Answering these questions should help you prepare responses to possible objections. If you feel you need a better idea of how others are likely to feel about your proposal, talk to a few people involved with the problem. The more you know about your readers' concerns, the better able you will be to anticipate their reservations and preferred alternative solutions.

Testing Your Choice

Now examine the problem and your chosen solution to see whether they will result in a strong proposal. Start by asking the following questions:

- Is this a significant problem? Do other people in the community or group really care about it, or can they be persuaded to care?
- Will my solution really solve the problem? Can it be implemented?
- Can I answer objections from enough people in the community or group to win support for my solution?

As you plan and draft your proposal, you will probably want to consider these questions again. If at any point you decide that you cannot answer them affirmatively and confidently, you may want to find another solution or even to write about some other problem.

Now is a good time to get together with two or three other students and run your chosen topics by one another. Assess their awareness of the problem, and "try out" your solution on them. Are they convinced that it is a possible solution? A good solution? What objections or reservations do they offer? What alternative solutions do they suggest? Does the problem you have chosen still seem important, and your solution feasible?

Offering Reasons for Your Proposal

To make a convincing case for your proposed solution, you need to offer your readers good reasons for adopting your proposal.

Listing Reasons

Write down every plausible reason you could give that might persuade readers to accept your proposal. These reasons should answer readers' key question: "Why is this the best solution?"

Choosing the Strongest Reasons

Keeping your readers in mind, look over your list of reasons and put an asterisk next to the strongest ones. If you do not consider two or three of your reasons strong, you may anticipate difficulty developing a strong proposal and should reconsider your topic.

Developing Your Strongest Reasons

Now look at your strongest reasons and explain briefly why you think each one will be effective with your particular readers. Then take around five minutes to write about each reason, developing your argument on its behalf.

Considering Alternative Solutions

Even if your readers are likely to consider your proposal reasonable, they will probably want to compare your proposed solution with other possible solutions. List alternative solutions that might be offered, and consider the advantages and disadvantages of each one relative to your solution. You might find it helpful to chart the information as follows:

Possible Solutions	*Advantages*	*Disadvantages*
My solution		
Alternative solution 1		
Alternative solution 2		

Doing Research

Thus far you have relied largely upon your own knowledge and instincts for ideas about solving the problem. You may now feel that you need to do some research to learn more about the causes of the problem and to find more technical information about implementing the solution. (For guidelines on conducting research, see Chapter 10.)

If you are proposing a solution to a problem about which others have written, you will want to find out how they have defined it and what solutions they have proposed. You may need to acknowledge these solutions in your essay, either accommodating or refuting them. Now is a good time—before beginning to draft—to get any additional information you need.

PLANNING AND DRAFTING

To help you plan your essay and begin drafting, review what you have done so far, set some specific goals for yourself, and prepare an outline.

Seeing What You Have

Reread your invention notes, asking yourself whether you have a good topic—an interesting problem with a feasible solution. If at this point you are doubtful about the significance of the problem or the success of your proposed solution, you might want to look for a new topic. If you are unsure about these basic points, you cannot expect to produce a persuasive draft.

If your invention material seems thin but promising, however, you may be able to strengthen it with additional invention writing. Consider the following questions:

- Could I make a stronger case for the seriousness of the problem?
- Could I find more reasons for readers to support my solution?
- Are there any other ways of refuting attractive alternative solutions or troubling questions about my own proposed solution?

Setting Goals

Before beginning to draft, think seriously about the overall goals of your proposal. Not only will the draft be easier to write once you have clear goals, but it will almost surely be more convincing as well.

Following are some goal-setting questions to consider now. You may find it useful to return to them while drafting, for they are designed to help you focus on exactly what you want to accomplish with this proposal.

Your Readers

- What do my readers already know about this problem?
- Are they likely to welcome my solution or resist it?
- Can I anticipate any specific reservations or objections they may have?

- How can I gain readers' enthusiastic support? How can I get them to help implement the solution?
- What kind of tone would be most appropriate? How can I present myself so that I seem both reasonable and authoritative?

The Beginning

- How can I immediately engage my readers' interest? Should I open with a dramatic scenario, like O'Malley? With statistics that highlight the seriousness of the problem, like Kibler? By quoting an authority on the problem? With a question, like Weisman?
- What information should I give first?

Defining the Problem

- How much do I need to say about the problem's causes or history?
- How can I show the seriousness of the problem? Should I use statistics, like Kibler and Weisman? Stress negative consequences, like O'Malley?
- Is it an urgent problem? How can I emphasize this? Should I redefine the problem, like Kibler?
- How much space should I devote to defining the problem? Only a little space, like O'Malley, or much space, like Kibler?

Proposing a Solution

- How can I present my solution so that it looks like the best way to proceed? Should I show how to implement it in stages, like Kibler? Focus on reasons to support it, like O'Malley?
- How can I make the solution seem easy to implement? Or should I acknowledge that the solution may be difficult to implement and argue that it will be worth the effort?

Anticipating Objections

- Should I mention every possible objection to my proposed solution? How might I choose among them?
- Has anyone raised these objections? Should I name the person?
- Should I accommodate certain objections?
- What specific reasons can I give for refuting each objection? How can I support these reasons?
- How can I refute the objections without seeming to attack anyone?

Rejecting Alternative Solutions

- How many alternative solutions do I need to mention? Which ones should I discuss?
- Should I indicate where these alternatives come from? Should I name those who proposed them?
- What reasons should I give for rejecting the alternative solutions? Like O'Malley, can I offer any evidence in support of my reasons?

■ How can I reject these other solutions without seeming to criticize their proponents? Both Weisman and O'Malley succeed at this.

The Ending

■ How should I conclude? Should I end by restating the problem and summarizing the solution, as Kibler does? By arguing that the solution is workable and might bring about cultural change? By arguing that some readers' preferred solution is sure to fail, as Weisman does? Or simply by summarizing my solution and its advantages, as does O'Malley?

■ Is there something special about the problem itself I should remind readers of at the end?

■ Should I end with an inspiring call to action or a scenario suggesting the consequences of a failure to solve the problem?

■ Would a shift to humor or satire be an effective way to end?

Outlining

After setting goals for your proposal, you are ready to develop a working outline. The basic outline for a proposal is quite simple:

the problem
the solution
the reasons for accepting the solution

This simple plan is nearly always complicated by other factors, however. In outlining your material you must take into consideration many other details, such as whether readers already recognize the problem, how much agreement exists on the need to solve the problem, how many alternative solutions are available, how much attention must be given to the other solutions, and how many objections should be expected.

Here is a possible outline for a proposal where readers may not understand the problem fully and other solutions have been proposed:

presentation of the problem
   its existence
   its seriousness
   its causes
consequences of failing to solve the problem
description of the proposed solution
list of steps for implementing the solution
discussion of reasons to support the solution
   acknowledgment of objections
   accommodation or refutation of objections
consideration of alternative solutions and their disadvantages
restatement of the proposed solution and its advantages

See page 170 for another sample outline.

Your outline will of course reflect your own writing situation. As you develop it, think about what your readers know and feel, and about your own writing goals. Once you have a working outline, you should not hesitate to change it as necessary while writing. For instance, you might find it more effective to hold back on presenting your own solution until you have dismissed other possible solutions. Or you might find a better way to order the reasons for adopting your proposal. The purpose of an outline is to identify the basic features of your proposal and help you organize them effectively, not to lock you into a particular structure.

Most of the information you will need to develop each feature can be found in your invention writing and research notes. How much space you devote to each feature is determined by the topic, not the outline. Do not assume that each entry on your outline must be given one paragraph—in the preceding example, each of the reasons for supporting the solution may require a paragraph, but you might present the reasons, objections, and refutations all in one paragraph.

Drafting

After reviewing your outline, start drafting the proposal. Let the outline help you write, but don't hesitate to change it if you find that drafting takes you in an unexpected direction. If you get stuck in drafting, return to the invention activities earlier in this chapter. As you draft, keep in mind the two main goals of proposal writing: (1) to establish that a problem exists and is serious enough to require a solution; and (2) to demonstrate that your proposed solution is feasible and is the best possible alternative. You might want to review the general advice on drafting on pages 11–13.

GETTING CRITICAL COMMENTS

Now is the time for your draft to get a good critical reading. All writers find it helpful to have someone else read and comment on their drafts. Your instructor may schedule such a reading as part of your coursework; otherwise, you can ask a classmate, friend, or family member to read it over. If your campus has a writing center, you might ask a tutor to read and comment on your draft. In this section are guidelines designed to be used by *anyone* reviewing an essay proposing a solution to a problem. (If you are unable to get someone else to review your draft, turn to the Revising and Editing section on pp. 183–85 for guidelines on reading your own draft with a critical eye.)

To provide focused, helpful comments, your critical reader must know your intended audience and purpose. At the top of your draft, write out the following information:

Audience: Who are your readers?

Purpose: What do you hope will happen as a result of your proposal?

Reading with a Critical Eye

Reading a draft critically means reading it more than once, first to get a general impression and then to analyze its basic features.

Reading for a First Impression

Read first to get a basic understanding of the problem and the proposed solution to it. As you read, try to notice any words or passages that contribute either favorably or unfavorably to your impression. After reading the draft, briefly write out your impressions. How convincing do you think the essay will be for its particular readers? What do you notice about the way the problem is presented and the solution argued for?

Reading to Analyze

Now read to focus on the basic features of proposal papers. (See pp. 171–72 to review the basic features.) Consider the following questions:

How Well Is the Problem Defined?

Decide whether the problem is stated clearly. Is enough information given about its causes and consequences? What more might be done to establish its seriousness? Is there more that readers might need or wish to know about it?

How Clearly Is the Solution Presented?

Restate the solution. Is it clear? How could its presentation be strengthened? Are steps for implementation laid out? If not, might readers expect or require them? Does the solution seem practical? If not, why?

How Convincing Is the Argument for the Solution?

Look at the reasons and evidence offered to support this solution. Are they sufficient? Which are most and least convincing? Why?

Consider the treatment of objections to the proposed solution. What reasons and evidence refuting objections seem most convincing? Which seem least convincing? Why? Are there other objections or reservations that need to be acknowledged?

Are alternative solutions discussed and either accommodated or refuted? What are the most convincing reasons given against any other solutions? Which are least convincing, and why?

How Appropriate Is the Tone?

Is the proposal advanced in a reasonable tone, one that argues forcefully yet finds some common ground with readers who may advocate alternative solutions? Are such solutions accommodated or rejected without a personal attack on those who propose them?

How Effective Is the Organization?

Evaluate the *overall plan* of the proposal, perhaps by outlining it briefly. Would any parts be more effective earlier or later? Look closely at the ordering of the argument for the solution—the presentation of the reasons and the accommodation or refutation of objections and alternative solutions. How might the sequence be revised to strengthen the argument? Point to any gaps in the argument.

Is the *beginning* engaging? If not, how might it be revised to capture readers' attention? Does it adequately forecast the main ideas and plan of the proposal? Can you think of other ways to begin?

Evaluate the *ending*. Does it frame the proposal by echoing or referring to something at the beginning? If not, how might it do so? Does the ending convey a sense of urgency? Can you think of a stronger way to conclude?

What Final Thoughts Do You Have?

What is the strongest part of this proposal? What part most needs more work?

REVISING AND EDITING

This section will help you identify problems in your draft and revise and edit to solve them.

Identifying Problems

To identify problems in your draft, you need to read it objectively, analyze its basic features, and study any comments you've received from other readers.

Getting an Overview

Consider the draft as a whole, trying to see it objectively. It may help to do so in two steps:

1. *Reread.* If at all possible, put the draft aside for a day or two before rereading it. When you reread, start by reconsidering your audience and purpose. Then read the draft straight through, trying to see it as your intended readers will.
2. *Outline.* Make a scratch outline to get an overview of the essay's development. This outline can be sketchy—words and phrases instead of complete sentences—but it should identify the basic features as they appear.

Charting a Plan for Revision

Use a double-columned chart to keep track of problems you need to solve. In the left-hand column list the basic features of proposals. As you analyze your draft and study any comments from others, note in the right-hand column the problems you want to solve. Here is an example:

Basic Features	*Problems to Solve*
Definition of the problem	
Presentation of the solution	
Argument for the solution	
Acknowledgement of alternative solutions	
Tone	
Organization	

Analyzing the Basic Features of Your Draft

Turn now to the questions for analyzing a draft on pages 182–83. Using these as guidelines, identify problems in your draft. Note anything you need to solve on your revision chart.

Studying Critical Comments

Review any comments you've received from other readers, and add to your chart any points that need attention. Try not to react defensively to these comments; by letting you see how others respond to your draft, they provide invaluable information about how you might improve it.

Solving the Problems

Having identified problems in your draft, you now need to find solutions and to carry them out. You have three ways of finding solutions: (1) review your invention notes for additional information and ideas; (2) do further invention to answer questions your readers raised; and (3) look back at the readings in this chapter to see how other writers have solved similar problems.

Following are suggestions to get you started on solving some of the problems common to writing proposals. For now, focus on solving those problems identified on your chart. Avoid tinkering with sentence-level problems; that will come later, when you edit.

Definition of the Problem

- If the problem is not clearly defined, consider sketching out its history, including past attempts to deal with it, discussing its causes and consequences more fully, dramatizing its seriousness more vividly, or comparing it to other problems readers may be familiar with.

Presentation of the Solution

- If the solution is not adequately described, try outlining the steps or phases in its implementation. Help readers see how easy the first step will be, or acknowledge the difficulty of the first step.

Argument for the Solution

- If the argument seems weak, think of more reasons for readers to support your proposal.
- If your refutation of any objection or reservation seems unconvincing, consider accommodating it by modifying your proposal.
- If you have left out any likely objections readers will have to the solution, acknowledge those objections and either accommodate or refute them.
- If you neglected to mention alternative solutions some readers are likely to prefer, do so now. Consider whether you want to accommodate or reject these alternatives. For each one, try to acknowledge its good points but argue that it is not as effective a solution as your own. You may, in fact, want to strengthen your own solution by incorporating into it some of the good points from alternatives.

Tone

- ▪ If your tone seems too adversarial, revise to acknowledge your readers' fears, biases, and expectations.

Organization

- ▪ If the argument or the essay is hard to follow, find a better sequence for the major parts. Try to put reasons supporting your solution in a more convincing order— leading up to the strongest one rather than putting it first, perhaps. Shift refutation of objections or alternative solutions so that they do not interrupt the main argument. Add explicit cues to keep the reader on track: previews of what comes next, transitional phrases and sentences, brief summaries of points just made. (For more on cues, see Chapter 7.)
- ▪ If the beginning is weak, is there a better place to start? Would an anecdote or an example of the problem engage readers more effectively?
- ▪ If the ending doesn't work, consider framing your proposal by mentioning something from the beginning of your essay, or ending with a call for action that expresses the urgency of implementing your solution.

Editing and Proofreading

In working on your draft so far, you may have corrected some obvious errors, but grammar and style have not been a priority. Now is the time to check carefully for errors in usage, punctuation, and mechanics, as well as to consider matters of style. You may find that studying your draft in separate passes—first for paragraphs, then for sentences, and finally for words—will help you recognize problems.

Once you have edited your draft and produced a final copy, proofread it carefully to be sure there are no typos, misspellings, or other mistakes.

A Writer at Work

STRENGTHENING THE ARGUMENT

This section focuses on student writer Patrick O'Malley's successful efforts to strengthen the argument for his proposed solution in "More Testing, More Learning." Read the following three paragraphs from his draft. Then compare them with paragraphs 4–6 of his revision on pages 165–68. As you read, take notes on the differences you observe between his draft and revision.

> The predominant reason students perform better with multiple exams is that they improve their study habits.

Greater regularity in test taking means greater regularity in studying for tests. Students prone to cramming
will be forced to open their textbooks more often, keeping them away from long, "kamikaze" nights of studying.
Regularity prepares them for the "real world" where you
rarely take on large tasks at long intervals. Several
tests also improve study habits by reducing procrastination. An article about procrastination from the Journal
of Counseling Psychology reports that "students view exams as difficult, important, and anxiety provoking."
These symptoms of anxiety leading to procrastination
could be solved if individual test importance was less-
ened, reducing the stress associated with the perceived
burden.

       With multiple exams, this anxiety decrease will free
students to perform better. Several, less important
tests may appear as less of an obstacle, allowing the
students to worry less, leaving them free to concentrate
on their work without any emotional hindrances. It is
proven that "the performance of test-anxious subjects
varies inversely with evaluation stress." It would also
be to the psychological benefit of students if they were
not subjected to the emotional ups and downs of large exams where they are virtually worry-free one moment and
ready to check into the psychiatric ward the next.

       Lastly, with multiple exams, students can learn how to
perform better on future tests in the class. Regular
testing allows them to "practice" the information they
learned, thereby improving future test scores. In just
two exams, they are not able to learn the instructor's
personal examination style, and are not given the chance
to adapt their study habits to it. The American Psychologist concludes: "It is possible to influence teaching
and learning by changing the type of tests."

One difference you may have noted between O'Malley's draft and revision
paragraphs is in the sequencing of specific reasons readers should accept the solution and take action on it. Whereas the draft moves in three paragraphs, from
improving study habits to decreasing anxiety to performing better on future tests,
the revision moves from learning more and performing better on major exams to
improving study habits to decreasing anxiety. These changes were made after a
response from a classmate and a conference with his instructor helped O'Malley
see that the most convincing reason for his particular readers (professors) would
probably be the improved quality of students' learning, not their study habits and
feelings. As he continued thinking about his argument and discovering further

relevant research, he shifted his emphasis from the psychological to the intellectual benefits of frequent exams.

You may also have noticed that the paragraphs of the revision are better focused than in the draft. The psychological benefits (reduced anxiety as a result of less procrastination) are now discussed mainly in a single paragraph (the third), whereas in the draft they are mixed in with the intellectual benefits in the first two paragraphs. O'Malley also uses more precise language in his revision; for example, changing "future tests" to "major exams, projects, and papers."

Another change you may have noticed is that all of the quoted research material in the draft has been replaced in the revision. Extending his library research for evidence to support his reasons, O'Malley discovered the very useful Harvard report. As his argument found a more logical sequence, more precise terms, and fuller elaboration, he saw different ways to use the research studies he had turned up initially and quoted in the draft.

A final difference is that in the revision O'Malley argues his reasons more effectively. Consider the draft and revised paragraphs on improved study habits. In the draft paragraph O'Malley shifts abruptly from study habits to procrastination to anxiety. Except for study habits, none of these topics is developed; and the quotation adds nothing to what he has already said. By contrast, the revision paragraph (5) focuses strictly on study habits. O'Malley keeps the best sentences from the draft for the beginning of the revised paragraph, but he adds several new sentences to help convince readers of the soundness of his argument that frequent exams improve students' study habits. These new sentences serve several functions: they anticipate a possible objection ("It might be argued . . . "), note a contrast between complex academic learning and familiar survival skills, and assert claims about the special requirements of regular academic study. The quotation from the Harvard report supports, rather than merely repeats, O'Malley's claims, and it effectively concludes the paragraph.

Reflecting on Your Writing

By this point, you have had considerable experience with proposals—reading them, talking about them, and writing one of your own. Now, then, is a good time to think critically about what you've learned about this genre. Reflecting on your own writing process will help you discover what you learned about solving problems you encountered in writing a proposal paper.

Begin by gathering your invention and planning notes, drafts and critical comments, revision plan, and final revision. Review these materials as you complete the following writing tasks.

▪ Identify *one* writing problem you needed to solve as you worked on your proposal essay. Don't be concerned with sentence-level problems; concentrate, instead, on a problem unique to developing a proposal essay. For example: Did you puzzle over how to convince readers that your proposed solution would actually solve the problem you identified? Did you find it difficult to outline the steps required to implement the solution? Did you have trouble coming up with alternative solutions your readers might favor?

▪ How did you recognize the writing problem? When did you first discover it? What called it to your attention? If you didn't become aware of the problem until someone else pointed it out to you, can you now see hints of it in your invention writings? If so, where specifically? When you first recognized the problem, how did you respond?

▪ Reflect on how you went about trying to solve the problem. Did you reword a passage, cut or add details about the problem or solution, or move paragraphs or sentences around? Did you reread one of the essays in this chapter to see how another writer handled the problem, or did you look back at the invention suggestions? If you discussed the writing problem with another student, a tutor, or your instructor, did talking about it help? How useful was the advice you got?

▪ Finally, write a page or two telling your instructor about the problem, how you discovered it, and how you tried to solve it. Be as specific as possible in reconstructing your efforts. Quote from your invention, draft, others' critical comments, your revision plan, and your revised essay to show the various changes your writing underwent as you tried to solve the problem. If you're still uncertain about your solution, say so. The point is not to prove that you've solved the problem perfectly, but to show what you've learned about problem solving in the process of writing a proposal.

7 Strategies for Cueing Readers

In order to guide readers through a piece of writing, a writer can provide four basic kinds of cues or signals: (1) thesis and forecasting statements, to orient readers to ideas and organization; (2) paragraphing, to group related ideas and details; (3) cohesive devices, to connect ideas to one another and bring about coherence and clarity; and (4) transitions, to signal relationships or shifts in meaning. This chapter examines how each of these cueing strategies works.

ORIENTING STATEMENTS

To help readers find their way, especially in difficult and lengthy works, you can provide two kinds of orienting information: a thesis statement, which declares the main point, and a forecasting statement, which both states the thesis and previews subordinate points showing the order in which they will be discussed in the essay.

Thesis Statements

Although they may have a variety of forms and purposes, all essays are essentially assertive. That is, they assert or put forward the writer's point of view on a subject. We call this point of view the essay's *thesis*, or main idea.

To help readers understand what is being said about a subject, writers often provide a thesis statement early in the essay. The *thesis statement* operates as a cue by letting readers know which is the most important, general idea among the writer's many ideas and observations. Like the focal point of a picture, the thesis statement directs the reader's attention to the one idea that brings all the other ideas and details into perspective. Here are two thesis statements from essays in Part One:

> *Roseanne* the sitcom, which was inspired by Barr the standup comic, is a radical departure simply for featuring blue-collar Americans—and for depicting them as something other than half-witted greasers and low-life louts.
> —*Barbara Ehrenreich,* Chapter 4: Justifying an Evaluation

> Now, much as I like the talk shows, I'm also from New England, and I can say that there's a big difference between the Rush Limbaugh show and a town meeting. And much as I like town meetings, they are not as effectively democratic as they could be. —*Donella H. Meadows,* Chapter 5: Arguing a Position

The second thesis statement requires two sentences. Most thesis statements

189

can be expressed in a single sentence; others require two or more sentences. Sometimes writers choose to imply the thesis rather than state it directly. For example, William L. Kibler indicates that his proposal to combat plagiarism (Chapter 6) includes positive and negative reinforcement:

> The solution I propose, based on my recent research, is built on the concept that the most effective way to prevent cheating is to actively promote academic integrity, while at the same time effectively confronting those who do cheat.

Readers naturally look for something that will tell them the point of an essay, a focus for the many diverse details and ideas they encounter as they read. The lack of an explicit thesis statement can make this task more difficult. Therefore, careful writers keep in mind the needs and expectations of readers in deciding whether to state the thesis explicitly or to imply it.

Another important decision is where to place the thesis statement. Most readers expect to find some information early on that will give them a context for the essay. They expect the essay to open with a thesis statement, and they need that statement to orient them, particularly if they are reading about a new and difficult subject. A thesis statement placed at the beginning of an essay helps give readers a sense of control over the subject, enabling them to anticipate the content of the essay and more easily understand the relationship between its various ideas and details.

Occasionally, however, particularly in fairly short, informal essays and in some argumentative essays, a writer may save a direct statement of the thesis until the conclusion. Such a thesis is designed to bring together the various strands of information or evidence introduced over the course of the essay and to suggest the essay's overall point. In many such cases, a concluding thesis is also used to point the way toward future developments or goals.

Forecasting Statements

A special kind of thesis statement, the *forecasting statement*, not only identifies the thesis but also gives an overview of the way that thesis will be developed. For example, note the role of the forecasting statement in this opening paragraph from an essay by William Langer on the bubonic plague:

> In the three years from 1348 through 1350 the pandemic of plague known as the Black Death, or, as the Germans called it, the Great Dying, killed at least a fourth of the population of Europe. It was undoubtedly the worst disaster that has ever befallen mankind. Today we can have no real conception of the terror under which people lived in the shadow of the plague. For more than two centuries plague has not been a serious threat to mankind in the large, although it is still a grisly presence in parts of the Far East and Africa. Scholars continue to study the Great Dying, however, as a historical example of human behavior under the stress of universal catastrophe. In these days when the threat of plague has been replaced by the threat of mass human extermination by even more rapid means, there has been a sharp renewal of interest in the history of the

14th-century calamity. With new perspective, students are investigating its manifold effects: demographic, economic, psychological, moral and religious.

—*William Langer, "The Black Death"*

This paragraph informs us that Langer's article is about the effects of the Black Death. His thesis, however, is not stated explicitly. It is implied by the forecasting statement that concludes the paragraph. With this sentence, Langer states that the study of the plague currently is focused on five particular categories. As a reader would expect, Langer then goes on to divide his essay into analyses of these five effects, taking them up in the order in which they appear in the forecasting statement.

EXERCISE 7.1

Read one of the essays in Chapter 3, "Explaining a Concept," underlining the forecasting statement. If you do not find any sentences that perform this function, try drafting one yourself. Reflect on the usefulness of this cueing device.

PARAGRAPHING

Paragraph Cues

The indentation that signals the beginning of a new paragraph is a relatively modern printing convention. Old manuscripts show that paragraph divisions were not always marked. In order to make reading easier, scribes and printers began to use the symbol ¶ to mark paragraph breaks. Later, indenting became common practice, but even that relatively modern custom has changed in some forms of writing today. Instead of indenting, most business writers now distinguish one paragraph from another by leaving an extra line of space above and below each paragraph.

The lack of paragraph cues makes reading extremely difficult. To illustrate this fact, the paragraph indentions have been removed from the following introductory section of a chapter in Stephen Jay Gould's book *Ever Since Darwin*. Even with proper paragraphing, this passage might be difficult for some readers because it includes unfamiliar information and technical language. Without paragraphing, however, Gould's logic is hard to follow, and the reader's mind and eye long for a momentary rest. (Each of the thirty sentences in the passage is numbered at the beginning.)

(1) Since man created God in his own image, the doctrine of special creation has never failed to explain those adaptations that we understand intuitively. (2) How can we doubt that animals are exquisitely designed for their appointed roles when we watch a lioness hunt, a horse run, or a hippo wallow? (3) The theory of natural selection would never have replaced the doctrine of divine creation if evident, admirable design pervaded all organisms. (4) Charles Darwin understood this, and he focused on features that would be out of place in a world constructed by perfect wisdom. (5) Why, for example, should a sensible

designer create only on Australia a suite of marsupials to fill the same roles that placental mammals occupy on all other continents? (6) Darwin even wrote an entire book on orchids to argue that the structures evolved to insure fertilization by insects are jerry-built of available parts used by ancestors for other purposes. (7) Orchids are Rube Goldberg machines; a perfect engineer would certainly have come up with something better. (8) This principle remains true today. (9) The best illustrations of adaptation by evolution are the ones that strike our intuition as peculiar or bizarre. (10) Science is not "organized common sense"; at its most exciting, it reformulates our view of the world by imposing powerful theories against the ancient, anthropocentric prejudices that we call intuition. (11) Consider, for example, the cecidomyian gall midges. (12) These tiny flies conduct their lives in a way that tends to evoke feelings of pain or disgust when we empathize with them by applying the inappropriate standards of our own social codes. (13) Cecidomyian gall midges can grow and develop along one of two pathways. (14) In some situations, they hatch from eggs, go through a normal sequence of larval and pupal molts, and emerge as ordinary, sexually reproducing flies. (15) But in other circumstances, females reproduce by parthenogenesis, bringing forth their young without any fertilization by males. (16) Parthenogenesis is common enough among animals, but the cecidomyians give it an interesting twist. (17) First of all, the parthenogenetic females stop at an early age of development. (18) They never become normal, adult flies, but reproduce while they are still larvae or pupae. (19) Secondly, these females do not lay eggs. (20) The offspring develop live within their mother's body—not supplied with nutrient and packaged away in a protected uterus but right inside the mother's tissues, eventually filling her entire body. (21) In order to grow, the offspring devour the mother from the inside. (22) A few days later, they emerge, leaving a chitinous shell as the only remains of their only parent. (23) And within two days, their own developing children are beginning, literally, to eat them up. (24) *Micromalthus debilis*, an unrelated beetle, has evolved an almost identical system with a macabre variation. (25) Some parthenogenetic females give birth to a single male offspring. (26) This larva attaches itself to his mother's cuticle for about four or five days, then inserts his head into her genital aperture and devours her. (27) Greater love hath no woman. (28) Why has such a peculiar mode of reproduction evolved? (29) For it is unusual even among insects, and not only by the irrelevant standards of our own perceptions. (30) What is the adaptive significance of a mode of life that so strongly violates our intuitions about good design? —*Stephen Jay Gould,* Ever Since Darwin

A major difficulty in reading this passage without paragraph breaks is the need to hold the meaning of each sentence "in suspension" as you read ahead, because the meaning of an earlier sentence may be affected by the meaning of succeeding sentences. For instance sentence 2 clarifies the meaning of the first sentence by giving specific examples; sentence 3 restates the idea, while sentences 4–7 clarify and illustrate it. Without paragraphing, you are forced to remember each sentence separately and even to anticipate such close connections among sentences in order to make sense of the text.

Paragraphing helps readers by signaling when a sequence of related sentences begins and ends. The use of such paragraph signals tells you when you can stop holding meaning in suspension. The need for this kind of closure is a major consideration of writers. Gould, for example, begins a new paragraph with sentence 8 to draw a sharp distinction between the examples and the general principle. Similarly, he begins a new paragraph with sentence 24 to signal a shift from a description of the reproductive mode of the cecidomyian gall midge to that of *Micromalthus debilis*. In this way, paragraphing keeps readers from being overloaded with information and at the same time helps them follow the development of ideas.

Paragraphing also helps readers judge what is most important in what they are reading. Writers typically emphasize important information by placing it at the two points where readers are most attentive—the beginning and ending of a paragraph. Many writers put information to orient readers at the beginning of a paragraph and save the most important information for last, as Gould does when he ends a paragraph with sentence 27.

You can give special emphasis to information by placing it in a paragraph of its own. Gould, for example, puts sentences 11 and 12 together in a separate paragraph. These two sentences could have been attached to either the preceding or following paragraphs. But Gould gives them a separate paragraph to emphasize the general point he wants to make. In addition, this paragraph serves as an important transition between the general discussion of how science explains things that go against intuition and the specific example of the bizarre adaptation of the cecidomyian gall midge.

EXERCISE 7.2

Here is how the original Gould passage is divided into six paragraphs: sentences 1–7, 8–10, 11–12, 13–23, 24–27, 28–30. Put a paragraph symbol ¶ in your own book before the opening sentence of each paragraph. Later exercises will ask you to analyze aspects of Gould's paragraphing.

Paragraph Conventions

Some writing situations call for fairly strict conventions for paragraphing. Readers may not be conscious of these conventions, but they would certainly notice if the custom were not observed. For example, readers would be surprised if a newspaper did not have narrow columns and short paragraphs. This paragraphing convention is not accidental; it is designed to make newspaper reading easy and fast and to allow the reader to take in an entire paragraph at a glance. Business writing also tends to have short paragraphs. Memo readers frequently do not want an excess of details or qualifications. Instead, they prefer a concise overview.

College instructors, in contrast, expect students to qualify their ideas and support them with specifics. They care not so much about how long it takes to read a paragraph as about how well developed the writing is. Therefore, paragraphs in college essays usually have several sentences. In fact, it is not unusual to find quite long paragraphs, as this example from an undergraduate history essay on the status of women in Victorian England illustrates:

> A genteel woman was absolutely dependent upon the two men in her life: first her father, and then her husband. From them came her economic and social status; they were the center of her thoughts and the objects of any ambitions she might have. The ideal woman did not live for herself; she barely had a self, because her entire existence was vicarious. Legally, a woman had almost no existence at all. Until her marriage, a daughter was completely in the power of her father; upon her marriage, she was legally absorbed by her husband. Any money she had became his, as did all of her property, including her clothes and even those things that had been given her as personal gifts before her marriage. Any earnings she might make by working belonged to her husband. A woman could not be sued for debt separately from her husband because legally they were the same person. She could not sign a lease or sue someone in court without having her husband be the complainant, even in cases of long separation. In cases of a husband's enmity, she had almost no legal protection from him. Under English law, divorces could be obtained, in practice, only by men. A man could divorce his wife on the grounds of adultery, but the reverse was not the case.

If any rule for paragraphing is truly universal, it is this: paragraphs should be focused, unified, and coherent. That is, the sentences in a paragraph should be meaningfully related to one another, and the relationships among the sentences should be clear. The following sentences—although they may look like a paragraph—do not constitute a meaningful paragraph because they lack focus, unity, and coherence.

> Maturity and attitude go together because both determine why you want to become a model. I went to the university for two years, not because I wanted to but because I was pushed into it. I used to think models were thought of as dumb blondes, but after being here at the university I realized that people still have respect for modeling and know all the hard work put in it.

Even though each of these sentences mentions either modeling or the university or both, the two topics are not connected. With each sentence, the focus shifts—from the general desire to become a model, to the writer's attending a university, to the stereotypical attitude of people toward models. There is no paragraph unity because no single idea controls the sentences. The various elements of the writing do not "stick together" to form a coherent meaning, and the reader may well become disoriented. The topic-sentence strategies discussed in the following section are useful for ensuring paragraph coherence.

EXERCISE 7.3

Look again at the Gould passage earlier in this chapter. Analyze how Gould's paragraphing helps you follow his meaning. Is each paragraph focused, unified, and coherent? How could you have paragraphed this passage differently?

Topic-Sentence Strategies

A *topic sentence* lets readers know the focus of a paragraph in simple and direct terms. It is a cueing strategy for the paragraph much as a thesis or forecasting statement is for the whole essay. Because paragraphing usually signals a shift in focus, readers expect some kind of reorientation in the opening sentence. They need to know whether the new paragraph will introduce another aspect of the topic or develop one already introduced.

Announcing the Topic

Some topic sentences simply announce the topic. Here are a few examples taken from Barry Lopez's book *Arctic Dreams*:

> A polar bear walks in a way all its own.
>
> What is so consistently striking about the way Eskimos used parts of an animal is the breadth of their understanding about what would work.
>
> Distinctive landmarks that aid the traveler and control the vastness, as well as prominent marks on the land made inadvertently in the process of completing other tasks, are very much apparent in the Arctic.
>
> The Mediterranean view of the Arctic, down to the time of the Elizabethan mariners, was shaped by two somewhat contradictory thoughts.

These topic sentences do more than merely identify the topic; they also indicate how the topic will be developed in subsequent sentences—by citing examples, describing physical features, presenting reasons and evidence, relating anecdotes, classifying, defining, comparing, or contrasting.

Following is one of Lopez's paragraphs that shows how the topic sentence (underlined) is developed:

> <u>What is so consistently striking about the way Eskimos used parts of an animal is the breadth of their understanding about what would work.</u> Knowing that muskox horn is more flexible than caribou antler, they preferred it for making the side prongs of a fish spear. For a waterproof bag in which to carry sinews for clothing repair, they chose salmon skin. They selected the strong, translucent intestine of a bearded seal to make a window for a snowhouse—it would fold up for easy traveling and it would not frost over in cold weather. To make small snares for sea ducks, they needed a springy material that would not rot in salt water—baleen fibers. The down feather of a common eider, tethered at the end of a stick in the snow at an aglu, would reveal the exhalation of a quietly surfacing seal. Polar bear bone was used anywhere a stout, sharp point was required, because it is the hardest bone. —*Barry Lopez,* Arctic Dreams

---

EXERCISE 7.4

Read Adam Paul Weisman's essay in Chapter 6. Mark the paragraphs that begin with topic sentences. Then explain how these sentences help you anticipate the paragraph's topic and method of development.

Forecasting Subtopics

Other topic sentences actually give readers a detailed overview of subtopics that
follow. In the following paragraph the subtopics mentioned in the opening sentence appear later in the paragraph. The subtopics are underscored in the first
sentence and then connected by lines to the point in the paragraph where they
subsequently appear.

Notice that the subtopics are taken up in the same order as in the opening
sentence: education first, followed by economic independence, power of office,
and so on. This correlation makes the paragraph easy to follow. Even so, one
subtopic may be developed in a sentence while another requires two or more
sentences. The last two subtopics—equality of status and recognition as human
beings—are not directly brought up but are implied in the last sentence.

> Oppressed groups are denied education, economic independence, the
> power of office, representation, an image of dignity and self-respect, equality of
> status, and recognition as human beings. Throughout history women have been
> consistently denied all of these, and their denial today, while attenuated and
> partial, is nevertheless consistent. The education allowed them is deliberately
> designed to be inferior, and they are systematically programmed out of and
> excluded from the knowledge where power lies today—e.g., in science and
> technology. They are confined to conditions of economic dependence based on
> the sale of their sexuality in marriage, or a variety of prostitutions. Work on a
> basis of economic independence allows them only a subsistence level of life—
> often not even that. They do not hold office, are represented in no positions of
> power, and authority is forbidden them. The image of woman fostered by cul-
> tural media, high and low, then and now, is a marginal and demeaning exis-
> tence, and one outside the human condition—which is defined as the prerog-
> ative of man, the male. —*Kate Millett,* Sexual Politics

Asking a Rhetorical Question

Occasionally, writers put topic sentences in a question-answer format, posing a
rhetorical question in one sentence, which is then answered in the next sentence.
Question-answer topic sentences do not always appear at the beginning of a paragraph. A question at the end of one paragraph may combine with the first sentence of the following paragraph. Here is a paragraph illustrating the rhetorical
question strategy:

> Why, then do so many people believe in astrology? One obvious reason is
> that people read into the generally vague astrological pronouncements almost
> anything they want to, and thus invest them with a truth which is not inherent
> in the pronouncements themselves. They're also more likely to remember true
> "predictions," overvalue coincidences, and ignore everything else. Other rea-
> sons are its age (of course, ritual murder and sacrifice are as old), its simplicity
> in principle and comforting complexity in practice, and its flattering insistence
> on the connection between the starry vastness of the heavens and whether or
> not we'll fall in love this month.
>
> —*John Allen Paulos,* Innumeracy: Mathematical Illiteracy and Its Consequences

---

EXERCISE 7.5

Look at the selection by David Quammen in Chapter 3 or by Adam Paul Weisman in Chapter 6. Where does the writer use the rhetorical question as a topic-sentence strategy? How well does it work? Explain briefly.

Making a Transition

Not all topic sentences simply point forward to what will follow. Some also refer back to earlier sentences. Such sentences work both as topic sentences, stating the main point of the paragraph, and as transitions, linking that paragraph to the previous one. Here are a few topic sentences from "Quilts and Women's Culture" by Elaine Hedges that use specific transitions (underscored) to tie the sentence to a previous statement:

> Within its broad traditionalism and anonymity, <u>however</u>, variations and distinctions developed.
>
> Regionally, <u>too</u>, distinctions were introduced into quilt making through the interesting process of renaming.
>
> <u>With equal inventiveness</u> women renamed traditional patterns to accommodate to the local landscape.
>
> <u>Finally</u>, out of such regional and other variations come individual, signed achievements.
>
> Quilts, <u>then</u>, were an outlet for creative energy, a source and emblem of sisterhood and solidarity, and a graphic response to historical and political change.

Sometimes the first sentence of a paragraph serves as a transition, while a subsequent sentence—in this case, the last—states the topic. The underscored sentences illustrate this strategy in the following example:

> . . . What a convenience, what a relief it will be, they say, never to worry about how to dress for a job interview, a romantic tryst, or a funeral!
>
> <u>Convenient perhaps, but not exactly a relief.</u> Such a utopia would give most of us the same kind of chill we feel when a stadium full of Communist-bloc athletes in identical sports outfits, shouting slogans in unison, appears on TV. Most people do not want to be told what to wear any more than they want to be told what to say. In Belfast recently four hundred Irish Republican prisoners "refused to wear any clothes at all, draping themselves day and night in blankets," rather than put on prison uniforms. Even the offer of civilian-style dress did not satisfy them; they insisted on wearing their own clothes brought from home, or nothing. <u>Fashion is free speech, and one of the privileges, if not always one of the pleasures, of a free world.</u> —*Alison Lurie,* The Language of Clothes

Occasionally, whole paragraphs serve as transitions, linking one sequence of paragraphs with those that follow. See how the next transition paragraph summarizes what went before (evidence of contrast) and sets up what will follow (evidence of similarity):

Yet it was not all contrast, after all. Different as they were—in background, in personality, in underlying aspiration—these two great soldiers had much in common. Under everything else, they were marvelous fighters. Furthermore, their fighting qualities were really very much alike.

—Bruce Catton, "Grant and Lee: A Study in Contrasts"

Positioning the Topic Sentence

Although topic sentences may occur anywhere in a paragraph, stating the topic in the first sentence has the advantage of giving readers a sense of how the paragraph is likely to be developed. The beginning of the paragraph is therefore the most commonly favored position for a topic sentence.

A topic sentence that does not open a paragraph is most likely to appear at the end. When placed in the concluding position, a topic sentence usually summarizes or generalizes preceding information. In the following example, the topic is not stated explicitly until the last sentence.

Even black Americans sometimes need to be reminded about the deceptiveness of television. Blacks retain their fascination with black characters on TV: Many of us buy *Jet* magazine primarily to read its weekly television feature, which lists *every* black character (major or minor) to be seen on the screen that week. Yet our fixation with the presence of black characters on TV has blinded us to an important fact that *Cosby*, which began in 1984, and its offshoots over the years demonstrate convincingly: There is very little connection between the social status of black Americans and the fabricated images of black people that Americans consume each day. The representation of blacks on TV is a very poor index to our social advancement or political progress.

—Henry Louis Gates, Jr., "TV's Black World Turns—But Stays Unreal"

When a topic sentence is used in a narrative, it often appears as the last sentence as a way to evaluate or reflect on events:

I hadn't known she could play the piano. She wasn't playing very well, I guess, because she stopped occasionally and had to start over again. She concentrated intensely on the music, and the others in the room sat absolutely silently. My mother was facing me but didn't seem to see me. She seemed to be staring beyond me toward something that wasn't there. All the happy excitement died in me at that moment. Looking at my mother, so isolated from us all, I saw her for the first time as a person utterly alone. *—Russell Baker, Growing Up*

In rare cases, the topic sentence for one paragraph appears at the end of the preceding paragraph, as in this example:

. . . And apart from being new, psychoanalysis was particularly threatening. French psychiatrists tended to look at the sufferings of their patients either as the result of organic lesions or moral degeneration. In either case, the boundary between the "healthy" doctor and the "sick" patient was clear. Freud's theory makes it hard to draw such lines by insisting that if the psychiatrist knew himself better, he would find more points in common with the patient than he might have thought. . . . *—Sherry Turkle, Psychoanalytic Politics*

In addition, it is possible for a single topic sentence to introduce two (or more) paragraphs. Subsequent paragraphs in such a series consequently have no separate topic sentence of their own. Following is a two-paragraph sequence in which the topic sentence opens the first paragraph:

> <u>Anthropologists Daniel Maltz and Ruth Borker point out that boys and girls socialize differently.</u> Little girls tend to play in small groups or, even more common, in pairs. Their social life usually centers around a best friend, and friendships are made, maintained, and broken by talk—especially "secrets." If a little girl tells her friend's secret to another little girl, she may find herself with a new best friend. The secrets themselves may or may not be important, but the fact of telling them is all-important. It's hard for newcomers to get into these tight groups, but anyone who is admitted is treated as an equal. Girls like to play cooperatively; if they can't cooperate, the group breaks up.
>
> Little boys tend to play in larger groups, often outdoors, and they spend more time doing things than talking. It's easy for boys to get into the group, but not everyone is accepted as an equal. Once in the group, boys must jockey for their status in it. One of the most important ways they do this is through talk: verbal display such as telling stories and jokes, challenging and sidetracking the verbal displays of other boys, and withstanding other boys' challenges in order to maintain their own story—and status. Their talk is often competitive talk about who is best at what. —*Deborah Tannen,* That's Not What I Meant!

EXERCISE 7.6

Now that you have seen several topic-sentence strategies, look again at the Gould passage earlier in this chapter and identify the strategies he uses. Then evaluate how well his topic sentences work to orient you as a reader.

COHESIVE DEVICES

Certain cohesive devices can be used to guide readers, helping them follow the writer's train of thought by connecting key words and phrases throughout a passage. Among such devices are pronoun reference, word repetition, synonyms, repetition of sentence structure, and collocation.

Pronoun Reference

One common cohesive device is pronoun reference. As noun substitutes, pronouns refer to nouns that either precede or follow them, and thus serve to connect phrases or sentences. The nouns that come before the pronouns are called antecedents. In the following paragraph, the pronouns (all *it*) form a chain of connection with their antecedent, *George Washington Bridge*.

> In New York from dawn to dusk to dawn, day after day, you can hear the steady rumble of tires against the concrete span of the <u>George Washington</u>

Bridge. The bridge is never completely still. <u>It</u> trembles with traffic. <u>It</u> moves in the wind. <u>Its</u> great veins of steel swell when hot and contract when cold; <u>its</u> span often is ten feet closer to the Hudson River in summer than in winter.

—*Gay Talese, "New York"*

This example has only one pronoun-antecedent chain, and it comes first so all the pronouns refer back to it. When there are multiple pronoun-antecedent chains with references forward as well as back, writers have to be sure that readers will not mistake one pronoun's antecedent for another's.

Word Repetition

To avoid confusion, writers often repeat words and phrases. This device is used especially if a pronoun might confuse readers:

The first step is to realize that in our society we have permitted the kinds of vulnerability that characterize the victims of <u>violent crime</u> and have ignored, where we could, the hostility and alienation that enter into the making of <u>violent criminals</u>. No rational person condones <u>violent crime,</u> and I have no patience with sentimental attitudes toward <u>violent criminals.</u> But it is time that we open our eyes to the conditions that foster <u>violence</u> and that ensure the existence of easily recognizable victims.

—*Margaret Mead, "A Life for a Life: What That Means Today"*

In the next example several overlapping chains of word repetition prevent confusion and help the reader follow the ideas:

<u>Natural selection</u> is the central concept of Darwinian theory—the <u>fittest survive</u> and spread their favored traits through populations. <u>Natural selection</u> is defined by Spencer's phrase "<u>survival</u> of the <u>fittest,</u>" but what does this famous bit of jargon really mean? Who are the <u>fittest</u>? And how is "<u>fitness</u>" defined? We often read that <u>fitness</u> involves no more than "differential reproductive success"—the production of more <u>surviving</u> offspring than other competing members of the population. Whoa! cries Bethell, as many others have before him. This formulation defines <u>fitness</u> in terms of <u>survival</u> only. The crucial phrase of <u>natural selection</u> means no more than "the <u>survival</u> of those who <u>survive</u>"—a vacuous <u>tautology.</u> (A <u>tautology</u> is a phrase—like "my father is a man"—containing no information in the predicate ["a man"] not inherent in the subject ["my father"]. Tautologies are fine as definitions, but not as testable scientific statements— there can be nothing to test in a statement true by definition.)

—*Stephen Jay Gould, Ever Since Darwin*

Notice that Gould uses repetition to keep readers focused on the key concepts of "natural selection," "survival of the fittest," and "tautology." These key terms may vary in form—*fittest* becomes *fitness* and *survival* changes to *surviving* and *survive*— but they serve as links in the chain of meaning.

Synonyms

In addition to word repetition, you can use synonyms, words with identical or very similar meanings, to connect important ideas. In the following example, the author develops a careful chain of synonyms and word repetitions:

> Over time, small bits of knowledge about a region accumulate among local residents in the form of stories. These are remembered in the community; even what is unusual does not become lost and therefore irrelevant. These narratives comprise for a native an intricate, long-term view of a particular landscape. . . . Outside the region this complex but easily shared "reality" is hard to get across without reducing it to generalities, to misleading or imprecise abstraction.
>
> —*Barry Lopez,* Arctic Dreams

Note the variety of synonym sequences: "region," "particular landscape"; "local residents," "community," "native"; "stories," "narratives"; "accumulate," "remembered," "does not become lost," "comprise"; "intricate long-term view," "complex . . . reality," "without reducing it to generalities." The result is a coherence of paragraph development that constantly reinforces the author's point.

Sentence-Structure Repetition

Writers occasionally repeat the same sentence structure to emphasize the connections among their ideas. For example:

> But the life forms are as much part of the structure of the Earth as any inanimate portion is. It is all an inseparable part of a whole. If any animal is isolated totally from other forms of life, then death by starvation will surely follow. If isolated from water, death by dehydration will follow even faster. If isolated from air, whether free or dissolved in water, death by asphyxiation will follow still faster. If isolated from the Sun, animals will survive for a time, but plants would die, and if all plants died, all animals would starve.
>
> —*Isaac Asimov,* "The Case against Man"

From the third sentence to the last, Asimov repeats the "If this . . . then that" sentence structure to emphasize his various points.

Collocation

Words collocate when they occur together in expected ways around a particular topic. For example, in a paragraph on a high school graduation, a reader might expect to encounter such words as *valedictorian, diploma, commencement, honors, cap and gown,* and *senior class.* Collocations occur quite naturally to a writer, and they usually form a recognizable network of meaning for readers. The paragraph that follows uses five collocation chains:

1. housewife—cooking—neighbor—home
2. clocks—calculated cooking times—progression—precise
3. obstinacy—vagaries—problem
4. sun—clear days—cloudy ones—sundial—cast its light—angle—seasons—sun—weather
5. cooking—fire—matches—hot coals—smoldering—ashes—go out—bedwarming pan

The seventeenth-century housewife not only had to make do without ther-
mometers, she also had to make do without clocks, which were scarce and dear
throughout the sixteen hundreds. She calculated cooking times by the progression of the sun; her cooking must have been more precise on clear days than
on cloudy ones. Marks were sometimes painted on the floor, providing her with
a rough sundial, but she still had to make allowance for the obstinacy of the sun
in refusing to cast its light at the same angle as the seasons changed; but she
was used to allowing for the vagaries of sun and weather. She also had a problem
starting her fire in the morning; there were no matches. If she had allowed the
hot coals smoldering under the ashes to go out, she had to borrow some from
a neighbor, carrying them home with care, perhaps in a bed-warming pan.

—*Waverly Root and Richard de Rouchement,* Eating in America

EXERCISE 7.7

Now that you know more about pronoun reference, word repetition, synonyms,
sentence-structure repetition, and collocation, look again at the Gould passage
earlier in this chapter and identify the cohesive devices you find in it. How do
these cohesive devices help you read and make sense of the passage?

TRANSITIONS

A *transition*, sometimes called a connective, serves as a bridge, connecting one
paragraph, sentence, clause, or word with another. Not only does a transition
signal a connection, it also identifies the kind of connection by indicating to readers how the item preceding the transition relates to that which follows it. Transitions help readers anticipate how the next paragraph or sentence will affect the
meaning of what they have just read. There are three basic groups of transitions,
based on the relationships they indicate: logical, temporal, and spatial.

Logical Relationships

Transitions help readers follow the logic of an argument. How such transitions
work is illustrated in this tightly—and passionately—reasoned paragraph by
James Baldwin:

The black man insists, by whatever means he finds at his disposal, that the
white man cease to regard him as an exotic rarity <u>and</u> recognize him as a human
being. This is a very charged and difficult moment, <u>for</u> there is a great deal of
will power involved in the white man's naivete. Most people are not naturally
malicious, <u>and</u> the white man prefers to keep the black man at a certain human
remove <u>because</u> it is easier for him <u>thus</u> to preserve his simplicity <u>and</u> to avoid
being called to account for crimes committed by his forefathers, <u>or</u> his neighbors.
He is inescapably aware, <u>nevertheless</u>, that he is in a better position in the world
<u>than</u> black men are, <u>nor</u> can he quite put to death the suspicion that he is hated
by black men <u>therefore</u>. He does not wish to be hated, <u>neither</u> does he wish to

change places, <u>and</u> at this point in his uneasiness he can scarcely avoid having recourse to those legends which white men have created about black men, the most unusual effect of which is that the white man finds himself enmeshed, so to speak, in his own language which describes hell, <u>as well as</u> the attributes which lead one to hell, <u>as being</u> black as night.

—James Baldwin, "Stranger in the Village"

Transitions Showing Logical Relations

To introduce another item in a series: first, second; in the second place; for one thing . . . for another; next; then; furthermore; moreover; in addition; finally; last; also; similarly; besides; and; as well as

To introduce an illustration or other specification: in particular; specifically; for instance; for example; that is; namely

To introduce a result or a cause: consequently; as a result, hence; accordingly; thus; so; therefore; then; because; since; for

To introduce a restatement: that is; in other words; in simpler terms; to put it differently

To introduce a conclusion or summary: in conclusion; finally; all in all; evidently; clearly; actually; to sum up; altogether; of course

To introduce an opposing point: but; however; yet; nevertheless; on the contrary; on the other hand; in contrast; still; neither . . . nor

To introduce a concession to an opposing view: certainly; naturally; of course; it is true; to be sure; granted

To resume the original line of reasoning after a concession: nonetheless; all the same; even though; still; nevertheless

Temporal Relationships

In addition to showing logical connections, transitions may indicate temporal relationships—a sequence or progression in time—as this example illustrates:

<u>That night,</u> we drank tea and <u>then</u> vodka with lemon peel steeped in it. The four of us talked in Russian and English about mutual friends and American railroads and the Rolling Stones. Seryozha loves the Stones, and his face grew wistful <u>as we spoke</u> about their recent album, *Some Girls.* He played a tape of "Let It Bleed" <u>over and over,</u> until we could translate some difficult phrases for him; <u>after that,</u> he came out with the phrases <u>at intervals during the evening,</u> in a pretty decent imitation of Jagger's Cockney snarl. He was an adroit and oddly formal host, inconspicuously filling our teacups and politely urging us to eat bread and cheese and chocolate. <u>While he talked to us,</u> he teased Anya, calling her "Piglet," and she shook back her bangs and glowered at him. It was clear that theirs was a fiery relationship. <u>After a while,</u> we talked about ourselves. Anya told us about painting and printmaking and about how hard it was to buy supplies in Moscow. There had been something angry in her dark face <u>since the beginning of the evening;</u> I thought <u>at first</u> that it meant she didn't like Americans; but <u>now</u> I realized that it was a constant, barely suppressed rage at her own situation. —*Andrea Lee,* Russian Journal

Transitions Showing Temporal Relationships

To indicate frequency: frequently; hourly; often; occasionally; now and then; day after day; again and again

To indicate duration: during; briefly; for a long time; minute by minute

To indicate a particular time: now; then; at that time; in those days; last Sunday; next Christmas; in 1996; at the beginning of August; at six o'clock; first thing in the morning; two months ago

To indicate the beginning: at first; in the beginning; since; before then

To indicate the middle: in the meantime; meanwhile; as it was happening; at that moment; at the same time; simultaneously; next; then

To indicate the end and beyond: eventually; finally; at last; in the end; subsequently; later; afterwards

Spatial Relationships

Spatial transitions orient readers to the objects in a scene, as illustrated in this paragraph:

On Georgia 155, I crossed Troublesome Creek, then went through groves of pecan trees aligned one with the next like fenceposts. The pastures grew a green almost blue, and syrupy water the color of a dusty sunset filled the ponds. Around the farmhouses, from wires strung high above the ground, swayed gourds hollowed out for purple martins.

The land rose again on the other side of the Chattahoochee River, and Highway 34 went to the ridgetops where long views over the hills opened in all directions. Here was the tail of the Appalachian backbone, its gradual descent to the Gulf. Near the Alabama stateline stood a couple of LAST CHANCE! bars. . . . —*William Least Heat Moon,* Blue Highways

Transitions Showing Spatial Relationships

To indicate closeness: close to; near; next to; alongside; adjacent to; facing

To indicate distance: in the distance; far; beyond; away; there

To indicate direction: up/down; sideways; along; across; to the right/left; in front of/behind; above/below; inside/outside; toward

---

EXERCISE 7.8

Return to the Gould passage on pages 191–92, and underline the logical, temporal, and spatial transitions. How do they help to relate the many details and ideas?

---

8 Strategies for All-Purpose Invention

The invention strategies described in this chapter are not mysterious or magical. They are tricks of the trade available to everyone, and they should appeal to your common sense and experience in solving problems. Once you've mastered these all-purpose invention strategies—clustering, listing, cubing, dialoguing, dramatizing, looping, and questioning—you can use them to tackle any writing situation you encounter in college or on the job. The best time to use them is as you write an actual essay. Part One, Chapters 2–6, shows you when these strategies can be most helpful and how to make the most efficient use of them. The Guides to Writing in those chapters offer easy-to-use adaptations of these general strategies, adaptations designed to satisfy the special requirements of each kind of writing.

CLUSTERING

Clustering is a strategy for revealing possible relations among facts and ideas. Unlike listing (the next strategy), clustering requires a brief period of initial planning. You must first come up with a tentative division of the topic into subparts or main ideas. Clustering works as follows:

1. In a word or phrase, write your topic in the center of a piece of paper. Circle it.
2. Also in words or phrases, write down the main parts or central ideas of your topic. Circle these, and connect them to the topic in the center.
3. The next step is to generate facts, details, examples, or ideas related in any way to these main parts. Cluster these around the main parts.

Clustering can be useful for any kind of writing. You can use it in the early stages of planning an essay to find subtopics and to organize information. You may try out and discard several clusters before finding one that is promising. Many writers use clustering to plan brief sections of an essay as they are drafting or revising. A model of clustering appears on page 206.

LISTING

Listing is a familiar activity. We make shopping lists and lists of errands to do or people to call. Listing can also be a great help in planning an essay. It enables you

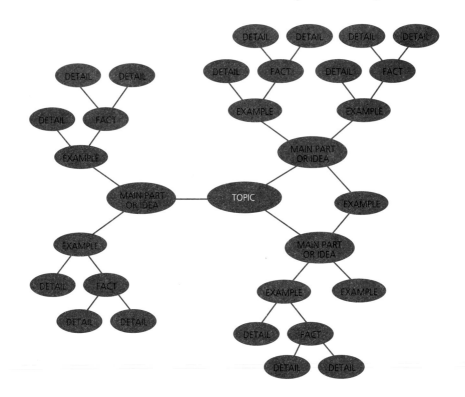

A Model of Clustering

to recall what you already know about a topic and suggests what else you may need to find out. It is an easy way to get started with your invention writing, instead of just worrying about what you will write. A list rides along on its own momentum, the first item leading naturally to the next.

A basic activity for all writers, listing is especially useful to those who have little time for planning—for example, reporters facing deadlines and college students taking essay exams. Listing lets you order your ideas quickly. It can also help as a first step in discovering possible writing topics.

Listing is a solitary form of brainstorming, a popular technique of problem solving in groups. When you work with a group to generate ideas for a collaborative writing project, you are engaged in true brainstorming. Here is how listing works best for invention work:

1. Give your list a title that indicates your main idea or topic.
2. Write as fast as you can, relying on short phrases.
3. Include anything that seems at all useful. Do not try to be judgmental at this point.

4. After you have finished, or even as you write, reflect on the list and organize it in the following way. This is a very important step, for it may lead you to further discoveries about your topic.

    Put an asterisk by the most promising items.
    Number key items in order of importance.
    Put items in related groups.
    Cross out items that do not seem promising.
    Add new items.

CUBING

Cubing is useful for quickly exploring a writing topic, probing it from six different perspectives. It is known as cubing because a cube has six sides. Following are the six perspectives in cubing:

Describing: What does your subject look like? What size is it? Color? Shape? Texture? Name its parts.

Comparing: What is your subject similar to? Different from?

Associating: What does your subject make you think of? What connections does it have to anything else in your experience? Be creative here—include any connection you can think of.

Analyzing: How is your subject made? Where did it come from? Where is it going? How are its parts related?

Applying: What can you do with your subject? What uses does it have?

Arguing: What arguments can you make for your subject? Against it?

Following are some guidelines to help you use cubing productively:

1. Select a topic, subject, or part of a subject. This can be a person, scene, event, object, problem, idea, or issue. Hold it in focus.

2. Limit your writing to three to five minutes for each perspective. The whole activity should take no more than a half hour.

3. Keep going until you have written about your subject from *all six* perspectives. Remember that the special advantage of cubing is the quick *multiple* perspectives it generates.

4. As you write from each perspective, begin with what you know about your subject. However, do not limit yourself to your present knowledge. Indicate what else you need to know about your subject, and suggest where you might find that information.

5. Reread what you have written. Look for bright spots, surprises. Recall the part that was easiest for you to write. Recall the part where you felt a special momentum and pleasure in the writing. Look for an angle or an unexpected insight. These special parts may suggest a focus or a topic within a larger subject, or they may provide specific details to include in a draft.

DIALOGUING

A dialogue is a conversation between two or more people. You can use dialoguing to search for topics, find a focus, explore ideas, or consider opposing viewpoints. As an invention strategy, writing a dialogue requires you to make up most or all parts of the conversation. Imagine two particular people talking, or hold a conversation yourself with some imagined person, or simply talk out loud to yourself. Follow these steps:

1. Write a conversation between two speakers. Label the speakers "A" and "B," or make up names for them.
2. If you get stuck, you might have one of the speakers ask the other a question.
3. Write brief responses in order to keep the conversation moving fast. Do not spend much time planning or rehearsing responses. Write what first occurs to you— just as in a real conversation, where people take quick turns to prevent any awkward silences.

Dialogues can be especially useful with personal experience and persuasive essays because they help you remember conversations and anticipate objections.

DRAMATIZING

Dramatizing is an invention activity developed by the philosopher Kenneth Burke as a way of thinking about how people interact and as a way of analyzing literature and the arts.

Thinking about human behavior in dramatic terms can be very productive for writers. Drama has action, actors, setting, motives, and methods. Since stars and acting go together, you can use a five-pointed star to remember these five points of dramatizing:

Each point on the star provides a different perspective on human behavior. We can think of each point independently and in combination. Let us begin by looking at each point to see how it helps us analyze people and their interactions.

Action.   An action is anything that happens, has happened, will happen, or could happen. Action includes events that are physical (running a marathon), mental (thinking about a book you have read), and emotional (falling in love). This category also refers to the results of an activity (a term paper).

Actor.   The actor is involved in the action. He or she may be responsible for the action or simply be affected by it. The actor does not have to be a person. It can be a force, something that causes an action. For example, if the action is a rise in the price of gasoline, the actor could be increased demand or short supply. Dramatizing may also include a number of co-actors working together or at odds.

Setting.   The setting is the situation or background of the action. We usually think of setting as the place and time of an event, but it may also be the historical background of an event or the childhood of a person.

Motive.   The motive is the purpose or reason for an action. It refers to the intention actors may have or the end an action serves.

Method.   The method explains how an action occurs, including the techniques an actor uses. It refers to whatever makes things happen.

Each of these five points suggests a simple invention question:

Action   = What?
Actor   = Who?
Setting = When and where?
Motive   = Why?
Method   = How?

This list looks like the questions reporters typically ask. But dramatizing goes further because it enables us to ask a much fuller set of invention questions generated by considering relations between these five elements. We can think about actors' motives, the effect of setting on the actors, the relations between actors, and so on.

You can use this invention strategy to learn more about yourself or about other significant people in your life. You can use it, as well, to explore, analyze, or evaluate characters in stories or movies. Moreover, dramatizing is especially useful in analyzing the readers you want to inform or convince.

To use dramatizing, imagine the person you want to understand better in a particular situation. Holding this image in mind, write answers to any questions in the following list that apply. You may draw a blank on some questions, have little to say to some, and a lot to say to others. Be exploratory and playful with the questions. Write responses quickly, relying on words and phrases, even drawings.

- What is the actor doing?
- How did the actor come to be involved in this situation?
- Why does the actor do what he or she does?

- What else might the actor do?
- What is the actor trying to accomplish?
- How do other actors influence—help or hinder—the main actor?
- What do the actor's actions reveal about him or her?
- What does the actor's language reveal about him or her?
- How does the event's setting influence the actor's actions?
- How does the time of the event influence what the actor does?
- Where did this actor come from?
- How is this actor different from what he or she used to be?
- What might this actor become?
- How is this actor like or unlike the other actors?

LOOPING

Looping—the strategy of writing quickly but *returning* to your topic—is especially useful for the first stages of exploring a topic. From almost any starting point, no matter how general or unfocused, looping enables you to find a center of interest and eventually a thesis. The steps are simple:

1. Write down your area of interest. You may know only that you have to write about another person or a movie or cultural trend that has caught your attention. Or, you may want to search for a topic in a broad historical period or one related to a major political event. Although you may wander from this topic as you write, you will want to keep coming back to it. Your purpose is to find a focus for writing, perhaps even a thesis.

2. Write nonstop for ten minutes. Start with the first thing that comes to mind. Write rapidly, without looking back to reread or correct anything. *Do not stop writing. Keep your pencil moving.* That is the key to looping. If you get stuck for a moment, rewrite the last sentence. Trust the act of writing to lead you to new insights. Follow diversions and digressions, but keep returning to your topic now and then.

3. At the end of ten minutes, pause to reread what you have written. Decide what is most important—a single insight, a pattern of ideas, an emerging theme, a visual detail, anything at all that stands out. Some writers call this a "center of gravity" or a "hot spot." To complete the first loop, express this center in a single sentence.

4. Beginning with this sentence, write nonstop for ten minutes.

5. Summarize in one sentence again to complete the second loop.

6. Keep looping until one of your summary sentences produces a focus or thesis. You may need only two or three loops; you may need more.

QUESTIONING

Asking questions about a subject is a way to learn about it and decide what to write. However, when you first encounter a subject, your questions may be scattered. Also, you are not likely to think right away of all the important questions you ought to ask. The advantage of a basic list of questions for invention, like the ones for cubing and for dramatizing discussed earlier in this chapter, is that it provides a systematic approach to exploring a subject.

The questions that follow come from both classical rhetoric (what Greek philosopher Aristotle called *topics*) and a modern approach to invention called *tagmemics*. Based on the work of American linguist Kenneth Pike, tagmemics provides questions about all the ways we make sense of the world, all the ways we sort and classify experience and come to understand it.

Here are the steps in using questions for invention:

1. Think about your subject. (A subject could be any event, person, problem, project, idea, or issue—in other words, anything you might write about.)

2. Start with the first question in the following list, and move right through the list. Try to answer each question at least briefly with a word or phrase. Some questions may invite several sentences, or even a page or more of writing. You may draw a blank on a few questions. Skip them. Later, with more experience with questions for invention, you can start anywhere in the list.

3. Write your responses quickly, without much planning. Follow digressions or associations. Do not screen anything out. Be playful.

What is your subject?

- What is your subject's name? What other names does it have? What names did it have in the past?
- What aspects of the subject do these different names emphasize?
- Imagine a still photograph or moving picture of your subject. What would it look like?
- What would you put into a time capsule to stand for your subject?
- What are its causes and results?
- How would it look from different vantage points or perspectives?
- What particular experiences have you had with the subject? What have you learned?

What parts or characteristics does your subject have and how are they related?

- Name the parts or characteristics of your subject.
- Describe each one, using the questions in the preceding subject list.
- How is each part or characterisic related to the others?

How is your subject similar to and different from other subjects?

- What is your subject similar to? In what ways are they alike?
- What is your subject different from? In what ways are they different?
- Of all the things in the world, what seems to you most unlike your subject? In what ways are they unlike each other? Now, just for fun, note how they are alike.

How much can your subject change and still remain the same?

- How has your subject changed from what it once was?
- How is it changing now—from moment to moment, day to day, year to year?
- How much can it change and still remain the same?
- What are some different forms your subject takes?
- What does it become when it is no longer itself?

Where does your subject fit in the world?

- When and where did your subject originate?
- What would happen if at some future time your subject ceased to exist?
- When and where do you usually experience the subject?
- What is this subject a part of and what are its parts?
- What is the relationship between the subject and that of which it is a part?
- What do other people think of your subject?

Strategies for Reading Critically

All writers rely on information in books, articles, letters, and other documents. Working with such sources calls on you to be a writer *and* a reader— to gather, analyze, select, and organize the information you find.

This chapter presents strategies to help you read *with a critical eye*. That means not just comprehending passively and remembering what you read, but also scrutinizing actively and making thoughtful judgments about your reading. The strategies for reading critically include:

- *Annotating:* Recording your reactions to, interpretations of, and questions about a text as you read it.
- *Contextualizing:* Placing a text in its historical, biographical, and cultural contexts.
- *Reflecting on challenges to your beliefs and values:* Critically examining the bases of your personal responses to a text.
- *Outlining and summarizing:* Identifying the main ideas in a text and restating them in your own words.
- *Evaluating the logic of an argument:* Determining whether a claim is adequately supported by evidence.
- *Recognizing emotional manipulation:* Identifying texts that unfairly and inappropriately use emotional appeals based on false or exaggerated claims.
- *Judging the writer's credibility:* Considering whether writers represent different points of view fairly and know what they're writing about.

These critical reading strategies can help you connect information from different sources and relate it to what you already know; distinguish fact from opinion; uncover hidden assumptions; examine your own beliefs and values; and subject both what you read and what you know to reasoned inquiry. You can readily learn these strategies and apply them not only to the selections in Part One of this text but also to your other college reading. Although mastering the strategies will not make critical reading easy, it can make your reading much more satisfying and productive and thus help you handle even difficult material with confidence.

ANNOTATING

Annotations are the underlinings, highlightings, and comments you make directly on the text you're reading. *Annotating* can be used to record immediate reactions and questions, outline and summarize main points, and evaluate and relate the

213

reading to other ideas and points of view. Especially useful for studying and preparing to write, it is also an essential element of many other critical reading strategies. In fact, all of the sections on other strategies in this chapter refer back to these annotations.

Your annotations can take many forms: underlining key words, phrases, or sentences; writing comments or questions in the margins; bracketing important sections of the text; connecting ideas with lines or arrows; numbering related points in sequence; and making note of anything that strikes you as interesting, important, or questionable. (If writing on the text itself is impossible or undesirable, you can annotate on a photocopy.)

Most readers annotate in layers, adding further annotations on second and third readings. Annotations can be light or heavy, depending on the reader's purpose and the difficulty of the material. Your purpose for reading also determines how you use your annotations. You can, for example, build on and extend your annotations by *taking inventory*: analyzing and classifying your annotations, searching systematically for patterns in the text, and interpreting their significance. An inventory is basically a list. When you take inventory, you make various kinds of lists to explore patterns of meaning you find in the text. For instance, in reading and annotating the following passage from a text by Martin Luther King, Jr., you might notice that many famous people are named or that certain similes and metaphors are used. By listing the names (Socrates, Jesus, Luther, Lincoln, and so on) and then grouping them into categories (people who died for their beliefs, leaders, teachers, and religious figures) you could better understand why the writer refers to these particular people. Obviously, taking inventory of your annotations would be very helpful in writing about a text you're reading.

Following is an illustration of annotating. The text that has been annotated comes from a famous essay by the Reverend Martin Luther King, Jr. King wrote it in 1963, when he was imprisoned after nonviolent marches and sit-ins he had led to protest racial segregation in Birmingham, Alabama, were met by violence. A group of local clergymen, fearing more violence, urged King to abandon his efforts and return to his home in Montgomery, Alabama. King responded with a long letter, which has became known as "Letter from Birmingham Jail."

1. White moderates block progress. . . . I must confess that over the past few years I have been gravely 1 disappointed with the <u>white moderate</u>. I have almost reached the regrettable conclusion that the Negro's [great stumbling block in his stride toward freedom] is not the White Citizen's Counciler or the Ku Klux Klanner, but the white moderate, who is more devoted to "<u>order</u>" than *order vs. justice* *negative vs. positive* to <u>justice</u>; who prefers a <u>negative peace</u> which is the <u>absence of tension</u> to a <u>positive peace</u> which is the <u>presence of justice</u>; who constantly says: "I agree with you in the <u>goal</u> you seek, but I cannot agree with *ends vs. means* *treating others like children* your <u>methods</u> of direct action"; who (paternalistically) believes he can set the timetable for another man's freedom; who lives by a mythical concept of time and who constantly advises the Negro to wait for a "more convenient season." <u>Shallow understanding from people of good will</u> is more frustrating than <u>absolute misunderstanding</u> from people <u>of ill will.</u> Lukewarm acceptance is much more bewildering than outright rejection.

2. Tension necessary for progress.

I had hoped that the white moderate would understand that <u>law and order exist for the purpose of establishing justice</u> and that when they fail in this purpose they become the [dangerously structured <u>dams</u> that block the flow of social progress.] I had hoped that the white moderate would understand that the <u>present tension</u> in the South is a <u>necessary phase of the transition</u> from an obnoxious <u>negative peace,</u> in which the Negro passively accepted his unjust plight, to a substantive and <u>positive peace</u> in which all men will respect the dignity and worth

Tension already exists anyway.

of human personality. Actually, <u>we who engage in nonviolent direct action are not the creators of tension. We merely bring to the surface the hidden tension</u> that is already alive. We bring it out in the open, where it can be seen and dealt with. [Like a boil that can never be cured

True?

so long as it is covered up but must be opened with all its ugliness to the natural medicines of air and light, injustice must be exposed, with all the tension its exposure creates, to the <u>light of human conscience</u> and the air of national opinion before it can be cured.]

Simile: hidden tension is like a boil

3. Questions clergymen's logic: Condemning his actions = condemning victims, Socrates, Jesus.

In your statement you assert that <u>our actions,</u> even though peaceful, must be <u>condemned</u> because they precipitate violence. But is this a logical assertion? <u>Isn't this like condemning</u> a robbed man because his possession of money precipitated the evil act of robbery? <u>Isn't this like condemning</u> (Socrates) because his unswerving commitment to truth and his philosophical inquiries precipitated the act by the misguided populace in which they made him drink hemlock? <u>Isn't this like condemning</u> Jesus because his unique God-consciousness and never-ceasing devotion to God's will precipitated the evil act of crucifixion? We must come to see that, as the federal courts have consistently affirmed, it is wrong to urge an individual to cease his efforts to gain his <u>basic constitutional rights</u> because the question may precipitate violence. [<u>Society must protect the robbed and punish the robber.</u>]

Yes!

example of a white moderate

I had also hoped that the white moderate would reject the <u>myth concerning time</u> in relation to the struggle for freedom. I have just received a letter from a white brother in Texas. He writes: "All Christians know that the colored people will receive equal rights eventually, but it is possible that you are in <u>too great a religious hurry.</u> It has taken Christianity almost two thousand years to accomplish what it has. The teachings of Christ take time to come to earth." Such an attitude stems from a tragic misconception of time, from the strangely irrational notion that there is something in the very flow of time that will inevitably cure all ills. Actually, time itself is neutral; it can be used either destructively or constructively. More and more I feel that the people of ill will have used time much more effectively than have the people of good will. We will have to repent in this generation not merely for the hateful words and actions of the bad people but for the appalling silence of the good people. Human progress never rolls in on wheels of inevitability; it comes through the tireless efforts of men willing to be co-workers with God, and without this hard work, time itself becomes an ally of the forces of social stagnation. We must use time creatively, in the knowledge that the time is always ripe to do right. Now is the time to make real the promise of democracy and transform our pending national elegy into a creative psalm of brotherhood. Now is the time to lift our national policy from the quicksand of racial injustice to the solid rock of human dignity.

Silence as bad as hateful words and actions.

4. Time must be used to do right.

metaphor

not moving

metaphors

You speak of our activity in Birmingham as extreme. At first I was   5 rather disappointed that fellow clergymen would see my nonviolent efforts as those of an extremist. I began thinking about the fact that I stand in the middle of two opposing forces in the Negro community. One is a force of complacency, made up in part of Negroes who, as a result of long years of oppression, are so drained of self-respect and a sense of "somebodiness" that they have adjusted to segregation; and in part of a few middle-class Negroes, who because of a degree of academic and economic security and because in some ways they profit by segregation, have become insensitive to the problems of the masses. The other force is one of bitterness and hatred, and it comes perilously close to advocating violence. It is expressed in the various black na-tionalist groups that are springing up across the nation, the largest and best-known being Elijah Muhammad's Muslim movement. Nourished by the Negro's frustration over the continued existence of racial dis-crimination, this movement is made up of people who have lost faith in America, who have absolutely repudiated Christianity, and who have concluded that the white man is an incorrigible "devil."

5. King in middle of two extremes: complacent & angry.

King accused of being an extremist.

Malcolm X?

I have tried to stand between these two forces, saying that we need   6 emulate neither the "do-nothingism" of the complacent nor the hatred and despair of the black nationalist. For there is the more excellent

6. King offers better choice.

How did nonviolence become

way of love and nonviolent protest. I am grateful to God that, through *part of* the influence of the Negro church, the way of nonviolence became an *King's* integral part of our struggle. *movement?*

7. *King's movement prevented racial violence.*

Threat?

If this philosophy had not emerged, by now many streets of the 7 South would, I am convinced, be flowing with blood. And I am further *Gandhi?* convinced that if our white brothers dismiss as "rabble-rousers" and *The church?* "outside agitators" those of us who employ nonviolent direct action, and if they refuse to support our nonviolent efforts, millions of Negroes will, out of frustration and despair, seek solace and security in black- *comfort* nationalist ideologies—a development that would inevitably lead to a frightening racial nightmare.

If . . . then

Oppressed people cannot remain oppressed forever. The yearning 8 for freedom eventually manifests itself, and that is what has happened to the American Negro. Something within has reminded him of his birthright of freedom, and something without has reminded him that it can be gained. Consciously or unconsciously, he has been caught up *worldwide* by the Zeitgeist and with his black brothers of Africa and his brown *spirit of* *uprising* and yellow brothers of Asia, South America and the Caribbean, the *the times* *against* United States Negro is moving with a sense of great urgency toward *injustice* the promised land of racial justice. If one recognizes this vital urge that has engulfed the Negro community, one should readily understand why public demonstrations are taking place. The Negro has many pent- up resentments and latent frustrations, and he must release them. So let him march; let him make prayer pilgrimages to the city hall; let him go on freedom rides—and try to understand why he must do so. If his repressed emotions are not released in nonviolent ways, they will seek *Not a* expression through violence; this is not a threat but a fact of history. *threat?*

8. *Discontent is normal & healthy, but must be channeled.*

So I have not said to my people: "Get rid of your discontent." Rather, I have tried to say that this normal and healthy discontent can be chan- neled into the creative outlet of nonviolent direct action. And now this approach is being termed extremist.

But though I was initially disappointed at being categorized as an 9 extremist, as I continued to think about the matter I gradually gained a measure of satisfaction from the label. Was not Jesus an extremist for love: "Love your enemies, bless them that curse you, do good to them that hate you, and pray for them which despitefully use you, and per- *Hebrew* secute you." Was not Amos an extremist for justice: "Let justice roll *prophet* down like waters and righteousness like an ever-flowing stream." Was

Christ's disciple

English preacher

not Paul an extremist for the Christian gospel: "I bear in my body the marks of the Lord Jesus." Was not Martin Luther an extremist: "Here I stand; I cannot do otherwise, so help me God." And John Bunyan: "I will stay in jail to the end of my days before I make a butchery of my conscience." And Abraham Lincoln: "This nation cannot survive half slave and half free." And Thomas Jefferson: "We hold these truths to be self-evident, that all men are created equal . . ." So the question is not whether we will be extremists, but what kind of extremists we will be. Will we be extremists for hate or for love? Will we be extremists for the preservation of injustice or for the extension of justice? In that dramatic scene on Calvary's hill three men were crucified. We must never forget that all three were crucified for the same crime—the crime of extremism. Two were extremists for immorality, and thus fell below their environment. The other, Jesus Christ was an extremist for love, truth and goodness, and thereby rose above his environment. Perhaps the South, the nation and the world are in dire need of creative extremists.

Founded Protestantis

9. Creative extremists are needed.

No choice but to be extremists. But what kind?

Disappointed in the white moderate.

I had hoped that the white moderate would see this need. Perhaps 10 I was too optimistic; perhaps I expected too much. I suppose I should have realized that few members of the oppressor race can understand the deep groans and passionate yearnings of the oppressed race, and still fewer have the vision to see that injustice must be rooted out by strong, persistent and determined action. I am thankful, however, that some of our white brothers in the South have grasped the meaning of this social revolution and committed themselves to it. They are still all too few in quantity, but they are big in quality. Some—such as Ralph McGill, Lillian Smith, Harry Golden, James McBride Dabbs, Ann Braden and Sarah Patton Boyle—have written about our struggle in eloquent and prophetic terms. Others have marched with us down nameless streets of the South. They have languished in filthy, roach-infested jails, suffering the abuse and brutality of policemen who view them as "dirty nigger-lovers." Unlike so many of their moderate brothers and sisters, they have recognized the urgency of the moment and sensed the need for powerful "action" antidotes to combat the disease of segregation. . . .

10. Some whites have supported King.

Who are they?

what they did

left unaided

CONTEXTUALIZING

All texts were written sometime in the past and often embody historical and cultural assumptions, values, and attitudes different from your own. To read critically, you need to become aware of these differences. *Contextualizing* is a critical reading strategy that enables you to make inferences about a reading's historical and cultural context and to examine the differences between its context and your own. To contextualize:

1. Annotate any language or ideas in the text that seem different to you—reflecting attitudes, assumptions, or values that strike you as different or out of style.

2. Reflect on what you know about the time and place in which the selection was written. Your knowledge may come from other reading, television or film, school, or elsewhere. (If you know nothing about the historical and cultural context, you could do some library research.)

3. In a paragraph or two, explore the differences you see between the writer's assumptions, values, and attitudes and those current in your culture today. Consider how these differences affect your understanding and judgment of the reading.

The excerpt from King's "Letter from Birmingham Jail" is a good example of a text that benefits from being read contextually. If you knew little about the history of slavery and segregation in the United States, of Martin Luther King, Jr., or of the civil rights movement, it would be very difficult to understand the passion for justice and impatience with delay expressed in this essay. Most Americans have seen television documentaries or newsclips showing demonstrators being attacked by dogs, doused by fire hoses, beaten by helmeted police. Such images provide a sense of the violence, fear, and hatred that King was responding to.

Comparing the context when King was in Birmingham Jail to present times reveals that things have changed since the sixties. Segregation has ceased to be legal. The term *Negro* is no longer used. Many African Americans hold powerful leadership positions. Nevertheless, as in Dr. King's time, many African Americans today are still pressing for fair treatment and equal opportunity.

REFLECTING ON CHALLENGES TO YOUR BELIEFS AND VALUES

To read critically, you need to scrutinize your own assumptions and attitudes as well as those expressed in the text you're reading. The difficulty is that our assumptions and attitudes are so ingrained, we're usually not aware of them. A good strategy for getting at these underlying beliefs and values is to identify and reflect on the ways the text challenges you—makes you feel disturbed, threatened, ashamed, combative, or whatever.

1. Identify challenges by annotating the text, marking each point where you feel your beliefs and values are being opposed, criticized, or unfairly characterized.

2. Select one or two of the most troubling challenges you've identified and write a few paragraphs trying to understand why you feel as you do. Don't defend your feelings; instead, analyze them to see where they come from.

    For example, if you are disturbed (as many of his original readers were) by King's criticism in paragraph 1 of readers who are "more devoted to 'order' than to justice," consider why. Which do you value more: order or justice? How does your preference reflect your situation, upbringing, religious beliefs, gender, sexual orientation, social class, race, or ethnicity? For what purposes—if any—do you think it would be okay to disturb the peace other people enjoy? What should those who experience injustice do to remedy their situation?

OUTLINING AND SUMMARIZING

Summarizing is a helpful strategy for understanding the content and structure of a reading. Many writers find it useful to outline a text as a preliminary to summarizing. *Outlining* reveals the basic structure of the text, whereas summarizing synopsizes its main action, details, or argument.

Outlining may be part of your annotating process, or it may be done separately. Writing a brief outline in the margins of the text as you read and annotate makes it easier to find things later. An outline written on a separate piece of paper gives you more space to work with and therefore allows for more detail. Either way, your goal is to identify the text's main ideas.

The key to both outlining and summarizing is being able to distinguish between the main ideas and the supporting ideas and examples. The main ideas form the backbone, the strand that holds the various parts of the text together. Outlining the main ideas helps you discover this structure. As you outline, you need to decide which are the most important ideas. Since importance is a relative term, different readers can make different—and equally reasonable—decisions based on what interests them in the reading. Outlining is further complicated when you use your own words rather than words from the text, for rephrasing can shift meaning or emphasis. Reading is never a passive or neutral act; the processes of outlining and summarizing show it to be a constructive one.

You don't have to make a complicated outline with roman numerals and letters. An informal scratch outline that identifies the main idea of each paragraph will do. Paragraphs typically organize material around a single topic, with the topic usually stated in a word or phrase and referred to throughout the paragraph. For example, the opening paragraph of the King excerpt (on p. 214) makes clear that its topic is "the white moderate."

Once you've found the topic of the paragraph, you need to figure out what is being said about it. To return to our example: if the white moderate is the topic of the opening paragraph, then what King says about it can be found in the second sentence, where he announces the conclusion he has come to—namely, that the white moderate is "the Negro's great stumbling block in his stride toward freedom." The rest of the paragraph specifies the ways the white moderate blocks progress.

When you outline a reading, it is best to use your own words. An outline of the King excerpt appears in the margins of the selection, with numbers for each paragraph. Here is the same outline, slightly expanded and reworded:

Sample Informal Outline

1. White moderates block progress in the struggle for racial justice.
2. Tension is necessary for progress.
3. The clergy's criticism is not logical.
4. Time must be used to do right.
5. Clergy accuse King of being extreme, but he stands between two extreme forces in the African American community.
6. King offers a better choice.
7. King's movement has prevented racial violence by African Americans.
8. Discontent is normal and healthy but it must be channeled creatively rather than destructively.
9. Creative extremists are needed.
10. Some whites have supported King.

Unlike an outline, a summary goes beyond merely listing the main ideas to recomposing them to form a new text. Whereas outlining depends on close analysis of each paragraph, summarizing requires creative synthesis. Putting the ideas together again—in your own words and in a condensed form—shows how reading critically truly is a constructive process of making meaning and leading to deeper understanding of any text.

One reader's summary is likely to differ—sometimes significantly—from another reader's. By using their own words when summarizing and by focusing on different aspects of the text, two readers may summarize the same text differently. They may well have different purposes for reading. Also, there is no exact formula for how long and detailed a summary should be.

Following is a sample summary of the King excerpt. It is based on the preceding outline, but is much more detailed. Most important, it fills in connections between the ideas that King left for readers to make.

Sample Summary

King expresses his disappointment with white moderates who, by opposing his program of nonviolent direct action, have become a barrier to progress toward racial justice. He acknowledges that his program has raised tension in the South, but he explains that tension is necessary to bring about change. Furthermore, he argues that tension already exists. But because it has been unexpressed, it is unhealthy and potentially dangerous.

He defends his actions against the clergymen's criticisms, particularly their argument that he is in too much
of a hurry. Responding to charges of extremism, King
claims that he has actually prevented racial violence by
channeling the natural frustrations of oppressed African
Americans into nonviolent protest. He asserts that extremism is precisely what is needed now--but it must be
creative, rather than destructive, extremism. He concludes by again expressing disappointment with white moderates for not joining his effort as many other whites
have.

EVALUATING THE LOGIC OF AN ARGUMENT

An argument has two basic parts: a claim and support. The *claim* asserts a conclusion—an idea, an opinion, a judgment, or a point of view—that the writer
wants readers to accept. The *support* includes *reasons* and *evidence* (facts, examples,
statistics, and expert testimony) that give readers the basis for accepting the conclusion. Three conditions must be met for an argument to be considered logically
acceptable—what we call the ABC test:

A.   The support must be *appropriate* to the claim.
B.   All of the statements must be *believable*.
C.   The statements must be *consistent* with one another and not contradictory.

Testing for Appropriateness

As a critical reader, you must decide whether the statements intended to support
the claim are actually appropriate and clearly related to it. To test for appropriateness, ask: How does each reason or piece of evidence relate to the claim? Is the
connection between support and claim clear and compelling? Or is the support
irrelevant or only vaguely related to the claim?

Appropriateness of support comes most often into question when the writer
argues by analogy or by invoking authority. For example, in paragraph 2, King
argues that if law and order fail to establish justice, "they become the dangerously
structured dams that block the flow of social progress." The analogy asserts
the following logical relationship: law and order are to progress toward justice
what a dam is to water. If you do not accept this analogy, then the argument
fails the test of appropriateness. King uses both analogy and authority in the
following passage: "Isn't this like condemning Socrates because his unswerving
commitment to truth and his philosophical inquiries precipitated the act by the
misguided populace in which they made him drink hemlock?" (paragraph 3).
You must not only judge the appropriateness of comparing the Greek populace's
condemnation of Socrates to the white moderates' condemnation of King's actions, but you must also judge whether it is appropriate to accept Socrates as an
authority on this subject. Since Socrates is generally respected for his teaching on

justice, his words and actions are likely to be considered appropriate to King's situation in Birmingham.

There are several common flaws or fallacies in reasoning that cause an argument to fail the test of appropriateness:

- *False analogy*, when two cases are not sufficiently parallel to lead readers to accept the claim.
- *False use of authority*, when writers invoke as expert in the field being discussed a person whose expertise or authority lies not in the given field but in another.
- *Non sequitur* (Latin for "it does not follow"), when one statement is not logically connected to another.
- *Red herring*, when a writer raises an irrelevant issue to draw attention away from the central issue.
- *Post hoc, ergo propter hoc* (Latin for "after this, therefore because of this"), when the writer implies that because one event follows another, the first caused the second. Chronology is not the same as causality.

Testing for Believability

You also must look critically at each statement supporting the claim to see whether it is believable. While you may find some statements self-evidently true, the truth of others will be less certain. To test for believability, ask: On what basis am I being asked to accept this assertion as true? If it can't be proved true or false, how much weight does it carry?

In judging facts, statistics, examples, and authorities, consider the following:

Facts are statements that can be proven objectively to be true. The believability of facts depends on their *accuracy* (they should not distort or misrepresent reality), *completeness* (they should not omit important details), and the *trustworthiness* of their sources (sources should be qualified and unbiased). King, for instance, asserts as fact that the African American will not wait much longer for racial justice (paragraph 8). His critics might question the factuality of this assertion by asking: Is it true of all African Americans? How much longer will they wait? How does King know what African Americans will and will not do?

Statistics, often mistaken as facts, are actually only interpretations of numerical data. The believability of statistics depends on the *comparability* of the data (apples cannot be compared to oranges), the *accuracy* of the methods of gathering and analyzing data (representative samples should be used and variables accounted for), and the *trustworthiness* of the sources (sources should be qualified and unbiased).

Examples and *anecdotes* are particular instances that if accepted as believable lead readers to accept the general claim. The believability of examples depends on their *representativeness* (whether they are truly typical and thus generalizable) and their *specificity* (whether particular details make them seem true to life). Even if a vivid example or gripping anecdote does not convince readers, it strengthens argumentative writing by clarifying the meaning and dramatizing the point. In paragraph 5 of the King excerpt, for example, King supports his generalization that some African American nationalist extremists are motivated by bitterness and hatred by citing the specific example of Elijah Muhammad's Muslim movement. Conversely, in paragraph 9, he refers to Jesus, Paul, Luther, and others as examples of extremists motivated by love and Christianity. These examples support his assertion that extremism is not in itself wrong, and that any judgment of it must be based on its motivation and cause.

Authorities are people to whom the writer attributes expertise on a given subject. Such authorities not only must be appropriate, as mentioned earlier, but they must be believable as well. The believability of authorities depends on their *credibility*, on whether the reader accepts them as experts on the topic at hand. King cites authorities repeatedly throughout his essay. He refers to religious leaders (Jesus and Luther) as well as to American political leaders (Lincoln and Jefferson). These figures are certain to have a high degree of credibility among King's readers.

In addition, you should be aware of the following fallacies in reasoning that undermine the believability of an argument:

- *Begging the question*, when the believability of the support itself depends on the believability of the claim. Another name for this kind of fallacy is *circular reasoning*.
- *Failing to accept the burden of proof*, when the writer asserts a claim but provides no support for it.
- *Hasty generalization*, when the writer asserts a claim on the basis of an isolated example.
- *Sweeping generalization*, when the writer fails to qualify the applicability of the claim and asserts that it applies to "all" instances instead of to "some" instances.
- *Overgeneralization*, when the writer fails to qualify the claim and asserts that "it is certainly true" rather than "it may be true."

Testing for Consistency

In looking for consistency, you should be concerned that all the support works together and that none of the supporting statements contradicts any of the other statements. In addition, the support, taken together, should provide sufficient reason for accepting the claim. To test for consistency, ask: Are any of the supporting statements contradictory? Do they provide sufficient support for the claim? Are there opposing arguments that are not refuted?

A critical reader might regard as contradictory King's characterizing himself first as a moderate between the forces of complacency and violence, and later as an extremist opposed to the forces of violence. King attempts to reconcile this apparent contradiction by explicitly redefining extremism in paragraph 9. Similarly, the fact that King fails to examine and refute every legal recourse available to his cause might allow a critical reader to question the sufficiency of his supporting arguments.

In evaluating the consistency of an argument, you should also be aware of the following fallacies:

- *Slippery slope*, when the writer argues that taking one step will lead inevitably to a next step, one that is undesirable.

- *Equivocation*, when a writer uses the same term in two different senses in an argument.
- *Oversimplification*, when an argument obscures or denies the complexity of the issue.
- *Either/or reasoning*, when the writer reduces the issue to only two alternatives that are polar opposites.
- *Double standard*, when two or more comparable things are judged according to different standards; often involves holding the opposing argument to a higher standard than the one to which the writer holds his or her own argument.

RECOGNIZING EMOTIONAL MANIPULATION

Many different kinds of essays appeal to readers' emotions. Tobias Wolff's remembered event essay (in Chapter 2) may be terrifying to some readers, Donella Meadows's position paper (in Chapter 5) may anger fans of talk-show host Rush Limbaugh, whom she characterizes as "funny and pompous and a scape-goater and hatemonger."

Writers often try to arouse emotions in readers, to excite their interest, make them care, move them to take action. There's nothing wrong with appealing to readers' emotions. What's wrong is manipulating readers with false or exaggerated appeals. As a critical reader, you should be suspicious of writing that is overly or falsely sentimental, that cites alarming statistics and frightening anecdotes, that demonizes others and identifies itself with revered authorities, or that uses symbols (flagwaving) or emotionally loaded words (such as *racist*).

King, for example, uses the emotionally loaded word *paternalistically* to refer to the white moderate's belief that "he can set the timetable for another man's freedom" (paragraph 1). In the same paragraph, King uses *symbolism* to get an emotional reaction from readers when he compares the white moderate to the "Ku Klux Klanner." To get readers to accept his ideas, he also relies on *authorities* whose names evoke the greatest respect, such as Jesus and Lincoln. Some readers might consider the discussion of African American extremists in paragraph 7 of the King excerpt to be a veiled threat designed to frighten readers into agreement. Or some readers might object that comparing King's crusade to that of Jesus and other so-called leaders of religious and political groups is pretentious and manipulative.

Following are some fallacies that may occur when the emotional appeal is misused:

- *Loaded or slanted language*, when the writer uses language that is calculated to get a particular reaction from readers.
- *Bandwagon effect*, when it is suggested that great numbers of people agree with the writer and if you continued to disagree, you would be alone.
- *False flattery*, when readers are praised in order to get them to accept the writer's point of view.
- *Veiled threat*, when the writer tries to alarm or frighten readers into accepting the claim.

JUDGING THE WRITER'S CREDIBILITY

Writers often try to persuade readers to respect and believe them. Because readers may not know them personally or even by reputation, writers must present an image of themselves in their writing that will gain their readers' confidence. This image cannot be made directly but must be made indirectly, through the arguments, language, and the system of values and beliefs implied in the writing. Writers establish credibility in their writing in three ways:

> by showing their knowledge of the subject
>
> by building common ground with readers
>
> by responding fairly to objections and opposing arguments

Testing for Knowledge

Writers demonstrate their knowledge through the facts and statistics they marshal, the sources they rely on for information, the scope and depth of their understanding. As a critical reader, you may not be sufficiently expert on the subject yourself to know whether the facts are accurate, the sources reliable, and the understanding sufficient. You may need to do some research to see what others say about the subject. You can also check credentials—the writer's educational and professional qualifications, the respectability of the publication in which the selection first appeared, any reviews of the writer's work—to determine whether the writer is a respected authority in the field. King brings with him the authority that comes from being a member of the clergy and a respected leader of the Southern Christian Leadership Conference.

Testing for Common Ground

One way writers can establish common ground with their readers is by basing their reasoning on shared values, beliefs, and attitudes. They use language that includes their readers (*we*) rather than excludes them (*they*). They qualify their assertions to keep them from being too extreme. Above all, they acknowledge differences of opinion and try to make room in their argument to accommodate reasonable differences. As a reader, you will be affected by such appeals.

King creates common ground with readers by using the inclusive pronoun *we*, suggesting shared concerns between himself and his audience. Notice, however, his use of masculine pronouns and other references ("the Negro . . . he," "our brothers"). Although King addressed his letter to male clergy, he intended it to be published in the local newspaper, where it would be read by an audience of both men and women. By using language that excludes women, King misses the opportunity to build common ground with half his readers.

Testing for Fairness

Writers display their character by how they handle objections to their argument and opposing arguments. As a critical reader, you want to pay particular attention to how writers treat possible differences of opinion. Be suspicious of those who ignore differences and pretend everyone agrees with their viewpoint. When objections or opposing views are represented, you should consider whether they have been distorted in any way; if they are refuted, you want to be sure they are challenged fairly—with sound reasoning and solid evidence.

One way to gauge the author's credibility is to identify the tone of the argument, for it conveys the writer's attitude toward the subject and toward the reader. Examine the text carefully for indications of tone: Is the text angry? Sarcastic? Evenhanded? Shrill? Positive? Negative? Do you feel as if the writer is treating the subject—and you, one reader—with fairness? King's tone might be characterized as patient (he doesn't lose his temper), as respectful (he refers to white moderates as "people of good will"), as pompous (comparing himself to Jesus and Socrates).

Following are some fallacies that can undermine the ethical appeal:

- *Guilt by association*, when someone's credibility is attacked by associating that person with another person whom readers consider untrustworthy.
- *Ad hominem* (Latin for argument "against the man"), when the writer attacks his or her opponents personally instead of finding fault with their argument.
- *Straw man*, when the writer directs the argument against a claim that nobody actually holds or that everyone agrees is weak; often involves misrepresentation or distortion of the opposing argument.

10 Strategies for Doing Research in the Library and on the Internet

A college library contains thousands of texts organized in various ways. A library's resources are so immense and so diverse that complete mastery of them is something only professional librarians have. With the help of librarians and the advice in this chapter, however, you will be able to manage the research assignments in this text as well as those for your other college courses.

Until recent years, students had to rely almost exclusively on the resources available at their college libraries. With increased access to the Internet, however, students now have more sources of information than ever before. Therefore, this chapter also provides strategies for using the Internet to your best advantage.

One way to make your college library or the Internet seem more manageable is to think of their diverse materials as two different types of resources: the actual materials for your research, and the resources or tools that enable you to find these materials. The search for research materials requires patience, careful planning, good advice, and even luck. Nevertheless, the rewards are great. One of life's greatest intellectual pleasures is to learn about a subject and then be able to put diverse information together in a new way—for yourself and others.

ORIENTING YOURSELF TO THE LIBRARY

Make a point of taking a tour of the library. Then, when you first research a subject, be sure you understand your research task well. Consult a reference librarian if you need help.

Taking a Tour

Your instructor may arrange a library orientation tour for your composition class. If not, you can join one of the regular orientation tours scheduled by the librarians. Unless you are already using the library frequently, a tour is essential because nearly all college libraries are more complex and offer more services than typical school or public libraries. On a library tour, you will learn how the library catalog and reference room are organized, how to access computer catalogs and databases, whom to ask for help if you are confused, and how to get your hands on books, periodicals, and other materials.

Consulting a Librarian

Librarians at the information or reference desk are there to provide reference services, and most have years of experience answering the very questions you are likely to ask. You should not hesitate to approach them with any questions you have about locating sources. Remember, however, that they can be most helpful when you can explain your research assignment clearly.

Knowing Your Research Task

Before you go to the library to start an assigned research project, learn as much as you can about the assignment. Should you need to ask a librarian for advice, it is best to have the assignment in writing. Ask your instructor to clarify any confusing terms and to define the purpose and scope of the project. Find out how you can narrow or focus the project once you begin the research. Asking a question or two in advance can prevent hours—or even days—of misdirected work.

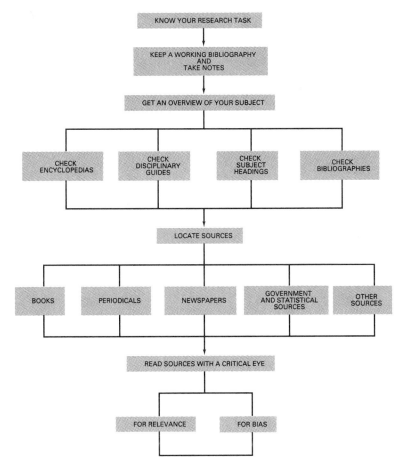

OVERVIEW OF A SEARCH STRATEGY

KNOW YOUR RESEARCH TASK

KEEP A WORKING BIBLIOGRAPHY AND TAKE NOTES

GET AN OVERVIEW OF YOUR SUBJECT

CHECK ENCYCLOPEDIAS — CHECK DISCIPLINARY GUIDES — CHECK SUBJECT HEADINGS — CHECK BIBLIOGRAPHIES

LOCATE SOURCES

BOOKS — PERIODICALS — NEWSPAPERS — GOVERNMENT AND STATISTICAL SOURCES — OTHER SOURCES

READ SOURCES WITH A CRITICAL EYE

FOR RELEVANCE — FOR BIAS

A RECOMMENDED SEARCH STRATEGY

In order for your library research to be manageable and productive, you need to work carefully and systematically. The search strategy presented in this chapter was developed by college librarians with undergraduate needs firmly in mind. Although specific search strategies may vary to fit the needs of individual research tasks, the general process presented here should help you get started, keep track of all your research, use library materials to get an overview of your subject, locate the sources you need, and read those sources with a critical eye.

KEEPING TRACK OF YOUR RESEARCH

As you research your topic, you want to keep careful records of all your sources by setting up a working bibliography.

Keeping a Working Bibliography

A working bibliography is a preliminary, ongoing record of books, articles, pamphlets—all the sources of information you discover as you research your subject. In addition, you can use your working bibliography as a means of keeping track of any encyclopedias, bibliographies, and indexes you consult, even though you do not use these resources in an essay or a research review.

Practiced researchers keep their working bibliography on index cards, in a notebook, or in a computer file. They may keep bibliographical information separate from notes they take on the sources. Many researchers find index cards most convenient because they are so easily alphabetized. Others find them too easy to lose and prefer instead to keep everything—working bibliography, notes, and drafts—in one notebook. Researchers who use computers set up working bibliographies in word-processing programs or bibliographic management programs, such as Endnote Plus, that work in conjunction with word-processing programs. Whether you use cards, a notebook, or a computer, the important thing is to make your entries accurate and complete. If the call number for a book is incomplete or inaccurate, for example, you will not be able to find the book in the stacks.

Because you must eventually choose a documentation style for your essay, you may want to select it now, at the beginning of your research, so that all sources listed in your working bibliography will conform to the documentation style of your essay. Chapter 11 presents two different documentation styles, one adopted by the Modern Language Association (MLA) and widely used in the humanities, and the other advocated by the American Psychological Association (APA) and used in the social sciences. Individual disciplines often have their own preferred styles of documentation, which your instructor may wish you to use.

Taking Notes

After you are oriented to your research topic and have found a way to focus it, you will want to begin taking notes from relevant sources. If you own the work or can obtain a copy of the relevant parts, you may want to annotate right on the page. Otherwise, you should paraphrase, summarize, and outline useful information as separate notes. In addition, you will want to write down quotations you might use in your essay.

You may already have a method of note-taking you prefer. Some researchers like to use index cards for notes as well as for their working bibliography. They use 3″ × 5″ cards for their bibliography and larger ones (4″ × 6″ or 5″ × 7″) for notes. Some even use a different color card for each of their sources. Other people prefer to keep their notes in a notebook, and still others enter their notes into a computer. Whatever method you use, be sure to keep accurate notes.

Care in note-taking is of paramount importance in order to minimize the risks of copying facts incorrectly and of misquoting. Another common error in note-taking is to copy the author's words without enclosing them in quotation marks. This error could lead easily to plagiarism, the unacknowledged use of another's words or ideas. Double-check all your notes, and be as accurate as you can. (See p. 262 for tips on avoiding plagiarism.) You might consider photocopying materials from sources that look especially promising. Photocopying can facilitate your work, allowing you to reread and analyze important sources as well as to highlight material you may wish to quote, summarize, or paraphrase.

GETTING STARTED

"But where do I start?" That common question is easily answered. You first need an overview of your topic. If you are researching a concept or an issue in a course you are taking, then your textbook or other course materials provide the obvious starting point. Your instructor can advise you about other sources that provide overviews of your topic. If your topic is just breaking in the news, then current newspapers and magazines might be sufficient. For all other topics—and for background information—encyclopedias and disciplinary guides are often the place to start.

Consulting Encyclopedias

Specialized encyclopedias can be a good place to start your research. General encyclopedias, such as *Encylopaedia Britannica* and *Encyclopedia Americana,* cover many topics superficially, whereas specialized encyclopedias cover topics in the depth appropriate for college writing. In addition to providing an overview of a topic, a specialized encyclopedia often includes an explanation of issues related to the topic, definitions of specialized terminology, and selective bibliographies of additional sources.

As starting points, specialized encyclopedias have two further advantages: (1) they provide a comprehensive introduction to key terms related to your topic, terms that are especially useful in identifying the subject headings used to locate material in catalogs and indexes; and (2) they provide a comprehensive presentation of a subject, enabling you to see many possibilities for focusing your research on one aspect of it. Specialized encyclopedias can be found in the catalog under the subject heading for the discipline, such as "psychology," and the subheading "dictionaries and encyclopedias."

Two particular reference sources can help you identify specialized encyclopedias covering your topic:

> *ARBA Guide to Subject Encyclopedias and Dictionaries* (1986). Lists specialized encyclopedias by broad subject category, with descriptions of coverage, focus, and any special features.
>
> *First Stop: The Master Index to Subject Encyclopedias* (1989). Lists specialized encyclopedias by broad subject category and provides access to individual articles within them. By looking under the key terms that describe a topic, you can find references to specific articles in any of over four hundred specialized encyclopedias.

Consulting Disciplinary Guides

Once you have a general overview of your topic, you will want to consult one of the research guides in that discipline. The following guides can help you identify the major handbooks, encyclopedias, bibliographies, journals, periodical indexes, and computer databases in the various disciplines. You need not read any of these extensive works straight through, but you will find them to be valuable references.

General	*Guide to Reference Books*, 10th ed. (1986). Edited by Eugene P. Sheehy.
Humanities	*The Humanities: A Selective Guide to Information Sources*, 4th ed. (1994). By Ron Blazek and Elizabeth S. Aversa.
Science and Technology	*Scientific and Technical Information Sources*, 2nd ed. (1987). By Ching-chih Chen.
Social Sciences	*Sources of Information in the Social Sciences: A Guide to the Literature*, 3rd ed. (1986). Edited by William H. Webb.
Anthropology	*Introduction to Library Research in Anthropology* (1991). By John M. Weeks.
Art	*Visual Arts Research: A Handbook* (1986). By Elizabeth B. Pollard.
Education	*Education: A Guide to Reference and Information Sources* (1989). By Lois Buttlar.
Film	*On the Screen: A Film, Television, and Video Research Guide* (1986). By Kim N. Fisher.
History	*A Student's Guide to History*, 6th ed. (1994). By Jules R. Benjamin.
Literature	*Reference Works in British and American Literature* (1990). By James K. Bracken.
	Literary Research Guide: A Guide to Reference Sources for the Study of Literatures in English and Related Topics, 2nd ed. (1993). By James L. Harner.
Music	*Music: A Guide to the Reference Literature* (1987). By William S. Brockman.

Philosophy	*Philosophy: A Guide to the Reference Literature* (1986). By Hans E. Bynagle.
Political Science	*Information Sources of Political Science*, 4th ed. (1986). By Frederick L. Holler.
Psychology	*Library Research Guide to Psychology: Illustrated Search Strategy and Sources* (1984). By Nancy E. Douglas.
Sociology	*A Guide to Reference and Information Sources* (1987). By Stephen H. Aby.
Women's Studies	*Introduction to Library Research in Women's Studies* (1985). By Susan E. Searing.

Checking Subject Headings

To carry your research beyond encyclopedias, you need to find appropriate subject headings. Subject headings are specific words and phrases used in libraries to categorize the contents of books and periodicals. As you read about your subject in an encyclopedia or other reference book, you should look for possible subject headings.

To begin your search for subject headings, consult the *Library of Congress Subject Headings (LCSH)*, which usually can be found near the library catalog. This reference book lists the standard subject headings used in catalogs and indexes and in many encyclopedias and bibliographies. Following is an example from the *LCSH*:

Home schooling *(May Subd Geog)* ← **Place names may follow heading**
     Here are entered works on the provision of compulsory education in the home by parents as an alternative to traditional public or private schooling. General works on the provision of education in the home by educational personnel are entered under Domestic Education.

Used for ——→	UF	Education, Home	
		Home-based education	
		Home education	**NT = Narrower term**
		Home instruction	**SA = See also**
		Home teaching by parents	
		Homeschooling	
		Instruction, Home	
		Schooling, Home	
Broader Term ——→	BT	Education	
Related Term ——→	RT	Education—United States	
		Education—Parent participation	

Subject headings provide you with various key words and phrases to use as you look through catalogs and indexes. For example, the preceding entry proved particularly useful because when the student found nothing listed in the library catalog under "home schooling," she tried the other headings until "Education—Parent participation" and "Education—United States" yielded information on three books. Note, too, that this entry explains the *type* of articles that would be found under these headings—and those that would be found elsewhere. Keep in mind that the terms listed in the *LCSH* might not be the *only* ones used for your subject; don't be reluctant to try terms that you think might be relevant.

Consulting Bibliographies

A bibliography is simply a list of publications on a given subject. Whereas an encyclopedia may give you only background information on your subject, a bibliography gives you an overview of what has been published on the subject. Its scope may be broad or narrow. Some bibliographers try to be exhaustive, including every title they can find, but most are selective. To discover how selections were made, check the bibliography's preface or introduction.

The best way to locate a comprehensive, up-to-date bibliography on your subject is to look in the *Bibliographic Index*. A master list of bibliographies that contain fifty or more titles, the *Bibliographic Index* includes bibliographies from articles, books, and government publications. A new volume is published every year. (Note that because this index is not cumulative, you should check back over several years, beginning with the most current volume.)

Even if you attend a large research university, your library is unlikely to hold every book or journal article a bibliography might direct you to. The library catalog and serial record (a list of the periodicals the library holds) can tell you whether the book or journal is available.

Determining the Most Promising Sources

As you follow a subject heading into the library catalog and bibliographic and periodical indexes, and discover many seemingly relevant books and articles, how do you decide which ones to track down and examine? With little to go on but author, title, date, and publisher or periodical name, you may feel at a loss; but these facts actually provide useful clues. Look, for example, at the following entry from *Education Index*, a periodical index:

> **Home schooling**
> Charter 'profit' [Noah Webster Academy, a new electronic charter 'school' in Michigan] D. Harrington-Lueker. *Am Sch Board J* v181 p27–8 S '94
> Educating children at home: implications for assessment and accountability. S. E. Marlow. bibl *Educ Urban Soc* v26 p438–60 Ag '94
> A home school/school district partnership. M. Terpstra. il *Educ Leadership* v52 p57–8 S '94
> Home schoolers as public school tutors. M. Shepherd. il *Educ Leadership* v52 p55–6 S '94
> Perspectives from a home-schooling educator. J. Riemer. il *Educ Leadership* v52 p53–4 S '94
> Why parents choose home schooling. C. Jeub. il *Educ Leadership* v52 p50–2 S '94
> **Suits and claims**
> In re Marriage of Riess (198 Ill.Dec. 305, 632 N.E.2d 635). *West's Educ Law Rep* v90 p722–31 Je 30 '94

This entry lists articles that address different aspects of home schooling, briefly describing some of the articles. You can see that the first article deals with an electronic school and the second focuses on assessment. The subheading "suits and claims" provides further help in identifying quickly whether the article could be useful by telling you that it is about a court case.

When you look in catalogs and indexes, consider the following points to help you decide whether you should track down a particular source:

- *Relevance to your topic.* Do the title, subtitle, description, subject headings, abstract, or periodical title help you determine just how directly a particular source addresses your topic?
- *Publication date.* How recent is the source? For current controversies, emerging trends, and continuing technical or medical developments, you must see the most recent material. For historical or biographical topics, you will want to start with contemporary perspectives, but keep in mind that older sources offer authoritative perspectives.
- *Description.* Does the length indicate a brief or an extended treatment of the topic? Does the work include illustrations that may elaborate on concepts discussed in the text? Does the work include a bibliography that could lead you to other works or an index that could give you an overview of what is discussed in the text? Does the abstract tell you the focus of the work?

From among the sources that look promising, select at least one book, one research report in an academic journal, and one article in a popular magazine. Or select three or four publications that you can tell from their titles concern different aspects of your topic or approach it from different perspectives. In this first look beyond an encyclopedia, avoid selecting sources by the same author, from the same publisher, or in the same journal. Common sense will lead you to an appropriate decision about diversity in source materials.

LOCATING SOURCES

When you tour your college library, or when you begin your research project, find out how best to gain access to the various resources you will need. Many libraries now offer access to their on-line card catalog, periodical holdings, periodical and newspaper indexes, government documents, some specialized CD-ROM products, or even the holdings of other libraries through public access terminals. Check the menu screen of one of the terminals; it usually indicates the resources that are available through the system.

Following are guidelines for finding books, periodical articles, newspaper articles, government documents and statistical information, and other types of sources.

Finding Books

The primary source for books is the library catalog. Now nearly every college library offers a computerized catalog, sometimes called an on-line catalog. The library may also maintain a card catalog consisting of cards filed in drawers. The on-line catalog provides more flexibility in searching subject headings and may even tell you whether the book has already been checked out. Another distinct advantage is its ability to print out source information, making it unnecessary for you to copy it by hand. Since an on-line catalog often contains material received and catalogued only after a certain date, however, you should check both catalogs.

Library catalogs organize sources by author, subject, and title. For each book there is a card or computer entry under the name of each author, under the title, and under each subject heading to which the book is related. Author, title, and subject cards or entries all give the same basic information.

1. The *call number*—always in the upper left-hand corner of cards in a card catalog, indicates the numerical code under which the book is filed in the library. Call numbers are assigned according to subject. Most college libraries use the Library of Congress subject headings and numbering system. Call numbers have at least two rows of numbers. The top row indicates the general subject classification, and the second row places the book within this classification. Subsequent rows identify the copyright and publication date for multiple editions. In an on-line catalog, the call number usually appears on a separate line.

2. The *author*—appears last name first, followed by birth and death dates. If there are multiple authors, there is an author card or entry under each author's name.

3. The *title*—appears exactly as it is printed on the title page of the book, except that only the first word and proper nouns and adjectives are capitalized.

4. The *publication information*—includes the place of publication (usually just the city), publisher, and year of publication. If the book was published simultaneously in the United States and abroad, both places of publication and both publishers are included.

5. The *physical description*—offers information about the book's length and size. A roman numeral indicates the number of pages used for front matter (such as a preface, table of contents, and acknowledgments).

6. *Notes*—indicate any special features (for example, a bibliography or an index).

7. *Subject headings*—indicate how the book is listed in the subject catalog. These may be headings you can use to find other books related to your subject.

In a card catalog, the title and subject cards for a book are just like the author card except that they have headings printed at the top, above the author's name. On the title card, the heading is the title (which appears again below the author's name). On the subject card the heading is one of the subject headings from the bottom of the card. Note that for a book, a separate catalog card or on-line entry exists for each subject heading listed. When you search for books on a particular subject, rather than by author or title, it's a good idea to check the *Library of Congress Subject Headings* (see p. 233) for key words related to your subject, before searching the catalog for a subject heading you have formulated on your own. This extra step will often save you time later on.

Here is one college library's on-line catalog display of the author entry for a recent book on home schooling in its collection. Notice the call number along the bottom line.

AUTHOR:	Guterson, David, 1951-
TITLE:	Family matters: Why home schooling makes sense/ David Guterson
EDITION:	1st Harvest ed.
PUBLISHER:	San Diego: Harcourt Brace & Co., c1992
PHYSICAL DESC:	x, 254 p.; 18 cm.
NOTES:	Includes bibliographical references and index.
SUBJECTS:	Education—United States
	Education—parent participation
	Teaching methods

LOCATION / CALL NUMBER	STATUS
UCSD Undergrad / 649.68 g 1993	Available

Finding Periodical Articles

The most up-to-date information on a subject usually is found not in books but in articles in magazines and journals, or periodicals. Articles in periodicals usually are not listed in the library catalog; to find them, you must instead use periodical indexes and abstracts. Indexes list articles, whereas abstracts summarize as well as list them. Library catalogs list the indexes and abstracts held in the library and note whether they are available in printed form, as microforms, or as computer databases. Those indexes listed in this section that are available as computer databases are labeled on-line and/or *CD-ROM* (for compact disc—read only memory). Names for these databases, if different from the print index, are also given. Check with a librarian to see what databases are available at your library.

Periodical indexes and abstracts are of two types: general and specialized.

General Indexes

General periodical indexes list articles in nontechnical, general-interest publications and cover a broad range of subjects. Most have separate author and subject listings as well as a list of book reviews. Following are some general indexes, beginning with one you may already be familiar with:

Readers' Guide to Periodical Literature (1900–; on-line and CD-ROM, 1983–); updated quarterly. Covers about two hundred popular periodicals and may help you start your search for sources on general and current topics. Even for general topics, however, you should not rely on it exclusively. Nearly all college libraries house far more than two hundred periodicals, and university research libraries house twenty thousand or more. The *Readers' Guide* does not attempt to cover the research journals that play such an important role in college writing. Here is a sample entry for "home education":

HOME EDUCATION
   Better off at home? I. Lyman. *National Review* v45 p60 + S 20 '93
   The economics of teaching your kids at home. K. Davis and K. Quillen. il
     Kiplinger's Personal Finance Magazine v47 p30 Jl '93
   Legally speaking [home schooling] K. House. *The Mother Earth News* v139
     p54 Ag/S '93
   The ultimate school choice: no school at all. D. Churbuck. il *Forbes* v152
     p144-5 + O 11 '93
   Understanding home schooling. J. A. Natale. *The Education Digest* v58 p58-
     61 Mr '93
                   Canada
   Home schooling. D. S. Smith. il *The Mother Earth News* v139 p53-4 + Ag/S
     '93

Magazine Index. On microfilm (1988–), on-line (1973–), and on CD-ROM as part of InfoTrac (1973–); see below. Indexes over four hundred magazines.

InfoTrac. On CD-ROM. Includes three indexes: (1) the *General Periodicals Index* (current year and past four), which covers over 1,100 general-interest publications, incorporating the *Magazine Index* and including the *New York Times* and *Wall Street Journal*; (2) the *Academic Index* (current year and past four), which covers four hundred scholarly and general-interest publications, including the *New York Times*; and (3) the *National Newspaper Index* (current year and past three), which covers the *Christian Science Monitor, Los Angeles Times, New York Times, Wall Street Journal,* and *Washington Post.* Some entries also include abstracts of articles.

Humanities Index (1974–; also on-line and on CD-ROM). Covers archaeology, history, classics, literature, performing arts, philosophy, and religion.

Social Sciences Index (1974–; also on-line and on CD-ROM). Covers economics, geography, law, political science, psychology, public administration, and sociology.

Public Affairs Information Service Bulletin (PAIS) (1915–; also on-line and on CD-ROM). Covers articles and other publications by public and private agencies on economic and social conditions, international relations, and public administration. Subject listing only.

Specialized Indexes and Abstracts

Specialized periodical indexes list or abstract articles devoted to technical or scholarly research. The following example from *Sociological Abstracts*, which indexes and summarizes articles from a wide range of periodicals that publish sociological research, is typical of entries found in specialized indexes:

> **91X2727**
> **Mayberry, Maralee & Knowles, J. Gary** (Dept Sociology U Nevada, Las Vegas 89154), **Family Unity Objectives of Parents Who Teach Their Children: Ideological and Pedagogical Orientations to Home Schooling,** ∪M *The Urban Review,* 1989, 21, 4, Dec, 209-225.
> ¶ The objectives of parents who teach their children at home are examined, using results from 2 qualitative studies: (1) a study conducted in Ore in 1987/88, consisting of interview & questionnaire data (N = 15 & 800 families, respectively); & (2) an ongoing ethnographic study being conducted in Utah (N = 8 families). Analysis suggests that while families have complex motives for teaching their children at home, most respondents felt that establishing a home school would allow them to maintain or further develop unity within the family. It is concluded that a family's decision to home school is often made in an attempt to resist the effects on the family unit of urbanization & modernization. Policy implications are discussed. 36 References. Adapted from the source document.

Here is a list of specialized periodical indexes that cover various disciplines:

Accountant's Index (1944–).

American Statistics Index (1973–).

Applied Science and Technology Index (1958–). On-line, CD-ROM.

Art Index (1929–).

Biological and Agricultural Index (1964–). CD-ROM.

Education Index (1929–). On-line, CD-ROM.

Engineering Index (1920–).

Historical Abstracts (1955–).

Index Medicus (1961–). On-line, CD-ROM (called MEDLINE).

MLA International Bibliography of Books and Articles in the Modern Languages and Literature (1921–). On-line, CD-ROM.

Music Index (1949–).

Philosopher's Index (1957–). On-line.

Psychological Abstracts (1927–). On-line (called PsycINFO), CD-ROM (PsycLIT).

Physics Abstracts (1898). On-line (called INSPEC).

Science Abstracts (1898–).

Sociological Abstracts (1952–). On-line, CD-ROM (called Sociofile).

Many periodical indexes and abstracts use the Library of Congress subject headings, but some have their own systems. *Sociological Abstracts*, for example, has a separate volume for subject headings. Check the opening pages of the index or abstract you are using, or refer to the system documentation, to see how it classifies its subjects. Then look for periodicals under your chosen Library of Congress subject heading or the heading that seems most similar to it.

Computer Databases

Your library may subscribe to *on-line* database networks and may own *CD-ROM* machines that are accessed through the library's computer terminals. Most research databases—like those noted in the preceding lists are electronic indexes listing thousands of books and articles.

You may be able to use a CD-ROM database yourself, but you will probably need a librarian to conduct an on-line search. When you use a CD-ROM database, check the first screen, which should let you know what information you are accessing. Some large databases may require more than one disc, usually separated by date. In such cases, the reference librarian can help you obtain the disc you need. Although you can search a database by author or title, most likely you will use *descriptors*, or key words describing subjects. Make your descriptors as precise as possible so that your database search results in a manageable list of sources relevant to your topic. Most databases include a thesaurus of descriptors and a set of guidelines for combining terms to narrow your search. In addition, most CD-ROMs include a browse function. When you enter a descriptor, the system automatically lists the terms that are close to it alphabetically. If you enter a very general descriptor, the system provides that general term along with subtopics. Use these subtopics to further narrow your search before you ask the system to retrieve records.

Once you have typed in your descriptors, the computer searches the database and lists every reference to them it finds. If your search is extensive, you can usually download the records to your own disc. Because you may be charged for access time and printing for an on-line search, or given a limit on time at the terminal and number of entries you can print from a CD-ROM database, you may want to talk with a librarian before consulting a database. Also keep in mind that because most electronic indexes cover only the most recent years of an index, you may need to consult older printed versions as well.

In addition to the database versions of the indexes listed earlier, many libraries subscribe to computer services that provide abstracts and/or the full text of articles, either in the database (so you can see them on screen) or by mail or fax for a fee, and that list books in particular subject areas. The use of computers for scholarly research is becoming more widespread, with new technology being developed all the time, so be sure to check with a librarian about what's available in your library. Some common computer services include the following:

ERIC (*Educational Resources Information Center*) (1969–). Indexes, abstracts, and gives some full texts of articles from 750 education journals. Here is an example of a work on home schooling listed in ERIC:

SilverPlatter 3.1   **ERIC 1982-June 1993**
                                          1 of 28

AN ACCESSION NUMBER: EJ442388
AU PERSONAL AUTHOR: Knowles,-J.-Gary; And Others
TI TITLE: From Pedagogy to Ideology: Origins and Phases of Home
Education in the United States, 1970-1990.
PY PUBLICATION YEAR: 1992
JN JOURNAL CITATION: American Journal of Education; v100 n2
p195-235 Feb 1992
IS ISSN:0195-6744
AV AVAILABILITY: UMI
CH CLEARINGHOUSE: UD
FI SOURCE FILE: EJ
DT TYPE NUMBER: 080; 141
DT DOCUMENT TYPE: Journal Articles (080); Reports—Descriptive (141)
DE Descriptors: Civil—Liberties; Court—Litigation; Educational—Change;
Educational History—Home schooling; Ideology—Teaching methods
ID IDENTIFIERS: Social Movements
LA LANGUAGE: English
AB ABSTRACT: Examines issues of home education since 1970 by
surveying the home-schooling movement in the broader historical
context. The twenty-year growth period illustrates the fluid nature of
home education as a social movement. Contemporary home-
schooling is not closely tied to the liberal goals of home education.

Business Periodicals Ondisc (1988–) and ABI/INFORM (1988–). Provides the full
text of articles from business periodicals. If your library has a laser printer
attached to a terminal, you can print out articles, including illustrations.

PsycBooks (1987–). A CD-ROM database that indexes books and book chapters
in psychology.

Carl/Uncover (1988–). An on-line document delivery service that lists over three
million articles from twelve thousand journals. For a fee, you can receive the
full text of the article by fax, usually within a few hours.

Interlibrary networks. Known by different names in different regions, these networks allow you to search in the catalogs of colleges and universities in your
area and across the country. In many cases, you can request a book, periodical
article, or newspaper article by interlibrary loan. It may take several weeks
for you to receive your material.

Locating Periodicals in the Library

When you identify a promising magazine or journal article in a periodical index,
you must go to the library serial record or on-line catalog to learn whether the
library subscribes to the periodical and, if so, where you can find it. Recent issues
of periodicals are usually arranged alphabetically by title on open shelves. Older
issues are either bound like books and filed by call numbers or filmed and available
in microform.

Finding Newspaper Articles

Newspapers provide useful information for many research topics in such areas as foreign affairs, economic issues, public opinion, and social trends. Libraries usually miniaturize newspapers and store them on microfilm (reels) or microfiche (cards) that must be placed in viewing machines to be read.

Newspaper indexes, such as the *Los Angeles Times Index, New York Times Index,* and the London *Times Index,* help you locate specific articles on your topic. College libraries usually have indexes to local newspapers as well.

Your library may also subscribe to newspaper article and digest services, such as the following:

National Newspaper Index. On microfilm (1989–), on-line (1979–), and on CD-ROM, as part of InfoTrac (see p. 238). Indexes the *Christian Science Monitor, Los Angeles Times, New York Times, Wall Street Journal,* and *Washington Post.*

NewsBank (1970–). On microfiche and CD-ROM. Full-text articles from five hundred U.S. newspapers. A good source of information on local and regional issues and trends.

Newspaper Abstracts (1988–). An index and brief abstracts of articles from nineteen major regional, national, and international newspapers.

Facts on File (weekly). A digest of U.S. and international news events arranged by subject, such as foreign affairs, arts, education, religion, and sports.

Editorials on File (twice monthly). Editorials from 150 U.S. and Canadian newspapers. Each entry includes a brief description of an editorial subject followed by fifteen to twenty editorials on the subject, reprinted from different newspapers.

Editorial Research Reports (1924–). Reports on current and controversial topics, including brief histories, statistics, editorials, journal articles, endnotes, and supplementary reading lists.

Foreign Broadcast Information Service (*FBIS*) (1980–). Foreign broadcast scripts, newspaper articles, and government statements from Asia, Europe, Latin America, Africa, Russia, and the Middle East.

Finding Government and Statistical Information

Following is a list of government publications and sources of statistical information that report developments in the federal government. The types of material they cover include congressional hearings and debates, presidential proclamations and speeches, Supreme Court decisions and dissenting opinions, as well as compilations of statistics. Frequently, government documents are not listed in the library catalog. Ask a reference librarian for assistance if you have trouble finding them.

Congressional Quarterly Almanac (annual). A summary of legislation, election results, roll-call votes, and significant speeches and debates.

Congressional Quarterly Weekly Report. Up-to-date summaries of committee actions, votes, and executive branch activities.

Statistical Abstract of the United States (annual). Generated by the Bureau of the Census, includes social, economic, and political statistics.

American Statistics Index (1974–; annual with monthly supplements). Federal government publications containing statistical information.

Statistical Reference Index (1980–). American statistical publications from sources other than the U.S. government.

The Gallup Poll: Public Opinion (1935–). Results of public opinion polls.

Finding Other Sources

Libraries hold a vast amount of useful materials other than books and periodicals. Some of the following sources and services may be appropriate for your research.

Vertical file. Pamphlets and brochures from government and private agencies.

Special collections. Manuscripts, rare books, materials of local interest, and the like.

Audio collections. Records, audiocassettes, and compact discs of all kinds of music, readings, and speeches.

Video collections. Slides, filmstrips, and videocassettes.

Art collections. Drawings, paintings, and engravings.

Interlibrary loans. Many libraries will borrow books from another library; be aware that interlibrary loans often take some time.

Computer resources. Many libraries house interactive computer programs that combine text, video, and audio resources in history, literature, business, and other disciplines.

USING THE INTERNET FOR RESEARCH

The *Internet* is a global network that connects computers and that enables computer users to share information and resources quickly and easily. Using the Internet, people can send and receive electronic mail (E-mail), read documents or post them for others to read, communicate with other people who share similar interests, and store, send, and receive documents, graphic images, videos, and computer applications. Your school may provide its students with access to the Internet, possibly at little or no cost. Using a computer and a modem or a direct network connection, students can gather information about a research subject from sources all over the world. If you are interested in ecology, for example, you can locate government reports and news articles on the environment, information from environmental action groups, ongoing forums discussing a wide range of environmental topics, and information about current scientific research in ecology. To find out whether you can access the Internet on campus, check with the reference librarian or computer services office. Much of the software you need to access the network is widely available for free or for a small fee through campus services, computer-user groups, electronic bulletin boards, or commercial services.

If you cannot gain access to the Internet through your university or college, you may use your own computer and modem to access a commercial Internet service provider. Service providers charge a fee; in return they provide all the software you need and a dial-up phone number to connect to the Internet. Some services charge a flat monthly or annual fee, while others base their charges on the amount of time you are connected. Some well-known commercial on-line services are CompuServe, Prodigy, and America Online; until recently, these large services provided only information storage, electronic mail, and chat forums for their members, but they now provide access to the Internet as well. Using these large services can become expensive, however. In most areas of the country, less expensive local Internet service providers now exist. Check with local computer stores or computer-user groups to compare pricing among the services available in your area.

Research on the Internet is very different from library research. Information is stored on many different computers, each with its own system of organization. There is no central catalogue, reference librarian, or standard classification system for the vast resources on the Internet. As a result, it can be difficult to determine the sources of information and to evaluate their reliability. Depending on your topic, purpose, and audience, the sources you find on the Internet may not be as credible or authoritative as library sources (see pp. 252–54 for information on determining the credibility of sources). When in doubt about the reliability or acceptability of on-line sources for a particular assignment, be sure to check with your instructor. In most cases, you will probably need to balance or supplement on-line sources with library sources. As with sources you locate in the library, you need to include proper documentation for all on-line sources that you cite (see Chapter 11).

Since the Internet is so large and relatively unorganized, you may wonder how to find information relevant to your topic. Various resources have been developed to make it easier to find information on the Internet. One popular resource is the WorldWide Web; others include Telnet, File Transfer Protocol, Archie, and Gopher.

Searching the WorldWide Web

The *WorldWide Web* was initially developed to allow scientists to link related information wherever that information might be located. Using the Web, for example, a physicist in California who published a paper on the Internet could create a link to a related paper by a colleague in Sweden. Anyone reading the first paper could simply click on the link for instant access to the second paper.

Since its inception, the WorldWide Web has grown and developed rapidly to include many other uses. People may now include not only text but also graphic images, sound, animation, and even video in documents, all of which can be shared with others. New programs make it much easier to search, view, and create Web documents. Presently, more than 2.6 million sources of information exist on the WorldWide Web, and its explosive growth continues as businesses, educa-

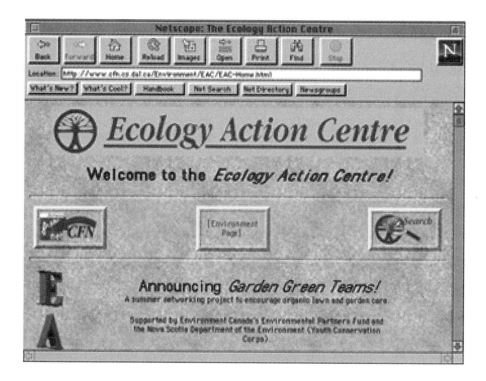

A sample home page from the Web site of the Ecology Action Centre, using the Netscape graphic browser.

tional institutions, government agencies, libraries, museums, and private individuals have rushed to set up their own Web sites.

Becoming Familiar with Web Sites

A particular *Web site* usually consists of a home page and the pages connected with it on a specific computer. A *home page* is the page you most often find first when you access a Web site; it typically provides a title heading, a brief introduction, and a table of contents consisting of *links* to the information available at that site. At the bottom of the home page you will usually find the name of the person or group responsible for the site and an E-mail address. The illustration above shows a home page from the Ecology Action Centre. However, you should note that home pages and Web sites vary in content, design, and organization.

On a WorldWide Web home page, links to other information are often indicated by underlined text (sometimes the words may be in bold type or highlighted in another way). In the example from the Ecology Action Centre, *Search EAC's Pages* is one such link. Note also that the boxes on the home page are buttons that, when clicked, link readers to further information. On a color monitor, links to additional information are indicated by a different color. After a color-coded link has been clicked on and the reader returns to the original page, the link changes color (usually to red) to show that it has been visited. In addition to providing connections to other documents, the links on a home page can perform many other functions: for example, they may open a form to be filled out by the reader, start a video, play music or sound, or provide a form for sending an E-mail message to the author, among other uses.

There are Web sites for people interested in finding the text of a recently passed law, browsing a college catalogue, listening to a jazz performance, or viewing prehistoric cave art from France. You can find Web pages that serve as indexes to information about particular topics and Web pages that allow browsers to search the Web using keywords for topics or names. Increasingly, many Web pages are interactive, allowing browsers to send comments or questions to the Web page author, respond to a survey, contribute to a collaborative work of fiction, or make purchases via the network.

Each Web page has its own address or *Uniform Resource Locator (URL)*, which functions much like a traditional telephone number. The URL allows people anywhere in the world to locate a particular Web page. In the example on page 245, the URL for the Ecology Action Center appears in the "Location" box near the top of the home page, and its three main parts are typical of most URLs: *http:// www.cfn.cs.dal.ca/Environment/EAC/EAC-Home.html*. The first part of a URL usually consists of the standard abbreviation *http://* (meaning "hypertext transfer protocol"); it tells the sending and receiving computers the type of information being sent and how to transfer it. The second part of the URL includes the standard *www.*, to establish that the location being accessed is on the WorldWide Web, as well as the Internet address of the institution, government agency, corporation, or organization (and the country, if outside of the United States) where the document is located (*cfn.cs.dal.ca* is the address of the Ecology Action Center). After a slash, the third part of the URL (which may be quite lengthy) gives the address of the directory and file where the page is found as well as the name of the specific page itself (as in *Environment/EAC/EAC-Home.html*).

When you find a Web page that you think you may want to visit again, it's a good idea to create a "bookmark" for that page by choosing the "Add bookmark" function from the Web program menu. The address of the Web page will be added to a list in the bookmark menu.

You may access a particular URL in several ways:

▪ By typing the URL directly into the location box and then hitting "Return" or "Enter" on your keyboard
▪ By selecting "Open Location" from the file menu and typing the URL into the dialogue box
▪ By pasting or copying the URL into the location box from some other source, such as the computer's scrapbook or clipboard

▪ By selecting the URL from the bookmark menu, if you have previously saved a bookmark for that page

The method you use to access a URL may depend on your Web browser.

Using Web Browsers

A *Web browser,* also called a *Web client program,* is software that allows you to display a Web page, including any graphic images, video, or sound that is included on that page. A Web browser also allows you to navigate among Web pages. For example, you may return to previous pages by clicking on an arrow icon (such as the "Back" button in the top left corner of the sample home page on p. 245) or by accessing a menu that lists recently visited pages. In addition, a browser helps you find, read, download, and save the text of documents, graphic images, video, or sounds.

The first graphic Web browser, MOSAIC, was created at the University of Illinois. Currently, the most widely used graphic browsers are Netscape (shown in the sample Web page on p. 245) and MacWeb, while other programs are under development. A plain-text browser, Lynx, does not display graphics or video and is used for computer or modem connections that lack the processing speed needed for graphic browsers such as MOSAIC and Netscape. Web browsers differ slightly in their format and features, though they share similarities that make them easy to use. Web browsers exist for virtually every computer platform, including IBM, Macintosh, and UNIX, and they are widely available at no cost to students and others at academic institutions.

Searching the Web for Information on Your Topic

A Web page often provides links to additional information about a subject at other Web sites. You may also use one of the special search engines on the Web itself. *Search engines* are resources available for searching the WorldWide Web. They are found on pages especially set up to allow you to enter a keyword or phrase. The search engine scans the Web for your keyword and produces a list of direct links to pages containing the keyword. Usually, the list includes a brief description of each page. The program searches both the titles of Web pages and the actual text of those pages for the keyword. By clicking on one of the links returned by the search, you can directly access a specific Web page. For example, by clicking the button "Net Search" shown in the example on page 245, you could directly access several popular search engines, such as Lycos and Webcrawler.

The well-known Lycos search engine, located at Carnegie Mellon University, offers two levels of searching: a quick search from among a relatively small selection of sites, and an in-depth search of the entire collection of Web sites. The sample Lycos search form shown on page 248 can be accessed through the URL given in the location box. To use Lycos, you type in one or more keywords and select the maximum number of sources, or "hits," you would like listed. Many

A sample Lycos search form for locating sources on a topic.

other search engines are available in various locations, and some large Web sites with many documents in their archives provide their own search engines.

Because the WorldWide Web is in demand by computer users, you might have to request access to a particular site several times before you are successful. If you receive a message such as "Unable to locate host" or "Access denied," try again later.

In addition, the success of a Web search depends on the keywords you choose; if a search yields few sources or irrelevant ones, try rephrasing your keywords or choosing more specific ones to locate the most useful information. If your topic is *ecology*, for example, you may find information under the terms *ecosystem, environment, pollution,* and *endangered species,* as well as a number of other related keywords, depending on the focus of your research. As with library searches, however, you may need to narrow your topic in order to keep the number of sources manageable. When you find a source that seems promising, be sure to create a bookmark for the Web page so you can return to it easily later on.

Finally, while the Web cannot provide the helpful advice and expertise of a reference librarian, you can contact authors of Web pages by E-mail to find additional resources.

Using Other Tools to Access the Internet

In addition to the WorldWide Web, other resources for accessing information on the Internet include Telnet, File Transfer Protocol (FTP), Archie, and Gopher. Helpful in research, these resources are available on the Internet, through computer-user groups, and from Internet service providers.

Telnet

Telnet is a software networking tool that allows you to log on to another computer—called the *host computer*—through your modem or a direct network connection. The host computer may be in the same room or on the other side of the world. Once connected, you can access any services or information that the host computer makes available. For example, you might browse the card catalogues of various college libraries or read newspaper articles, government documents, and reports of recent scientific research. Many different kinds of information can be located through Telnet. Telnet makes it possible for you to use FTP, Archie, and Gopher to find and download information stored in thousands of host computers all over the world.

File Transfer Protocol (FTP)

File Transfer Protocol (FTP) is a standard communication format that allows files to be transferred across computer networks, even across networks composed of different kinds of computers. For example, documents created on a Macintosh computer may be downloaded and read on an IBM-compatible computer through FTP. Although similar in function to Telnet in that it allows you to log on to and read information stored in host computers, FTP can also transfer that information to your computer, provided you are granted access. FTP also allows you to create, delete, and rename files on a remote system when you have been granted these privileges.

Generally, when people refer to FTP as a research tool, they are referring to *anonymous FTP*—a special "public" space provided by many host computers for storing documents that may be accessed freely by anyone. To retrieve a file using anonymous FTP, you log on to the host computer using the login name *anonymous* and any password (usually your E-mail address). You then search the directories and files of the public archives on that host computer and download the file you wish to retrieve. FTP works best when you know the location of the information you are seeking.

Archie

Because the Internet is such a large collection of networks, it can be difficult for you to find and keep track of the locations of all the information you seek. *Archie* is a system that indexes files on host computers that allow the general public to gain access to them, and thereby provides a way of searching for specific kinds of information. Under this system, host computers register as Archie servers; once a month, each Archie server is asked to update its list of files on the system's master index.

You can conduct an on-line search of the Archie index by file name (or part of it) using an Archie client program, such as Anarchie, which is available on-line as well as from service providers and computer-user groups. Following the Archie search, you would use FTP to access the host computer where the file is located.

Gopher

The *Gopher* system functions like the subject cards in a library's card catalogue, allowing you to browse by topic, rather than by file name or location, and to find information on the same subject grouped together. In addition, you can browse the Internet by choosing resources from menus. When you find a source that interests you, Gopher can retrieve it for you to read or save without using FTP. Most Gopher client programs, like WorldWide Web browsers, also include the bookmark feature, which makes it easy to return to sources.

Gopher indexing services vary, particularly in the way subjects are organized and classified. Therefore, you need to be resourceful, trying out different approaches to locate information on a particular topic.

Using Special Interest Groups on the Internet

Joining Discussion Groups

To conduct research on a particular topic on the Internet, you may also find it helpful to join a *computer discussion group* on your topic. Discussion groups operate like large mailing lists. Members of a group communicate with each other through E-mail. A message sent by any group member to the list is automatically distributed to everyone who subscribes to that list.

Various discussion groups and their E-mail addresses can be found in computer publications, special interest magazines, print directories in the library, and by word of mouth. You may also conduct on-line searches to find discussion groups on particular topics. Many discussion groups are managed by special software such as listserv, which automatically takes care of the details of operating the list: adding new subscribers, distributing messages, and deleting the addresses of members who leave the group (unsubscribing). You can subscribe to most discussion groups at no cost. To subscribe to a particular group, you simply send an E-mail request to the group's listserv E-mail address. Once you are a member, any messages sent to the group are automatically sent to you, and any messages you send are automatically distributed to the other members of the group.

Participating in Newsgroups

Newsgroups are similar to discussion groups except that membership is not required. You can read and post messages to a newsgroup even if you do not subscribe to it. Messages sent to the newsgroup are posted for anyone to read and respond to, much like a public bulletin board. Readers can browse the messages, dropping in and following a discussion that interests them and ignoring the rest.

Thousands of newsgroups currently exist on the Internet. As with discussion groups, they are organized primarily by topic. Software programs such as Nuntius and Newswatcher are widely available and make it easy to browse, read, and save newsgroup messages.

Using Discussion Groups and Newsgroups

Although discussion groups and newsgroups are not authoritative sources of factual information in the same way that published library sources are, they can serve many useful functions in research and writing. A computer group can help you conduct preliminary research on a topic or seek some general background information on a controversy—how it developed and whether it has been resolved.

- For a paper proposing changes in public schools, a group focusing on child development may alert you to some interesting new research on how play supports language development, suggesting new models for learning environments.
- For a paper explaining the concept of ecology, you may find that there are various interpretations of the concept among scholars in the field. Reading messages posted to a group on ecology can give you a good sense of the major questions, issues, and trends related to your topic.

Discussion groups and newsgroups can provide a means of conducting field research on a topic. For example, you might conduct an informal public opinion poll, sample the current thinking about a topic, or post a question you'd like answered. Groups can also help you find and evaluate useful sources on a topic.

- For a paper arguing the position that there ought to be import quotas on Japanese cars, you might send a message to a discussion group or newsgroup on trade issues, asking for recent sources of information on trade practices.
- For a paper proposing a solution to the problem of endangered species, you might post a request for help in evaluating sources: "What are the three most important books or articles to read on the preservation of critical habitats?"
- For an essay arguing the position that the government should be more flexible in seeking to preserve wetlands, you may have found two important sources that contradict each other. You might describe the contradiction, and ask the group members whether recent opinion has favored one point of view over the other.

Discussion groups vary from lively to nearly inactive; members may be extremely polite or openly combative; and the level of discussion may range from technical and scholarly to casual. Read enough messages from a particular group to get a sense of the tone and level of the discussion before subscribing or posting a message to the group yourself. Be polite when asking for help, and gracious in thanking those who respond.

Establishing E-Mail Contact with Experts

Another advantage of using the Internet for research is that you can contact other researchers—authors, scholars, scientists, government officials, and so on—directly by sending E-mail. Of course, you may also contact these experts by letter or telephone, but you are most likely to receive a response if you send an E-mail message. Many people are willing to respond to specific requests for information. For instance, if you have additional questions after reading an article on your topic, you might send your questions to the author. To locate a person's E-mail address, try looking at published papers, books, or on-line documents, many of which now include the writer's E-mail address.

You may also find E-mail useful for requesting an interview with an expert. In your E-mail message, introduce yourself, briefly describe the purpose and general topic of the interview, and request a time and place convenient for the person you wish to interview. You might even conduct the interview by E-mail if the interviewee cannot meet with you personally. After the interview, be sure to send a note of thanks via E-mail or regular mail.

The following sources of information about the Internet can help you learn more about this valuable research tool.

> Hahn, Harley, and Rick Stout. *The Internet Complete Reference.* Berkeley: Osborne McGraw-Hill, 1994.
>
> Krol, Ed. *The Whole Internet User's Guide and Catalogue.* Sebastopol, CA: O'Reilly & Associates, 1994.
>
> LaQuey, Tracy. *The Internet Companion: A Beginner's Guide to Global Networking.* 2nd ed. Reading: Addison-Wesley, 1994.

READING SOURCES WITH A CRITICAL EYE

From the very beginning of your search, you should evaluate potential sources to determine which ones to use in your essay. (Suggestions for deciding which sources to consult at an early stage of your research are given on pp. 234–35.) Obviously, you must decide which sources provide information relevant to the topic. But you also must read sources with a critical eye to decide how credible or trustworthy they are. Just because a book or essay appears in print does not necessarily mean the information or opinions within it are reliable.

Selecting Relevant Sources

Begin your evaluation of sources by narrowing your working bibliography to the most relevant works. Consider them in terms of scope, date of pubication, and viewpoint.

Scope and Approach

To decide how relevant a particular source is to your topic, you need to examine the source in depth. Do not depend on title alone, for it may be misleading. If the source is a book, check its table of contents and index to see how many pages are devoted to the precise subject you are exploring. In most cases you will want an in-depth, not a superficial, treatment of the subject. Read the preface or intro- duction to a book or the abstract or opening paragraphs of an article and any biographical information given about the author to determine the author's basic approach to the subject or special way of looking at it. As you look at these elements, consider the following questions:

- Does the source provide a general or specialized view? General sources are helpful early in your research, but you then need the authority or up-to-date coverage of specialized sources. Extremely specialized works, however, may be too technical.
- Is the source long enough to provide adequate detail?
- Was the source written for general readers? Specialists? Advocates? Critics?
- Is the author an expert on the topic? Does the author's way of looking at the topic support or challenge your own views?

Date of Publication

Although you should always consult the most up-to-date sources available on your subject, older sources often establish the principles, theories, and data upon which later work rests and may provide a useful perspective for evaluating it. Since many older works are considered authoritative, you may want to become familiar with them. To determine which sources are authoritative, note the ones that are cited most often in encyclopedia articles, bibliographies, and recent works on the subject.

Viewpoint

Your sources should represent a variety of viewpoints on the subject. Just as you would not depend on a single author for all of your information, so you do not want to use authors who all belong to the same school of thought. For suggestions on determining authors' viewpoints, see the next section, Identifying Bias.

Using sources that represent different viewpoints is especially important when developing an argument for one of the essay assignments in Chapters 4–6. During your invention work in those chapters, you may want to research what others have said about your subject to see what positions have been staked out and what arguments have been made. You will then be able to define the issue more care- fully, collect arguments supporting your position, and anticipate arguments op- posing it.

Identifying Bias

One of the most important aspects of evaluating a source is identifying any bias in its treatment of the subject. Although the word *bias* may sound like a criticism or drawback, it simply refers to the fact that most writing is not neutral or objective and does not try or claim to be. Authors come to their subjects with particular viewpoints. In using sources, you must consider carefully how these viewpoints are reflected in the writing and how they affect the way authors present their arguments.

Although the text of the source gives you the most precise indication of the author's viewpoint, you can often get a good idea by looking at the preface or introduction or at the sources the author cites. When you examine a reference, you can often determine the general point of view it represents by considering the following elements:

- *Title.* Does the title or subtitle indicate the text's bias? Watch for "loaded" words or confrontational phrasing.
- *Author.* What is the author's professional title and/or affiliation? What is the author's perspective? Is he or she in favor of something or at odds with it? What has persuaded the author to take this viewpoint? How might the author's professional affiliation affect his or her perspective? What is the author's tone? Information on the author may also be available in the book or article itself or in biographical sources available in the library.
- *Presentation of argument.* Almost every written work asserts a point of view or makes an argument for something the author considers important. To determine this position and the reason behind it, look for the main point. What evidence does the author provide as support for this point? Is the evidence from authoritative sources? Is the evidence persuasive? Does the author accommodate or refute opposing arguments?
- *Publication information.* Was the book published by a commercial publisher, a corporation, a government agency, or an interest group? What is that organization's position on the topic? Is the author funded by or affiliated with the organization?
- *Editorial slant.* What kind of periodical published the article—popular, academic, or alternative? Knowing some background about the publisher or periodical can help determine bias, because all periodicals have definite editorial slants. In cases where the publication title does not indicate bias, there are reference sources that may help you determine this information. Two of the most common are the *Gale Directory of Publications and Broadcast Media* (1990) and *Magazines for Libraries* (1992).

11 Strategies for Using and Acknowledging Sources

Much of the writing you do in college requires you to use sources in combination with your own firsthand observation and analysis. Any time you get information and ideas from others—whether from reading, interviews, computer bulletin boards, lectures, or other print and nonprint material—you are using sources.

In college, using sources is not only acceptable, it is expected. No matter how original their thinking, educated people nearly always base their original thought on the work of others. When you cite material from another source, you need to acknowledge the source, usually by giving the author and page or date (depending on the documentation system) in parentheses in your text and including a list of works cited or references at the end of your paper. This chapter provides guidelines for using sources effectively and acknowledging them accurately.

USING SOURCES

Writers commonly use sources by quoting directly as well as by paraphrasing and by summarizing. This section provides guidelines for deciding when to use each of these three methods and how to do so effectively.

Deciding Whether to Quote, Paraphrase, or Summarize

As a general rule, quote only in these situations: (1) when the wording of the source is particularly memorable or vivid or expresses a point so well that you cannot improve it without destroying the meaning; (2) when the words of reliable and respected authorities would lend support to your position; (3) when you wish to highlight the author's opinions; or (4) when you wish to cite an author whose opinions challenge or vary greatly from other experts'. Paraphrase those passages whose details you wish to note completely but whose language is not particularly striking. Summarize any long passages whose main points you wish to record selectively as background or general support for a point you are making.

Quoting

Quotations should duplicate the source exactly. If the source has an error, copy it and add the notation *sic* (Latin for "thus") in brackets immediately after the error to indicate that it is not yours but your source's:

According to a recent newspaper article, "Plagirism [sic] is a problem among journalists and scholars as well as students" (Berensen 62).

However, you can change quotations (1) to emphasize particular words by underlining or italicizing them, (2) to omit irrelevant information or to make the quotation conform grammatically to your sentence by using ellipses, and (3) to make the quotation conform grammatically or to insert information by using brackets.

- *Underlining or italicizing for emphasis.* In quotations, underline or italicize the words you want to emphasize, and add the notation *emphasis added* in parentheses at the end of the sentence.

  In a review of psychosocial literature on adolescence, Elder (1975) concludes: "Adolescents who fail to receive guidance, affection, and concern from parents—whether by parental inattention or absence—are likely to rely heavily on peers for emotional gratification, advice, and companionship, *to anticipate a relatively unrewarding future,* and to engage in antisocial activities" (emphasis added).

- *Using ellipses for omissions.* An ellipsis—three spaced periods (. . .)—signals that something has been left out of a quotation. A writer may decide to leave certain words out of a quotation because they are not relevant to the point being made or because they add information readers will not need in the new context in which the quotation is being used. When you quote only single words or phrases, you don't need to use an ellipsis because it is obvious that you have left out some of the original. However, when you omit words from within a quotation, you must use an ellipsis to mark the missing words. When the omission occurs within the sentence, put a space *before* and *after* each of the three periods:

  Hermione Roddice is described in Lawrence's *Women in Love* as a "woman of the new school, full of intellectuality and . . . nerve-worn with consciousness" (17).

  When the omission falls at the end of the sentence, place a sentence period *directly after* the last word, followed by three spaced periods, for a total of four periods:

  But Grimaldi's recent commentary on Aristotle contends that for Aristotle rhetoric, like dialectic, had "no limited and unique subject matter upon which it must be exercised. . . . Instead, rhetoric as an art transcends all specific disciplines and may be brought into play in them" (6).

  A period plus an ellipsis can indicate the omission of the rest of a sentence as well as of whole sentences, paragraphs, even pages. When a parenthetical reference follows the ellipsis at the end of a sentence, place the three spaced periods after the quotation, and place the sentence period after the final parenthesis:

  But Grimaldi's recent commentary on Aristotle contends that for Aristotle rhetoric, like dialectic, had "no limited and unique subject matter upon which it must be exercised . . ." (6).

▪ *Using brackets for insertions or changes.* Use brackets around an insertion or a change needed to make a quotation conform grammatically to your sentence, such as a change in verb tense or a change in the capitalization of the first letter of the first word of a quotation, or to replace an unclear pronoun. In this example from an essay on James Joyce's "Araby," the writer adapts Joyce's phrases "we played till our bodies glowed" and "shook music from the buckled harness" to fit the tense of her sentences:

> In the dark, cold streets during the "short days of winter," the boys must generate their own heat by "[playing] till [their] bodies glowed." Music is "[shaken] from the buckled harness" as if it were unnatural, and the singers in the market chant nasally of "the troubles in our native land" (30).

You may also use brackets to add or substitute explanatory material in a quotation.

> Guterson notes that among Native Americans in Florida, "education was in the home; learning by doing was reinforced by the myths and legends which repeated the basic value system of their [the Seminoles'] way of life" (159).

Several kinds of changes necessary to make a quotation conform grammatically to another sentence may be made without any signal to readers: (1) a period at the end of a quotation may be changed to a comma if you are using the quotation within your own sentence, and (2) double quotation marks enclosing a quotation may be changed to single quotation marks when that quotation is enclosed within a longer quotation.

Integrating Quotations

Depending on its length, a quotation may be integrated into your text by enclosing it in quotation marks or set off from your text in a block without quotation marks.

In-Text Quotations

Incorporate brief quotations (no more than four typed lines of prose or three lines of poetry) into your text. You may place the quotation virtually any place in your sentence:

At the Beginning
"To live a life is not to cross a field," Sutherland quotes Pasternak at the beginning of her narrative (11).

In the Middle
Woolf begins and ends by speaking of the need of the woman writer to have "money and a room of her own" (4)—an idea that certainly spoke to Plath's condition, especially in her impoverished and harassed last six months.

At the End
In *The Second Sex*, Simone de Beauvoir describes such an experience as one in which the girl "becomes as object, and she sees herself as object" (378).

Divided by Your Own Words

"Science usually prefers the literal to the nonliteral term," Kinneavy writes,
"—that is, figures of speech are often out of place in science" (177).

When you quote poetry within your text, use a slash with spaces before and after
(/) to signal the end of each line of verse:

> Alluding to St. Augustine's distinction between the City of God and the Earthly
> City, Lowell writes that "much against my will / I left the City of God where it
> belongs" ("Beyond the Alps" lines 4–5).

Block Quotations

Put in block form prose quotations of five or more typed lines and poetry quotations of four or more lines. For APA style, use block form for quotations of 40
or more words. If you are using MLA style, indent the quotation an inch (or ten
spaces) from the left margin, as shown below. If you're using the APA style, indent
the block quotation five to seven spaces, keeping your indents consistent throughout your paper. Double-space between lines just as you do in your text. *Do not*
enclose the passage within quotation marks. Use a colon to introduce a block
quotation, unless the context calls for another punctuation mark or none at all.
When quoting a single paragraph or part of one, do not indent the first line of
the quotation more than the rest. In quoting two or more paragraphs, indent the
first line of each paragraph an extra quarter inch (or three spaces). If you are using
the APA style, the first line of subsequent paragraphs in the block quotation indents an additional five to seven spaces from the block quotation indent.

```
In "A Literary Legacy from Dunbar to Baraka," Margaret
Walker says of Paul Lawrence Dunbar's dialect poems:
                He realized that the white world in the United
                States tolerated his literary genius only be-
                cause of his "jingles in a broken tongue," and
                they found the old "darky" tales and speech
                amusing and within the vein of folklore into
                which they wished to classify all Negro life.
                This troubled Dunbar because he realized that
                white America was denigrating him as a writer
                and as a man. (70)
```

Punctuating Introductory Statements

Statements that introduce quotations take a range of punctuation marks and lead-
in words. Here are some examples of ways writers typically introduce quotations:

Introducing a Quotation with a Colon

As George Williams notes, protection of white privilege is critical to patterns of
discrimination: "Whenever a number of persons within a society have enjoyed
for a considerable period of time certain opportunities for getting wealth, for

exercising power and authority, and for successfully claiming prestige and social deference, there is a strong tendency for these people to feel that these benefits are theirs 'by right' " (727).

Introducing a Quotation with a Comma

Similarly, Duncan Turner asserts, "As matters now stand, it is unwise to talk about communication without some understanding of Burke" (259).

Introducing a Quotation Using that

Noting this failure, Alice Miller asserts that "the reason for her despair was not her suffering but the impossibility of communicating her suffering to another person" (255).

Introducing a Quotation Using as . . . said

The token women writers authenticated the male canon without disrupting it, for as Ruth Bleier has said, "The last thing society desires of its women has been intellectuality and independence" (73).

Punctuating within Quotations

Although punctuation within a quotation should reproduce the original, some adaptations may be necessary. Use single quotation marks for quotations within the quotation:

Original Passage

E. D. Hirsch also recognizes the connection between family and learning, suggesting in his discussion of family background and academic achievement "that the significant part of our children's education has been going on outside rather than inside the schools" (Guterson 16–17).

Quoted Version

Guterson claims that E. D. Hirsch "also recognizes the connection between family and learning, suggesting in his discussion of family background and academic achievement 'that the significant part of our children's education has been going on outside rather than inside the schools' " (16–17).

If the quotation ends with a question mark or an exclamation point, retain the original punctuation:

"Did you think I loved you?" Edith later asks Dombey (566).

If a quotation ending with a question mark or an exclamation point concludes your sentence, retain the question mark or exclamation point and put the parenthetical reference and sentence period outside the quotation marks:

Edith later asks Dombey, "Did you think I loved you?" (566).

Avoiding Grammatical Tangles

When you incorporate quotations into your writing, and especially when you omit words from quotations, you run the risk of creating ungrammatical sentences.

Here are three common errors you should try to avoid: verb incompatibility, ungrammatical omissions, and sentence fragments.

Verb Incompatibility

When this error occurs, the verb form in the introductory statement is grammatically incompatible with the verb form in the quotation. When your quotation has a verb form that does not fit in with your text, it is usually possible to use just part of the quotation, thus avoiding verb incompatibility.

> The narrator suggests his bitter disappointment when ~~"I~~ *he*
> ~~saw myself~~ *describes seeing himself "* as a creature driven and derided by vanity"
>
> (35).

An Awkward Omission

Sometimes the omission of text from a quotation results in an ungrammatical sentence. Two ways of correcting the grammar are (1) by adapting the quotation (with brackets) so that its parts fit together grammatically and (2) by using only one part of the quotation.

> From the moment of the boy's arrival in Araby, the bazaar
>
> is presented as a commercial enterprise: ''I could not
>
> find any sixpenny entrance and . . . hand~~ing~~ *[ed]* a shilling
>
> to a weary-looking man'' (34).

OR

> From the moment of the boy's arrival at Araby, the bazaar
>
> is presented as a commercial enterprise: ~~''I~~ *he* "could not
>
> find any sixpenny entrance" and ~~. . . handing a shilling~~ *so had to pay a shilling to get in (34).*
>
> ~~to a weary-looking man'' (34).~~

An Incomplete Introductory Sentence

Sometimes when a quotation is a complete sentence, writers carelessly neglect the introductory sentence—for example, by forgetting to include a verb. Even though the quotation is a complete sentence, the total statement is then a sentence fragment.

> The girl's interest in the bazaar ~~leading~~ *leads* the narrator to
>
> make what amounts to a sacred oath: ''If I go . . . I will
>
> bring you something'' (32).

Paraphrasing and Summarizing

In addition to quoting sources, writers have the option of paraphrasing or summarizing what others have written. In a *paraphrase*, writers accurately and thoroughly state in their own words all the relevant information from a passage, without any additional comments or elaborations. A paraphrase is useful for recording details of the passage when the order of the details is important but the source's wording is not. Because all the details of the passage are noted, a paraphrase is often about the same length as the original passage.

In a *summary*, writers boil down a long passage—several pages or even a whole chapter or work—to its main ideas using their own words. Unlike a paraphrase, a summary conveys the gist of a source, using just enough information to record the points the summarizer chooses to emphasize. In choosing what to include in a summary, be sure not to distort the author's meaning.

To avoid plagiarizing inadvertently, you must use *your own words and sentence structures* when paraphrasing or summarizing. If you include some of the author's words, enclose them in quotation marks. Note that even though a paraphrase or summary is restated in your own words, you still need to include a parenthetical citation that identifies the original source of the ideas.

Here is a passage from a book on home schooling and an example of a paraphrase of it.

Original Passage

Bruner and the discovery theorists have also illuminated conditions that apparently pave the way for learning. It is significant that these conditions are unique to each learner, so unique in fact, that in many cases classrooms can't provide them. Bruner also contends that the more one discovers information in a great variety of circumstances the more likely one is to develop the inner categories required to organize that information. Yet life at school, which is for the most part generic and predictable, daily keeps many children from the great variety of circumstances they need to learn well.

—*David Guterson,* Family Matters: Why Homeschooling Makes Sense (p. 172)

Paraphrase

According to Guterson, the discovery theorists, particularly Bruner, have identified the "conditions" that allow learning to take place. Because these conditions are specific to each individual, many children are not able to learn in the classroom. According to Bruner, when people can explore information in different situations, they learn to classify and order what they discover. The general routine of the school day, however, does not provide children with the diverse activities and situations that would allow them to learn these skills (172).

Here is an example of a summary of the longer section that contains the original passage printed above:

Summary

In looking at different theories of learning that discuss individual-based programs (such as home schooling) versus the public school system, Guterson describes

the disagreements among "cognitivist" theorists. One group, the discovery theorists, believe that individual children learn by creating their own ways of sorting
the information they take in from their experiences. Schools should help students
develop better ways of organizing new material, not just present them with
material that is already categorized, as traditional schools do. Assimilationist
theorists, on the other hand, believe that children learn by linking what they
don't know to information they already know. These theorists claim that traditional schools help students learn when they present information in ways that
allow children to fit the new material into categories they have already developed (171–75).

Introducing Cited Material

Notice in the preceding examples that the source is acknowledged by name. Even
when you use your own words to present someone else's information, you generally must acknowledge that you borrowed the information. The only types of
information that do not require acknowledgment are common knowledge (John
F. Kennedy was assassinated in Dallas), familiar sayings ("haste makes waste"),
and well-known quotations ("All's well that ends well").

The documentation guidelines later in this chapter present various ways of
citing the sources you quote, paraphrase, and summarize, but in general you
should be sure your readers can tell where a source's words or ideas begin and
end. You can accomplish this most readily by separating your words from those
of the source's with such phrases as "According to Smith," "Peters claims," "As
Jones asserts," and so on. When you cite a source for the first time, use the author's
full name; afterwards, use just the last name.

Avoiding Plagiarism

Writers—students and professionals alike—occasionally misuse sources by failing
to acknowledge them properly. The word *plagiarism*, which derives from the Latin
word for "kidnapping," refers to the unacknowledged use of another's words,
ideas, or information. Students sometimes get into trouble because they mistakenly
assume that plagiarizing occurs only when another writer's exact words are used
without acknowledgment. Keep in mind, however, that you need to indicate the
source of any ideas or information you have taken note of in your research for a
paper, whether you have paraphrased, summarized, or quoted from the source.

Some people plagiarize simply because they do not know the conventions for
using and acknowledging sources. This chapter makes clear how to incorporate
sources into your writing and how to acknowledge your use of those sources.
Others plagiarize because they keep sloppy notes and thus fail to distinguish between their own and their source's ideas. Either they neglect to enclose their
source's words in quotation marks or do not indicate when they are paraphrasing
or summarizing a source's ideas and information. If you keep a working bibliography and careful notes, you will not make this serious mistake. (See pp. 230–31
for tips on keeping a working bibliography and taking notes.)

There is still another reason some people plagiarize: they feel unable to write the paper by themselves. They feel overwhelmed by the writing task or by the deadline or by their own and others' expectations of them. This sense of inadequacy is not experienced by students alone. In a *Los Angeles Times* article on the subject, a journalist whose plagiarizing was discovered explained why he had done it. He said that when he read a column by another journalist on a subject he was preparing to write about, he felt that the other writer "said what I wanted to say and he said it better." If you experience this same anxiety about your work, speak to your instructor. Don't run the risk of failing a course or being expelled because of plagiarizing.

ACKNOWLEDGING SOURCES: MLA AND APA DOCUMENTATION STYLES

Although there is no universally agreed-upon system for acknowledging sources, there is agreement on both the need for documentation and the items that should be included. Writers should acknowledge sources for two reasons: to give credit to those sources, and to enable readers to consult the sources for further information.

Most documentation styles combine some kind of in-text citations keyed to a separate list of works cited. The information required in the in-text citations and the order and content of the works-cited entries vary across the disciplines, but two styles predominate: the author-page system, used in the humanities and advocated by the Modern Language Association (MLA), and the author-year system, used in the natural and social sciences and advocated by the American Psychological Association (APA). Be sure to check with your instructor about which style to use, or whether you should use some other style.

This section presents the basic features of the MLA and APA documentation styles. In Part One of this book, you can find an example of a student essay that follows the MLA style (Jessica Statsky, Chapter 5) and one that uses the APA style (Patrick O'Malley, Chapter 6).

If you find that you need more information about these documentation styles, consult the *MLA Handbook for Writers of Research Papers*, Fourth Edition (1995), or the *Publication Manual of the American Psychological Association*, Fourth Edition (1994).

Parenthetical Citation in Text

The MLA author-page system requires that in-text citations include the author's last name and the page number of the original passage being cited. The APA author-year system calls for the last name of the author and the year of publication of the original work in the citation. If the cited material is a quotation, you also need to include the page number of the original. If the cited material is not a quotation the page number is optional.

| MLA | Dr. James is described as a "not-too-skeletal Ichabod Crane" (Simon 68). |
| APA | Dr. James is described as a "not-too-skeletal Ichabod Crane" (Simon, 1982, p. 68). |

Notice that the APA style uses commas to separate author, year, and page as well as *p.* for "page" (Simon, 1982, p. 68), whereas the MLA uses no punctuation between author and page (Simon 68). Note also that the parenthetical citations in both cases come before the final period. With block quotations, however, the citation comes after the final period preceded by a space (see p. 258 for an example).

If the author's name is mentioned in your text, put the page reference in parentheses as close as possible to the quoted material, but without disrupting the flow of the sentence. For the APA style, cite the year in parentheses directly following the author's name, and place the page reference in parentheses before the final sentence period.

| MLA | Simon describes Dr. James as a "not-too-skeletal Ichabod Crane" (68). |
| APA | Simon (1982) describes Dr. James as a "not-too-skeletal Ichabod Crane" (p. 68). |

To cite a source by two or three authors, the MLA uses all the authors' last names; for works with more than three authors, it uses all the authors' names or just the first author's name followed by *et al.* To cite works with three to five authors in the APA style, use all the authors' last names the first time the reference occurs and the last name of the first author followed by *et al.* subsequently. If a source has more than six authors, the APA uses only the last name of the first author and *et al.* at first and subsequent references.

MLA	Dyal, Corning, and Willows identify several types of students, including the "Authority-Rebel" (4).
APA	Dyal, Corning, and Willows (1975) identify several types of students, including the "Authority-Rebel" (p. 4).
MLA	The Authority-Rebel "tends to see himself as superior to other students in the class" (Dyal, Corning, and Willows 4).
APA	The Authority-Rebel "tends to see himself as superior to other students in the class" (Dyal et al., 1975, p. 4).

To cite one of two or more works by the same author(s), the MLA includes the author's last name, a shortened version of the title, and the page. The APA uses the author's last name plus the year (and the page, if you are citing a quotation). When more than one work being cited was published by an author in the same year, the APA style uses lowercase letters with the date (*1973a, 1973b*).

| MLA | When old paint becomes transparent, it sometimes shows the artist's original plans: "a tree will show through a woman's dress" (Hellman, *Pentimento* 1). |

| APA | When old paint becomes transparent, it sometimes shows the artist's original plans: "a tree will show through a woman's dress" (Hellman, 1973, p. 1). |

To cite a work listed only by its title, both the MLA and the APA use a shortened version of the title.

| MLA | An international pollution treaty still to be ratified would prohibit all plastic garbage from being dumped at sea ("Awash" 26). |
| APA | An international pollution treaty still to be ratified would prohibit all plastic garbage from being dumped at sea ("Awash," 1987). |

To quote material taken not from the original source but from a secondary source that quotes the original, both the MLA and the APA give the secondary source in the list of works cited, and acknowledge that the original was quoted in a secondary source in the text.

| MLA | E. M. Forster says "the collapse of all civilization, so realistic for us, sounded in Matthew Arnold's ears like a distant and harmonious cataract" (qtd. in Trilling 11). |
| APA | E. M. Forster says "the collapse of all civilization, so realistic for us, sounded in Matthew Arnold's ears like a distant and harmonious cataract" (as cited in Trilling, 1955, p. 11). |

List of Works Cited or References

Providing full information for the parenthetical citations in the text, the list of works cited identifies all the sources the writer uses. Every source cited in the text must refer to an entry in the works-cited list. And, conversely, every entry in the works-cited list must correspond to at least one parenthetical citation in the text.

Whereas the MLA style recommends the title *Works Cited,* the APA prefers *References.* Both alphabetize the entries according to the first author's last name. However, when several works by the same author are listed, the APA provides the following rules for arranging the list:

- Same name single-author entries precede multiple-author entries:

```
Aaron, P.   (1990).

Aaron, P., & Zorn, C. R.   (1985).
```

- Entries with the same first author and different second author should be alphabetized according to the second author's last name:

```
Aaron, P., & Charleston, W.   (1987).

Aaron, P., & Zorn, C. R.   (1991).
```

- Entries by the same authors should be arranged by year of publication, in chronological order:

```
Aaron, P., & Charleston, W.   (1987).

Aaron, P., & Charleston, W.   (1993).
```

▪ Entries by the same author(s) with the same publication year should be arranged alphabetically by title (according to the first word after *A*, *An*, or *The*), and low-ercase letters (*a*, *b*, *c*, and so on) should follow the year within the parentheses:

```
Aaron, P.  (1990a).  Basic . . .

Aaron, P.  (1990b).  Elements . . .
```

In the MLA style, multiple works by the same author (or same group of authors), are alphabetized by title. The author's name is given for the first entry only; in subsequent entries, three hyphens and a period are used.

```
Vidal, Gore.  Empire.  New York: Random, 1987.

---.  Lincoln.  New York: Random, 1984.
```

The essential difference between the MLA and APA styles of listing sources is the order in which the information is presented. The MLA follows this order: author's name; title; publication source, year, and page. The APA puts the year after the author's name. In the examples that follow, note also the differences in capitalization and arrangement between the two documentation styles.

The MLA style requires a "hanging indent," which means that the first line of a works-cited entry is not indented but subsequent lines of the entry are indented. The MLA specifies an indent of half an inch, or five spaces.

The APA recommends that only the *first* line of each entry be indented five to seven spaces for papers intended for publication; for student papers, however, it notes that a hanging indent of five to seven spaces may be preferred. The following examples demonstrate a hanging indent of five to seven spaces for both documentation styles.

Books

A Book by a Single Author

```
MLA      Guterson, David. Family Matters: Why Homeschooling
             Makes Sense. San Diego: Harcourt, 1992.

APA      Guterson, D. (1992). Family matters: Why home-
             schooling makes sense. San Diego: Harcourt
             Brace.
```

A Book by an Agency or Corporation

```
MLA      Association for Research in Nervous and Mental
             Disease. The Circulation of the Brain and
             Spinal Cord: A Symposium on Blood Supply. New
             York: Hafner, 1966.

APA      Association for Research in Nervous and Mental
             Disease. (1966). The circulation of the brain
             and spinal cord: A symposium on blood supply.
             New York: Hafner.
```

A Book by More Than One Author

MLA   Gottfredson, Stephen G., and Sean McConville.
          America's Correctional Crisis. Westport:
          Greenwood, 1987.

APA   Gottfredson, S. G., & McConville, S. (1987).
          America's correctional crisis. Westport, CT:
          Greenwood.

MLA   Dyal, James A., William C. Corning, and Dale M.
          Willows. Readings in Psychology: The Search
          for Alternatives. 3rd ed. New York: McGraw,
          1975.

APA   Dyal, J. A., Corning, W. C., & Willows, D. M.
          (1975). Readings in psychology: The search
          for alternatives (3rd ed.). New York: McGraw-
          Hill.

For works by more than three authors, the MLA lists all the authors' names or the name of the first author followed by *et al.* The APA cites all authors' names regardless of the number.

MLA   Nielsen, Niels C., Jr., et al. Religions of the
          World. 3rd ed. New York: St. Martin's, 1992.

A Book by an Unknown Author   Use title in place of author.

MLA   Rand McNally Commercial Atlas. Skokie: Rand, 1993.

APA   Rand McNally commercial atlas. (1993). Skokie, IL:
          Rand McNally.

A Book with an Author and Editor

APA   Arnold, M. (1966). Culture and anarchy (J. Dover
          Wilson, Ed.). Cambridge: Cambridge University
          Press. (Original work published 1869)

If you refer to the text itself, begin the entry with the author:

MLA   Arnold, Matthew. Culture and Anarchy. Ed. J. Dover
          Wilson. Cambridge: Cambridge UP, 1966.

If you cite the editor in your paper, begin the entry with the editor:

MLA   Wilson, J. Dover, ed. Culture and Anarchy. By
          Matthew Arnold. 1869. Cambridge: Cambridge
          UP, 1966.

An Edited Collection

MLA   Carter, Kathryn, and Carole Spitzack, eds. Doing
          Research on Women's Communication. Norwood:
          Ablex, 1989.

APA   Carter, K., & Spitzack, C. (Eds.). (1989). <u>Doing research on women's communication.</u> Norwood, NJ: Ablex.

A Work in an Anthology or Collection

MLA   Fairbairn-Dunlop, Peggy. "Women and Agriculture in Western Samoa." <u>Different Places, Different Voices</u>. Ed. Janet H. Momsen and Vivian Kinnaird. London: Routledge, 1993. 211-26.

APA   Fairbairn-Dunlop, P. (1993). Women and agriculture in western Samoa. In J. H. Momsen & V. Kinnaird (Eds.), <u>Different places, different voices</u> (pp. 211-226). London: Routledge.

A Translation

APA   Tolstoy, L. (1972). <u>War and peace.</u> (C. Garnett, Trans.). London: Pan Books. (Original work published 1868-1869)

If you refer to the work itself, begin the entry with the author:

MLA   Tolstoy, Leo. <u>War and Peace</u>. Trans. Constance Garnett. London: Pan, 1972.

If you cite the translator in your text, begin the entry with the translator's name:

MLA   Garnett, Constance, trans. <u>War and Peace</u>. By Leo Tolstoy. London: Pan, 1972.

An Article in a Reference Book

MLA   Suber, Howard. "Motion Picture." <u>Encyclopedia Americana</u>. 1991 ed.

APA   Suber, H. (1991). Motion picture. In <u>Encyclopedia Americana</u> (Vol. 19, pp. 505-539). Danbury, CT: Grolier.

An Introduction, Preface, Foreword, or Afterword

MLA   Holt, John. Introduction. <u>Better Than School</u>. By Nancy Wallace. Burnett: Larson, 1983. 9-14.

APA   Holt, J. (1983). Introduction. In N. Wallace, <u>Better than school</u> (pp. 9-14). Burnett, NY: Larson.

A Government Document

MLA   United States. Cong. Senate. Subcommittee on Con-
                stitutional Amendments of the Committee on
                the Judiciary. Hearings on the "Equal Rights"
                Amendment. 91st Cong., 2nd sess. S. Res. 61.
                Washington: GPO, 1970.

APA   U.S. Department of Health, Education and Welfare.
                (1979). Healthy people: The surgeon general's
                report on health promotion (DHEW Publication
                No. 79-55071). Washington, DC: U.S. Govern-
                ment Printing Office.

An Unpublished Doctoral Dissertation

MLA   Bullock, Barbara. "Basic Needs Fulfillment among
                Less Developed Countries: Social Progress
                over Two Decades of Growth." Diss. Vanderbilt
                U, 1986.

APA   Bullock, B. (1986). Basic needs fulfillment among
                less developed countries: Social progress
                over two decades of growth. Unpublished doc-
                toral dissertation, Vanderbilt University,
                Nashville, TN.

Articles

An Article from a Daily Newspaper

MLA   Wilford, John Noble. "Corn in the New World: A
                Relative Latecomer." New York Times 7 Mar.
                1995, late ed.: C1+.

APA   Wilford, J. N. (1995, March 7). Corn in the New
                World: A relative latecomer. The New York
                Times, pp. C1, C5.

An Article from a Weekly or Biweekly Magazine

MLA   Glastris, Paul. "The New Way to Get Rich." U.S.
                News & World Report 7 May 1990: 26-36.

APA   Glastris, P. (1990, May 7). The new way to get
                rich. U.S. News & World Report, 108, 26-36.

An Article from a Monthly or Bimonthly Magazine

MLA   Rohn, Alfie. "Home Schooling." Atlantic Monthly
                Apr. 1988: 20-25.

APA   Rohn, A. (1988, April). Home schooling. Atlantic
                Monthly, 261, 20-25.

An Article in a Scholarly Journal with Continuous Annual Pagination   The volume number follows the title of the journal.

MLA   Natale, Jo Anna. "Understanding Home Schooling."
             Education Digest 9 (1993): 58-61.

APA   Natale, J. A. (1993). Understanding home school-
             ing. Education Digest, 9, 58-61.

An Article in a Scholarly Journal That Paginates Each Issue Separately   The issue number appears after the volume number. For the MLA, a period separates the two numbers; for the APA, the issue number is in parentheses.

MLA   Epstein, Alexandra. "Teen Parents: What They Need
             to Know." High/Scope Resource 1.2 (1982): 6.

APA   Epstein, A. (1982). Teen parents: What they need
             to know. High/Scope Resource, 1(2), 6.

An Anonymous Article

MLA   "Awash in Garbage." New York Times 15 Aug. 1987,
             sec. 1: 26.

APA   Awash in garbage. (1987, August 15). The New York
             Times, p. A26.

An Editorial

MLA   "Stepping Backward." Editorial. Los Angeles Times
             4 July 1989: B6.

APA   Stepping backward. (1989, July 4). [Editorial].
             The Los Angeles Times, p. B6.

A Letter to the Editor

MLA   Rissman, Edward M. Letter. Los Angeles Times 29
             June 1989: B5.

APA   Rissman, E. M. (1989, June 29). [Letter to the
             editor]. The Los Angeles Times, p. B5.

A Review

MLA   Anders, Jaroslaw. "Dogma and Democracy." Rev. of
             The Church and the Left, by Adam Minchik. New
             Republic 17 May 1993: 42-48.

If you don't know the author, start with the title. If the review is untitled, begin with the words *Rev. of* and alphabetize under the title of the work being reviewed.

APA   Anders, J. (1993, May 17). Dogma and democracy
             [Review of the book The church and the left].
             The New Republic, 208, 42-48.

Other Sources

Computer Software

MLA SPSS/PC+ Studentware Plus. Diskette. Chicago:
     SPSS, 1991.

APA SPSS/PC+ Studentware Plus [Computer software].
     (1991). Chicago: SPSS.

Material from Newsbank

MLA Sharpe, Lora. "A Quilter's Tribute." Boston Globe
     25 Mar. 1989. NewsBank: Social Relations
     (1989): fiche 6, grids B4-6.

Material from a Database on CD-ROM If publication data is available for the work, it should be included. For MLA, the electronic publication date appears at the end of the reference.

MLA Braus, Patricia. "Sex and the Single Spender."
     American Demographics 15.11 (1993): 28-34.
     ABI/INFORM. CD-ROM. UMI-ProQuest. 1993.

APA Braus, P. (1993). Sex and the single spender
     [CD-ROM]. American Demographics, 15(11),
     28-34. Available: ABI/INFORM.

When print and electronic versions of the material are identical, APA prefers a reference to the print version.

Material from an On-line Computer Service Both the MLA and the APA include publication information (if available), the medium, and the name of the service. Because information available through a computer service may not be the same as the original print version, the MLA includes the date the information was accessed. So that readers can locate the article, APA provides the path number at the end of the reference. Notice that the MLA uses a nonhyphenated spelling of the word *online*, while the APA uses a hyphenated spelling, *on-line*.

MLA Reece, Jerry S. "Measuring Investment Center Per-
     formance." Harvard Business Review 56.3
     (1978): 28-40. Online. Dialog. 7 Mar. 1995.

APA Reece, J. S. (1978). Measuring investment center
     performance. Harvard Business Review [On-
     line] 56(3), 28-40. Available: Dialog file
     107, item 673280 047658

Notice that final periods are omitted from entries that end with electronic addresses or with path, file, or item numbers.

Article from an On-line Journal   The MLA includes the volume number and issue number, if given, after the title of the journal. The number of pages or paragraphs appears after the colon, if the source gives them; otherwise, *n. pag.* (for "no pagination") appears. The date of access appears at the end. In the MLA style, the electronic address for the document is optional. If given, it appears after the date of access, preceded by the word *Available* and a colon. The APA requires an availability statement that includes the specific information (such as path, directory, file name, and so on) needed to access the source.

MLA   Moulthrop, Stuart. "You Say You Want a Revolution? Hypertext and the Laws of Media." Postmodern Culture 1.3 (1991): 53 pars. Online. BITNET. 10 Jan. 1993.

APA   Nielsen, R. (1995, March). Radon risks [16 paragraphs]. Carcinogens [On-line serial], 4 (12). Available FTP: Hostname: princeton.edu Directory: pub/carcinogens/1995 File: radon.95.3.12.radonrisks

A WorldWide Web Site   The following MLA format is from an adaptation of MLA style guidelines prepared by Janice W. Walker and approved by the Alliance for Computers and Writing ("ACW Style Sheet," jwalker@chuma.cas.usf.edu). The author's name appears first, if known. Otherwise, begin with the title. If the file is part of a larger work, the title of the complete work follows the title of the work you are citing. The http address and date of access complete the reference. The APA format is derived from the APA's general guidelines for citing on-line sources.

MLA   Burka, Lauren P. "A Hypertext History of Multi-User Dimensions." MUD HISTORY. http://www.ccs.neu.edu/home/lpb/mud-history.html (5 Dec, 1994)

APA   Burka, L, (1994). "A hypertext history of multi-user dimensions." MUD HISTORY [On-line]. Available: http://www.ccs.neu.edu/home/lpb/mud-history.html

A Posting on a Discussion Group or Newsgroup   The following MLA format is from an adaptation of MLA style guidelines prepared by Janice W. Walker and approved by the Alliance for Computers and Writing ("ACW Style Sheet," jwalker@chuma.cas.usf.edu). The name of the author appears first, followed by the subject line and the address of the listserv or newslist. The date appears last. If the author's name is not known, begin with the subject. The APA format is derived from the APA's general guidelines for citing on-line sources.

MLA   Seabrook, Richard H. C. "Community and Progress." cybermind@jefferson.village.virginia.edu (22 Jan. 1994).

APA   Seabrook, R. H. C. Community and progress [On-
line]. Available:cybermind@jefferson.village.
virginia.edu

The APA requires that electronic conversations carried out via an electronic discussion group be cited within the text.

Performances

MLA   <u>Hamlet</u>. By William Shakespeare. Dir. Jonathan
Kent. Perf. Ralph Fiennes. Belasco Theatre,
New York. 20 June 1995.

A Television Program

MLA   "The Universe Within." <u>Nova</u>. Narr. Stacy Keach.
Writ. Beth Hoppe and Bill Lattanzi. Dir. Goro
Koide. PBS. WNET, New York. 7 Mar. 1995.

APA   Hoppe, B., & Lattanzi, B. (1995). The universe
within (G. Koide, Director). In P. Apsell
(Producer), <u>Nova.</u> Boston: WGBH.

A Film

MLA   <u>Boyz N the Hood</u>. Writ. and Dir. John Singleton.
Perf. Ice Cube, Cuba Gooding, Jr., and Larry
Fishburne. Columbia. 1991.

APA   Singleton, J. (Writer and Director). (1991). <u>Boyz
n the hood</u> [Film]. New York: Columbia.

A Music Recording   Unless the medium is a compact disc, the MLA indicates the medium ahead of the name of the manufacturer for an audiocassette, audiotape, or LP.

MLA   Beethoven, Ludwig van. Violin Concerto in D Major,
op. 61. U.S.S.R. State Orchestra. Cond.
Alexander Gauk. David Oistrikh, violinist.
Audiocassette. Allegro, 1980.

            Springsteen, Bruce. "Dancing in the Dark." <u>Born in
the U.S.A.</u> Columbia, 1984.

APA   Beethoven, L. van. (1806). Violin concerto in D
major, op. 61 [Recorded by USSR State Or-
chestra]. (Cassette Recording No. ACS 8044).
New York: Allegro. (1980)

            Springsteen, B. (1984). Dancing in the dark. On
<u>Born in the U.S.A.</u> [CD]. New York: Columbia.

If the recording date differs from the copyright date, APA requires that it should appear in parentheses after the name of the label. If it is necessary to include a number for the recording, use parentheses for the medium; otherwise, use brackets.

An Interview

MLA   Lowell, Robert. "Robert Lowell." Interview with
                Frederick Seidel. <u>Paris Review</u> 25 (1975): 56-
                95.

        Franklin, Ann. Personal interview. 3 Sept. 1983.

When using the APA style, do not list personal inteviews in your references list. Simply cite the person's name in your text, and in parentheses give the notation *personal communication* and the date of the interview. For published interviews, use the appropriate format for an article.

Index

Instructor's Resource Manual to Accompany

SECOND EDITION

The *Concise Guide to Writing*

RISE B. AXELROD
CHARLES R. COOPER

Instructor's Resource Manual

to Accompany

The Concise Guide to Writing

Second Edition

Rise B. Axelrod

California State University, San Bernardino

Charles R. Cooper

University of California, San Diego

St. Martin's Press

New York

Manufactured in the United States of America.
09876
f e d c b a

For information, write:
St. Martin's Press
175 Fifth Avenue
New York, NY 10010

ISBN: 0-312-11704-3

Contents

Section **I**

OVERVIEW AND SUGGESTED COURSE PLANS

OVERVIEW OF THE TEXT

The Concise Guide to Writing opens with a chapter that addresses the central concerns of this book: why and how we write. This introductory chapter focuses on the writing process, describing it through writers' testimony and offering practical advice on how to manage the process. The rest of the book divides into two parts:

Part I: Writing Activities (Chapters 2–6)

These chapters cover five kinds of nonfiction prose—autobiography, concept explanation, evaluation, position paper, and proposal. The writing assignments are versatile, producing short or long essays, based on personal experience and observation or on library research. Each chapter includes the following components:

- illustrative academic assignments
- group inquiry activities
- reading selections, each followed by questions for discussion and analysis and by a commentary
- a summary of the basic features of the kind of writing illustrated by the readings
- a writing assignment based on the kind of writing treated in the chapter
- a Guide to Writing that includes strategies for invention and research, planning and drafting, getting critical comments, and revising and editing
- a Writer at Work profile of one student's writing process
- a metacognitive activity to help students learn from their own writing processes.

Part II: Strategies for Writing and Research (Chapters 7–11)

This section offers methods of cueing readers (thesis statements, paragraphing, cohesive devices, and transitions) as well as strategies for invention, such as clustering, listing, cubing, looping, dramatizing, and questioning. The critical reading strategies include annotating, outlining and summarizing, evaluating the logic of an argument, and recognizing emotional manipulation. The section also includes techniques for library research and research on the Internet, as well as guidance on using and acknowledging sources following both the

Modern Language Association (MLA) and the American Psychological Association (APA) styles.

SUGGESTED COURSE PLANS

The Concise Guide to Writing is a versatile teaching tool. With this textbook, you can organize a writing course in many different ways and with quite diverse emphases. With it, you can design a course in which students base their writing solely on personal experience and knowledge or one in which they regularly use library resources. You can emphasize critical thinking and reading skills by focusing on the reading selections and their analysis questions along with the guides for critically reading a draft. You can develop a course around a problem of general interest by asking students to write reflective, explanatory, and argumentative essays about the same subject. You can help novice writers grasp the fundamentals of written English or challenge experienced writers to stretch their abilities by focusing on the stylistic options. You can structure your class around lectures, discussions, workshops, and conferencing.

For your convenience, here is an outline of Part I that briefly defines each chapter's assignment:

Chapter 2: Remembering Events. Students write a narrative that conveys the significance of an experience.

Chapter 3: Explaining a Concept. Students investigate a concept and explain it to their readers.

Chapter 4: Justifying an Evaluation. Students explain and justify their judgment of something.

Chapter 5: Arguing a Position. Students examine an issue and present an argument to support their position.

Chapter 6: Proposing a Solution. Students analyze a problem and develop a case for their own solution.

The assignments in Part I move from reflective to informative to argumentative forms of writing. The reflective essay—Chapter 2, on remembered events—stresses the exploration of memory and feeling. Students learn to find meaning in personal experience. They also learn to present their experience so that their readers can understand its significance and possibly relate it to their own lives as well as to human experience in general.

The informative essay—Chapter 3, on concept explanation—shifts the focus from the personal and subjective to the public and objective. Students learn to gather, analyze, and synthesize information by using invention heuristics as well as research strategies (Chapter 10). In presenting what they have learned to their readers, students learn to organize the information and use an array of explanatory strategies such as classifying, comparing and contrasting, narrating a process, explaining known causes and effects, and, of course, defining.

The argumentative essays—Chapters 4–6—require students not only to gather and analyze information and ideas but also to deliberate upon them and to present the results of their deliberation in a carefully reasoned, well-supported argument. Evaluative writing (Chapter 4) provides a good transition from presenting information to arguing an assertion. Students learn to consider how much information about the subject their readers need to understand the writer's judgment. The position paper (Chapter 5) introduces students to the special rhetorical demands of argumentation. The proposal (Chapter 6) develops the idea that arguing can be a constructive, collaborative activity, one that enables groups of people to take action together to solve common problems.

Any of the informative and argumentative essays in Part I can be used as the basis of a library-research paper project, large or small.

Most instructors and programs seem to prefer giving assignments following our chapter sequence, with Chapter 7 usually integrated with Chapter 3. Other sequences are possible, however. In fact, though there are obvious relations between certain chapters, they can be assigned in any sequence, as each is independent of the others. For example, since Proposing Solutions may be completed quite successfully without library research, it could efficiently precede Arguing a Position. We have from time to time assigned Remembering Events last, as a reward to students for persisting with researched argument.

If you want to conclude your course with a library-research essay, either Explaining a Concept or Arguing a Position is the best choice. Keep in mind, however, that neither of these chapters requires library research, should you want students to rely on their own knowledge. You might want to review Invention in each of these chapters to see how the no-library-research option is possible for students.

The course-making flexibility of *The Concise Guide to Writing* is one of its great advantages. Not only can assignments be made in any sequence, but they can also be adjusted to challenge capable student writers or to accommodate inexperienced student writers. For example, capable writers could carry out extended library research in Explaining a Concept and Arguing a Position and write multiple drafts.

Section **II**

TEACHING STRATEGIES
FOR CHAPTERS 2 THROUGH 6

Each of the five chapters in Part I focuses on a different kind of nonfiction prose that you may have your students write. The chapters all follow the same plan.

Chapter Introduction

- Writing in Your Other Courses shows illustrative academic assignments from diverse disciplines, which help students recognize that they are likely to encounter the chapter's writing situation (or genre) again both as a parallel assignment in another college course and as a strategy that will play a central role in a different kind of assignment
- For Group Inquiry activities (one at the beginning of the chapter and another at the Testing Your Choice stage of invention work) enable students to rehearse the writing situation they are beginning to explore

Readings and Accompanying Activities

- Readings, Questions for Analysis, and Commentaries indicate the range of writing strategies used to achieve various purposes for particular audiences
- Questions for Discussion following each reading draw students into discussion of a main idea in the reading in terms of their own experience
- Questions for Your Own Writing start students generating possible topics and speculating about how they might develop them

Analysis of Purpose and Audience and Summary
of Basic Features

- An analysis of Purpose and Audience followed by a summary of Basic Features provide an overview of the readings

Guide to Writing

- Invention and Research followed by Planning and Drafting help students discover ideas and gather information as well as solve the problems they encounter during the process of writing each kind of essay
- Getting Critical Comments helps students read one another's drafts critically and constructively
- Revising and Editing leads students to revise their writing thoughtfully and systematically

A Writer at Work

- A Writer at Work profiles one student's attempt to solve a particular writing problem

Reflecting on Your Writing

- Reflecting on Your Writing invites students to review their writing process and to recognize that they now have the resources to solve many of the problems in their writing

In the chapter-by-chapter discussion in Section III, we will suggest ways of approaching each individual chapter. Here, we examine each of the components listed above to suggest ways of handling them in the classroom.

CHAPTER INTRODUCTION

Writing in Your Other Courses

Each chapter opens with three or four typical assignments from college courses across the disciplines. We made up very few of these; nearly all came from current academic texts or instructors' manuals. We did revise several of them to foreground aspects of the rhetorical situation, making explicit what the student is expected to know and do. Unfortunately, not all academics consistently make clear to students what is required in essay-exam questions or paper topics.

There is much you can do to involve students in analyzing these academic assignments:

- you can help them analyze one or two, emphasizing their thinking/ writing demands, and then they can analyze another (either in small groups or as a class)
- you can ask each student to find another assignment in a textbook in another course or to construct a likely one based on information in the text

For Group Inquiry

The purpose of the group inquiry activity early in each chapter is to engage students immediately in an interactive, oral rehearsal of the situation they will encounter when they write the chapter's essay assignment.

You'll notice that each group inquiry divides distinctly into two parts: first, the rehearsal of the writing situation and, second, a reflection on what happened and what students learned. You may have to help students make this shift. The whole activity need not take more than twenty minutes or so. Because students *experience* the writing situation early in the chapter, we have found they are much more interested in the readings and questions. It starts them into a chapter in a surprisingly productive way. Don't skip this activity!

READINGS AND ACCOMPANYING ACTIVITIES

In each of the chapters of Part I, there are three readings illustrating the kind of writing that the chapter presents. Some of the readings are complete essays, while some are edited pieces. Most are by recognized authors, but we have included in each set one essay written by a college freshman using earlier versions of this book. At the end of each chapter in A Writer at Work, we include part of the writing process (invention, drafting, or revision) of one of these student essays.

Each of the readings is followed by these sections:

- For Discussion: a topic for small-group or whole-class discussion of an idea in the reading
- For Analysis: four or five questions for analysis requiring close reading
- For Your Own Writing: suggestions for topics students can consider writing about
- Commentary: our comments on the reading, pointing out noteworthy features, without answering any of the questions in the For Analysis section

As a set, the Commentary sections present all of the rhetorical concepts students need to understand and produce the kind of writing treated in the chapter. Moreover, the Commentary and For Analysis sections make cross-references to specific writing strategies discussed and illustrated in Part II of the *Guide*.

Readings

We have selected the reading carefully to represent a variety of examples of each kind of writing. They illustrate the full range of features and most of the strategies that characterize the type of writing. The readings in each chapter, therefore, work together as a set, and we try to assign as many of them as we can.

The purpose of the readings is to introduce writers to each kind of writing, showing them how various good writing of that kind can look, before they begin their own essays. Novice writers may be encouraged to see that other students have used earlier versions of this book to learn to write.

Readings play an important role in each chapter of this book because we believe that writers benefit from studying good professional writing. We do *not* prescribe the readings as models for students to imitate but as examples of the many possible directions in which they can take their own writing. A few carefully chosen readings allow us to demonstrate some of the choices available to writers, and also to point out the basic features of the type of writing as they appear in each of the readings. We can show students how the readings differ and also what they have in common. We believe that, used carefully, readings can inspire writers rather than intimidate them. Readings help them develop a sense of the problems they must face in each kind of writing and equip them with options for solving these problems. A specific kind of learning is involved here—learning the possibilities and boundaries of a genre. Knowing about a genre is a heuristic, not a constraint, in our view.

For Discussion

A For Discussion section following each reading lets students engage the ideas in the reading, before analyzing it rhetorically. The discussion task is set so that students can connect their personal experience to an idea in the text. It gives students practice in talking about ideas in texts, something few of them do every day; and we believe it increases their interest in a text and makes them more willing to analyze it rhetorically.

We have had excellent results with this follow-up assignment: immediately after the discussion in class of the For the Discussion Topic, students individually take notes about their ideas; later they draft an extended journal entry; and then at the next class meeting they share their ideas with members of their discussion group. This activity extends, refines, and clarifies each student's ideas.

For Analysis

The analysis questions draw students into many different talking and writing activities:

- to locate and identify features of the reading and strategies the writer has used
- to analyze the writer's use of these strategies and their effects
- to put themselves in the writer's position and to consider reasons for the writer's choices and solutions to the problems
- to evaluate these choices and solutions and to suggest alternatives and improvements

The analysis questions aim to engage students actively with the readings, leading them to explore beneath the surface of each reading and to examine structural features and strategies they find there. The questions give students practice in thinking about the issues and problems that writers of each kind of writing must address as well as the decisions they must make. We find that this helps novice writers understand what they are trying to do in the assignment. Looking at what other writers have done to see what works and why it works helps them to set and pursue goals in their own writing.

For Your Own Writing

This section anticipates the first invention step in the Guide to Writing: listing topics and choosing one. Even before they arrive at invention, students begin generating possible topics and considering the possibilities and constraints of the assignment. If they read all three readings and consider the writing possibilities following each one, they will be well prepared to identify their own essay topics.

You can profitably approach this activity as an occasion for whole-class brainstorming. Each student can contribute at least one topic and speculate about its appeal and requirements. You can then single out topics that seem especially promising. Each student could then take any topic and bring notes to class about how he or she would approach it.

Commentary

The purpose of the commentary on each reading selection is to introduce selected basic features and strategies illustrated in the readings. The commentaries complement the For Analysis questions. In most cases a particular feature or strategy identified in one commentary becomes the subject of a question in succeeding readings. Sometimes, an analysis question introduces a feature or strategy that is taken up in the commentary for the next reading. This recursiveness is designed to reinforce students' learning.

The commentaries also introduce concepts discussed in further detail in other parts of the book, primarily the Writing Strategies in Part II. Page references have been set out in the margin to make cross-reference easier.

The commentaries are intended to model close rhetorical analysis of the readings and to stimulate further discussion. They are neither exhaustive nor definitive. We expect you and your students to find places where you can extend, illustrate, or disagree with our analysis. The point is to get students thinking and talking about how writing is put together. We encourage our students to imagine themselves in the writer's place in order to speculate about why the writer might have made particular choices. We also urge students to think about the wisdom of those choices and to consider ways in which the essay could be revised.

Using the Readings and Analysis Questions in Class.   The readings and questions are adaptable enough to suit a variety of class plans. To cover all the readings and questions in depth takes at least two class periods and some homework assignments, so in each chapter you may want to concentrate on just one or two of the readings and discuss the others briefly. Another way to save time is to address only two or three of the questions following each reading.

If you follow the sequence of each chapter, discussion of the readings precedes students' work on invention for their own essays. This ensures that they will have a solid grounding in each kind of writing before they attempt it. They will have read several good examples and thought about the issues raised by the analysis questions. The summary of Basic Features then reviews and consolidates the important issues for each kind of writing, preparing students to begin the invention process.

An alternative scheme would be to have students begin their invention while they are reading the selections. You could introduce the invention activities by discussing particular readings. If you choose to integrate the invention task with discussion of the readings, the summary of Basic Features, which follows the readings in each chapter, can be a preview for students before they begin invention and a review before they begin their first drafts. You may also want to save one of the readings—perhaps a student essay—to discuss at this point.

When we discuss the readings in class, we use the analysis questions in two formats: an open forum, with the instructor acting as moderator, or small groups of three or four students, each group discussing a question about one of the texts. Discussion by the whole class allows you to steer the discussion of the readings directly. One good way to ensure that everyone has something to contribute to the discussion is to assign an informal, one-page response to one of the analysis questions, in their journals if you have students keep journals. You can then call on some students to read aloud what they have written. This response can be written as homework before the class, or it can be written in five or ten minutes at the beginning of the class period.

These short written responses to the analysis questions can also help initiate discussion in small groups with one student in each group reading his or her response to the others in the group. In large classes this format allows more students to participate, and it can elicit responses from students who would not speak in front of the whole class. After ten or fifteen minutes, a student from each group can make a brief oral summary of the group's discussion for the rest of the class. These summaries can lead naturally into a whole-class discussion of the readings or a brief lecture by the instructor on some specific writing issue that appears in the readings.

Successful Class Discussions of the Readings.   Since the primary purpose of discussing the readings is to help students write essays of the same kind, we make frequent connections between the features we find in the readings and those that students will be generating in their invention writing. We usually make these connections as we summarize the main points of the discussion. Often we summarize by listing discourse features and strategies on the chalkboard, inviting students to help us make the lists. Students then have a visual reminder of the key points they are learning, and the instructor can happily avoid the role of Inspector of Responses in favor of being the leader and recorder of the discussion.

In our most successful class discussions, the students do most of the talking and talk to one another rather than just to us. The best discussions also have momentum: students are able to sustain discussion instead of merely answering our questions. This is why the analysis questions focus on important writing issues but do not ask students simply for facts. We intend the questions to open up discussion and engage students with the problems they will be facing in their own essays, not merely test their comprehension of the readings.

ANALYSIS OF PURPOSE AND AUDIENCE AND A SUMMARY OF BASIC FEATURES

Between the Readings and the Guide to Writing sections, each chapter contains a discussion of the rhetorical possibilities and a summary of the basic features for that kind of writing. The purpose and audience analysis draws students' attention to the rhetoric of the selections and helps them think about their own purposes and potential readers. This section summarizes the main points raised in the readings by the analysis questions and the commentaries, thus giving students a chance to review and consolidate the information they have learned so far before trying to apply it in their own essays. If students understand the basic features of each kind of writing and have seen how they work in the readings, it should be easier for them to respond to the invention tasks. Student writers often have difficulty coming up with much useful material until they learn the value of the features that the invention tasks ask them to generate. Referring students to the Purpose and Audience and Basic Features sections during the composing process reminds them of the key rhetorical issues for their writing.

GUIDE TO WRITING

The Guide to Writing assists the student in learning how to write the type of prose under consideration. Each Guide to Writing is tailored to consider special challenges the student will meet during the writing process. This section of the manual presents overall advice and specific teaching strategies for each of the sections that appear in the nine Guides to Writing: Invention and Research, Planning, Drafting, and Getting Critical Comments, and Revising and Editing.

Invention and Research

Each guide includes a sequence of invention activities designed specifically to help students ask themselves questions and generate ideas and information useful for their essays. Since so few students have ever participated in systematic invention, we are especially careful to introduce them to the invention activities. We ask the students to open their books to the invention section and then briefly explain the purpose of each activity. By having students turn the pages and skim the invention exercises while you preview them orally for the students, you will be able to reduce students' apprehension about these unfamiliar activities and greatly increase the probability that they will successfully complete the invention section before beginning their draft.

This is also the time to remind students of the time frame for invention: suggest that they begin work right away, but spread the work out over several sessions; tell them what day the invention will be due, and that you will be checking it on that day to ensure that their invention base is adequate to begin planning and drafting.

You could do the first part of the invention, listing possible subjects, in class as whole-class brainstorming or in small groups, beginning by reading the lists in the book and moving to other topics the students can think of. Students then move to choosing a topic and exploring it. Students will progress through the invention sequence at different rates, but you can help them stay on track by requiring that they reach a certain point by a certain class meeting. If you ask them to bring their invention-in-progress to every class meeting, you can ask them to share certain sections with their peers in pairs or small groups, while you circulate and examine each student's work-to-date.

Research is comfortably included in our broad definition of invention—everything that happens before and during writing to produce ideas and evaluate them. Except for the writing activities in Chapter 2 on reflective writing, all the other writing activities (Chapters 3 through 6) can include formal research. In our discussion about how to teach these activities later in this chapter, we explain how students can complete these assignments either with or without formal research. For example, depending on their topics, students can explain a concept that they already know without using or documenting any sources, or they can research new topics, relying entirely on sources (Chapter 3: Explaining Concepts).

Where research is appropriate, the Guide to Writing invites it. You can decide how much research students should do or leave it to them to decide. We provide additional guidance in Chapter 10: Doing Research in the Library and on the Internet and Chapter 11: Strategies for Using and Acknowledging Sources.

Planning and Drafting

The Planning and Drafting section in each chapter in Part I is organized as follows:

- Seeing What You Have
- Setting Goals (focused on each chapter's type of writing)
- Outlining
- Drafting

Invention may produce a number of complete paragraphs, several lists, free writing, an interview, or notes on library research—a plethora of material that must be organized before the student can write a draft. This much material poses for many students a new problem: what to do with all of it.

The Guide to Writing in each chapter urges students to consider several alternative plans before settling on one. Often students are unaware of alternatives; we find it helpful to illustrate several, sometimes from the reading selections and sometimes from topics suggested by students.

Each planning section reminds students, as they go on to draft, that what they have developed is only a plan. In other words, it is expendable. The final test for the paper is not whether it follows the outline, but whether it works. Like many other parts of the Guide to Writing, this may demand from inexperienced writers a new approach, a new order of priorities.

Up to the drafting stage, the student has been dealing with pieces or facets; now for the first time the student will attempt to see the material as a whole. We suggest that students write their first rough drafts in a single sitting lasting about two to three hours. The drafting session resembles extended free writing: it lasts longer, it allows the student to pause much more, and of course the writer is trying for a more ordered product, but as in free writing, the writer should work as fast as possible and not worry too much about grammatical details or spelling.

The object of this approach is to keep the student focused on the larger shape of the essay, not on distracting details. Research shows that most competent writers occasionally write garbled sentences in their first drafts and that writers who struggle to perfect each sentence as it is written are inefficient. Of course, there are exceptions, and students should remember that the Guide to Writing is just that—a guide, not a set of inflexible orders.

Getting Critical Comments

The part of this section called Reading with a Critical Eye guides students in analyzing a classmate's draft. Like the invention sequence, this section is specific to the particular discourse type. Nevertheless, in the various chapters these guides follow a general pattern, having two main sections:

Reading for a First Impression.   The student reads the draft straight through and gives a general impression in just a few sentences.

Reading to Analyze.   During close reading and rereading, the student analyzes the discourse features and strategies of the particular kind of writing being worked on. This section consists of several close-reading tasks that ask the student to *describe* and *evaluate* the draft. The tasks mirror the discourse issues central to the readings, questions, and commentaries at the beginning of each chapter, the summary of basic features, the invention activities, and the advice on drafting. This circling back again and again to the central discourse issues for a kind of writing makes each chapter an integrated system of reading, analyzing, inventing, drafting, critical reading, and revising. Attentive students who have come this far—and who are able to analyze their own and other students' drafts thoughtfully—are in a surprisingly strong position to produce a solid revision.

Students may use the analysis section in various ways: (1) to guide an in-class written analysis of another student's draft; (2) to guide an at-home written analysis of another student's draft, in order to prepare for a conference or class discussion or just to turn over the analysis to the other student; and (3) to guide their discussions of drafts in pairs, small groups, or in a whole-class workshop.

We recommend starting with a written analysis. To eliminate problems of duplicating and exchanging papers in advance of class meetings, we schedule class time for a written analysis of each draft. (Then we move on to some form of talk about the drafts. See Organizing Workshops in the teaching practices section of this manual.) Students need fifteen to twenty-five minutes to complete a thorough analysis, though, of course, you could ask for a quicker analysis.

The written analysis—as homework or in class—adds still another piece of writing to the class, writing of a type generally different from the essay the student is writing. It holds students' attention closely to the written text as they search for evidence to substantiate their evaluations. It is a writing-to-learn exercise *par excellence,* requiring review and use of the discourse concepts presented in the chapter. We have found that it also produces better workshop discussions of drafts.

In each chapter, before students use Reading with a Critical Eye, we recommend that you orient them to it carefully, even taking them through each step to ensure that they understand how to read and respond to the draft. Encourage them to write as much as they can, being as specific as possible without worrying about being right or straining to say something wise. Each student should just try to give a full response as one thoughtful reader.

Good papers pose a special problem: often students find nothing to say about them. We try to encourage the student facing a fine essay to figure out precisely what is fine about it, to tell the author what she or he did well. Often this exercise will lead the reader to notice something that was not in fact so fine, something that can be improved. But this is not the only point of the exercise; it also helps the reader learn to analyze, and it often points out to the writer features and strategies of her or his own work that she or he may not have noticed.

These peer critiques not only make it possible for every student to receive some reaction to a rough draft before revising, but they also help teach students the critical and editing techniques they need to use on their own papers. With coaching and practice, students can write apt, detailed, and insightful criticism. As they realize their own successes, students will come to respect both themselves and their classmates as readers and helpers. This respect improves every other classroom activity; most particularly it does wonders for small-group work when students must look to one another rather than to the teacher for help or ideas.

Revising and Editing

This section has a revising plan that is organized as follows:

Identifying Problems
    Getting an overview
    Charting a plan for revision
    Analyzing the basic features of your draft
    Studying critical comments
Solving the Problems (focused on each chapter's type of writing)
Editing and Proofreading

Students are now on their own, perhaps with advice from other students and from you, to improve their drafts. The second stage above, Solving the Problems, takes them back through the possibilities of the assignment they are working on. It gives very specific advice about how they can solve problems they recognize in their drafts.

It will be an excellent use of class time to ask students to make or at least begin their plan for revision under your guidance. If they are able to reread their drafts carefully, compose a scratch outline, and study their peers' comments while they are in the classroom with you available as a resource for question answering, they will be well launched into the process and able to complete it and then revise their drafts on their own. Alternatively, students could write out their revision plans outside of class and you could review them at the next class meeting to ensure that they're on track. Then you could select and duplicate the best revision plan and ask the writer to present it to the class as a model.

The last step in revising is editing and proofreading—locating and correcting errors in grammar, spelling, and punctuation. By making this the last step, we hope to stress the importance of editing and proofreading.

A WRITER AT WORK

Each chapter includes among its readings one written by first-year college students using this Guide to Writing. The Writer at Work section focuses on an earlier stage in the writing of one of those papers. The subject of the essay and the issues facing the student are discussed, followed by a typed version of the student's notes.

As a group, the selections cover many writing issues and all the key stages that a paper written according to the guidelines in this book will go through.

The Writer at Work sections also allow students to see what good work looks like before it is finished. A good essay bears few, if any, traces of its genesis; its surface is polished, smooth, impenetrable. Student writers can find no evidence there that they could do such work. To see a flawed first draft or jumbled free writing—the sort of thing they can do—may help them believe that they can do the other as well.

REFLECTING ON YOUR WRITING

Coming at the end of the chapter after students have written and edited their final revision, this section may seem to be merely an afterthought. But in our teaching, it has become an integral part of students' work in each kind of writing they do in Part I. This reflective or "metacognitive" activity brings closure to students' work in the chapter. It reinforces what students have learned and consolidates that learning—helping students remember and value their learning.

When we grade and respond to the revised essay, we make a point of referring to the students' own reflections on how they discovered and tried to solve a particular problem in their writing. If their solution doesn't work very well, for example, we may be able to suggest other ways of reworking the essay. Often we can offer some additional ideas on how they can avoid the problem in the future. Sometimes, we point out another problem and invite the student to revise the essay one more time, trying to solve that particular problem. We might also refer them to strategies used in one or two of the readings that they might be able to adapt to their purposes.

We also find students' written reflections useful for periodic conferences and for midterm class discussions. Often in conference we can suggest specific ways a student could use the invention activities to avoid a recurrent kind of problem, or how the student could find in the readings strategies for solving problems. Midterm discussion with the entire class could reinforce students' image of themselves as problem solvers, capable of learning from reading as well as from others. These two activities are especially useful if you are asking students to assemble a portfolio with a self-statement evaluating what they have learned during the course.

CHAPTER PLANS

Chapter **1**
Introduction

This brief introductory chapter begins by arguing that writing makes important contributions to thinking, learning, success, personal development, and communication. Exercise 1.1 invites students to reflect on these ideas in relation to their own writing. The introduction then explains how writing is learned by identifying three things students need to know: how written texts work, how the writing process works, and how to think critically about learning. Each of these sections discusses how we can learn what we need to know and includes an exercise that could be used along with the quotations as the basis for class discussion.

How Written Texts Work introduces the concepts of purpose, audience, and genre or kind of writing. These are concepts central to the writing assignments chapters in Part I, each of which focuses on a different genre. We define genres as social acts: different rhetorical situations call for different genres. We talk about the predictability as well as the variability of genres. The point is that genres have conventions, patterns that help readers understand them, but they should not be thought of as formulaic or static. By placing genres in their social context, we can see how they reflect as well as affect the values and assumptions of the people who use them. Different kinds of discourse privilege different kinds of experience, different ways of knowing. You might use Exercise 1.2 to reinforce this idea that kinds of writing differ according to the context in which they are used.

The second section, *How the Writing Process Works*, introduces the idea that writing is a complex and recursive process. We refer here to writing as creative problem solving, a notion that we come back to in the new critical thinking activity at the end of each Part I chapter, Reflecting on Your Writing. We also introduce the important idea that writing is not always a solitary activity but often involves collaboration. Since *The Concise Guide to Writing* offers many opportunities for collaboration, you might want to reinforce this idea by putting students into small discussion groups and having them exchange the metaphors and similes they've thought of for Exercise 1.3.

Under the heading *How We Learn a Writing Process That Works*, we introduce the Guides to Writing in each of the Part I chapters. The Guides, as we explain, provide procedural scaffolding to help students recognize the full potential of the writing process. They help students resist the impulse to be done even before they've begun exploring their topic. They also make the process somewhat less imposing by suggesting how students might break it into smaller, more focused tasks.

Exercise 1.4 could be used to get students to reflect on what they typically do when they write. Many students will say they are satisfied with the process they currently use, even if that involves what we've called the "dangerous method." The Guides to Writing try to increase their repertoire of strategies for invention, planning, revising, and editing. They offer an array of heuristic questions specific to the genre that encourages students to think more about their subject as well as to think more systematically.

How to Think Critically about Your Learning introduces students to the idea of metacognition, thinking about thinking. There's ample evidence to suggest that learners learn better when they reflect on what they are learning. Conscious reflection seems also to help writers in the process of writing. Writers often can rely on strategies they have used many times before, but when the subject is especially challenging or they are writing in a genre that is new to them, writers— no matter how expert—shift to a heightened state of awareness so they can use all of the resources at their command. Exercise 1.5 invites students to reflect on their strengths and weaknesses as writers and to set some goals for themselves in the course.

The section called *Using This Book* forecasts the plan of the book, emphasizing the Guides to Writing in the writing assignment chapters of Part I. Some general advice about invention, drafting, revising, and editing concludes the chapter.

Chapter **2**

Remembering Events

THE WRITING ASSIGNMENT

Write an essay about a significant event in your life. Choose an event that will be engaging for readers and that will, at the same time, tell them something about you. Tell your story dramatically and vividly, giving a clear indication of its autobiographical significance.

The Nature of the Writing Assignment

This assignment has two pedagogical goals: to teach students to write a coherent narrative and to introduce the rhetorical concepts of purpose and audience. Students learn how to sequence the action chronologically, to shape the structure of their narratives meaningfully around a central conflict, and to use a consistent point of view.

By focusing the writing assignment on the significance of the event, the chapter also draws students' attention to the way in which purpose and audience control the selection as well as the presentation of details. Students writing about significant events must decide how much they want to disclose about themselves and to discover ways of connecting to their readers' experience. This assignment involves students, sometimes for the first time, in reflecting seriously about their own experience and about human experience in general. It encourages students to make discoveries about themselves and to share these insights with others through writing. For inexperienced writers, this use of writing as discovery can lead to an important new commitment to writing, a commitment that subsequent assignments attempt to foster.

Autobiographical writing is treated here as not merely an exercise in storytelling but as a meaningful intellectual activity. In learning about autobiographical writing, students discover the basic process of all writing—making meaning from experience. That is, they learn how to present their experience so that readers can recognize, believe, and understand what has happened and why it is important.

Chapter 2: Remembering Events encourages students to do reflective writing, writing that relies on the invention strategies of memory search and analysis as well as the writing strategies of narration and description. Many instructors like to begin writing courses with a unit on reflective writing, assigning autobiography because students can use a fairly straightforward narrative organization for their essays.

Special Problems of This Writing Assignment

We have noticed that students facing this assignment for the first time may have problems developing a well-paced, dramatic narrative and achieving the self-disclosure necessary to reveal the event's significance.

In their first drafts of essays about events, student writers tend to draw on what they know of storytelling conventions. Typically this involves beginning with a general introduction, setting the scene, or declaring the significance of the event in broad terms. The succession of events is then played out in the body of the paper without much alteration in pace to include descriptive details, the writer's feelings at the time, and reflections with hindsight. A writer often forgets to show as well as tell, to bring an experience alive with sensory detail rather than merely to record the sequence of events.

Many writers have initial difficulties managing the pace of a narrative, not realizing that the climax of an event can easily be undercut if pages of incidental events have misdirected readers' expectations. We find it useful to spend some time with the readings explaining how writers adjust the flow of time and create suspense.

For many writers, the companion to the convention of beginning a story with a general introduction is the convention of ending it with a moral. Unused to probing the personal significance of events they write about, inexperienced writers tend to translate this convention into a moralistic conclusion. Again we use the readings to point out ways in which reflection on the significance of an event can be woven into the narrative and how to avoid simplistic conclusions. We encourage students to go deeper—to look at reasons for their actions and re-actions, to explore the humorous or absurd possibilities of their topics and the personal insights that these can provide.

Promising and Unpromising Topics

The writing assignment in this chapter gives students a wide choice of topics. This choice, as students soon discover, presents problems as well as opportunities. The chief problem comes when students choose events from which they do not have enough distance or events in which the significance is too obvious.

When asked to choose a significant event, students frequently want to write about the first topic that comes to mind, often a recent experience or a traumatic one. An event that happened very recently may appear to be important only because it is on the writer's mind. While writing about such an event will help the writer understand it, the event may turn out not to have much meaning after all. Traumatic events may also be problematic as topics, not because they lack significance but because they are too meaningful. Writing about a traumatic event may involve more self-disclosure than seems appropriate given the writing situation.

Looking back over the events of their lives for possible topics, writers understandably tend to think big. Major emotional landmarks readily suggest themselves: graduation, making the team, having an accident, passing or failing the big test. In the Guide to Writing, we suggest that students also consider events from the following categories:

- Any "first," such as when you first realized you had a special skill, ambition, or problem; when you first felt needed or rejected; when you first became aware of some kind of altruism or injustice

- Any memorably difficult situation: when you had to make a tough choice, when someone you admired let you down (or you let someone else down), when you struggled to learn or understand something
- Any occasion when things did not turn out as expected: when you expected to be praised but were criticized, when you were convinced you would fail but succeeded
- Any incident that challenged your basic values or assumptions
- Any humorous event, one you still laugh about, perhaps one that seemed awkward or embarrassing at the time
- Any event that shaped you in a particular way, perhaps making you independent, proud, insecure, fearful, courageous, ambitious
- Any incident charged with strong emotions such as love, fear, anger, embarrassment, guilt, frustration, hurt, pride, happiness, joy
- Any incident that changed your relationship with a parent, spouse, or child

Some of these peak experiences are initiations or rites of passage. They are prominent in the minds of many students and can make excellent autobiographical topics. The events featured in all the readings in this chapter also may be said to involve rites of passage.

A problem with these topics, however, is that many of them are common experiences, familiar to almost everyone. The challenge in writing about such an event is to avoid the cliché, to find something distinctive in the experience, or to give readers a new perspective on it. We encourage students to think twice before writing about their first experience on the ski slopes, the prom that was not all it promised to be, the event that would have embarrassed anyone. Experiences such as these that exactly match expectations contain nothing surprising for readers, no new insights or discoveries. Students would do better to look beyond the obvious and consider some of the subtler experiences they may have had—moments of intense awareness, realizations, important changes that took place within themselves.

CHAPTER INTRODUCTION

Writing in Your Other Courses

We wouldn't want to overemphasize the number of times students will be asked to write about their personal experience in their college courses. In fact, you may want to take this opportunity to discuss with them the value of writing about personal experience. Freshmen, both the eighteen-year-old variety and the older student, are often struck by the abstractness of their college studies. Some instructors may even appear to disdain self-examination. The four sample assignments—from psychology, sociology, political science, and linguistics—suggest ways in which personal experience can inform our studies of academic subjects. You might point out that connecting what one is learning to one's own life, though certainly not a requisite of learning, can be a stimulant.

For Group Inquiry

If you decide to have your students do this group inquiry activity, you will find that their interest in the chapter will be enhanced along with their confidence that they will be able to write an interesting remembered event essay. This activity guides them through a rehearsal for the essay they will write later and prepares them to think seriously about the genre.

If you are beginning the course with this chapter, this particular group inquiry activity provides a good starting point. It has students tell one another stories, which is always fun. And it gives students a chance to get to know one another and begin to form a good working relationship.

READINGS

All of the readings in this chapter involve fairly early childhood experiences. That is not to say, of course, that students must be limited in their own topic choice. But "childhood" is recognized as an important subgenre of autobiography by literary theorists, and writing about childhood is seen as an important way to organize memory and find meaning in one's life by certain cognitive psychologists. Writing about one's childhood gives writers the advantage of emotional distance. Childhood is an appropriate topic for eighteen-year-olds as well as for older students.

One recurrent theme in autobiography appears to be the desire for independence, or, put more generally, the relationship between the child and parent figure. All the writers in this chapter contend with this issue. Lorde's essay about losing a school election dramatizes her somewhat ambivalent relationship with her mother. Wolff works hard to keep his secret, and disturbing, activities from his mother and her boyfriend. And Brandt, the student author in the collection, centers her essay on her parents' reactions to her act of rebellion, if you can call shoplifting rebellion. The Writer at Work section demonstrates Brandt's growing awareness of the role her parents play in making this event significant for her.

Other themes are suggested in the For Discussion and For Your Own Writing sections following each reading, and you will undoubtedly see still other thematic connections worth making.

Topics in Analysis Questions and Commentaries

These lists can serve as a quick reference to help you plan your discussion of discourse features either in class or in conference.

Lorde

For Analysis
1. narrative pace
2. reporting thoughts and feelings

3. dialogue
4. significance

Commentary
purpose and audience
dialogue: quoting and
    paraphrasing

Wolff

For Analysis	*Commentary*
1. significance	creating tension
2. structure of narrative	pacing
3. beginning	specific narrative action
4. voice	naming and detailing

Brandt

For Analysis	*Commentary*
1. dialogue	deciding what to disclose
2. naming, detailing, and comparing	learning through the process
3. framing	
4. significance	

"THE ELECTION" BY AUDRE LORDE

Most students find this selection dramatic and affecting. The brief introduction to the piece asks students to consider Lorde's motivation for running for office and her mother's response to her running; students may be somewhat surprised by the parental attitude toward the child's ambition.

For Discussion

Here students are invited to consider, either in small groups or as a class, both the personal and the cultural significance of the event. While Lorde's narrative might seem on the surface merely to deal with the fairly universal experience of childhood trials and defeats, this For Discussion section encourages students to place the event within its specific social and historical context, adding depth to the significance of the narrative.

For Analysis

1. If you have not already discussed narrative strategies with your students, you might use this reading selection as an opportunity to do so. This question focuses specifically on narrative pacing, inviting students to note that writers may skim quickly over less important periods of time, and then slow the narrative to dramatize incidents more central to the significance of the story.

2. This question helps students see how writers use both telling and showing in writing about their experiences. In the paragraphs highlighted in the question, Lorde alternates between reporting her thoughts and feelings and dramatizing her reaction to her loss through specific narrative action. Students may note that the relatively high proportion of reported thoughts and feelings—telling—in this section serves to heighten the drama of the following paragraphs when Lorde's mother enters the scene.

3. Students may be hesitant to use dialogue in their own narrative. The point of this question is to help students recognize the centrality of dialogue in contemporary autobiography: not only does it dramatize the story, but it implicitly gives information about each speaker, and, especially, about the relationship

between the speakers. Students should note that Lorde's use of dialogue in this section of her story is particularly dramatic for several reasons: she uses directly quoted speech rather than summary or paraphrase; she allows her mother's Grenadian dialect to add color and verisimilitude; and she uses short phrases and repetition within the quoted speech to further heighten the drama of the scene.

    4. This question focuses on an underlying theme of the reading selections in this chapter: the relationships between the writers and their parents. Students are likely to have little trouble identifying a certain amount of ambivalence on the part of each writer toward his or her parents; this question should help students recognize that human emotions are rarely unequivocal in close relationships, and that this very ambivalence can provide rich material for autobiographical writing.

For Your Own Writing

Here students are asked to recall events that, like the one Lorde writes about, involved an emotional confrontation. While many students shy away from writing about highly emotional situations, this suggestion reminds them that emotionally laden incidents can make for good autobiographical writing, particularly if they are from one's distant childhood.

Commentary

This commentary focuses on Lorde's purpose and audience. Students are asked to consider Lorde's aim in telling a fairly predictable story and to speculate about how Lorde expects her audience to react to her narrative.

The commentary also considers Lorde's use of dialogue, already highlighted in the third question For Analysis. You might invite students to practice writing dialogue on their own or in small collaborative groups.

"ON BEING A REAL WESTERNER" BY TOBIAS WOLFF

Wolff's is a compelling narrative, brilliantly told. In our experience students respond strongly to this selection—some empathize with the boy, while others are repulsed by his behavior. The challenge with this piece is to use the initial responses to analyze it as a piece of autobiographical writing. The following activity for discussion tries to make this transition.

For Discussion

This activity can be handled in small groups or by the class as a whole. It asks students to think about both the essay's personal and broader cultural significance. We begin by inviting students to look at what Wolff seems to be saying about playing soldier and cowboy. Then, in the second paragraph, we ask them to reflect on the values embodied by stereotypical male and female roles. Finally, we ask students to reconsider Wolff's purpose in presenting these stereotypes.

Be sure that students think about Wolff's statement in the final paragraph: "All my images of myself as I wished to be were images of myself armed. Because I did not know who I was, any image of myself, no matter how grotesque, had power over me."

For Analysis

1. You might want to call students' attention to the end of paragraph 7 and to paragraph 8 where Wolff reflects on power. Note that we introduce at this point the idea that the personal significance of an experience might also be generally significant—in other words, that the artistic rendering of experience often has the power to touch readers deeply by connecting to their own feelings and values even if their experience is nothing like that being represented.

2. Since this question requires a close rereading of the story, you might assign it for homework and begin class by discussing what students found. Another possibility is to continue the group work begun in the For Discussion section. Students could reread the essay aloud in their groups, stopping to discuss where each new stage beings. Then, the recorder for each group could put its findings on the board and the class could see at a glance where everyone agrees and differs.

Here's the progression we came up with. You and your students may find other ways of describing the story's movement toward its climax.

step 1: getting the rifle (paragraph 1)
step 2: keeping the promise (paragraph 5)
step 3: cleaning the rifle (paragraph 5)
step 4: marching with it (paragraph 5)
step 5: posing with it (paragraph 5)
step 6: dressing in Roy's army uniform (paragraph 5)
step 7: acting like a sniper and making shooting sounds (paragraph 6)
step 8: finding the ammunition and putting it into his own hiding place (paragraph 7)
step 9: loading the rifle and drawing a bead on passersby (paragraph 7)
step 10: shooting the squirrel (paragraph 9)

In addition to conveying personal significance, essays about remembered events also occasionally have other purposes. You might read Wolff's story, for example, as an argument about gun control. Looked at this way, the progression we see in the story might be interpreted as a "slippery slope" kind of argument for gun control. You might want to raise this possibility to bring out the implications of a work's structure. Even though students are not now writing arguments, they will benefit from seeing how personal narratives often make implicit arguments.

3. Students are likely to disagree on this question. It draws their attention to the role of beginnings. You might want them to see that these opening paragraphs explain how the boy got the rifle so they fill in important exposition. They also introduce the idea of soldiering; the boy puts Roy "under siege" (paragraph 2) and Roy does the same thing to the mother (paragraph 3).

23

4. In their analysis of paragraphs 9–13, students should notice that the boy's first response is to hide. Then when his mother comes home, he plays a role. He pretends to be innocent and cries. (You might ask them why Wolff uses the word "blubbered" instead of "wept.") That night, he prays and blissfully goes to sleep. Students might argue over Wolff's tone here, but it seems to us that he is quite sardonic in this self-portrait.

For Your Own Writing

This may be a question to which only selected students will be able to respond. Most of us can readily recall occasions when power was used on or against us but seldom recall occasions when we used or abused power. Students might feel more comfortable thinking about the last question: "How did you feel" when you were in a position of power? That might include occasions when one sibling had power over another, probably a younger sibling. Power situations also include occasions when decisions—however trivial—were made and one person had the deciding vote.

Commentary

This commentary gives you an opportunity to spend some time discussing and even practicing narrating strategies such as tension, pacing, naming, detailing, and comparing.

"CALLING HOME" BY JEAN BRANDT

This selection is written by a college freshman about an event that occurred when she was thirteen. Brandt is writing about an embarrassing event and with a good deal of honesty. By focusing on what she felt at the time of the event, Brandt avoids the predictable moral about crime not paying. She boldly presents her changing feelings: naive optimism, humiliation, excitement, shame, worry, relief.

Some of Brandt's invention writing and the first draft appear at the end of the chapter in the Writer at Work section. You might want students to read these pages before they read the revised version of the essay printed here. If you assign the draft, you could begin your analysis of the essay with question 4, which refers specifically to Brandt's refocusing of the essay as she revised it. You can use the Writer at Work section to prepare your own students to write an essay on a remembered event.

For Discussion

This activity, which might be handled in small groups or by the class as a whole, addresses the idea of taking responsibility for one's actions as well as the social dimensions of crime and punishment. Notice that students are invited to compare Brandt's essay with Wolff's. Students are often intrigued by the subject of transgression. Opinion tends to be strong and quite polarized, leading to a lively discussion. To make it a little less abstract, you might ask them each to write on a piece of paper (which they keep and do not need to show to others in the class) a "crime" they have committed. It doesn't, of course, need to be a criminal act, but it should definitely break the rules. A key question to ask is "Whose interests are served by these rules?"

For Analysis

1. Brandt uses dialogue throughout this essay: a brief exchange with her sister (end of paragraph 3 and beginning of 4), a summarized dialogue with the man from the store in paragraph 6, an extended exchange with her sister in paragraphs 7–15, a summary of what the police officers said to her in paragraphs 16 and 18, the phone conversation with her father and mother in paragraphs 19–34, and the final comment by her father (and silence by her mother) in paragraphs 36–38.

Students tend to be insightful about this parent–child relationship. Some will note that the father's anger is more open than the mother's reaction, and that he displaces the blame, converting his daughter into a victim of the authorities. As a victim, Brandt may consider herself freed from taking responsibility. Her mother, however, expresses disappointment and then appears to withdraw her love. When Brandt writes, in paragraph 9, about anticipating explaining to her parents, she focuses on her dread of her mother's reaction, perhaps because she knows her mother will respond by withdrawing love. Students familiar with the concept of "tough love" may interpret the mother's reaction positively.

2. This is a good activity to have students do in groups. Searching together for examples should be fun, and discussing their evaluations should be particularly helpful in sharpening the students' sense of what makes descriptive language effective.

3. The strategy of framing an essay is simple but quite useful. Students will see that the story begins and ends with a car ride. You might ask them to contrast these two scenes. Many readers sense that not only was this experience sobering, but it also helped Brandt mature. In the opening scene she seems to be childish, and in the end she is much more reserved and chastened. You might ask them what Brandt seems to have learned at the time, and what she learned years later from writing about this remembered event.

4. This question pertains to Brandt's relations with her parents but also focuses on the process of clarifying the event's significance that Brandt went through as she drafted and revised the essay.

For Your Own Writing

The focus here is on actions that are atypical, times when you did something that even surprised you. We stress that these do not have to be negative experiences. In fact, many are likely to be quite positive, even liberating.

Commentary

Here we raise the issue of personal disclosure and stress that students must decide what they want to disclose about themselves. In the Writer at Work section near the end of the chapter, students see Brandt struggling not to oversimplify her feelings or whitewash her actions. They should note that it is through this struggle, during the writing process itself, that Brandt is able to discover the deeper significance of the event.

PURPOSE AND AUDIENCE

This section of the chapter reminds students that essays about remembered events have important rhetorical constraints. You might want to discuss the various motives autobiographers have for writing about their own experiences. A way to begin is by asking students about their own choices. Why are they willing to share some memories and not others? How much is their choice affected by their assumptions about readers?

In the reading selections, for example, Lorde provides so many details about her thinking process that one may suspect her motives for telling readers all this. Many students are surprised that Brandt chose to relate an embarrassing experience like breaking the law and being arrested. One wonders what to make of her obvious pride when she thinks she has successfully stolen the Snoopy button. Is she writing to confess her guilt or to brag, or both?

Writers frequently have multiple and even contradictory motives. We want to show our weaknesses but be liked in spite of them or even because of them. Wolff risks alienating readers by scaring them, but, at the same time, he appeals to their sympathy.

BASIC FEATURES OF ESSAYS ABOUT REMEMBERED EVENTS

This section reviews the most important features of writing about autobiographically significant events:

- a well-told story
- a vivid presentation of significant scenes and people
- autobiographical indication of the significance

We discuss these features in detail and illustrate them with specific reference to the selections.

You might want to discuss them before students plan and draft their own essays and review them again before they read one another's drafts to see how well they used and developed these features in their own writing.

GUIDE TO WRITING

Invention

We recommend the following invention activities to help students choose a promising subject and probe it fully:

- Choosing an event to write about
- Recalling key people
- Testing your choice
- Exploring the significance

We designed this sequence of invention activities to address the special problems that the assignment poses: choosing an appropriate event with autobiographical significance and telling a vivid, engaging story about it.

We offer a list of topics—kinds of events students might consider writing about. The For Your Own Writing section after each reading can also help them think of topics.

Once students have an event to work with, the guide invites them to recall specific sensory details and key people associated with it. These heuristics lead writers to imaginatively re-create the scene, inhabited with people and echoing with language. The idea is that this reenactment will allow them to gain insight into the event's significance. They then sketch out the story and test their choice, in part by rehearsing it for others in their group.

Next comes a set of heuristics designed to get them systematically to probe the event's significance. They try to recall their feelings at the time of the experience and contrast these remembered feelings with their present perspective. We find that this procedure, when performed thoughtfully, can be enormously powerful. It enables the writer to create the remembered self as the subject of discourse, often freeing the writer to present the thick texture of experience.

For Group Inquiry

Here students are urged to meet with other students to rehearse their stories. Trying out the story in this informal way can help students get a better sense of how to structure the narrative to make it interesting to readers. It also helps them decide whether their choice is a good one.

Planning and Drafting

You might help students plan their essays by holding conferences with them about the goals they've set for the essay. In this conference, the student would do most of the talking. Your role would be primarily to help students clarify their global goals—those dealing with purpose and audience.

Getting Critical Comments

This section provides a guide that will help students read one another's drafts and respond constructively. Reading for a First Impression directs the reader to get an overall sense of the essay before looking at its basic features.

You will notice that Reading to Analyze is organized according to the basic features. Students could be asked to answer every question, or they could be encouraged to focus on the areas that seem to them to need special attention. Or the writer could ask the reader to focus on certain questions. We also ask students to end with a few final thoughts or suggestions on what the writer should work to improve.

Revising and Editing

This section urges students to think of revising as problem solving. Analyzing specific features and considering readers' critical comments can help students focus on the aspects of the essay that need substantial revision. The idea of revising as problem solving is addressed in the concluding sections under Reflecting on Your Writing.

A WRITER AT WORK

Since this is the first writing assignment, this Writer at Work section gives an overview of Jean Brandt's writing process from invention through drafting to revising. We recommend having students read Brandt's Writer at Work before or after they've studied her completed essay. You might also refer to it as a way of introducing the Guide to Writing.

REFLECTING ON YOUR WRITING

Because we have found that students' experience with each genre is made richer through retrospective examination, each assignment chapter in the text concludes with a series of activities for guided reflection on the students' writing experiences. Students choose which aspect of their writing process to focus on. The purpose of this activity is not for students to justify what they wrote but to get them to think of themselves as problem solvers, writers who have many ways of improving their writing.

Although students need to do this reflection on their own writing process, we've found that saving class time even for a brief discussion of their findings helps to consolidate their learning. You could begin by listing on the board the problems students chose to reflect on. When advising students about revising their drafts, you will want to focus on the unique constraints and possibilities of autobiographical writing. We have found the following list of typical problems helpful because it reminds us of where students predictably come up short and of language we can use to focus our criticism and advice.

Subject

- The essay does not meet the criteria for an event essay but seems more like a person essay, reflection essay, or some other type of writing.
- The topic is too broad ("my childhood," "our championship season").
- The event does not seem important to the writer.
- The essay either trivializes a major event or overstates a minor one (this second case can be effective if handled humorously).

Narrative Structure of the Event

- The event sprawls out over too much time or space.
- The event is not clearly framed for the reader; it should begin or end at another point.
- The narrative drags in places or skips over important episodes too quickly.
- The narrative lacks dramatic tension or suspense.
- The dialogue is undramatic and uninteresting; it does not move the action forward.

Anecdotes and Scenes

- Are either too brief, or much too extended.
- Do not seem to relate well to the event, are poorly chosen or badly framed.
- The essay lacks telling details to build a dominant impression.
- The writer has not selected relevant details or includes too many seemingly trivial, irrelevant ones.
- People do not seem believable in their actions or dialogue.

Significance to the Writer

- There is no apparent significance, stated or implied.
- The significance is heavy-handed, inflated, oversimplified, or sentimentalized; the writer moralizes about the event.
- The essay is not very thoughtful in exploring the event's significance; the writer may come off as a hero or a blameless victim.
- The essay has not given the reader a vivid impression of the writer.

PREPARING FOR CONFERENCES

If you hold conferences with your students on their drafts, you could have them prepare for the conference by filling in the form on the following page.

PREPARING FOR A CONFERENCE: CHAPTER 2

Before the conference, write answers to the questions below. Bring your invention writing and first draft to the conference.

1. Briefly describe the event you are writing about. How did you come to choose it? Why is it important in your life?

2. List the scenes (locations) and people in your essay. Be prepared to talk about which ones are most vividly presented and which may need further detailing or less.

3. Explain briefly how you organized your telling of this event. What other possibilities could you consider for beginning, ending, and organizing the essay?

4. Event essays involve both self-discovery and self-presentation. What, if anything, has writing this draft led you to discover about yourself? What kind of self does your draft now present to readers?

5. What are you most pleased with in this draft? Be specific.

6. What specifically do you need to do next to revise your draft? List any problems you see in the draft or problems that another reader has pointed out. Say briefly how you might attempt to solve these problems. Use the back of this form for these notes. (If you have completed the text's Revising plan, bring it with you to the conference instead of answering this question.)

Chapter *3*
Explaining a Concept

THE WRITING ASSIGNMENT

Write an essay that explains a concept. Choose a concept that interests you and that you want to study further. Consider carefully what your readers already know about it and how your essay might add to what they know.

The Nature of the Writing Assignment

This assignment gives students practice in the most common kind of writing they are likely to encounter: writing to convey helpful and interesting information. We like to give students a fairly free rein in choosing their concepts. We urge them to be guided by their academic or extracurricular interests, but we require that their subjects be significant and their information new and interesting for a number of readers.

Aside from requiring fresh, interesting information, this assignment's main demand of a writer is clarity. Reporting information is an exercise in organization, in marshaling available information into a pattern that will be easy for readers to see. Basic Features of Explanatory Essays and Using Writing Strategies review for students a set of strategies including definition, classification, narration, illustration, and comparison and contrast. The assignment invites the student writer to use these strategies in a combination that suits the subject, the readers, and the writer's point.

The essay that explains a concept may be used to introduce students to techniques of library research and to styles of documenting sources (Chapter 11: Strategies for Using and Acknowledging Sources), and it can become an extended term paper. This chapter introduces students to strategies that they will need again when they write arguments in subsequent chapters, as well as essay exams or reports for classes. As they gain control of these writing strategies, students learn new ways to organize information, to phrase it in their own words, and thus to make it their own.

In this chapter, we focus on a particular aim of explanatory writing—writing to explain concepts. This focus enables students to work on the kind of explanation they are reading and writing in most of their courses. Throughout the disciplines, particularly in introductory courses, students are learning basic concepts. They learn by reading and by writing. Understanding the rhetoric of explanatory discourse can help them become better learners as well as more effective explainers.

Special Problems of This Writing Assignment

In our experience, the main problems that student writers have in this assignment fall into two categories: choosing an appropriate concept and then analyzing and synthesizing the available information on it. One solution to the problem of topic choice is to encourage students to write about subjects introduced in their other courses. In the section Invention and Research, mainly academic subjects are suggested. If students lack confidence in writing about academic subjects, you might allow them to write about concepts drawn from their extracurricular interests.

Students may ask you "What *is* a concept?" We propose an answer that paraphrases the dictionary definition: *a general idea derived from specific instances.* Each reading in this chapter enables students to understand that concepts are formed from many specific observations or instances. It is also interesting to consider that certain concepts can be intuited or fully recognized long before they are named.

Students will need your help in finding a focus for their essay. Most concepts are too big—too much is known about them—for a college essay, even a long research paper. Consequently, you may want them to write about only one *aspect* of the concept. Notice how the invention activities are set up to lead students first to a broad overview of the concept and then to a focus on one interesting aspect of it. Only with a focus in mind do they begin collecting research information.

When we teach this assignment, we discuss with students their concept-choice and the concept-focus. We involve the whole class in assessing each other's topic choices and foci.

Presenting a technical concept in a way that is clear and interesting to a general audience challenges student writers. Students may become very concerned with the specificity and accuracy of the information they report and, in the process, forget about holding readers' interest. The purpose of the essay is to give readers interesting new knowledge. The greatest challenge of this assignment may not be the analysis and selection of information but the presenting of information in a way that allows readers to understand key terms, follow the organization of the essay, and remain interested in the topic. To succeed with this challenge, students will need to pay particular attention to the tone they use, the cues they provide for readers, and the defining and classifying strategies they use.

The assignment can also be a good way to introduce students to library research. The student who knows little about a concept but is curious about it can gather information from the library, from the Internet, or by talking with experts. You may want to require some research from all students, referring them to Chapter 10: Strategies for Doing Research in the Library and on the Internet and Chapter 11: Strategies for Using and Acknowledging Sources.

The most important problem students have with this writing task is that they may allow themselves to be eclipsed by their sources. Their essays then become dumping grounds for unprocessed information, leaving readers to guess at its significance. One of the hardest things for student writers to do is to discover what they want readers to learn about the information. Without this particular purpose, the essay will be a pointless collection of facts, drifting like an abandoned ship.

Related to discovering an informative purpose is the problem of selecting and arranging the information, using the range of available strategies to achieve the purpose. Student writers often have difficulty designing a plan that will organize the information in a way that readers will find interesting and comprehensible. A common problem is the essay that grasps at a simple, ready-made structure, often following the writer's process of discovering the information and ignoring what readers know or need to know about the subject. Again, analyzing the structure of the readings can show students how to avoid this problem.

Promising and Unpromising Topics

The least problematic topics are those that are established concepts, such as existentialism or bilingualism. Students who choose such topics will probably have little difficulty finding and maintaining a conceptual focus. Other kinds of topics are no less promising, but they can be problematic in different ways:

- *Concepts undergoing change:* Some concepts may be treated from a static and historical perspective. For example, the concept of musical harmony can be considered to be stable and fixed. It might appear this way if one researched it only through reference sources and books. On the other hand, if one researched extensively in specialized periodicals, one could discover challenges by avant-garde musicians to traditional concepts of harmony. In this case, either treatment seems justified, depending on the purpose and audience. For certain other concepts, however, acknowledgment of recent developments and rapidly evolving trends seems vital to an accurate portrayal of the concept; notions of mental illness, for example, have undergone major transformations in recent years.
- *Concepts about controversial issues:* If your course will cover both explanatory writing (Chapter 3) and persuasive writing (Chapters 4–6), now is the time to begin discussing with your students the differences between the two genres. For this essay, we emphasize that their opinion should not be foregrounded or obviously stated, though it will certainly guide their selection and presentation of material. Students who have chosen a concept they have strong feelings about, e.g., racism or recycling, will need your guidance to help them shape a balanced, informative treatment of the topic, rather than a partisan, argumentative one.
- *Concepts about personal life:* Some students may be attracted to concepts for which personal experience will be their sole resource, topics like friendship, success, and maturity. Students may be more likely to choose these topics if the class has already done personal experience writing (Chapter 2). While this focus is certainly valid, you may want to encourage students to move beyond personal experience to published sources. Your guidance here can be supportive and enlightening: many students will be surprised to discover that library sources are available on such concepts as friendship and maturity, and that material from these sources may be interwoven with personal experience anecdotes to create an effective essay.

CHAPTER INTRODUCTION

Writing in Your Other Courses

These examples of explaining concepts come from college courses in disparate academic domains: hard science, social science, and humanities. Working through this chapter and writing their own essays on a concept will familiarize students with the central role concept definition and explanation plays in all fields of inquiry.

For Group Inquiry

This activity gives students their first classroom opportunity to explain a concept—in this case orally, briefly, and informally—to a small group of their peers. This activity shouldn't take more than fifteen minutes. If the list of possible concepts does not allow sufficient choice, you could lead a class brainstorming session to come up with other possible concepts. Before they begin the activity, you could review with students the interactive nature of the exercise: following each mini-presentation, listeners share with the presenter something they learned about the concept. Whole-class follow-up can focus on the questions in the last paragraph of the activity; this discussion should be productive as students will already have begun to answer these questions in their small groups.

READINGS

Topics in Analysis Questions and Commentaries

For your convenience, we list below all the discourse topics addressed in each of the For Analysis and Commentary sections. This list can serve as a quick reference in class or in conference to direct a student's attention to an essay question or Commentary that addresses an area the student needs to work on in revising his or her draft. For example, if a student's draft would benefit from the definition of key terms, you could suggest reviewing Castro from the perspective of question 2.

Quammen

For Analysis	Commentary
1. organization	focus in introduction
2. cueing the reader	engaging readers' interest
3. explaining a process	pacing of information
4. examples	use of process narration

Castro

For Analysis	Commentary
1. answering readers' questions	using sources
2. defining key terms	organization
3. comparison and contrast	sentence structure
4. authority	

Murayama

"IS SEX NECESSARY?" BY DAVID QUAMMEN

Students will find this to be a thoroughly entertaining and informative essay. It shows that explanatory writing need not be dry or dull and that scientific concepts can be truly fascinating. Quammen comes across as an expert on the subject, but he is not a professional scientist. His expertise, like that of students themselves, comes from research into secondary sources.

For Discussion

This discussion activity will engage students' interest in the essay. By beginning with their own life experiences, they will become motivated to analyze and understand the topic of the essay. This kind of activity is supported by research in both schema theory and reader response criticism. Using their own prior science education and attitudes about it as a basis, students can build on the known and the familiar toward a more focused discussion of the content and rhetoric of the essay. This For Discussion section could be assigned first as a written journal entry. In-class follow-up could include whole-class or small-group discussion.

For Analysis

Here we invite students to reread the text closely, analyzing its strategies and features. If these questions are answered thoughtfully, they can demystify for students some of the ways writers achieve their effects.

We find students benefit most from writing out their answers to the questions. We regularly use these responses as a basis for analyzing the texts in class, either as part of a whole-class discussion or in small groups.

1. Here's an overview of the essay's organization:

paragraph 1:	introduces and defines the concept of parthenogenesis.
paragraph 3:	asserts that it is widespread, supporting this claim with various examples.
paragraphs 4–8:	explain the process of reproduction in the aphid.
paragraphs 9–12:	explain the advantages of this system of reproduction.
paragraph 13:	cites an even more extreme example of parthenogenesis.
paragraphs 14–16:	discuss the ultimate disadvantage of parthenogenesis as compared with sexual reproduction.

2. You might want to point out how Quammen's introductory paragraph engages readers' curiosity before he even names and defines the concept in the penultimate sentence. He uses humor in paragraph 2 to keep readers' interest and to provide a transition between the definition in paragraph 1 and the explanation that follows. Paragraph 3 begins with a topic sentence forecasting the list of examples. Paragraph 4, like paragraph 2, uses direct address to get readers' attention and also serves as a transition, forecasting the remainder of the essay. Paragraph 9 serves as another transition, summarizing the conclusion drawn from the preceding paragraphs (that this system of reproduction produces "a zillion aphids") and forecasting the following paragraphs ("what is the point of it?"). The essay concludes with a summary ("So it is necessary, at least intermittently") and a return to the witty tone of the opening paragraph.

3. The obvious time markers are the names of months—March, May, and September—but other markers are more subtle. Try to get students to identify words such as "suddenly" (paragraph 5), "and so on," "then again," "before long" (paragraph 6), and "continues" (paragraph 7). The verb tense is consistently present, which makes the "story" of the aphids seem as if it is happening before us.

4. Students should not have any difficulty finding all the examples Quammen gives in these two paragraphs, but they may not know what to say about how the examples serve Quammen's explanatory purpose. You might point out that in paragraph 1, Quammen needs to give examples of parthenogenetic birds and bees in order to counter the Cole Porter song lyric with which he wittily opens the essay. The purpose for the many examples given in paragraph 3 is stated explicitly in the opening topic sentence: to support the assertion that parthenogenesis is practiced within almost every group of animals. Quammen emphasizes this fact from the start to give readers a reason for learning about parthenogenesis.

Listing so many names is likely to impress readers with the surprising variety of parthenogenetic animals. The focus in the last five sentences of paragraph 3 on the various ways insects practice parthenogenesis sets the stage for the extended example of the aphid developed in paragraphs 4–10.

For Your Own Writing

This activity could function as a pre-invention exercise. Though you need not present it to students as a way to think of possible topics for their own essay (indeed, to do so might inhibit their listing), you might ask them to refer to these lists during invention. Here is a list of some possible concepts to include in this activity: hydrostatic pressure, meiosis, biome, atomic mass, entropy, bird migration, hibernation, lithosphere, breccia, geologic time scale, plate tectonics, rapid-eye movement (REM) sleep, steroids, aerobic exercise.

Commentary

This commentary stresses Quammen's choices in focusing and limiting his information (paragraph 1), generating a high level of reader interest (paragraph 2), and regulating the pace of information (paragraph 3). These three considerations are important in writing about concepts.

"CONTINGENT WORKERS" BY JANICE CASTRO

Because many students—particularly older ones—may have experience as "contingent" workers, they are likely to have strong opinions about the impact of this trend and Castro's evidence for its existence. Some may share Castro's somewhat bleak outlook, while others may see the trend as an opportunity for increased flexibility in the work place.

For Discussion

This section, which could be assigned first as a written journal entry and then used as a basis for small-group or whole-class discussion, asks students to reexamine Castro's essay—particularly its disturbing predictions—in light of their own hopes and plans for the future. You might find that this essay provides a useful introduction to the concept of a *trend*.

For Analysis

1. This question calls students' attention to an element of concept explanation they may have overlooked: the ways in which, even in an apparently "neutral" essay, a writer selects and arranges her material in order to make a certain point about her subject. Students will probably locate the point of Castro's essay near the beginning, where she asserts that the burgeoning force of "contingent workers" is "the most important trend in business today" (paragraph 3). They should also note that most of the information Castro chooses to present deals either with the causes of this trend (increased savings for companies that hire "temps") or with its effects (less job security and fewer benefits, as well as lowered morale, for most of this "'disposable' work force" (paragraph 3).

2. Defining, whether of key or peripheral terms, is a crucial strategy in explaining concepts. Students will probably note that Castro's definition of "contingent workers" is itself somewhat contingent—a developing definition for a still-developing concept.

3. The rhetorical strategy of comparison and contrast helps to organize the information in this essay and to make it more accessible. Castro does not, however, use comparison and contrast in a simplistic manner—for instance, she does not cue readers with the obvious "in contrast" phrase—and students may need some guidance in sorting out the benefits and detriments of being a contingent worker.

4. This question asks students to consider to what extent they find Castro and Quammen trustworthy. Although Castro is not an economist, she is able to become at least a "temporary expert" on her subject. Students should note that she relies not on one or two but on a variety of sources, and that the qualifications of each source are included in the text itself. Students may also note that she invites the trust of her readers by appealing, however indirectly, to common experience. Quammen also cites authorities in paragraphs 11 and 16, but he relies primarily on his presentation of facts and his use of terminology to establish his credibility.

For Your Own Writing

Here, students are invited to consider writing about some aspect of the world of work, ranging from a variation on the concept explained in Castro's essay to a completely different concept such as the "glass ceiling." As many students will have had limited firsthand experience with the concepts mentioned in this section, you might point out that students who choose to write about this type of topic will be particularly reliant on secondary sources.

Commentary

This section discusses the use of sources, organization, and sentence structure. Students are once again asked to consider the variety of sources cited in Castro's essay; you might remind students that they will be expected to document their sources more thoroughly than Castro needs to. The following section of the Commentary highlights the ways in which writers organize the information they have gathered and plan their essays. Students will already have considered this challenge in the first question in For Analysis, but this section goes into more detail concerning Castro's selection and organization of her material. As students proceed with their own writing, they will find valuable guidelines for selection and organization in the Invention and Planning and Drafting sections of the Guide to Writing later in the chapter. Finally, the Commentary discusses the use of specific types of sentence structure in presenting information; you might reassure students that they do not need to know the technical grammatical terms for these types of sentences in order to use sentence combining to good effect in their own writing.

"SCHIZOPHRENIA: WHAT IT LOOKS LIKE, HOW IT FEELS" BY VERONICA MURAYAMA

For Discussion

Notice how this For Discussion question shifts midway from commenting on the subject of Murayama's essay to asking directly for the students' opinions on this subject: "How would you explain . . . ? What resources are you aware of . . . ?" This activity earnestly solicits the students' view; it validates their prior knowledge and their beliefs about mental illness as useful background for understanding the essay. It also teaches students how to talk about ideas in texts. Following class discussion—conducted in small groups or with the whole class—you could give students a few minutes to jot down some notes about the discussion to serve as the basis for a journal entry they will write outside of class.

For Analysis

1. Murayama seeks to engage readers' interest by launching quickly and directly into her topic; she explains what schizophrenics suffer from and provides evidence of the severity of the illness. Quammen begins on a light, playful note to draw readers in, and Castro opens with a kind of riddle to surprise readers.
2. By examining the beginnings and endings of these two essays, stu-

dents will see that framing an essay brings a sense of closure and completion. In an essay explaining a concept, it may highlight the importance of the concept. Murayama's essay, for example is framed by references to the fact that many homeless people are untreated schizophrenics, certainly a compelling reason to motivate a reader to learn more about schizophrenia. Quammen's framing is looser, but both his introduction and conclusion comment wittily on the connection between parthenogenesis and not having sex, and both obliquely include humans in the discussion.

3. Students should identify specific features of Murayama's essay that contribute to its logical organization and locate them by paragraph. Below we list three specific features and indicate where they are used:

- forecasting of the essay's focus: end of paragraph 3.
- excellent transitions linking topics of preceding paragraphs to topics introduced in new paragraphs: beginnings of paragraphs 3, 4, 5, 6, 8, 9.
- generalizations followed by examples and quotations: paragraphs 4, 5, 8, 10.

4. In paragraph 9, Murayama quotes, paraphrases, and summarizes from a source. Examining her source use by comparing the source with Murayama's writing, students will find a good example of judicious use of quotation set into a larger section of paraphrase and summary. Murayama obviously understands this source material well and adopts it to her own purpose. Students sometimes think they must either paraphrase a source *or* quote it. Here they witness what is actually more common: a brief quotation surrounded by a larger contextualizing segment of paraphrase and summary, and all of it appropriately credited to the original source.

For Your Own Writing

This section expands from the essay's focus on schizophrenia to the general subject of mental illness. Students can then refocus on different smaller topics; all mental disorders can be considered concepts and would be good choices for this essay. You could conduct a brief but lively whole-class brainstorming session and follow it up with a journal question giving students the opportunity to pick a topic and find out what they already know about it and what more they think they would need to find out.

Commentary

The commentary concentrates on purpose, forecasting, and strategies for quoting. Together with the questions, the commentary provides abundant material for you to work with, material that helps you present the essay to the students.

PURPOSE AND AUDIENCE

This section expounds the simple but worthy goals of explanatory writing: to instruct in a manner that is engaging and accessible to one's readers.

BASIC FEATURES OF EXPLANATORY ESSAYS

Here is a list of the features covered in this section. It is useful to have students read this section once before they begin work on invention and then to reread it again as they are making their revision plan.

- an appeal to readers' interests
- a logical plan
- clear definitions
- careful use of sources
- appropriate writing strategies

GUIDE TO WRITING

Invention and Research

Here is a list of the invention activities:

- Finding a concept
- Researching the concept
- Focusing the concept
- Testing your choice
- Considering explanatory strategies

It will be a good idea to familiarize your students with these steps before they actually begin the invention process. Suggest that they begin work right away, but spread the work out over several sessions. You can help them stay on track by requiring that they reach a certain point by a certain class meeting.

For Group Inquiry

At the Testing Your Choice stage of invention, we invite students to meet in small groups to try out their ideas on one another.

Planning and Drafting

The purpose of this section is to help students move smoothly from invention to drafting. After students take time to review their invention writings, they should set some goals for their essay. If there is time, students could explain their goals to you in a brief conference; or they could explain them to one another in small groups.

Getting Critical Comments

We usually urge students to write out comments and suggestions. Students who have participated in peer review of drafts in the past may have made only marginal comments on the draft itself and exchanged oral comments with another student. Getting comments in writing helps later when the writer is trying to make a revising plan.

Revising and Editing

Working with this section will enable your students to decide what changes they want to make and to carry out these revisions effectively. During this phase of the writing process, you might remind them that they can review the Basic Features summary or look at how the writers in this chapter solved similar problems, study the critical comments they received from their peers, or discuss their plans for revisions with you.

Students who seriously question their drafts in light of the guidelines in this section will probably revise their essays substantially. You could point out to students how recursive the process is; as we move from examining readings to doing invention to getting critical comments to making our revision plans, we lead ourselves back through the possibilities for developing an essay of this type, though the tasks are posed differently now.

We find it useful to emphasize to students the importance of rereading and considering the draft *as a whole* before contemplating specific revision changes. Some students resist this step; once they have secured feedback from their classmates, they want to proceed directly to revising their drafts.

You might ask students to make or at least begin their plan for revision under your guidance. If they are able to study their peers' comments, reread their drafts carefully, and compose a scratch outline while they are in the classroom with you available as a resource, they will be well launched into the process and able to complete it and then revise their drafts on their own. Alternatively, students could review them at the next class meeting to ensure that they're on track. Then you could select and duplicate the best revision plan and ask the writer to present it to the class as a model.

A WRITER AT WORK

This section is connected to the last essay in the chapter, the student essay written by Veronica Murayama. It discusses her use of sources: finding them, deciding which ones to use, and integrating them into her essay. Question 4 in the For Analysis section asks students to study A Writer at Work in conjunction with Murayama's essay and the Commentary following it.

REFLECTING ON YOUR WRITING

Once students have completed their own essays, we ask them to reflect carefully on their experience with writing concept explanations. See page 14 for more information on this activity.

RESPONDING TO ESSAYS EXPLAINING CONCEPTS

When advising students about revising their drafts, you will want to focus on the unique constraints and possibilities of concept explanations. We have found the following list of problems helpful because it reminds us of where students predictably fall short and of language we can use to focus our criticism and advice.

Concept

- The essay is unfocused. It is not clear what point the writer is trying to make about this concept.
- The writer apparently has not mastered the concept—relies too much on sources and jargon, lacks authority.
- The explanation seems inappropriate for the audience—telling them too much or too little.

Plan

- The essay is hard to follow.
- The writer neglects to forecast the plan and provide transitions.
- The information needs to be rearranged for greater clarity.

Definitions and Other Writing Strategies

- Definitions of terms likely to be unfamiliar to readers are inadequate.
- The writer has not made use of clearly relevant strategies of presenting information—comparison and contrast, classification, cause and effect, for example.
- Examples don't seem to have a clear purpose or point.
- The writer concentrates on recent developments, when readers need background information or historical information.
- Instead of explaining a concept, the writer takes a position on an issue related to the concept.

Sources

- The citations and sources reveal a superficial or incomplete search for information.
- Certain sources are inappropriate, dated, or peripheral.
- The essay relies too much or too little on quoted material.
- Quoted material is not integrated smoothly into the writer's text.
- Sources cited are not in the reference list.
- Citations and references do not consistently follow an accepted documentation style.

PREPARING FOR CONFERENCES

If you hold conferences with your students on their drafts, you could have them prepare for the conference by filling in the form on the following page.

PREPARING FOR A CONFERENCE: CHAPTER 3

Before the conference, write answers to the questions below. Bring your invention writing and first draft to the conference.

1.   What concept are you explaining? How did you come to choose it?

2.   Who are your readers? What do you assume they already know about your concept? How did these assumptions influence how you decided to focus your explanation?

3.   Explain briefly what writing strategies you decided to use—defining, classifying, comparing and contrasting, examining cause and effect, narrating a process—and why they seem appropriate.

4.   Describe your organizational plan. How does the essay begin and end? How did you sequence the strategies?

5.   What are you most pleased with in this draft? Be specific.

6.   What specifically do you need to do next to revise your draft? List any problems you see in the draft or any that have been pointed out by other readers. Say briefly how you might attempt to solve these problems. Use the back of this form for these notes. (If you have completed the text's Revising plan, bring it with you to the conference instead of answering this question.)

Chapter 4

Justifying an Evaluation

THE WRITING ASSIGNMENT

Choose a subject to evaluate. Write an essay assessing your subject addressed to a particular group of readers, giving them all of the background information, reasons, and evidence they will need to accept your evaluation. Your principal aim is to convince these readers that your judgment of this subject is informed and reasonable.

The Nature of the Writing Assignment

With this assignment, students begin the third and perhaps most challenging kind of writing featured in this book—argumentation. The sequence of three types of argumentative writing includes the evaluation (Chapter 4), position paper (Chapter 5), and the proposal (Chapter 6).

Evaluation essays are so well understood, their features so well established, that we can hold students to a standard of performance that may surprise them in its fullness and preciseness. Writing an evaluation requires students to consider carefully their reasons and to support them with appropriate evidence. Writing an evaluation nearly always draws students into comparison or contrast.

Special Problems of This Writing Assignment

This seems like a straightforward assignment: say whether you like or dislike something, and then say why. It can, nevertheless, go wrong in many ways the first time student writers try it. Students may not be willing to assert firm judgments, or they may not understand that they need to defend their judgments. In addition, because they are unaccustomed to being held to the rhetorical requirements of a specific writing situation, student writers may overlook the requirement to describe the subject for readers who are unfamiliar with it. They may also unwittingly merge or blur their reasons because they lack confidence in them.

These problems suggest that, before you ask students to analyze one another's drafts, you may want to have the class discuss sample essays to see how the writers meet the rhetorical requirements of the assignment. Furthermore, the problems of the assignment make the evaluation a good choice for a double assignment in which you ask students immediately to do a second essay on a different subject. For the first essay, you could give them two or three choices of subjects, such as the same story or movie, and then they could choose their own subjects for the second essay.

Perhaps the biggest problem of all arises when students risk doing this assignment from memory. To support an argument, writers need specific evidence.

A subject to be evaluated needs to be studied and restudied before and during invention and drafting. Students should not evaluate a movie unless they can see it two or three times, nor should they evaluate a novel unless they have time to reread parts of it.

Promising and Unpromising Topics

The first step in the Invention and Research section for this chapter asks students to list possible subjects for their evaluation essays. We provide a list of general topic areas to get students started, a list drawn from our own experience with successful and unsuccessful topics. As you can see, we suggest a range of possible topic areas—including media, arts, literature, education, government, campus, and leisure—that extends far beyond the few examples we have provided through the chapter readings.

Our experience has shown us that the most successful essays are those that draw heavily on the writer's interests and expertise. Students who express an avid interest in skateboarding often write fine essays on skateboard magazines, skateboard parks, or skateboard models. Not only are they familiar with the standards usually applied to that field of interest, but they are also able to make comparisons with and contrasts to related subjects (for example, other skateboard magazines, parks, or models) with some ease. The topics themselves can be quite ambitious—we had some remarkable essays evaluating such things as strategic nuclear arms treaties and UAW contracts—but they are successful only when the student has expertise in the topic. You should, by all means, encourage your students to draw on their own strengths, knowledge base, and interests when choosing topics.

By and large, students have the least amount of difficulty evaluating consumer products. Standards are fairly easy to establish, the essays themselves are not difficult to structure, and comparisons can be found in personal experience. Students, however, have a tendency to slip into a kind of Madison Avenue prose, uncritically touting the virtues of their chosen product and making claims of "comfort" or "style" that are unsupported by evidence. Personal taste often takes the place of more objective bases for evaluation in essays about consumer products. We discourage essays about consumer products; some instructors forbid them.

We are also wary of topics that try to evaluate abstract concepts such as "friendship" or "greed." Though it is theoretically possible to write such evaluations, it is extremely difficult to decide upon appropriate standards for judgment. Even more difficult is determining the kind of evidence that might be brought to bear on such a topic. Our students have occasionally written creditable essays evaluating "capitalism" or "democracy," but the key to their success seems to lie in the fact that these concepts can be illustrated by referring to specific examples of free market economics or democratic government.

Easily the most promising topics are discrete, tangible objects or events that can be revisited and analyzed—a story or novel, movie, musical recording, concert, play performance, essay in this book, magazine, restaurant, college program or service. Before drafting, students can revisit the subject, taking careful notes. They can revisit once again before revising, keeping the subject *present* throughout the writing process. Such immediate presence of the subjects makes it easier for students to amass the evidence or examples required in a strong evaluation essay.

CHAPTER INTRODUCTION

Writing in Your Other Courses

These four assignments represent some of the kinds of evaluative writing students may encounter in courses in the natural and social sciences, and the humanities. You might begin by asking students to add to the list assignments from their own courses requiring evaluation. Be careful to discriminate between assignments requesting evaluation from those simply asking for analysis.

Students may be surprised to learn that academics tend to be more concerned with analysis—what we often call criticism—than evaluation. Analysis, of course, may implicitly include some evaluation. But students will seldom find assignments in literature courses, for example, that ask them to evaluate a poem or novel. Even a request to analyze the artistry of a particular poem should not be misread as a request for evaluation. The question assumes that the poem is artistic. Students are being asked to demonstrate in what ways the poem displays artistry, not to judge whether or not—or even to what degree—it is artistic. Questions asking students to agree or disagree with a critical statement about a work of literature may also be misread as a request for evaluation. Although the answer will involve judgment of the statement or idea as it is applied to the text, the essay should focus more on elucidating the text than on evaluating the statement.

For Group Inquiry

This group inquiry activity is designed to engage students in the most basic and yet most difficult aspect of evaluative writing: choosing appropriate standards for judgment. Notice that the activity has two parts. First, students discuss the standards they would use for evaluating the kind of entertainment they have chosen and select the three they agree are most important. Then, they reflect on where these standards come from. The second part of the task will likely be new for them because few students—indeed few people other than experts in a field—think about the standards by which they judge things. Normally we just make judgments without thinking seriously about the values underlying our judgments. Through this group inquiry activity, you can lead students to recognize the importance of self-reflectiveness and critical analysis.

If students have difficulty coming up with standards, you might advise them to think of a particular instance they are all familiar with and to consider how they would judge that. The group inquiry activity asks them to see if they can reach a consensus about the three most important criteria. But even the process of consensus building may involve argument. They should expect to disagree on some things. Disagreement can help them anticipate objections readers may have to their written argument.

READINGS

Topics in Analysis Questions and Commentaries

Two of the reading selections in this chapter deal with popular culture—film and television. David Ansen evaluates the controversial film *Do the Right Thing*, and Barbara Ehrenreich reviews the popular television program *Roseanne*. Interestingly, both writers assume that to be good, popular art should include serious social commentary. This will come as a surprise to many students, and some may challenge this basis for judgment. Kevin Stewart's evaluation of an autobiographical essay from Chapter 2 of this book does not share this assumption.

For your convenience as quick reference, we list below the discourse topics addressed in each of the For Analysis questions and in the Commentary. You might use this list in class or in conference to refer students to particular discourse features they need to review.

Ansen

For Analysis
1. description of subject
2. comparison and contrast
3. refutation
4. credibility

Commentary
purpose and audience
argumentative strategy
criteria or bases for judgment
evidence

Ehrenreich

For Analysis
1. thesis statement
2. comparison and contrast
3. textual evidence
4. wit

Commentary
logical fallacy
topic sentences
use of the colon
repetition (*anaphora*)

Stewart

For Analysis
1. forecasting
2. reasons
3. cueing the reader
4. evidence

Commentary
choosing reasons
choosing writing strategies

"SEARING, NERVY, AND VERY HONEST" BY DAVID ANSEN

The brief introduction to this reading reminds students of the primary reason for reading movie reviews: to help us decide whether or not to see a film. With this understanding in mind, students should be able to recognize ways that movie reviewers try to influence readers' decisions. You might ask students if they ordinarily look at the reviews of movies they're considering seeing. How do they make their decisions? Many will no doubt say that they depend on advertising (especially the brief compilation of scenes called trailers that are shown prior to other films). Some may say they rely on what their friends who have seen the movie say about it. They should recognize that this word-of-mouth advertising is also a kind of film reviewing, and its strength lies in the credibility of the reviewer/friend and the assumption that you and your friends share the same bases for judging films.

It may help—but it is certainly not necessary—that students see *Do the Right Thing* to analyze Ansen's review. It is always possible to show the video in class, but that would divert attention away from Ansen's essay. If you want students to review a film, however, we do urge you to show the videotape in class and discuss it in detail. To write on a film, students need to be able to resee at least parts of it to find evidence.

For Discussion

This activity, which can be done with small groups or with the whole class, goes right to the heart of the controversy *Do the Right Thing* fostered. If the class has seen the film, you might want to focus on how they interpret the concluding events: the murder of Radio Raheem and the subsequent destruction of Sal's pizzeria. But they can discuss the general question of whether violence may or may not be justifiable without having seen the film. In fact, it may be more profitable for them to begin considering the issue in terms of their personal experience. We also suggest that, if there is time, you might want to have them read and discuss William Carlos Williams's short story "The Use of Force." It can be read aloud in about ten or fifteen minutes.

For Analysis

1. This question invites students to apply—and test the accuracy of—some assertions we've made about evaluative writing. You might have students work in groups rereading Ansen's essays to see if the features and strategies listed here can be found. This is a good way of previewing the chapter.

2. This question raises the issue of how writers use comparison and contrast in evaluation. Students can begin now to consider why evaluative writing relies so heavily on this particular writer's strategy.

Students will see that in one case Ansen uses comparison and in the other contrast. In paragraph 2, Ansen compares Spike Lee's "rude comic impulse" to that of comedians Lenny Bruce and Richard Pryor. (Lenny Bruce was repeatedly arrested in the 1950s for using obscenity in his act.) This comparison allows him to place Lee in the same class with two exceptional comedians. In paragraph 3, he contrasts Lee's handling of race relations on film.

3. Students familiar with the controversy over *Do the Right Thing* will not be surprised by Ansen's emphasizing this objection and his refutation of it. You might want to connect this question to the For Discussion section since both focus on the issue of racial violence raised by the film.

4. This question draws students' attention to the issue of credibility. Some students may feel that Ansen is trying to be nervy and honest himself by reporting Lee's tough language. While he uses a somewhat sophisticated vocabu-

lary ("invective," "soliloquies," and "noxious"), he does not talk down to his readers. In fact, his style is unpretentious and often colloquial ("blows away the pieties" and "stack the deck").

For Your Own Writing

This section asks students to consider writing a movie review of their own. It invites them to rehearse the composing process by making the kinds of decisions they will need to make when they actually write an evaluative essay: choosing a topic, making a judgment, determining their reasons, and anticipating readers' possible objections.

This is a challenging activity and one that you might want to support by taking class time to allow students to discuss their tentative decisions in small groups or with the whole class. You might consider grouping students according to current films they've seen and allow them to debate their evaluations in their groups.

Commentary

The commentary following this first selection introduces the main features and strategies of evaluative writing. Purpose and readers are discussed in order for students to recognize how the rhetorical situation in which they are writing will inform their argumentative strategy. You might ask students to infer the values Ansen assumes his readers share as well as the differences he ignores. Reading to analyze a writer's argumentative strategy can be quite challenging. But it can be very useful when students need to develop their own arguments.

Another point brought up in the commentary is that the center of an evaluation is an assertion, a value judgment. Some students are hesitant to assert themselves, while others may be only too eager to declare their judgments. You might discuss qualifying claims. Ansen, for example, does not qualify his claims. That is both to be admired and also to be questioned. For example, at the end of paragraph 3 he states: "The beauty of 'Do the Right Thing' is that all the characters, from the broadest cartoons to the most developed, are given their humanity and their due." A skeptical reader might very well question a sweeping assertion like this. Moreover, a critical reader might wonder just what Ansen means by a phrase like "given their humanity and their due." Vagueness and overgeneralizing are common pitfalls of argumentative writing. They seem to occur most often in evaluative writing when the writer adopts a tone that is either too enthusiastic in its praise or too damning in its criticism.

We also bring up the possibility that the basis for judgment might need to be explained or defended. Writers of evaluation have to decide not only on what criteria to base their judgment but also whether to discuss their choice of criteria. You might ask students whether they think Ansen needs to explain his criterion of portraying reality honestly without oversimplifying or whether he is right to assume that most readers would understand and accept it.

"THE WRETCHED OF THE HEARTH"
BY BARBARA EHRENREICH

Students may be surprised to find a television series, particularly a sitcom, being treated seriously. You might want to discuss with them Ehrenreich's unstated assumption that television is worth studying because it provides a mirror reflecting—and occasionally criticizing—some aspect of society. Some social critics—possibly including Ehrenreich—also argue that we construct ourselves through our self-representations. Therefore, television, as well as film and music, potentially could have an enormous influence on the kind of society we become.

For Discussion

The very first sentence of Ehrenreich's essay focuses attention on class: "*Roseanne* the sitcom . . . is a radical departure simply for featuring blue-collar Americans—and for depicting them as something other than half-witted greasers and low-life louts." She goes on to point out that the "working class does not usually get much of a role in the American entertainment spectacle." You might ask students to think of some television programs (current and past) that identify characters in terms of social and economic class and then to consider the ways we stereotype members of different classes.

Our questions attempt to move discussion away from the media's representation of class to the students' own perceptions and experiences. The focus on the American dream and whether it still exists should stimulate some interesting debate.

For Analysis

1. Ehrenreich's judgment, like most if not all evaluations, is essentially comparative. She argues that *Roseanne* challenges the stereotypes we've come to expect from popular culture's representations of blue-collar Americans.

2. In Paragraph 1, she refers to *Rocky, The Deer Hunter,* and *Saturday Night Fever* as a class of 1970s films representing working-class characters as "greasers" and "louts." Then she refers to Archie Bunker as another blue-collar type. (Students might not be familiar with this character or the television show, *All in the Family,* in which he appeared.) She contrasts *Roseanne* to both of these stereotypes of blue-collar Americans.

3. One aim of this question is to emphasize the importance of evidence in supporting the argument. But we also want students to notice that because Ehrenreich's judgment is about the series as a whole, she cannot depend solely on evidence from individual episodes. She has to demonstrate that what she is claiming is true throughout the series and not just true of one or two episodes. Evidence from specific episodes appears in paragraphs 4, 5, and 6, whereas general evidence from the series as a whole appears in paragraphs 3, 4, and 5.

4. This last question invites students to talk about tone and credibility. Some students will be responsive to Ehrenreich's rather sophisticated wit, while others will not. You might ask them to describe the person that comes across to them from reading this essay.

For Your Own Writing

Here students are urged to consider evaluating a series of some kind rather than a single, isolated subject. The problem of identifying appropriate criteria may be ameliorated by evaluating a series: thinking of something in terms of a series leads one to think about the ways we categorize and value things. For example, to evaluate several self-portraits by a single painter, a writer would want to think about what makes them self-portraits or what qualities people look for in self-portraits. Taken as a series, the paintings become studies in the genre of the self-portrait.

Commentary

This commentary treats several topics: balancing the judgment as well as using topic sentences and two stylistic factors. The point about balance might be applied to the other readings in this chapter. You could ask students to review the essays to see whether the writers avoid unqualified praise or blame. On the other hand, some students, in an attempt to balance their judgment, wind up making no clear judgment at all. You might discuss with them the difference between qualifying a judgment and waffling.

The paragraph on topic sentences reminds students that the writer bears some responsibility to make the essay readable. We discuss here only a few examples of Ehrenreich's use of cueing strategies; you could ask students to find other examples in this selection or in another selection they read in this chapter. The discussion of Ehrenreich's use of the colon and repetition might serve as an occasion for students to practice using these sentence strategies in their own writing.

"AN EVALUATION OF TOBIAS WOLFF'S 'ON BEING A REAL WESTERNER'" BY KEVIN STEWART

This selection is somewhat unusual in that it takes another selection from the text as its topic; you might consider giving your students this option as well (see the For Your Own Writing section).

For Discussion

This section asks students to look closely at the expression of emotion in writing or telling about personal experience; students who have worked with Chapter 2: Remembering Events may have an advantage here. You might begin this as a small-group activity, asking students to get together briefly in groups of two or three, before broadening the discussion to include the entire class.

For Analysis

1. Stewart's first paragraph introduces the main points of his essay—the reasons for his positive judgment of Wolff's story—and forecasts the order in which they are presented. Stewart's reasons include narrative strategies, detailing

of scenes and people, the relation of the story to his own experience, and the writer's expression of the significance of the event; most students should have little difficulty tracing Stewart's paragraph-by-paragraph presentation of his evidence in support of these reasons. Asked to examine whether other writers in this chapter have forecast their arguments in their opening paragraphs, students may note that Ansen's evaluation is singular among these selections in beginning *in media res;* while most students will agree that beginning an evaluation with a forecasting statement has the obvious advantage of helping the reader anticipate the writer's upcoming argument, they will probably also agree that Ansen's approach allows him to capture the reader's attention immediately by beginning with a specific scene.

2.   As the reasons for Stewart's judgment are explicitly based on the fairly authoritative commentary of an earlier chapter in the text, few students are likely to argue that they are inappropriate. However, close scrutiny of Stewart's reasons will help students to be especially conscious of the reasons they will eventually choose in support of their own judgments.

3.   Whereas the first question drew students' attention to Stewart's use of forecasting, this question focuses on another important cueing strategy: transitions. Students will probably note that as long as Stewart's argument focuses on his first set of reasons—"strategies of narrative action and detailing of the scene and people" in paragraphs 2–5—the topic sentences refer both to material from previous paragraphs and to the material in the paragraph to come. On the other hand, the topic sentences in paragraphs 6 and 7, each of which introduces a new reason, do not refer directly to the preceding paragraphs.

4.   Most students will probably agree that Stewart's support for the reason in paragraph 3—"the careful focus of the scene and action"—is less thorough and specific than the support in paragraph 5 for the detailing of objects and participants in the scene. Students are likely to have widely different responses to the evidence presented in paragraph 6. If some students suggest that the thread of Stewart's argument is lost in the long paragraph relating his own experience, you might remind them that Stewart announces in his first paragraph that the relation of Wolff's story to Stewart's personal experience is one of the reasons for his positive judgment of the story.

For Your Own Writing

Unless you plan on discouraging your students from evaluating essays in Part I of the text (or from evaluating literary texts), this activity should be a useful pre-invention exercise. In addition to helping students choose possible topics for their own evaluations, this activity guides students in identifying appropriate standards for evaluating particular topics.

Commentary

This brief section focuses on identifying both appropriate reasons for judgment and appropriate writing strategies for evaluation. In Stewart's case, a careful reading of Chapter 2: Remembering Events enabled him to choose appropriate reasons in support of his evaluation. Likewise, Stewart's thorough reading of

Chapter 2 helped him rule out at least one inappropriate writing strategy: comparing and contrasting.

PURPOSE AND AUDIENCE

This section gives you an opportunity to focus class discussion on the concepts of purpose and audience as they pertain to the writing of evaluation essays. The writing situations that open the chapter together with the illustrative academic assignments in the introduction should suggest the range of situations in which evaluative essays may be written.

Two of the essay selections exemplify a special use of evaluation: to review instances of popular culture such as films and television programs. If you ask students about the purpose of reviewing cultural artifacts like these, most students will answer in market terms: to help consumers decide which film to see. Although that is undoubtedly the way that readers of newspapers and magazines typically use reviews, the essays presented here (possibly with the exception of the student essay) attempt to do something more.

BASIC FEATURES OF EVALUATIONS

This section summarizes what students have learned from analyzing the readings. We emphasize four basic features:

- a well-presented subject
- a clear, well-balanced judgment
- a convincing argument
- pointed comparisons

This discussion of basic features forms a bridge from the readings to the students' own writing. The same features reappear in the Invention and Research activities, in the guide to Reading with a Critical Eye, and in the Revising and Editing section. You may want to refer students to this summary if they have problems with a particular feature.

GUIDE TO WRITING

Invention and Research

We recommend these activities to help students choose a subject, determine what they think about it, and develop a reasoned argument supporting their judgment for their particular readers:

- Choosing a subject
- Exploring your subject
- Analyzing your readers
- Developing an argumentative strategy
- Testing your choice

You might want to spend class time brainstorming possible subjects for evaluation. You could, of course, assign the whole class the same subject—an evaluation of a short story, an essay from a chapter in this book, or a film (you show on video). If you want to allow greater choice but also want to give students the benefit of collaborative learning, you could invite students to work together in small groups of three to five. These groups could discuss the subject they've chosen, debate their different judgments, and read one another's drafts. Some instructors have found it especially instructive for students to write the essay collaboratively. If you are attracted by this idea, be sure to consider—in advance—how you will grade the essay. Collaborative projects of this kind can be very productive, but they require careful planning and sensitive guidance to make them work well for everyone.

Probably the most difficult invention activity is Developing an Argumentative Strategy. Students tend to have two kinds of difficulty: identifying the standards underlying their judgment and finding evidence. You can address the first problem by having students (working together in pairs or in small groups) explain to one another why they think the reasons are appropriate. If students are already working together on the same subject, the topic of what standards they are applying will probably come up. Even if students are not familiar with the particular subject, the writer could describe the subject as fitting into a general class of things (e.g., horror films) and then the group could discuss the question: What makes a horror film good?

The second difficulty—finding evidence—requires that the writer have ready access to the subject being evaluated. If it is a film, the videotape should be available for students to replay. Also, students need to develop a system of note-taking that allows them to refer specifically to the film (for example, by quoting or paraphrasing particular bits of dialogue).

For Group Inquiry

This group activity invites students to rehearse their argument before drafting and to give one another feedback.

Planning and Drafting

This section offers advice on reviewing invention writing, setting goals, outlining, and drafting. You may want to spend some class time discussing the goals. They refocus the basic features in terms of actions students can take, given their particular rhetorical situation, to present the subject effectively and make their argument understandable and convincing.

Getting Critical Comments

This guide to critical reading helps students analyze one anothers' drafts the way they analyzed the readings at the beginning of the chapter. Once again, all the basic features of evaluation essays are the center of attention. Students are specifically asked to look at these features in the context of the writer's audience and purpose.

Revising and Editing

This section urges students first to get an overview of their own essays and a sense of their problems before attempting to solve any single problem. We also encourage students to put off considering readers' critical comments until they have made their own assessments of their essays' strengths and weaknesses.

A WRITER AT WORK

Since developing an argumentative strategy raises difficulties for many students, the Writer at Work section illustrates Kevin Stewart's efforts to complete the chart of reasons and evidence suggested in the Invention guidelines. You might have students compare Stewart's plan for his argument with the revised version of his essay that appears earlier in the chapter.

REFLECTING ON YOUR WRITING

As students complete their own evaluation essays, we ask them to reflect on what they have learned from the writing they've done in this genre. See page 14 for more information on this activity.

RESPONDING TO ESSAYS JUSTIFYING AN EVALUATION

When advising students about revising their drafts, you will want to focus on the unique constraints and possibilities of evaluative writing. We have found the following list of typical problems helpful because it reminds us of the language we can use productively to advise students and remind them of what they've read in the evaluation chapter.

Subject

- The subject is not within the limits set by your assignment (you assigned reviews of current movies and the student evaluates a fast-food place).
- The subject is too broad (jazz music rather than a particular jazz recording).
- The subject does not lend itself to evaluation (the homeless, cigarette smoking, school spirit).

Judgment

- The essay describes the subject or merely identifies its strong and weak points but does not express a clear judgment based on evidence.
- The judgment is overstated, without appropriate qualification or clarification.

Argument

- There is too much descriptive, historical, or biographical background, distracting from the argument.
- The argument consists of a string of unsupported value judgments ("The acting was good. The directing was excellent. The cinematography was well done.").
- There are too many reasons or too few.
- The reasons seem arbitrary and inappropriate, not based on standards usually applied to a subject of that kind.
- The reasons are not organized logically.
- The reasons do not support the judgment.
- The essay fails to provide enough evidence about the subject to be convincing.
- The essay falls back on "advertising language" or PR style.
- Faulty or circular logic: something is good because it is entertaining; something is "good" because it presents contemporary issues.
- Similarly, something is not necessarily "good" because it is "realistic," or "bad" because it is not. Conversely, something is not "good" simply because it is "unusual," "offbeat," or "strange" (e.g., rock stars).

Comparison and Contrast

- The essay misuses comparison and contrast, evaluating two subjects instead of one.
- The comparison or contrast seems mismatched to the subject.
- The comparison or contrast is not developed (the writer asserts only "*Star Wars* is a better movie than *Star Trek*" without giving examples or reasons).

PREPARING FOR CONFERENCES

If you hold conferences with your students on their drafts, you could have them prepare for the conference by filling in the form on the following page.

PREPARING FOR A CONFERENCE: CHAPTER 4

Before the conference, write answers to the questions below. Bring your invention writing and first draft to the conference.

1. What have you chosen to evaluate? How did you decide on this subject? What is your judgment of it?

2. Who are your readers, and what can you assume they know and think about your subject? How, specifically, do you hope to influence their thinking through your essay?

3. List the reasons for your judgment. Be prepared to talk about their appropriateness, sequence, and relationship.

4. List the comparisons and contrasts in your essay, and briefly describe the purpose for each one. What, exactly, does comparison/contrast contribute to your argument?

5. What are you most pleased with in this draft? Be specific.

6. What specifically do you need to do next to revise your draft? List any problems you see in the draft or ones others have pointed out. Say briefly how you might attempt to solve these problems. Use the back of this form for these notes. (If you have completed the text's Revising plan, bring it with you to the conference instead of answering this question.)

Chapter 5

Arguing a Position

THE WRITING ASSIGNMENT

Write a position paper on a controversial issue. Examine the issue critically, take a position, and develop a reasoned argument in support of your position.

The Nature of the Writing Assignment

When students take a position on a controversial issue, they discover not only that people differ but also that they have good reasons for their different views. They learn to respect the complexity of issues and the subtlety of others' reasoning. Because this chapter emphasizes the rhetorical aspects of argumentation, it helps students avoid polemics.

The writing assignment requires that students examine the issue critically. Instead of framing an argument to support an already-formed opinion, we encourage students to analyze and evaluate the pros and cons of the issue before reaching their own conclusions. We urge them to examine their own underlying assumptions as critically as they would those of their opponents. We want them to recognize the value of thinking through the issue and of basing their position on solid reasoning and evidence, not merely to convince others but for their own sake as well.

Special Problems of This Writing Assignment

Probably the greatest problem students encounter when they begin writing position papers is mistaking assertion for argumentation. This problem manifests itself in sweeping generalizations unsupported by reasons and evidence. Students with little experience developing an argument usually assume that all they need do is state what they think. They don't realize that they have to give the reasons for their position or offer evidence to support it. Nor do they recognize how important it is to anticipate readers' opposing arguments and either to modify their own position by acknowledging good points or to defend it by refuting arguments with which they disagree.

For some students, the essential problem is lack of experience setting out their reasons in a way that others can follow. For them, reading a diversity of arguments will provide instructive illustrations. If, however, the problem stems from the habit of relying on unexamined assumptions and biases, then the solution becomes more difficult. These students need first to accept the value of introspection and reasoning. They must recognize that the aim of argumentation is not merely to voice your own opinion but to examine it critically.

The root of the problem might be cognitive as well as emotional immaturity. Students who have not yet overcome their own egotism have little experience with other points of view; therefore, they have few strategies for self-analysis, let alone for audience analysis. They may be able to assert their own opinions forcefully but tend to have difficulty looking critically at their own assumptions or presenting to others their train of thought. In our experience, students with this kind of problem respond well when argumentative writing is presented as an act of communication rather than as an act of aggression. When the emphasis is on creating common ground instead of squashing your opponents into the ground, students feel less defensive and more open to alternative ways of seeing.

Promising and Unpromising Topics

We have found that there is no simple rule for prejudging the promise of topics for position papers. Many experienced instructors feel otherwise. For example, they often eliminate from consideration issues having to do with matters of faith like abortion and creationism. We find, however, that students can often handle issues such as these if they take seriously other points of view. What we find most limiting is lack of information. If students are not well informed about an issue and do not have time or inclination to inform themselves, then their argument is likely to be fatuous—full of generalization and lacking in reasons and evidence.

Without making the assignment a full-blown research project, you might encourage students to discuss the issue with others and to do some reading about it. Exploring opposing views should be a routine part of the invention process. Sometimes, however, students make their research one-sided. It is good to seek reasons and evidence to support a position, but students also need to learn about the other side. They need to be able to anticipate opposing arguments and to recognize values and concerns they may share with others.

In the Guide to Writing, we offer a list of possibilities to get students thinking about issues they could write about. Many of the topics we suggest are ones we think students will know and also care about. Caring about the topic is essential for good writing, particularly for argumentative writing. This requirement comes as a surprise to some students and may even be threatening to them. We have been amazed how many students are reluctant to express an opinion. Sometimes there is a cultural basis to their resistance. They may have been taught that it is inappropriate for them to argue assertively. Some have been made to feel that they know too little to have an opinion worth sharing. Others believe that they are in college to consume ideas and opinions, not to produce them. For these students, we emphasize the process over the product. We explain that taking a position teaches them to analyze issues critically and to evaluate arguments pro and con. With experience, students gain confidence in their reasoning abilities and come to enjoy developing a thoughtful, well-supported argument.

CHAPTER INTRODUCTION

Writing in Your Other Courses

Reading and writing about controversial issues is common throughout the curriculum. The examples included here suggest a range of courses—history, economics, sociology, and health sciences—where students can expect to encounter such assignments. Notice that these assignments do not ask students simply to summarize other people's arguments but to present and support their own.

For Group Inquiry

This activity lets students practice debating an issue. They can choose any issue they know something about. The debate will give them a sense of just how much information a writer actually needs to make a convincing argument. The most important part of the activity is the reflection at the end. You might ask each group to speak to the class for a few minutes about their experience.

READINGS

These three readings should be interesting to many of your students. One of the three directly involves young people, and the others treat talk shows and Native American claims, topics that have generated much debate.

Topics in Analysis Questions and Commentaries

These lists can serve as a quick reference to help you plan your discussion of discourse features either in class or in conferences.

Harjo

For Analysis	*Commentary*
1. posing questions	word choice
2. organization	metaphor
3. evidence	citing authorities
4. authority	using statistics

Meadows

For Analysis	*Commentary*
1. establishing credibility	refutation
2. appeals to logic	establishing credibility
3. comparison	making a claim
4. using examples	cueing the reader
	definition

Statsky

For Analysis	*Commentary*
1. organization	defining the issue
2. argumentative strategy	qualifying the thesis
3. authorities	
4. conclusion	
5. analysis of purpose and audience	

"LAST RITES FOR INDIAN DEAD"
BY SUZAN SHOWN HARJO

Students may be unfamiliar with the issue Harjo addresses in this essay.

For Discussion

This activity seeks to involve students in a discussion, in small groups or with the whole class, about traditional American values and the historical (and present-day) attitudes toward Native Americans as well as other ethnic minorities. Notice that students are asked to come up with at least one example to support their claims about today's values and attitudes.

For Analysis

1. Here we introduce the concept of the rhetorical question. Asking rhetorical questions is a strategy familiar to most students. But many have not looked at it with a critical eye. Students need to recognize that some readers become annoyed by questions like these because they feel manipulated by them. Clearly, the only possible answer to these particular questions is outrage. As Harjo says in the next paragraph, "The ordinary American would say [in response] there ought to be a law. . . ." On the other hand, rhetorical questions can effectively establish common ground between writer and readers and set the stage for the rest of the argument. Harjo's questions and follow-up in the second paragraph do this by pointing out the unfairness of the double standard, one for "the ordinary American" and another for Native Americans.

2. We expect that students will see that the argument basically falls into two parts: paragraphs 1–12 and 13–18. The first part makes the case against the storing of Native American remains, and the second part shows what is being done to remedy the situation and what still needs to be done. Here's our outline:

paragraphs 1–2:	raise the issue and state the claim
paragraphs 3–5:	attack the reason the heads were originally removed
paragraph 6:	argues that exhibiting Indian remains is dehumanizing
paragraphs 7–9:	criticize the market in Indian "artifacts" because it perpetuates the desecration of burial sites
paragraphs 10–12:	question the reason (research to benefit living Indians) given for keeping the remains
paragraph 13:	discusses laws to protect Indian burial sites
paragraphs 14–15:	tell of efforts by universities and the Smithsonian to return some Indian remains
paragraphs 16–18:	ask that action be taken to stop collectors and to return all Indian remains

You might want students to suggest that Harjo's argument would be stronger if it made better use of cueing devices, particularly forecasting and transition statements. You could review Chapter 7: Strategies for Cueing Readers and then have students add appropriate cueing.

3. In paragraphs 4 and 5, Harjo argues that the Army's "Indian Crania Study" was "pseudoscientific." To support this claim, she cites as evidence an officer's journal entry and the fact that there are no records of "overall comparisons, conclusions or final reports." To this criticism of past "research" she adds her objections to current research. She points out that even if the research were beneficial to living Indians, it would not justify keeping an estimated nineteen thousand bodies. Moreover, she quotes an impartial authority to prove that this claim to benefit Indians is itself bogus. Finally, in paragraph 12, Harjo acknowledges that studying Indian remains for racial biological studies could presumably be useful, but it is not ethical to conduct such research without the consent of relatives. By marshaling evidence to support her argument, Harjo strengthens her claim. She shows that claims to justify the storing of Indian remains for scientific research are suspect at the very least.

4. Students might think that paragraphs 13–15 indicate that the issue is moot, but Harjo indicates, in paragraphs 16–18, that it is still a controversial issue. She uses paragraphs 13–15 to show readers that many reasonable people—legislators, university museum and Smithsonian curators alike—recognize the legitimacy of her argument and are acting to remedy the situation.

For Your Own Writing

The focus here is on handling your own strong feelings as you argue your position on a controversial issue. Some people think that feelings ought to be avoided altogether in reasoned argument. The Harjo essay offers an excellent opportunity for you to discuss this issue with your students.

Commentary

The issue of feelings particularly as it affects word choice and the use of evidence is raised in the commentary. You might want to introduce such concepts as *slanted* and *loaded language* to help students become more sensitive to the way that arguments are made indirectly through word choice and images. An exercise that is both enjoyable and enlightening is to have students watch commercials on television and report on the way they use language and imagery to indirectly influence viewers' opinions.

Another topic discussed here is the use of statistics and authorities as evidence. These two kinds of evidence (often related) carry enormous weight in our culture. You might ask students to consider why that is so. Why do we have respect for numerical and authority figures?

"RUSH AND LARRY, COAST TO COAST: THIS IS NOT DEMOCRACY IN ACTION" BY DONELLA H. MEADOWS

This essay considers the role of media talk shows in a democracy; as the title suggests, Meadows argues that these shows are not the democratic forums that they are often assumed to be. Most students will be familiar with one or more of the programs Meadows mentions, and we ask them to reflect on their own opinions about these shows before reading Meadows's essay.

For Discussion

This activity gives students the opportunity to relate Meadows's ideas about arguing to her essay's argumentative structure. Following small-group or whole-class discussion, you could give students a few minutes to jot down notes on what was said and their reactions to it. Then ask them to organize, expand, and rewrite their notes as a journal assignment, which could be read out loud to the whole class or shared in small groups.

For Analysis

These questions require students to reread the text closely, analyzing its strategies and features. We find that students benefit most from these questions when we ask them to write out answers to them prior to class discussion.

1. This question asks students to begin considering the ways in which writers about controversial issues represent themselves to their readers. Astute students will not that Meadows's opening description of herself as a "talk-show junkie" can be seen as both a claim to expertise and an admission of weakness; thus, it establishes at once her credibility and her humanity. In somewhat the same way, her explanation that she is from New England (paragraph 4) lends her an authority about town meetings based on personal experience. Her comments about Rush Limbaugh's popularity in paragraph 7 may lead students to describe her as "liberal"; you might need to encourage students to expand on this characterization, but it serves as a good starting point for a discussion of how often argument is based on personal opinion and underlying assumptions—and of how it can nonetheless succeed as argument.

2. Here, we engage students in an analysis of Meadows's logical or syllogistic reasoning, asking them first to consider the role of representation within a democracy. Students are then asked to decide whether call-in talk shows are in fact representative of the population as a whole, and then to agree or disagree with Meadows's conclusion about the democratic quality of such programs. The question might best be addressed in small groups.

3. This question focuses on one of several strategies writers find especially useful when arguing about controversial issues: comparison. Students may already have noticed that Meadows's argument hinges on the similarities she draws between call-in talk shows and New England–style town meetings; this question asks them to consider both the validity of this comparison and its effectiveness in Meadows's argument.

4. The use of examples is another central strategy in argumentative writing. In addition to naming specific call-in shows (Rush Limbaugh's and Larry King's), Meadows provides examples of cases that represent the types of issues discussed on these programs (Ross Perot, Zoë Baird, congressional pay raises), as well as those cases untouched by the average talk show (Ron Brown, Yugoslavia, the savings and loan disaster). In considering these examples, students will probably note that Meadows uses this double set of examples to suggest that not only

are call-in shows not truly representative, but they "miss the biggest, most profound issues" (paragraph 9).

For Your Own Writing

This section asks students to consider writing an essay about a controversial issue involving the media—a rich source of topic possibilities for many students. Options suggested here—including piracy, monitoring, and outright censorship—revolve around regulation of various media. Whether students use these suggestions as starting points or come up with ideas of their own, this section reminds them that they will need to consider carefully their own assumptions about the issue. As students begin thinking of topics for their own writing, they may find it useful to refer back to this exercise for possibilities.

Commentary

This section discusses several important elements of writing about controversial issues: refutation, establishing credibility, making a claim, cueing the reader, and defining key terms. The scratch outline presented in the text helps students recognize the centrality of refutation in Meadows's argument. As is the case with many essays about controversial issues, refutation serves here both as a primary writing strategy and as the organizational principle of Meadows's essay. Students who have responded to the first For Analysis question will already have examined how Meadows establishes her credibility. Here, students are encouraged to note how her credibility as a "talk-show junkie" and a New Englander—and thus as somewhat of an expert on both call-in shows and town meetings—allows her to make the claim that, contrary to popular opinion, neither is truly democratic. This commentary section continues with a brief discussion of Meadows's use of transitions and other cues and concludes by asking students to focus on Meadows's use of definition—specifically, definition of her key term, democracy. The question of this particular definition, already foregrounded for students in the second For Analysis question, is central to Meadows's argument.

"CHILDREN NEED TO PLAY, NOT COMPETE" BY JESSICA STATSKY

This essays treats a topic with which some students may have had personal experience: organized sports for children. The headnote invites them to reflect on their experience, and you might make this the subject of class discussion.

For Discussion

This activity focuses on Statsky's basic assumption about traditional American values. The discussion may take place in small groups or with the whole class. Students are invited to test her assumption against their own experiences and observations. They are asked specifically to think about how the educational system deals with the ideas of cooperation and competition, and also to examine their treatment in the media and advertising. The point is to get them to come up with specific instances to support one point of view or the other.

For Analysis

1.   This is the second time in the chapter that we ask students to outline an argument. We emphasize outlining because it helps students to read critically. Outlining is valuable in writing as well as reading. One of the greatest difficulties students have in writing an argument is organizing it logically. In the Guide to Writing, we urge students to make an outline on two different occasions: before drafting and before revising the draft. The outline they make before drafting, though tentative and subject to revision as they draft, will help them to plan the draft by ordering the points they hope to cover. The outline they make before revising will help them to see the draft objectively (that is, see what they actually said rather than what they intended to say), and to reorder the points or clarify the organization.

You can expect students to notice the following cueing devices. Statsky does some forecasting, but her essay could be improved on this score. She forecasts the first reason at the end of paragraph 1 and repeats it again at the end of paragraph 2, where she also forecasts the second reason. Students should question this repetition. You might ask them to suggest language Statsky could have used to forecast concisely all three of her reasons.

She does a good job with topic sentences both to introduce the topic of the paragraph (as in paragraph 3) and to provide a summary/transition (as in paragraph 4). You might want to emphasize her use of explicit transitions: "For example" (paragraphs 3 and 8), "another reason" and "Consequently" (paragraph 7), and "Indeed" (paragraph 8).

2.   Students might point to a variety of passages and also differ in the way they interpret them. The point is to help them to explain why they interpret a particular passage in a particular way. In their own argumentative writing, students often cite what they consider to be evidence for a claim but fail to explain the connection to readers. This question gives them practice in making connections explicit.

3.   Statsky refers to as many as twelve authorities, including Dr. Tutko (paragraph 3), a mother of a Pee Wee Football player (paragraph 4), Rablovsky and several unidentified studies (paragraph 5), and so on.

4.   Students will notice that the conclusion restates the essay's major points. There are good reasons for doing this, but there are also other—perhaps more engaging—ways of concluding a position paper. You might discuss these possibilities with the class and even collaboratively draft one or two.

5.   This question directs students' attention to the Writer at Work section. In particular, it focuses on Statsky's purpose and audience analysis and how it changed as she drafted and revised the essay.

For Your Own Writing

Students will be surprised how many controversial issues related to childhood and adolescence they can come up with. You might generate the list in a class brainstorming session and then invite students to choose a topic and discuss it with the other students who chose that topic.

Commentary

This commentary treats important aspects of two basic features of position papers: defining the issue and qualifying the thesis. Statsky is careful (some readers may think overly careful) to state the issue precisely. You might ask students to consider whether each of her distinctions is really needed. For example, she specifies noncontact as well as contact sports. This distinction would be important if someone argued that contact sports might be dangerous to children but noncontact sports are not.

PURPOSE AND AUDIENCE

This section treats purpose and audience in position-paper writing. Purpose and audience are basic concepts for every type of writing but are essential for argumentation. The argumentative strategy writers devise depends on how well they can anticipate their readers' assumptions and values and adjust their purpose to their particular audience. We identify a spectrum of purposes and audiences. You might ask students to try to infer the writers' aims and assumptions about readers from the selections in this chapter.

BASIC FEATURES OF POSITION PAPERS

In this section we review the important characteristics of the position paper:

- a well-defined issue
- a clear position
- a convincing argument
- an appropriate tone

As you move through the argumentative writing chapters, you might want to point out that many of the same features are considered essential.

GUIDE TO WRITING

Invention and Research

We recommend the following invention activities to help students analyze the issue and develop an argument for particular readers:

- Choosing an issue
- Exploring the issue
- Considering your purpose and audience
- Stating your thesis

- Testing your choice
- Developing your reasoning
- Anticipating readers' concerns
- Restating your thesis

Under the first heading, we propose a list of possible topics to get students thinking of issues in which they have an interest. Throughout the guide, we encourage students to consider their purpose and audience, and also emphasize the deliberative aspects of argumentation, asking students to explore all sides of the issue.

For Group Inquiry

This group inquiry really serves as a further way for students to test their choice of topic. Students are asked to tell the others about the issue they have chosen to address in their essays. The task of briefly explaining an issue is not as simple as it may sound. To explain the issue, students need to have given it considerable thought and also need to have some sense of how much their auditors may know about it. If students find that their group members see the issue differently from the way they do, they may need to redefine it for the others, indicating why they see it as they do.

Some students may turn this into an occasion to explain their position on the issue or to rehearse their argument. And if the issue is one that the others in the group feel strongly about, they may wind up debating it. Although such a discussion could take up more time than your schedule allows, debating can be a very productive invention and critical thinking exercise.

Planning and Defining

If you have students working in groups, you might give them an opportunity to discuss their goals and plans. You could have them bring to class a tentative outline to present to the group. The group members could then query the writer as to how certain elements of the outline embody the writer's purpose and expectations about readers. Students might ask the writer, for example, what made her decide on a particular sequence of reasons or why she chose to refute a particular argument. Explaining her plans might lead the writer to clarify or even modify them. The group could also help the writer consider other possibilities. Such a discussion could help the writer not only develop her thinking on the issue but also possibly develop a better sense of audience.

Getting Critical Comments

Students are likely to take lightly the request that they identify their purpose and audience for their readers. For example, they may assume that all they need to say about purpose is that they are trying to convince readers to accept their position. Since readers seldom adopt writers' positions completely, however, writers dealing with highly controversial issues usually have more limited—and realistic— aims. They might aim, for example, to get readers to accept certain arguments even if they won't accept the writers' conclusions. You might want to spend some time discussing purpose so that students can better prepare their readers.

Since position papers are difficult intellectually as well as rhetorically, you might want to organize more than one reading, focusing each time on different features. A first reading, for example, might focus on presentation of the issue and statement of the thesis, while further readings might focus on the points in the argument and their organization.

Revising and Editing

You might want to point out to students that the guides to Reading to Analyze in the previous section and the plan for revising presented here both center on the basic features of position papers. The plan for revising leads them to identify problems having to do with the basic features in their draft. The advice under Solving the Problems is also organized by the basic features. The rationale for organizing all of this material around the basic features is that it gives students a way to focus their revision on one thing at a time.

Although the advice for solving problems is quite detailed, it is meant only to be suggestive. You might also remind students of how the writers they have read handled potential problems. If students have been working in groups, it might be profitable to have them discuss with their group members one or two of the problems with their drafts and their ideas for solving those problems. Getting students involved in actively discussing their drafts should encourage them to do some substantial revision.

A WRITER AT WORK

This section focuses on Jessica Statsky's invention process, specifically those activities that help her to clarify the rhetorical situation in which she is writing. The first activity involves exploring the issue by rehearsing both sides of the argument. Some students may resist examining both sides, feeling that they should concern themselves solely with developing an argument for their own side, whatever that happens to be. You might want to discuss why it is important intellectually as well as rhetorically to examine both sides.

Statsky decides, as a result of her exploration of the issue, to address her essay to parents who are undecided about involving their children in organized, competitive sports. Students may observe that in making this choice, Statsky avoids addressing questions about cultural attitudes toward competition and winning. You might point out, however, that her final, and most important, argument focuses on competition and winning.

REFLECTING ON YOUR WRITING

As students complete their own projects, we ask them to reflect carefully on their experience with writing essays that take positions on controversial issues. See page 14 for more information on this activity.

RESPONDING TO ESSAYS TAKING A POSITION

When advising students about revising their drafts, you will want to focus on the unique constraints and possibilities of taking a position. We have found the following list of typical problems helpful because it reminds us of where students predictably fall short and the language we can use productively to advise students and remind them of what they've read in the chapter on arguing a position.

Issue

- The issue the student is writing about is not really an issue—no one is debating it.
- The issue is not adequately described or opposing views are not clearly explained.

Position

- The writer does not assert a position on the issue; the writer may waffle, agreeing with one side and then the other, but never taking a stand.
- The writer merely reports opposing positions.
- The thesis is asserted too soon or too late.
- The key terms of the thesis do not seem appropriate and are not carried through the essay.

Argument

- It is difficult to see exactly why the writer takes the position; the reasons would be difficult or impossible to list.
- There is no explicitly cued, logical, step-by-step progression to the argument.
- The argument would be stronger if the points were arranged in a different order.
- Support is thin—relatively few examples, anecdotes, statistics, etc.
- The argument is adequately supported but seems flat, uncommitted, lacking surprises or insights, and likely to bore readers.
- The writer ignores readers—no objections or opposing arguments are accommodated or refuted.

Tone

- The tone seems inappropriate to the writer's purpose and assumed readers.

PREPARING FOR CONFERENCES

If you hold conferences with your students on their drafts, you could have them prepare for the conference by filling in the form on the following page.

Before the conference, write answers to the questions below. Bring your invention writing and first draft to the conference.

1. Which controversial issue are you writing about? How did you come to choose it? Why are people still debating it?

2. What is your position on the issue?

3. Who are your readers and how do you want to influence them?

4. For what reasons do you take this position? Be prepared to talk about their relation to one another, their sequence in your essay, and ways you might anticipate readers' objections to them.

5. What are you most pleased with in this draft? Be specific.

6. What specifically do you need to do next to revise your draft? List any problems you see in the draft or any that other readers have noticed. Say briefly how you might attempt to solve these problems. Use the back of this form for these notes. (If you have completed the text's Revising plan, bring it with you to the conference instead of answering this question.)

Chapter 6
Proposing a Solution

THE WRITING ASSIGNMENT

Write an essay proposing a solution to a problem. Choose a problem faced by a community or group to which you belong, and address your proposal either to one or more members of the group or to an outsider who might help solve the problem.

The Nature of the Writing Assignment

Proposal writing reinforces the aim of argument as positive and constructive—to convince readers to solve a common problem in a particular way. This view of argumentation (sometimes called Rogerian because it is based on the work of psychologist Carl Rogers) assumes that, in order to get readers to consider alternatives, it is necessary to reduce their sense of threat. Hence, argumentation becomes an effort not to defeat an opponent but to bridge differences by finding or creating common ground.

Learning to write a proposal directly engages students in learning to write for particular readers. For this reason, we have narrowed the scope of the writing task by asking students to propose solutions to problems plaguing communities or groups to which they belong. We want students to practice writing for particular readers whose interests and values they could imagine. In the Guide to Writing, we urge students to anticipate their readers' possible objections, foresee their alternative proposals, and figure out which reasons and evidence they would find most persuasive.

Special Problems of This Writing Assignment

Special difficulties students sometimes encounter as they write proposals involve topic choice and the need to establish the problem's existence and seriousness. Even though students are asked to write about a problem faced by a group to which they belong, they sometimes take on problems that are too abstract or complicated for them to handle effectively in a short time. It is understandable that students should want to solve some of the major problems we as a society face—such as the threat of nuclear annihilation, the lack of shelter for the homeless, or the deterioration of our industrial urban centers. As much as we do not want to discourage students from trying to understand these problems and even possibly contributing to their solution, we also do not want them to fail in their attempts to write successful proposals because their writing is too general. This chapter is designed to teach students how to gather the information they need to make their writing more specific.

A good proposal does two things: it defines a problem and argues for a particular solution. We have found that even the student who argues effectively for a solution may sometimes fail to establish the problem's existence and seriousness. Defining the problem actually requires careful assessment of the rhetorical situation. The student must decide just how aware of the problem the readers are and how best to convince them that it is worthy of their attention and possibly their time and money as well.

Promising and Unpromising Topics

Choosing an appropriate topic is probably the hardest part of proposal writing. Some students know immediately what they want to write about, while others are at a loss. Perhaps the greatest stumbling block is abstractness. The more distant the problem is from the writer's personal experience the harder it is to write about. That is why we urge students to choose a problem plaguing a community or group to which they belong. Even the most abstract problems can be treated in the context of a local group. Those concerned with broad educational problems, for example, might find evidence of the problem in their own high school or college. Those concerned with social and economic problems like homelessness and unemployment might look in their communities.

Writing about a problem in a group to which they belong will also help students with the crucial task of analyzing their readers. They can more easily anticipate possible objections to their solution and alternative solutions others might offer. They can also draw on common values, interests, and experience to establish the seriousness of the problem and argue for the feasibility of the proposed solution.

CHAPTER INTRODUCTION

Writing in Your Other Courses

These essay assignments from college classes in three disciplines all require analyzing a problem and proposing a solution to it. For two of the three cases, an audience is specified. You will want to discuss with students how the language of the assignments makes it clear that analyzing, researching, and explaining the problem are important steps for this writing purpose, but that they are all preliminary to and supportive of the main emphasis: the presentation of the solution.

For Group Inquiry

Participating in this group activity so early in the process, long before they begin to consider their own topics and even before they discuss the chapter readings, students will be drawn surprisingly quickly into the complexities and possibilities of proposing solutions to problems. This activity has the benefits of preparing the students for the readings and anticipating the entire chapter. After about fifteen minutes, shift the students to the set of questions at the end of the paragraph that ask them to step back and reflect together on the experience. After a few more minutes, shift the focus to whole-class discussion to share reflections on and reactions to the process of proposing solutions.

READINGS

These three readings should have appeal to most of your students. All are on important and controversial topics, and all make lucid and well-reasoned proposals to solve serious problems.

Topics in Analysis Questions and Commentaries

These lists can serve as quick reference, indicating where each rhetorical concern is addressed. In class or in conference, you can use it to direct a student's attention to a particular area the student needs to work on. For example, if a student's draft lacks an evaluation of alternative solutions, you could point him or her to Weisman–Commentary or O'Malley–question 4 and Commentary.

Kibler

For Analysis
1. features of proposals
2. presenting the problem
3. definition

4. cueing the reader
5. anticipating readers' reactions

Commentary
organization
strategies of argument
first-hand and second-hand research

Weisman

For Analysis
1. beginning
2. neutral tone
3. example
4. organization
5. advantages of solution, common values

Commentary
alternative solution
objection
respect for others' values

O'Malley

For Analysis
1. solution: define and qualify
2. forecasting of plan
3. reasons in support
4. alternative solutions (Weisman)
5. revision—A Writer at Work

Commentary
objections
alternative solutions
interviewing readers
plan
cueing

"CHEATING: INSTITUTIONS NEED A COMPREHENSIVE PLAN FOR PROMOTING ACADEMIC INTEGRITY" BY WILLIAM L. KIBLER

This example of proposal writing addresses a problem with which most students will be familiar; Kibler's proposed solution, however, may surprise them with its thoroughness. At the end of the introductory note, we ask students to speculate about the effectiveness of Kibler's proposal, as well as to consider its implications for students themselves.

For Discussion

This activity, which might be best carried out in small groups, gives students the opportunity to analyze the problem themselves, exploring ideas left out of Kibler's analysis. The discussion questions invite students to draw on their personal experiences, showing them that, as students, they may have some insight into the problem unavailable to teachers and administrators like Kibler. The questions also suggest that teachers might share some responsibility for the problem. Following in-class discussion, you could invite students to collaborate on a brief, one-page rebuttal to Kibler's argument.

For Analysis

These questions are very different from the questions in the For Discussion section: where the For Discussion section asks students to respond to ideas about the problem of academic cheating and Kibler's problem solution, here we require them to reread the text closely, analyzing its strategies and features. Working on these questions can be very challenging, and we find that students benefit most when we ask them to write answers to them in their journals as homework or discuss selected questions in small groups preparatory to class discussion.

1. This question asks students to test some of the assertions we've made about writing that proposes solutions. By looking for these features and strategies in Kibler's essay, students learn to read critically. This task might be done in small groups because students will disagree on such things as whether the writer takes a definite stand or strives to see the problem in new ways.

2. Students should note that Kibler spends almost the first third of his essay presenting the problem of academic cheating, establishing its existence and suggesting its seriousness. In the first three paragraphs, Kibler presents the problem by referring to the first-hand and second-hand research, demonstrating the existence of the problem through a startling set of statistics (paragraph 1) and pointing out its seriousness by referring to his own research (paragraph 3), which indicates the failure of most institutions to deal with the problem.

3. Here is a chance to ask your students to do some informal writing before they respond aloud in a class discussion. Ask students to articulate their own definitions of "cheating," possibly using an example drawn from their own experience, observation, or reading to illustrate their definition. In the writing or in the discussion you can ask students to compare their definitions with what Kibler implies in his essay.

4. Students should have little trouble in noting that Kibler helps his readers follow his argument for his solution by presenting it in a careful step-by-step format, devoting one paragraph to each step. This question presents an opportunity to discuss with students the value of explicit cueing. Many students resist it, thinking that it makes the writing too mechanical. We like to get students to look at cueing from a rhetorical perspective.

5. Anticipating readers' questions, objections, and reservations is a crucial element of all argument, and it is especially important in writing that proposes solutions. The introductory note to this selection points out that Kibler's projected readers include faculty members; some students will find Kibler's treatment of faculty concerns in paragraph 9 adequate, while others may see it as brief and somewhat slighting.

For Your Own Writing

This activity gives students the opportunity to "walk through" the process of planning a proposal essay, asking them to choose a local problem, identify an audience, and present the problem and a plausible solution. You might begin this activity with a whole-class brainstorming session.

Commentary

This commentary helps students focus on three fundamental elements of proposal writing: planning, strategies or argument, and research. The section begins by providing a scratch outline of Kibler's essay, allowing students to see at a glance that he has followed a careful plan in presenting both the problem and his proposed solution. The outline also helps students focus on the argumentative strategies upon which Kibler's proposal relies, including the use of statistics, careful consideration of his audience, and a specific step-by-step explanation of how his proposed solution could be implemented. Finally, this section points out that Kibler's essay makes use of both first-hand and second-hand research. Depending on the topics they choose, your students may find it necessary to use one or both types of research in their own writing; you might refer them to Chapter 10: Strategies for Doing Research in the Library and on the Internet.

"BIRTH CONTROL IN THE SCHOOLS"
BY ADAM PAUL WEISMAN

This essay deals with a problem students should be somewhat familiar with—teenage pregnancy. Weisman advocates a solution to the problem that is controversial. He proposes that birth-control clinics be located on high school campuses to provide students with contraceptives. We point out that the idea of school-based birth-control clinics is not original with Weisman. Your students may be surprised to find a proposal advocating someone else's idea. They should realize, however, that this often happens. The fact that a proposal has been tried already and has had some success should increase its chances of being accepted by readers.

For Discussion

This activity seeks to involve students in the debate. The discussion can take place in small groups or with the whole class. You might even set up a class debate on this proposal. Since many of your students will have just come from high school, they are likely to have something to say about the problem and whether basing clinics on high school campuses is likely to help ameliorate it.

For Analysis

1. Writers are always concerned with the writing problem of how to begin an essay. Experienced writers have a repertoire of potential opening gambits they can draw upon. Inexperienced writers, however, tend to get stuck when they don't know just how to begin an essay. It is important for students to develop a set of strategies for beginning and to understand the strategies' advantages and disadvantages in particular rhetorical situations.

Weisman combines two common strategies in his opening paragraph: beginning with a rhetorical question and citing authorities. His title identifies the proposed solution (birth-control clinics) and combines with the opening paragraph to orient readers and prepare them for the argument, which is the body of the proposal.

2. The appeal to trust, or ethos, is as important in proposal writing as it is in position papers, so we want students to pay close attention to the tone of this and the other essays in this chapter. In fact, you might have students work in small groups at some point to compare the selections for tone.

We suggest that Weisman adopts the tone of a neutral reporter as befits the rhetorical situation in which he is operating, writing for a newsmagazine. The argumentative strategy includes coming across to readers as a practical person, yet also sensitive to the ethical concerns of others. Weisman represents the arguments put forth for the alternative solution of sexual abstinence, quoting one of the leading spokesmen for this camp, then–Education Secretary William Bennett. He also includes this group's objections to the school clinic proposal.

3. Students should recognize that the example of the Johns Hopkins clinic is central to Weisman's argument because it proves that the proposed solution works. Evidence that a proposed solution works is inevitably the cornerstone of a proposal. There are, of course, other, perhaps equally important criteria as well. For example, there are practical questions such as whether the difficulty and cost of implementing the solution is justified by the results gained. There are also ethical questions such as whether the means used to solve the problem are justified by the ends they achieve. You will certainly want your students to consider all of the criteria in judging the persuasiveness of the argument.

4. Here's our outline:

paragraph 1:	raises the issue but does not state Weisman's stance
paragraph 2:	cites statistics showing severity of the problem
paragraphs 3–4:	summarize each side of the issue
paragraphs 5–9:	explain why contraception advocates' approach works
paragraph 10:	includes the abstinence advocates' counterargument
paragraphs 11–14:	challenge the abstinence advocates and present Weisman's stance

5. In addition to the argument discussed in question 3 that the proposed solution works, Weisman points to several additional advantages. For example, in paragraph 6, he notes that sexually inactive high school students who received professional counseling at the Hopkins clinic delayed initiating sexual activity for some period of time. This fact would surely appeal to those who advocate abstinence. (You might also want to discuss with your students the casual reasoning involved here.) Another advantage Weisman points out is that the clinics provide general health care to the students, many of whom would otherwise be without adequate care. This outcome should please everyone concerned about young people.

For Your Own Writing

This activity turns students' attention to the prospect of writing a proposal. It asks students to consider what problems a particular group—high school or perhaps college students—could help solve. Our intention is to get students to tap their own experience. This question will inspire good class discussion.

Commentary

We begin our commentary with the concept of the argumentative strategy. This concept helps students understand the rhetoric of writing a proposal. By analyzing the argumentative strategies of writers like Weisman, they begin to see how their own purpose is affected by the values and assumptions of their readers. Moreover, they consider strategically how they might present the problem and argue for their solution. They also take seriously the need to anticipate and respond to objections others might make to their argument. In addition, they recognize how central to proposal writing it is to anticipate alternative solutions.

"MORE TESTING, MORE LEARNING"
BY PATRICK O'MALLEY

This student essay shows students the advantages of careful invention, research, and revision. They should also note O'Malley's considerate treatment of readers' objections and alternative solutions. He adds to his credibility by his responsible use of publications from educational psychology and his reference to a Harvard study.

For Discussion

This activity connects students' personal experience with the subject of the essay. By discussing their own experience with frequent exams, their interest in O'Malley's proposal will be heightened and they will be more receptive to the subsequent rhetorical focus in the questions for analysis. Once again, this discussion can take place in small groups or with the whole class.

For Analysis

1. This question asks students to underline words or phrases in paragraph 3 that show how O'Malley defines and qualifies his solution. One possibility for getting students started on the questions for analysis would be to discuss the questions briefly after you have discussed the reading. You could even give students a few minutes in class to underline. (Question 3 also calls for underlining.) By providing time for your students to begin this work in class under your guidance, you can help them learn how to annotate a text, an essential strategy of critical reading. Then you could ask them to write out answers to the questions outside of class—to be turned in at the next class meeting.

A careful underlining of paragraph 3 will reveal that O'Malley explains his solution, gives examples of how it could work in two disciplines, and specifies frequency, length, and question type.

2. This question teaches students that many writers forecast to some degree early in their essay the organizational plan they will follow. This is a useful technique for students to learn; not only is it characteristic of much academic writing, but it also helps writers to become more aware of the organization they have chosen and to be more inclined to revise their plan for presentation if they discover a better one. In this case, the plan is partially forecast: the last sentence of paragraph 2 lists succinctly and in order the reasons that O'Malley will present in support of his proposal, but nothing is mentioned about the objections and alternatives that will be brought up or the research evidence that will be cited. Opinions among your students will probably differ on the question of whether these elements should have been included in the forecasting or whether the forecasting should have been more explicit, by stating, for example, "Three reasons will be provided for this proposal."

3. O'Malley presents the different parts of his argument—in this case the reasons for or benefits of his proposal—so clearly that they really stand out for the reader. This is the heart of his essay—the changes for the better that will ensue if his proposal is adopted. In each paragraph, the topic is introduced quickly and directly, with brief transitions for paragraphs 5 and 6.

paragraph 4: "the main reason . . . students learn more"
paragraph 5: "Another reason . . . improve their study habits"
paragraph 6: "Frequent exams should also decrease anxiety . . ."

4. O'Malley locates his alternative solutions late in his essay. Weisman puts his alternative solution much earlier—in paragraph 4—and he contrasts it directly with his own proposed solution presented in paragraph 3. By comparing and contrasting these two strategies, students will see that in their own writing they have different options for organization, options that have implications for their impact on their readers. In O'Malley's case, he doesn't reveal the alternative solutions until he has completely established his own argument. He seems fair and thorough to acknowledge three possible alternatives, showing that he understands why some people might prefer them; yet we know he will refute them, and he does, though it may be said that he accommodates the last one. Weisman, on the other hand, has only one alternative solution—abstinence—to present in opposition to his solution—contraception. By pairing them using a neutral tone (see Weisman, question 2), Weisman gives the appearance at first of objectivity, of considering both solutions as potentially equally valid. Only in paragraph 5 does Weisman begin to slip away from this position. By examining both essays together, students will realize that both build bridges of shared concerns with readers, but they do so using different strategies and with different effects.

   5.   This challenging question asks students to compare one paragraph of O'Malley's draft with one paragraph of his revision. The most obvious change is elaboration; the revised version elaborates much more extensively on the positive effects of frequent testing, while the draft only devotes two sentences to this. We also see better use of sources, with the well-integrated quotes from the Harvard study and the paraphrase from Fredericksen. Finally, the revision exhibits greater felicity of expression. Ask the students to compare the second sentences of each paragraph, which are on the same topic, for clarity, precision, and elegance.

For Your Own Writing

   This section asks students to write about a conventional practice that needs to be improved or refined. You could generate some potential topics for it through whole-class brainstorming and then assign a brief rehearsal of a chosen topic as journal writing.

Commentary

   This commentary accentuates the extreme care O'Malley takes with objections and alternative solutions. It also presents the strengths of his organization.

PURPOSE AND AUDIENCE

   As we have suggested, proposal writing, perhaps more than any other kind of writing, requires sensitivity to readers and careful thought to purpose. Throughout the chapter, we discuss the role the argumentative strategy plays in realizing the writer's understanding of the rhetorical situation. Here we remind readers of some of the problems proposal writers encounter with their readers and the ways in which they might try to solve them.

BASIC FEATURES OF PROPOSAL PAPERS

   Here we review the most important features of proposals:

- a well-defined problem
- a proposed solution
- a convincing argument
- a reasonable tone

   These are basically the same features discussed in Chapter 5: Arguing a Position, the only difference being the shift from issue and position to problem and solution.

GUIDE TO WRITING

Invention and Research

Here is a list of the invention activities:

- Choosing a problem to write about
- Analyzing and defining the problem
- Identifying your readers
- Finding a tentative solution
- Defending your solution
- Testing your choice
- Finding reasons for adopting your proposal
- Considering alternative solutions
- Doing research

You might want to give students an overview of the invention activities and discuss how much time you expect them to spend on them. You could do the first part of the invention, listing problems, in class as whole-class brainstorming or in small groups, beginning with the problems the students have generated in the For Your Own Writing sections and moving to other problems the students can think of. Students will progress through the invention sequence at different rates, but you can help them stay on track by requiring that they reach a certain point by a certain class meeting. If you ask them to bring their invention-in-progress to every class meeting, you can ask them to read aloud from it to begin class discussion or share certain sections with their peers in pairs or small groups.

For Group Inquiry

This activity will give your students the opportunity to rehearse orally their plans. By talking with one another in small groups, they will clarify the meanings they have created through the invention exercises. As group members discuss their essay plans, they should question one another about their intentions: "How will you convince readers that the problem is serious?" "Whom do you plan to address your proposal to?" They will also be able to offer suggestions: "Let me tell you one alternative solution I can think of. It would be to . . ." "You know, there's a group here in town working on that problem. It's called . . ."

Planning and Drafting

The purpose of this section is to help students move smoothly from invention to drafting. After students take time to review their invention writings, they should set some goals for their essay. If there is time, students could explain their goals to you in a brief conference; or they could explain them to one another in small groups. As students move into drafting, you can remind them to rely heavily on their invention for material; if they find that their invention is not providing them with enough material, they may need to do more invention writing.

Getting Critical Comments

Since we argue that proposal writing requires a strong sense of audience, getting comments on your draft is especially valuable. You might encourage readers in a draft workshop to pretend they are the readers addressed in the proposal. Roleplaying like this can be informative and enjoyable. Having two or three students listen as the writer reads the draft aloud might heighten attention to the draft's argument. The listeners/readers could discuss the proposal as if they were at a meeting to discuss its merits.

Revising and Editing

We find it useful to emphasize to students the importance of reading and considering their draft as a whole before contemplating specific revision changes. We know that successful writers take time to review their drafts from a global, holistic perspective prior to considering what modifications they will make. Some students resist this step; once they have secured feedback from their classmates, they want to proceed directly to revising their drafts. It would be an excellent use of class time to ask students to study their peers' comments, reread their drafts carefully, and compose a scratch outline while they are in the classroom. They can then discuss their revision plans in small groups with the students who listened to or read their draft.

A WRITER AT WORK

This section deals with the revision process of the student essay by Patrick O'Malley on frequent testing. It asks students to compare part of O'Malley's draft with his revision. Question 5 in the For Analysis section also relates O'Malley's essay and this section.

REFLECTING ON YOUR WRITING

Now that students have completed their own essays proposing solutions, we ask them to reflect on what they have learned about this genre, reviewing what they have learned about the genre through the reading selections in the chapter and through their own writing. See page 14 for more information about this activity.

RESPONDING TO ESSAYS PROPOSING SOLUTIONS

When advising students about revising their drafts, you will want to focus on the unique constraints and possibilities of proposals. We have found the following list of typical problems helpful because it reminds us of where students predictably fall short and the language we can use productively to advise students and remind them of what they've read in the chapter on proposing solutions.

Problem

- It is not clear to whom the proposal is being presented and what the writer expects readers to do about it.
- The problem is much too large or complex for the student writer to enter the debate on it authoritatively: poverty in America, terrorism.
- The problem is too insignificant or temporary to matter to readers (noise in the dorms, lack of school spirit, bad cafeteria food).
- The problem shifts in mid-essay to something different, usually a result of the writer's not framing the problem clearly enough in the beginning.

Alternative Solutions

- Alternative solutions are not presented, where there are obvious alternatives.
- The alternative solutions are represented unfairly.
- Alternative solutions are not effectively refuted or accommodated.

Proposed Solution

- The essay focuses on causes or effects of the problem rather than proposing a solution.
- The writer complains about the problem at length and only expresses a demand that it be solved, rather than presenting a feasible solution.
- The essay offers too many solutions, without arguing effectively for one, or for a two-pronged or three-pronged attack on the problem.
- The essay naively proposes an entirely inadequate solution to a large, complex problem, or the proposed solution does not seem workable (it may be frivolous, too complex, or costly).
- The essay does not argue effectively for the proposed solution: the proposed solution may lack reasons or evidence, or there may be logical fallacies in the argument.
- The essay ignores obvious or major obstacles or objections to the proposed solution.
- The solution doesn't match the problem (solving children's excessive TV watching by having teachers assign a weekly environmental project) or proposes a solution that has been tried unsuccessfully in the past (without showing why it could work this time).

Tone

- The essay moralizes, editorializes, or rails about the problem, lecturing the reader.
- The essay denounces those seen as causing the problem.
- The essay seems confused or unclear about the problem, lacks authority.

PREPARING FOR CONFERENCES

If you hold conferences with your students on their drafts, you could have them prepare for the conference by filling in the form on the following page.

PREPARING FOR A CONFERENCE: CHAPTER 6

Before the conference, write answers to the questions below. Bring your invention writing and first draft to the conference.

1. What problem are you trying to solve? Why is it significant? Who is affected by the problem, and how much do they know about it?

2. What solution are you proposing to solve the problem?

3. Who are your readers? (An individual, committee, group?) Be very specific in identifying your readers. What action do you want them to take?

4. Which of your reasons do you think would be most convincing to these readers? Briefly explain why. How have you anticipated readers' objections to your proposed solution? What else could you do?

5. What alternative solutions do you think your readers might be considering? How have you handled these alternatives? What else could you do?

6. What are you most pleased with in this draft? Be specific.

7. What specifically do you need to do next to revise your draft? List any problems you see in the draft or any problems pointed out by other readers. Say briefly how you might attempt to solve these problems. Use the back of this form for these notes. (If you have completed the text's Revising plan, bring it with you to the conference instead of answering this question.)

Chapter 7
Strategies for Cueing Readers

Whereas Part I introduces the possibilities and constraints of various kinds of nonfiction prose, Part II focuses on the craft of writing, the strategies a writer can use to achieve a particular purpose in a piece of writing. The opening chapter brings together several topics that are generally taught in isolation: thesis, paragraphing, and cohesion. We combine these topics in one chapter called Strategies for Cueing Readers because we want students to think of thesis statements, paragraphing, cohesive devices, and transitions as part of a signaling system that writers use to help readers read and comprehend their texts. In effect, these are strategies that writers use to establish and maintain focus in writing.

The chapter is divided into four sections:

Orienting Statements. To suggest how writers can provide a context so that readers will understand each succeeding sentence, we discuss thesis statements and forecasting statements.

Paragraphing. To indicate how writers can use paragraphing to help readers, we show how indention affects readers and also how writers can use topic-sentence strategies to orient readers.

Cohesive Devices. To show how writers can enhance coherence by connecting key words and phrases, we illustrate the following cohesive devices: pronoun reference, word repetition, synonyms, sentence-structure repetition, and collocation.

Transitions. To demonstrate how writers signal and identify connections for readers by linking ideas between sentences and paragraphs, we survey the following transition strategies: local, temporal, and spatial relationships.

We illustrate each of these strategies extensively with examples by professional writers. The exercises invite students to see how these cueing strategies work in longer pieces of discourse.

OVERVIEW OF THE EXERCISES

7.1 Find and underline the thesis and the forecasting in any of the essays in Chapter 3
7.2 Put paragraphing symbols in the Gould passage
7.3 Analyze paragraphing in the Gould passage
7.4 Analyze topic sentences in Weisman's "Birth Control in the Schools" (Chapter 6)
7.5 Analyze rhetorical questions in Quammen's "Is Sex Necessary?" (Chapter 3) or Weisman's "Birth Control in the Schools" (Chapter 6)
7.6 Analyze topic-sentence strategies in the Gould passage

7.7   Analyze cohesive devices in the Gould passage

7.8   Analyze transitions in the Gould passage

SUGGESTIONS FOR TEACHING THE EXERCISES

7.1   Find and underline the thesis and forecasting in any of the essays in Chapter 3.

You may use this exercise to emphasize the point that the thesis statement in an argument essay focuses details and orients readers. To appreciate how thesis statements guide readers, students might be encouraged to convert each of the thesis statements into questions. Some students wonder whether giving a detailed preview is advisable since it gives so much away. You might use this opportunity to discuss when writers need to forecast and how much forecasting they need to give. But recognize that this writing problem usually involves a broader one: how explicit should a writer be? Many inexperienced writers are afraid of being too obvious when stating a thesis or forecasting an essay.

7.2   Put paragraphing symbols in the Gould passage.

If you do not want this exercise to be merely clerical, you might ask your students to paragraph the Gould passage in class before they find out how it was originally paragraphed. Reading the passage aloud may help them sense where closure and orienting occur.

7.3   Analyze paragraphing in the Gould passage.

This exercise works well as a small-group activity because it encourages students to find explanations for Gould's paragraphing decisions or to justify their own choices. To stimulate analysis, you might play devil's advocate and suggest some alternative paragraphing possibilities if students do not propose any of their own. Students tend to think that there are no alternatives if the piece was written by a professional and published. You might try the same exercise with an unidentified piece of writing or a student draft.

7.4   Analyze topic sentences in Weisman's "Birth Control in the Schools" (Chapter 6).

In an argumentative essay like this one, the topic sentences do more than announce the topics of paragraphs—they also advance the argument and set up contrasts among opposing views or an opposing solution to the problem. Since topic sentences—their placement, form, and function—are not at all obvious to students, talk them through this essay paragraph by paragraph. Decide whether the first sentence is the topic sentence (we think it is in every case) and discuss its function at that point in the essay. Do not overlook the transitional role of many topic sentences.

After leading a discussion of the topic sentences in this essay, you could put students on their own in pairs or small groups to analyze topic sentences in another argument essay. To prepare carefully for such group discussion, they could first write out their analysis as homework in a journal.

7.5 Analyze rhetorical questions in Quammen's "Is Sex Necessary?" (Chapter 3) or Weisman's "Birth Control in the Schools" (Chapter 6).

Several paragraphs in these essays begin with questions, questions that serve both a rhetorical and a topical function. Discuss several of them with your students, noting their transitional and topical functions. Caution students about overreliance on questions as topic sentences. Some respected writers use them sparingly, others regularly. Argument seems to invite their use.

7.6 Analyze topic-sentence strategies in the Gould passage.

This exercise might be used as a follow-up to Exercise 7.3, with students analyzing their paragraphing decisions in terms of topic-sentence strategies. Students should find sentences 13, 24, and 28 fairly conventional topic-sentence strategies. Sentence 11, however, might surprise them. The object of this exercise is for them to examine how those topic sentences serve readers. To do this most effectively, students probably should work in groups.

7.7 Analyze cohesive devices in the Gould passage.

Students might find this easier to do if they work in small groups, each group looking for a different cohesive device. They also might find it easier to study cohesion within paragraphs.

7.8 Analyze transitions in the Gould passage.

Students will find lots of logical transitions and several temporal transitions but very few spatial ones in this passage. You might want to have them also analyze a passage with more spatial description. The purpose of this exercise, however, is not simply to locate transitions; it is to examine how they help readers make sense of what they are reading. Students should probably work in groups on this exercise and might also be asked to supply some alternative transitions Gould could have used.

Chapter **8**
Strategies for All-Purpose Invention

Because each writing-activity chapter in Part I has its own invention sequence, we do not discuss invention as a general topic early in our text. Instead, we engage students immediately in invention at the beginning of each Guide to Writing in Chapters 2 through 6.

In this chapter, we catalog the familiar all-purpose heuristics or strategies of invention: clustering, listing, cubing, dialoguing, dramatizing, looping, and questioning. You can orient students to this catalog and let them use it whenever they want, or you can make specific assignments from it, helping students learn to use some of the strategies. All of the strategies can support writing activities in Part I. Students learn to use many of the general strategies in this catalog by using the invention activities in the Guides to Writing. For example, in the Guide to Writing in Chapter 2: Remembering Events, students are directly or indirectly asked to *list, loop* (write and then stop to focus your thoughts), *write a dialogue,* and *outline.* Further, as students revise and edit their essays, they might use activities in this chapter to explore their subjects further or if they need to solve problems in their drafts.

Chapter **9**

Strategies for Reading Critically

In this chapter, we present various ways of using writing to think critically about your reading. To illustrate these strategies, we refer throughout the chapter to a sample reading selection— an excerpt from Martin Luther King Jr.'s "Letter from Birmingham Jail," provided near the beginning of the chapter.

The strategies include annotating, contextualizing, reflecting on challenges to one's beliefs and values, outlining and summarizing, evaluating the logic of an argument, recognizing emotional manipulation, and judging the writer's credibility.

As with the preceding chapter cataloguing invention strategies, you can introduce students to this catalog and encourage them to use it whenever they like, or you can make specific assignments from it. Some of these strategies, such as annotating, evaluating the logic of an argument, and judging the writer's credibility, are integrated into the Guides to Writing in Part I and can support the reading students do in that section of the text.

Chapter 10
Strategies for Doing Research
in the Library and on the Internet

This chapter and the next present freshmen with information that will help them to do library research, research on the Internet, and document a research paper. Knowing, however, is not the same as doing. We urge you to arrange a library tour for your students, one that not only follows the steps in the search strategy but that also gives students actual experience with many of the research materials—encyclopedias, bibliographies, card and on-line catalogs, indexes, abstracts, computer databases, government publications—introduced here.

We also urge you to have your students do research for several of their papers in your course. The only writing activity in Part I that does not invite library research is remembering events. Library or Internet research could be used for every other assignment. You would not have to make any of these essays a major research project. Research need not make writing seem more difficult or more time-consuming but should be viewed as a strategy used routinely like clustering or reading a draft critically.

Chapter 11
Strategies for Using and Acknowledging Sources

The first of the two sections in this chapter, Using Sources, teaches students how to integrate source material into their writing. Next, Acknowledging Sources surveys MLA and APA documentation style and format.

In this chapter, we briefly discuss plagiarism to clarify what is meant by plagiarism and to bring into the open some of the reasons why writers plagiarize. We define plagiarism broadly as the "unacknowledged use of another's words, ideas, or information." You may wish to discuss these issues in class, and you probably also will wish to inform students of your own and your institution's policy regarding plagiarism.

Most students who plagiarize, we assume, do not understand that the acknowledged use of other people's ideas, information, and even words is not only acceptable but expected of educated people. For this reason, if for no other, we believe students should routinely be asked to consult sources when they write. If this is done, students will begin to understand that, for the most part, academic writing is a dialogue between the writer and other writers on a given subject.

Plagiarism is, we also assume, in many cases simply evidence of students' unfamiliarity with academic conventions. They plagiarize because they do not know how to integrate source material into their own writing. Using Sources surveys various acceptable methods of quoting, paraphrasing, and summarizing source material. In many cases, we use illustrations from essays in Part I so that students can see how these strategies are used in the context of a whole selection. You might take some class time to discuss these strategies and suggest others students might add to their repertoire.

Section **IV**

TEACHING PRACTICES

In this section, we discuss ways you can conduct conferences with students, organize in-class workshops, have students keep journals, present and discuss readings, and set up collaborative learning groups. The methods we suggest here are ones we have borrowed from others or developed on our own while teaching the assignments in this book.

HOLDING CONFERENCES

Conferences with students are time-consuming and difficult to schedule when classes are large, but we recommend them highly as a teaching practice even if you can see students individually only once or twice during the course. Conferences allow the instructor to develop a rapport with students, thus building the trust and self-confidence that many students need before they will take the risks in their writing that lead to real progress. For many students, these conferences are their only opportunities to work individually with a college instructor.

A conference may be scheduled at any time during the composing process. We find it most useful after the first or second draft of an essay has been written, at a point when the student has spent some time thinking about the assignment, generating invention notes, and making at least one attempt to put the ideas into draft form but before the student has finished work on the essay. You could discuss the first draft in a conference and the second draft in a workshop with other students, or vice versa, before the student writes the final revision of the essay.

In the one-term (ten-week) courses we have taught, we like to see students in conference three times. The second of these, the midterm conference, allows us to review the student's progress and discuss the student's individual goals for the remainder of the course. (See the Midterm Progress Report form at the end of Section IV.)

Individual Conferences

We find that the best length for individual conferences is half an hour, although it is possible to make some progress in twenty minutes if the time is spent carefully.

The student comes to the conference with a draft in hand and may at first expect you to play the role of mechanic, making the necessary repairs on it while he or she waits in anxious silence. It is often tempting to take the draft from the student and go to work on it, but doing so defeats the object of conferencing, which is to help students learn to work on their own drafts. To this end, we leave the draft in the student's hands for most of the conference and usually begin by asking the student either to read it aloud or talk about it. In the most successful conferences, the students do at least half the talking; our comments merely draw them out and let them make discoveries for themselves.

In Section III of this manual, at the end of our discussion of teaching each part I chapter, you will find an example of a planning form for students.

Small-Group Conferences

An alternative to the individual conference is the small-group conference. Instead of meeting with each student for half an hour, the instructor might meet with three students for an hour, spending twenty minutes on each student's draft. In a typical group conference, each student brings copies of the draft for the other two students and the instructor. They each read their drafts aloud while the listeners make notes on their copies. At the end of each reading, the instructor leads a discussion about the draft, with the other two students contributing their views and suggestions. After twenty minutes, the writer collects the annotated copies, and attention turns to the next student's draft.

The group conference lacks the privacy of an individual conference, an important consideration for shy students. On the other hand, the group may generate ideas that would not emerge in a one-on-one conference. Some of the comments we make about the first student's draft usually apply to the other two as well, and students often see how to revise their own drafts after the discussion of another student's draft. Neither conference format is inherently better than the other; we recommend that you try both to decide which you prefer.

ORGANIZING WORKSHOPS

The workshop brings class members together to read and respond to work in progress—usually the first or second draft. There are many possible variations in the format of a workshop, including the following ones that have worked for us.

Written Response

Because students don't hear or remember everything a critical reader says about a draft, we find it helps when students write up their responses so that the writers can refer to them later when they actually revise. We also find that when students are given guidance and time, they can give a very thoughtful, useful response—one that helps them as writers as well as helping their workshop partner.

We typically begin by asking students to exchange their drafts with another class member. As students first exchange drafts, they could brief their partners on particular points they would like the partners to look at. Each student then spends twenty to forty minutes reading the partner's draft silently and writing a critical response to it. Activities and questions to guide this process can be found under Getting Critical Comments in each of the writing assignment chapters in Part I. They write their responses on separate sheets of paper, labeled at the top to look like this:

Proposal Essay Draft 2
Workshop Response for John Smith by Mary Gomez

While students are working silently on others' drafts, you may choose to move among them to offer advice. Alternatively, you can arrange in advance for one or two students to bring copies of their drafts for you to review during this time. When students have finished writing, they return the draft with their written comments, taking a few minutes to look over the response and ask the partner about anything confusing. To facilitate this critical exchange, you may want to pair students according to their writing abilities, changing the pairs so that each student receives comments from several others during the course. Another option is to organize students into small groups instead of pairs, each group including some stronger and weaker writers.

Novice writers tend to write their first workshop responses with some anxiety. A few will launch into devastatingly honest evaluations of a partner's draft, but most err on the side of conciliation. Influenced perhaps by the knowledge that their own drafts are undergoing similar scrutiny, they are usually eager to praise and offer little substantial criticism. At the beginning of the course, they also lack the experience to make recommendations to the writer.

One way to address this problem in the first workshop is to take students through the activities and questions in Getting Critical Comments, modeling for them the kind of critique that would let the writer know what works, what needs work, and what might be done to revise the essay. A good response points to specific things in the draft, describing their effect on the reader tactfully but honestly, and suggests options the writer might consider. Questions to the writer beginning "How about . . . ?" are often useful. To model such a critique, you can use copies of a class member's draft or copies of an anonymous draft written for a similar assignment in a previous course.

Discussion

Another way to organize the workshop is around oral reading and response. One possibility is to arrange in advance for one or two students to bring enough copies of their drafts for the other class members to share a copy between every two students. The writer tells the class about any particular problems he or she has had in the draft and then reads it aloud while the rest of the class follows along on the copies, making marginal notes where appropriate. The class will respond better if they hear and see the draft simultaneously. At the end of the oral reading, the instructor chairs a discussion of the draft, appointing a scribe to record the comments for the writer. The activities and questions in Getting Critical Comments can form the basis of this discussion. At the end of the discussion, the scribe gives the writer the discussion notes, and other students pass along their copies with marginal notes.

This whole-class discussion of one draft at a time simulates the traditional writers' workshop widely used in MFA programs. Many instructors using this workshop format ask that the writer not participate in the discussion. There are good reasons for this rule. At the draft stage, writers need to know the immediate personal responses and evaluative reflections of readers. They need to listen to the discussion, reflect thoughtfully on what readers say, what they have questions about. The writer needs to watch postures and facial expressions. Were the readers really interested in this draft, or is the discussion lifeless and perfunctory? What things do readers point to? What do they ignore? What seems to confuse them? What do they understand best and seem most pleased about? Is the discussion desultory, moving from one point to the next with little connection or sequence? Or does the discussion have a direction with many people involved making their contributions? From watching this sort of discussion of one's draft, a writer can know whether it struck readers as boring or engaging, pointless or informative, unsupported or convincing.

By concentrating initially on one or two papers with the whole class, you can remind students of the basic issues of that kind of writing. At the end of the discussion, you can summarize these basic issues on the chalkboard and relate them to points in Getting Critical Comments. This should give students more confidence in helping one another and keep them focused on the central issues of the assignment rather than the peripheral ones.

Working with the whole class on one draft also allows you to make observations that are relevant to the assignment and not just to the draft in hand. An alternative is to divide the class into small groups of four or five, with one member of each group bringing copies of his or her draft for the others in the group and reading it aloud to them. If there is time, a group could respond to several students' drafts—at least superficially. In a large class, this allows more students to receive group responses to their drafts and encourages the more reticent students to participate in the discussion. You can join one group or move among the groups. This format works best when students know what is expected and can work productively without your guidance.

Practical Considerations

1. When a student comes to class late or without a draft, you have several options, depending on which workshop format the class is using:

- conduct a conference with the student
- have the student join a pair and read a draft page by page as one partner finishes
- have the student respond to a copy of a draft that has been duplicated for the whole class

In all these cases, the student must be reminded that he or she is responsible for obtaining another student's response to his or her own draft. You could require the student to get a written comment from a writing center tutor. Specify that the tutor should follow the guidelines for Reading a Draft with a Critical Eye.

2. You can choose whether to have students work in pairs or small groups or whether to lead a discussion in which the entire class participates.

3. When the first and second draft of the same assignment are read in subsequent workshops, some instructors ask students to choose a different partner to respond to the second draft. Other instructors allow students to choose the same partner to read the second draft, so that the partner can comment on the progress the writer has made since the first draft.

4. Some instructors find it useful to have students put their phone numbers on their workshop responses, so that writers can call their workshop partners if they find they have questions as they revise their drafts.

5. Some instructors ask all students to bring an extra copy of their drafts. During the workshop, while pairs are quietly writing their critiques of one another's drafts, the instructor quickly reviews all drafts, noting the most glaring problems.

ASSIGNING JOURNALS

Many writing teachers appreciate the value of journals in a writing course. The brevity, frequency, and informality of entries in a journal allow students to use writing in many more ways than they do in formal essays. In our courses, students keep a journal in which they respond to questions in *The Concise Guide to Writing* or to questions and assignments provided by their instructors. Journal assignments can be used to challenge students to engage in a wide range of critical-thinking activities, including responding to readings and practicing various thinking and writing strategies. Although journal entries may be written outside of class, they can be written in class—for example, to begin discussion of the reading, to summarize a discussion, or to reflect on what they have learned, perhaps using the metacognitive activity at the end of each Part I chapter.

Practical Considerations: Assigning, Monitoring, and Responding to Journal Questions

Some instructors hand out a weekly set of three to five journal questions, while others provide students at the beginning of the quarter with a list of questions for the entire course, specifying weekly due dates. A few instructors collect journal entries only every few weeks; most, however, find it worthwhile to collect and respond to them on a weekly basis. Although some instructors ask students to keep their journals in spiralbound notebooks, you may want to have your students write each journal entry on a separate sheet of looseleaf notebook paper, labeled with their names, the week number, and the number of the entry (or whatever information best facilitates your record-keeping system). This makes collecting their completed journal entries for each week somewhat easier and enables them to use a computer if they like.

Responding to journal entries need not be time-consuming. A few suggestions or words of encouragement in the margins are generally sufficient to let students see that you've read their entries. Although some instructors use informal marking systems such as pluses, checks, and minuses, journal entries really should not be graded, not judged for mechanical correctness. Instead, they should be evaluated for quantity and for quality of thought. It is important that students understand from the very beginning that the journal, although informal, is neither a private diary nor busy-work but a serious component of the course, and that you will expect their journal entries to be thorough, thoughtful, even provocative.

Planning a Sequence of Journal Questions

It takes careful planning to coordinate journal questions with the reading selections for the course. Journal questions require students to go beyond superficial responses to the readings and give them the freedom to experiment with different kinds of writing. A planned sequence of journal questions allows students to reflect on what they have learned and to see connections between the various components of your course. In particular, journal questions can help them make connections between the assigned readings and their own writing.

Sample Journal Questions

In general, journal assignments help students to improve their writing skills by exercising their critical reading and thinking skills. Journal questions can guide students to identify certain strategies in the texts they're reading, and then practice these writing strategies on their own. The following list of kinds of questions, which is by no means exhaustive, suggests a range of possibilities for the journal.

Analyzing and Responding to Readings. Some instructors use the journal exclusively for this purpose, calling it a Reader's Journal instead of a Writer's Journal. They ask their students to answer questions following the readings in Part I chapters, as well as questions they pose about trade books they assign. You could also assign critical reading strategies from Chapter 9 or invite students to select the ones they find most useful.

See the discussion in the next section, Presenting and Discussing Readings, for ideas about using journal writing to encourage critical reading and to prepare for class discussions of assigned readings.

Applying Rhetorical Strategies. Other questions help students apply strategies they see in their reading to their own essays:

> In Chapter 7: Strategies for Cueing Readers you learned about various ways to make your writing more readable. Discuss one cueing strategy that would remedy a particular weakness that you have or someone else has noticed in your writing. Give an example of the problem in your writing, showing how you would use this cueing device to solve it.

Experimenting and Adapting. Many questions of this type encourage students to experiment with general rhetorical strategies, and to adapt these strategies to different types of discourse. These questions, some of which refer to reading passages provided by the instructor, help students develop an awareness of the many choices—voice, style, tone—involved in taking a particular rhetorical stance:

> Take an issue that you know a lot about and argue for or against it in the most *unauthoritative* voice you can.

"Translate" some fine writing into bureaucratese, as George Orwell does with the following biblical passage. Then reflect on what makes the writing good in one passage and bad in the other.

> I returned and saw under the sun, that the race is not to the swift, nor the battle to the strong, neither yet bread to the wise, nor yet riches to men of understanding, nor yet favor to men of skill; but time and chance happen to them all.

> Objective consideration of contemporary phenomena compels the conclusion that success or failure in competitive activities exhibits no tendency to be commensurate with innate capacity, but that a considerable element of the unpredictable must invariably be taken into account.

Preparing to Write Formal Essays. Some journal assignments help students prepare to write their own essays by testing ideas, practicing parts of essays, or writing mini-essays developing one basic feature of the genre. This type of journal question can be used as a supplement to the invention sequence for each Part I assignment:

> Write a mini-evaluation of one of your former teachers, developing *one* reason for your evaluation. One full page should be adequate. Be sure to follow the guidelines discussed in class and outlined in Chapter 4: Making an Evaluation.

> Write two different thesis paragraphs for the essay interpreting a story. You may want to try casting the same idea in two different ways, or you may make very different claims in each. State your thesis and indicate how you are going to support your claims.

Practicing Editing Skills. Some journal questions may ask students to practice editing skills, ranging from punctuation to the use and acknowledgment of sources. You could use the Editing and Proofreading guides in each chapter applied to the students' own writing or to passages you distribute.

> Made a works cited list for books used in this class, a short story in an anthology, a magazine article, and a newspaper article.

> Photocopy a page from your evaluation essay and staple it to your journal entry. Then do some close editing as we did in class today. Use the Editing and Proofreading guide to look for any problems.

Reflecting on Your Learning. Finally, you could use the journal as a place for students to reflect on what they are learning in the course as well as in other courses. The metacognitive activity Reflecting on Your Writing could be used here or you could devise additional journal questions, such as:

> How would you describe yourself as a writer at the beginning of the term? In what ways have you changed as a writer over the term?

Looking back over your other courses this term, list the kinds of writing you had to do. Then choose one kind of writing and describe its basic features.

You will no doubt think of still other ways of using a journal to complement *The Concise Guide to Writing*.

PRESENTING AND DISCUSSING READINGS

Reading plays a very important role in a writing course. We encourage students to read *as writers*—to examine not only the content of a text but also various features and strategies they can adapt for use in their own writing. We also want them to learn to read *with a critical eye*—to question rather than accept unsupported assertions, to differentiate between fact and opinion, to evaluate arguments, and to examine assumptions. Chapter 9 presents an array of critical reading strategies, and each Part I chapter follows readings with questions For Discussion and For Analysis. These could be used as the basis for small-group or whole-class discussion. We emphasize that our courses are discussion seminars and that we expect every student to participate in the discussions.

Helping Students Prepare for Successful Discussions

In order for discussions of the readings to succeed, we try to ensure not only that students have done the reading carefully but also that they are prepared to discuss it, with us and with one another. Instructors can use many different strategies both for ensuring that students do the reading in the first place and for guiding them to get the most out of class discussions.

Encouraging Students to Do the Reading. Simply letting students know on the syllabus that they will be expected to answer journal questions and participate in discussions (and that they will be evaluated on their journals and class participation) is enough to motivate most students, most of the time. However, many instructors find it worthwhile to take further measures to ensure that all of the students do all of the reading.

Nearly all instructors assign journal questions on the readings as homework and then call on several students at random to read their journal entries aloud at the beginning of the class. Some instructors use *in-class* journal questions on the readings as quizzes. Since the topics of these questions are not announced in advance, students know that they must complete the assigned reading in order to be prepared. You could use an informal grading system to arrive at a "preparation grade" for the course.

Helping Students Get the Most out of the Reading. Experienced writing teachers know that asking the right questions about reading can encourage close reading. Carefully planned journal questions—questions that do not merely test students' comprehension but ask students to read critically and to examine the text's rhetorical features and strategies—help students make thoughtful contributions to classroom discussion. The discussion and analysis questions that follow each reading in Part I of *The Concise Guide to Writing* are questions of this type.

Although annotation is not required in our assignments, students find it an indispensable technique for critical reading. Annotating is particularly useful in preparing students for discussions of the readings, as their annotations serve to remind them in the classroom of the features and patterns they note as they read each piece. Annotating is illustrated in Chapter 9: Strategies for Reading Critically.

Many instructors ask students to read some texts not once but several times, annotating for different features each time. They prepare students to annotate by listing and discussing these features. For instance, students might annotate first for organization of main ideas, then for the basic features of the discourse type, and finally to note the writer's particular rhetorical strategies.

Because the idea of annotation is likely to be new to most students, many instructors find it helpful to prepare students for making their own annotations by providing a sample of a thoroughly annotated text, or by talking students through a page of text as they annotate it. It is also a good idea to collect students' earliest tries at annotation in order to monitor and encourage their attempts.

Chapter 9 also offers other strategies for critical reading you can use as the basis for class discussion such as reflecting on challenges to your beliefs and judging the writer's credibility.

Facilitating Successful Classroom Discussions

Remind students of the connection between the reading and their own writing. To begin, you could call on several students to read their answers to journal questions or you can pair students up to work on different parts of the reading and then report their findings to the class. The aim is to involve them from the start in an active examination of the text, and also to engage them in collaboration of some kind. We find that the best way to do this is to ask "real" questions that require close analysis of how a particular strategy works or falls short, for example.

To complete the discussion, ask students to summarize the main things they have learned. Some instructors go around the room, asking each student to make a brief comment, pointing to a strategy they could imagine trying in their own writing or, conversely, something they will try to avoid doing. They might also compare and contrast different readings in the chapter.

Some Practical Considerations

Give up on discussions that don't seem to be going anywhere or that aren't engaging most of the students. Do not stay on a single point (or a single essay) for too long. Instead, keep the pace of the discussion fairly quick so that students stay attentive.

Try to involve every student in every discussion so that a few students are not doing all the talking. Many students are somewhat shy about speaking in class, so involving them may take some special effort on your part. One way to elicit a spoken response from even the shyest of students is to ask a simple, low-key question such as "What is memorable about the piece?" Most students should be able to answer this question on the spot, and they can be encouraged to speculate about what makes the piece memorable.

Many instructors find that group activities are a good way of getting students involved in discussions. Some instructors assign each essay in a chapter to a group of three or four students and ask each group to annotate its essay, either for a set of features or for a single feature. Each group then leads the discussion of its essay, beginning by reporting its observations to the rest of the class. This type of activity is particularly useful for involving students in discussion: the students in the audience are aware that they, too, will have to lead the class discussion, and this awareness makes them more likely to contribute.

SETTING UP COLLABORATIVE LEARNING GROUPS

There is a growing interest—and an expanding literature—in collaborative writing and learning. For twenty years or more in the schools there has been serious experimentation with collaborative learning indicating that students learn more through carefully planned small-group activities.

Collaborative learning has always been central, of course, to writing-workshop courses and to any composition course in which students discuss work in progress. For quite a while now, experienced, informed writing instructors have seen themselves as collaborators with students to improve their composing, rather than as error sleuths or test givers or even as evaluators.

And there is strong interest within composition studies in collaborative *writing*—those occasions in academia, business, and the professions when two or more writers collaborate to produce a single piece of writing. Several of the writing assignments in Part I lend themselves very well to collaboration. Explaining concepts (Chapter 3), especially if based on research, works well, and any of the argument chapters—4 through 6—could be used. Collaborating on the position paper would be especially challenging if students' views on the issue were opposed. The proposal is the most obvious choice and the one written collaboratively most often outside the classroom.

Collaborative Learning Assignments

We sometimes ask students to meet in small groups *outside of class* to discuss *readings* and either plan an oral report or complete tasks we pose. These meetings are occasions primarily for rereading and talking, though some writing usually results as well. We sometimes talk about these groups as collaborative *reading* groups.

Here are our two basic activities you might try:

Group Report on a Reading

Carefully read the essay assigned to your group and then meet with your group to prepare a presentation for the class. You may be asked to respond to the For Discussion or For Analysis question following the reading, or to a question posed in class.

You should expect other members of the class to be familiar with the essay you will present. Needless to say, be sure that you are familiar with the essays assigned to the other groups. You must be prepared to participate in the discussion about the essays that the other groups present.

Group Evaluation of Two Readings

Your group has been assigned two readings. Carefully read the two essays before you meet with your group. Before you read, though, review the Basic Features section. Then, as you read both readings, take notes on how they fulfill the basic features of the genre. Decide on your own which reading you think is more effective and why.

Then meet with your group and discuss each person's choice. Try to arrive at a consensus. If you cannot agree, feel free to file minority and majority reports. In your report (or reports) you should explain your group's judgment and the reasons for making it.

You should expect other members of the class to be familiar with these essays. Needless to say, be sure that you are familiar with the essays assigned to the other groups. You must be able to participate in the other groups' presentations of their evaluations.

You will see many possible variations on these basic activities. For example, for the evaluate-two-readings activity, you could ask groups to report on similarities and differences between the two readings rather than to argue that one is more effective than the other.

Give students an opportunity to meet in class to schedule a regular time to meet outside of class. Explain to them that the collaborative discussion of readings will contribute to their success in your course, and offer them general guidelines for collaboration. Their goal—at least in these two basic activities—is to prepare a brief report (five to eight minutes, depending on how many groups you have and how long your class meets) on what they learn about the readings. Tell them they must report as a *panel*, with each person contributing. Since the reports tend to sprawl, you will have to enforce time limits so that all groups may report and you will have time for other activities.

GENERAL GUIDELINES FOR RESPONDING TO STUDENT WRITING

This section offers general guidelines for responding to invention work, drafts, and revisions. It opens with a discussion of the basis for response, pointing to the sources of criteria and standards within each of the writing assignment chapters (2–6) in *The Concise Guide to Writing*.

The Criteria for Response

We need to consider first the basis for response. This basis comes from the writer's purpose and intended audience and from the genre constraints and possibilities of the particular writing situation. Possible purposes and stances toward readers are addressed in the Purpose and Audience discussion of each of the writing assignment chapters (2–6) in *The Concise Guide to Writing*. Genre possibilities are discussed and illustrated in the Basic Features section of the same chapters. These features and their characteristic—though varied—patterning define each genre, having evolved from writers' practices over many years in particular writing situations.

Students find themselves—thanks to you and the text—in the situation, let's say, of writing about a remembered event. There are many possibilities open to them for translating this remembered experience into a vivid, memorable, coherent story. Which possibilities they grasp—that is, which features they select and the way they pattern them—depends on how they want to present themselves to particular readers.

The Basic Features in each of the writing assignment chapters provide the basis for evaluating students' work. These become criteria for responding to a draft or revision when, with the student's purpose and readers in mind, you (or other students) ask: Given his or her purpose and readers, has the writer finally realized the possibilities of this genre? Has the writer overlooked any features? How well has the writer used the features he or she has chosen? These general questions are treated in several places in each writing assignment chapter:

- *For Analysis* questions following each reading
- *Testing Your Choice* in the Invention section
- *Setting Goals* in the Planning and Drafting section
- *Reading with a Critical Eye* in the Getting Critical Comments section
- *Solving the Problems* in the Revising and Editing section

They are illustrated, discussed, or experienced directly in various other places in Chapters 2–6, including the writing scenarios that open each chapter, the two group-inquiry activities, the readings and their commentaries, and the writer-at-work discussion that concludes each chapter.

The Concise Guide to Writing doesn't conceal its expectations of students. By the time they've worked their way through a chapter—analyzing readings, studying commentaries, reviewing Basic Features, completing invention—they should, if they've been at all alert, be ready to draft an essay that reflects a good understanding of the writing situation. With the help of the guidelines for Reading with a Critical Eye, they should then be prepared to respond confidently to a draft and to comprehend any suggestions that you might offer. When they revise, the suggestions for Solving the Problems should seem almost predictable. They should, in other words, know the criteria for evaluating writing of the type they are attempting. And having come this far with them, you should be confident about responding appropriately and helpfully to their final drafts.

Principles of Response

To complement your own insights about responding to student writing from your experience as a teacher and writer, *The Concise Guide to Writing* provides a clear basis for responding to student work in each of several diverse genres. This basis for response might be thought of as essential knowledge for fostering students' writing development. With this as a starting point, what principles, then, might guide an instructor's response to student writing? From long experience in the classroom and from devotion to the growing literature in composition studies, we've settled on the following principles.

- Students need response to their work at every stage of composition, not just at the revision stage. Response to a topic choice, to initial invention work, or to a first draft may be decisive in enabling the student to produce a revised essay that invites and justifies your thoughtful evaluation.
- Response at the draft stage should anticipate immediate revision and specifically encourage a student to persist through one or more revisions.
- Response to errors in grammar and usage, punctuation, and spelling should be reserved for later drafts.
- For response to lead to motivated, productive revision it must take account of the student's purpose and audience; the particular ideas in the essay; and the constraints and possibilities of the genre or writing situation. General advice, interchangeable from one essay to the next, is usually fruitless.
- Students most of all need their teachers to be genuine *readers* of their work, not merely judges and error hunters. A readerly response helps students understand that writing is an important and irreplaceable form of interaction with others. It also helps them to imagine readers' responses as they write.
- Response to drafts and revisions should be selective. Novice writers, like a beginner at any complex human performance, can be overwhelmed and discouraged by too much advice.
- Students should share the responsibilities for response in a writing course. They should read and respond to one another's writing and solve problems in their own writing. The goal is for students to be able on their own to write purposefully, to imagine readers' questions or objections, to revise in order to say what they want to say as well as it can be said, and to correct errors and stylistic infelicities.

Responding at the Invention Stage

If you require students to complete all of the invention work, you may want to devote some class time to coaching and response. We usually complete the first two steps in class, first listing topics and then choosing one. A whole-class effort always produces many more promising topics than students come up with on their own. Students first list some topics alone, but we then make one big list on the chalkboard from everyone. Some instructors begin evaluating topics here, pointing out those that are both problematic and promising. Students also comment on the proposed topics.

Once students have chosen a topic, even a tentative one, they can always use some response. We evaluate each topic carefully at this point, helping students see the implications of a topic choice. Students will learn a great deal about the assignment from this kind of response to their topics.

For the first assignment of the term, you may also with to schedule time for students to start exploring their topics in class. We ask three or four students to read these invention notes aloud and then we draw them out about what they seem to be learning. Our purpose is to overcome the strangeness of systematic invention work—few students, if any, have ever done it—and to help them see what productive invention writing might look like.

Many instructors find it best to set due dates over the next week or so for the remaining stages of invention work. We may again ask a few students to read aloud certain parts or allow some class time for them to work in small groups, to talk to one another about what they are learning about their topics through their invention work. This can also be a good time for students to be analyzing chapter readings or, if that is behind them, discussing essays in *The Great American Bologna Festival*, second edition, the collection of student essays that accompanies *The Concise Guide to Writing*. Because these essays were all written for the writing assignments in the *Guide*, they serve as trustworthy examples of the kind of writing students using our text are working to produce.

When the invention work has been completed, we think it's wise to collect it—if only for the first assignment—in order to find out whether students are getting something from it. We don't try to predict how useful a particular student's invention will turn out to be, but we know from many years of coaching and observation that the most productive invention work has an exploratory, even playful, quality. It is specific, or concrete, rather than general. It follows up on images, pushes ideas, rather than letting them drop. It is sometimes digressive and fragmentary, and it is relatively lengthy. It is rarely brief or cautious, and never perfunctory. In my program we comment briefly on students' work in these terms; and, most important, we photocopy four or five pieces that meet these criteria and discuss them with the class.

Responding at the Draft Stage

Responses at the draft stage can come in peer workshops (meeting in class or out), in conferences with you, or from you in writing.

In Workshops. The key workshop resource in *The Concise Guide to Writing* is the Getting Critical Comments section in each of the writing assignment chapters (2–6). These guidelines begin by helping students prepare their drafts for a critical reader by stating their purpose and readers in writing. Then, after exchanging drafts, they can follow the guidelines for Reading with a Critical Eye in order to analyze a draft and advise the writer about possible revisions. We ask students to write out their analyses, to deepen their understanding of the draft, and to provide the writer with a record of suggestions for revision. Peer discussion tends to be especially productive after students have spent a half hour or so doing this kind of thoughtful, written analysis, in or out of class. We allow fifteen or twenty minutes for student pairs to discuss what they have learned from one another.

We find that we need to prepare students to respond to one another's work. To do so, we review the guidelines for Getting Critical Comments and carefully explain that writers need to know *what the reader sees* and to garner *specific suggestions for revising*.

There are countless variations on this workshop scheme, all of them with merit. Advantages we claim for our scheme are that students follow assignment-specific guidelines and write before they talk.

Our instructors usually join in a group's discussion, instead of just looking on or listening in.

In Conferences. The key to successful conferences is to get students to prepare carefully so that when they come to see you, they can do most of the talking and take much of the responsibility for improving their drafts.

We give students a form to fill in before coming to the conference, a different form for each writing assignment. You will find specially designed forms for each of the writing assignments in *The Concise Guide to Writing*, ready for you to reproduce, in Section III of this book.

Responding at the Revision Stage

By the time students complete an essay assignment, they will have generated a good deal of writing. For instructors, the goal is to have a system of reading and responding to it that allows us to give students helpful feedback while processing the pile of student work in a reasonable amount of time.

Helping Students Organize an Assignment Package. You need to tell students exactly what materials are to be turned in with the final, revised essay. At the beginning of the course, we give students a handout that specifies what they are to turn in for each writing assignment. We ask for the following materials:

1. *Invention Notes*
2. *Drafts:* One or more drafts, legible and labeled with the student's name, the assignment title, and the draft number. The pages should be numbered.
3. *Critical Comments:* Written comments about one draft, done by a classmate. The classmate's name should be on the response.
4. *A List of Problems in the Draft:* From the analysis completed in the Revising and Editing section of the *Guide.*
5. *Revision:* The final, revised version of the essay, typed and proofread with any errors neatly corrected. It should be double-spaced, typed on one side of the page only, and numbered. The title page should be labeled in the top right-hand corner with the student's name, the chapter title for the assignment, the word *Revision,* and the date.
6. *Reflecting on Your Writing:* The student analyzes his or her problem-solving process in writing and revising the paper.

We also ask students to put this work into a file folder with their name, section, and the assignment written clearly on the outside. We find that this assignment package reduces confusion, eases our management of the large amounts of writing, and speeds the reading and response process.

Before reading the packet, you might read the student's written reflections in response to the Reflecting on Your Writing. The reflections on writing, with its focus on how the student identified and solved a problem in the essay, presents a self-portrait of the student as a writer. We try to applaud the student's problem-solving efforts in order to bolster the student's confidence and encourage revising. We might draw the student's attention to another problem that needs solving and invite another revision focusing on this problem.

Surveying the Package and Completing Records.   We start by skimming to see that all the assigned writing is there and to see what the student has accomplished in the invention and drafts. The invention tends to be a good indicator of the depth and thoroughness of the revised essay, and problems in the revision can often be traced to deficiencies in invention. We try to make this connection clear to students early in the course.

We keep track of each student's performance in all the various stages of the composing process for each assignment. (You will find the record sheet later in this chapter, ready for you to reproduce.) This sheet is for our own records, and students do not see it.

The students' self-evaluation (Reflecting on Your Writing in Chapters 2–6) prompts them to reflect critically on their composing process, to think about what they have written, and to take responsibility for the decisions they have made. At its worst, such a self-evaluation will say no more than "here-it-is-I-like-it-hope-you-do-too," as the student declines the invitation to take responsibility. At its best, however, it provides the student with an account of his or her composing process, and it provides you with a critical introduction to the essay. It can also reveal the student's level of involvement with the assignment. We usually read the self-evaluation carefully.

Responding to the Revised Essay.   Plan to spend several minutes responding to the revision. We make a few comments in the margins, noting both strong and weak points in the writing, and then we add a few sentences of comments at the end, on a separate sheet of paper. You may want to keep a copy of these comments for your own records. We try to find something in the essay to praise, and we find that critical comments work best when phrased in terms of what the student might have done in the essay or should try to do in the next one. Questions are useful, too, when they lead students to think about other ways they might have addressed the problems in the paper. This approach casts the instructor in the role of adviser rather than of judge.

You may choose to respond to your students' final drafts by following the guidelines in *The Concise Guide to Writing* for Reading with a Critical Eye. By doing so, you model for students the kind of written responses you expect of them in workshops.

When time is limited, you need to respond to features in the essay in order of priority. In an autobiographical essay, we begin by considering the larger rhetorical issues: what the writer has tried to accomplish in telling the story, its structure, the beginning and ending, and the pacing of the narrative. Next, we look at some particular features of the genre: the quantity and vividness of descriptive details, the writer's recollection of feelings at the time of the event or toward the person, the use of dialogue, and the proportion of narration, description, and commentary in the story. (In Section III you will find brief guidelines for responding to each of the assignments in *The Concise Guide to Writing*, listing the criteria for response and some typical problems.) Finally, we comment on the writer's style, diction, and sentence structure.

We advise against commenting on everything that could be improved in a paper. An inexperienced writer can be easily overwhelmed by too much criticism and become too discouraged to work on any of the problems. Rather, we try to focus on a few of the most important things that need attention, thereby giving the student achievable goals. We follow the same policy with mechanical errors and stylistic infelicities, assuming that if we mark every transgression in a weak writer's paper, the student may be overwhelmed. Later in this chapter is a plan for dealing with students' errors.

Finally, we do not hesitate to ask a student to revise still again an essay that fails to meet minimal requirements established by the readings, commentary, and Guide to Writing in each chapter. We find that this request sets standards more effectively than a low grade.

Some General Guidelines for Responding to Revised Essays

1. Check the package to be sure that all of the required parts are there. Note missing parts and comment on parts (the invention, for example) that please or disappoint you.
2. Read the revision through quickly to get the sense of it. Is it what you assigned? Does it look approximately right?
3. Decide first whether the package needs to be returned for further work before you can evaluate it. There are several reasons why you might want the student to do some additional work before you evaluate the package:

- The package is substantially incomplete; the invention, workshop responses, self-evaluation, or one or more drafts are missing, or perhaps only the final revision is there.
- The final revision is not typed, or is otherwise unreadable because of printer problems, worn-out ribbons, etc.
- The revision does not meet the rhetorical situation: it is a problem solution essay rather than a cause essay, a person essay rather than an event essay, an evaluation essay without adequate evidence from the thing being evaluated, and so on.
- The topic does not fall within the constraints of your assignment. (For example, you might have declared dormitory problems off-limits for the problem solution essay, and yet the student wrote about a dormitory problem.)
- The revision is seriously disorganized.
- The revision has major problems with style, mechanics, or English usage that seriously impair a reader's comprehension.

If you return an essay package for further work, outline your reasons briefly and ask the student to make an appointment for a conference to discuss his or her plan for revising. You might ask the student to review the readings and the Basic Features for this essay in *The Concise Guide to Writing*. Set a deadline (from one to two weeks) for resubmitting the package. You want to make it clear that although the package does not yet meet your standards, you are convinced that the student is capable of succeeding with this writing assignment. You might ask the writer to (a) start over with a new topic, (b) substantially revise an entire draft, or (c) revise only one part of a draft.

4. If the revision is ready to be evaluated, look first for the strengths in the paper. What did the student do well, or at least satisfactorily? Try to comment on some aspects of the paper of which you approve.

5. Does the revision show a grasp of the specific features of its type of writing? Usually, some features are represented more successfully than others. Which ones are handled well? Which ones could have been developed more successfully?

6. Does the revision seem coherent and organized? Are the transitions from one part to the next handled smoothly? Comment on structural elements that work well or that might be improved.

7. Consider writing style. College writers struggle to develop a natural yet authoritative style. They may write in a style that is too casual or childlike, or they may try to write a ponderous "academic" prose. Some will have a wonderful, natural voice, with appropriate modulations for different readers. You may want to comment on the essay's style, pointing to one or two specific examples from the revision if you can.

8. What about errors? We expect revised essays to have been carefully edited and proofread, but most students are just learning to identify and edit their own writing. Since even the best essays often have some sentence-level problems, we like the "minimal marking" scheme described later in this section. This scheme allows us to respond first to substantive issues and then to mark a student's errors in only a small part of the essay. This procedure reinforces the importance of editing but puts it in its proper place at the end of the writing process.

Grading. We do not grade individual essays, though you may wish to. Our reasoning is that a letter grade is at best a cryptic indication of performance, and that grades on individual essays can involve instructor and students in unproductive appeals and justifications. Furthermore, the risk of a low grade can discourage an inexperienced writer from taking creative chances. We recognize, however, that students need some indication of their progress before the obligatory letter grades at the end of the course, so we fill out midterm progress reports for all students indicating what grades they can expect at the end of the course if they continue at their present levels of performance. This form shows students where they need to focus their attention in the remainder of the course.

At the end of the course, we use a final course report form to write a response to the final essay submitted and an evaluative summary of the student's performance in the whole course. (You will find these forms, ready to reproduce, later in this chapter.) This summary, and the course grade, is based on a quick review of a student's revised essays—we ask that they be turned in along with the revision of the final essay. We also review our records of a student's attendance, reading journal entries, quizzes, workshop responses, and any other work we might have assigned. Then we give a final grade based on three criteria:

1. Whether all the assigned work has been completed in a timely fashion.
2. Whether the work has improved during the course.
3. Whether revised essays are fully realized rhetorically; that is, whether the student's revisions reveal substantial learning about the rhetorical and composing possibilities of the various genres assigned in the course.

RESPONDING TO ERROR

Responding to students' errors in mechanics, usage, and syntax is no small matter in writing course. First, it is not easy to reduce students' errors; second, it is only too easy for efforts at reducing errors to dominate a writing course, crowding out time for reading, thinking, and composing. For some time we searched for a sensible approach to responding to error and finally, in 1984, we found one we were willing to try: a scheme for "minimal marking" developed by Richard Haswell of Washington State University. Before looking at this scheme, however, we want to outline the principles supported by the current literature on error that guided our search.

Principles

Following are some widely accepted principles for dealing with error in a first-year college writing course.

- Attention to error must not prevent students from spending most of their time reading, discussing, inventing, researching, planning, drafting, and revising extended, multiparagraph discourse. This principle holds for all students, no matter how high their initial error rate.
- Too much emphasis on error limits students' focus to local sentence problems, when they should instead be focusing most of the time on global rhetorical problems. Over-attention to error makes students cautious when they need to be taking chances, both to discover something to say and to find the sentences to say it.
- Correct style and usage are more likely to be acquired through reading, writing, and revising than learned through grammar study, rules and maxims, and exercises.
- If grammatical and stylistic concepts are taught directly, they should be taught thoroughly by providing students with background information, adequate definitions, diverse examples and nonexamples carefully discussed, and practice with feedback. Too often, textbook explanations of grammatical concepts are clear to students only if they already know the concept.
- Error merits close attention only when students are editing and proofreading final drafts.
- Instruction and response to student work must ensure that students take responsibility for finding, diagnosing, and correcting their own errors. The instructor must follow up by checking these corrections and requiring still further work on unacceptable corrections. If the instruc-

tor indicates which lines or sentences contain errors, students can find and correct most of their errors in spelling, mechanics, and usage.

- If students analyze their errors, they will find patterns that can focus and simplify their efforts at overcoming those errors. If, for example, a student had problems with internal sentence punctuation, he or she might review appropriate handbook explanations of comma usage and complete some exercises.
- Instruction in error correction must be individualized. Whole-class instruction in grammar, usage, or style should occur only occasionally if at all. Students can also get help at campus writing centers and from peer-editing and tutoring teams.

These principles can guide your dealings with error even for students whose error rate is high, who speak a nonstandard dialect, or who still struggle with English as a second language. Only those students who are still in the earliest stages of learning English as a second language should require special instruction, which should be offered by ESL specialists. These principles justify heterogeneous classes for first-year college writing programs and call into question programs that track students. Where students are tracked, these principles indicate a similar pedagogy for students on different tracks.

Minimal Marking

How, in a writing class, can you observe the principles outlined above? Richard Haswell's "minimal marking" scheme provides one defensible, workable answer. Haswell's article appeared in the October 1983 issue of *College English*. Here's how we've adopted his scheme:

To mark a student's final draft, you indicate obvious sentence-level error (spelling, punctuation, capitalization, and usage) on one page of the essay by underlining the error or placing it in brackets. In the margin next to the error, you write the correction symbol. Students then are responsible to correct the errors you have checked. They can do this work right on their texts or on a separate page. They then return the essays to you so that you can review the corrections and either explain errors students were unable to correct or refer them to the appropriate section of a handbook. Students can also work in small groups, helping one another find and correct their errors.

Not only will this system reduce the time you must spend on error, but it involves students in doing the actual work. With Haswell's scheme, students are encouraged to be responsible for their own editing, rather than relying on the instructor to "correct" their essays. Also, this kind of marking can be done quite rapidly after you have responded to content. It provides an outlet for the part of our teaching brain that is dedicated to reducing error without bludgeoning students with criticism. On the other hand, it satisfies the part of the student brain that expects us to point out errors. Yet the student must identify, diagnose, and correct the error.

Some further practical considerations: You might want to check errors in one or two paragraphs only, or on one page only—on papers with many errors, for instance, or if your time is limited. Bracket the portion of the essay you marked. You might also indicate by page number or correction symbol the section of the handbook where the student can find an explanation of the error. You can schedule class time for students to complete (or at least begin) their corrections, or you can ask them to complete the corrections outside of class and return the essay at the next class meeting. The success of this scheme depends on your evaluating students' corrections and then following up in some way on each remaining error. After indicating errors that still remain, you could follow up in a number of ways:

- confer with a student, explaining the errors and helping with the corrections
- require the student to complete an appropriate handbook exercise
- ask students to meet with another student to work together on necessary revisions

MIDTERM PROGRESS REPORT

Student _____   Course _____

Instructor _____   Section _____

Date _____   Term _____

QUANTITY OF WORK   Has the student completed all assignments?

Invention _____   Journal Entries _____

Drafts & Revisions _____   Quizzes _____

Workshop Responses _____   Revision Plans _____

Self-Evaluations _____   Attendance _____

QUALITY OF WORK   To what extent has the student:

Used the Guide to Writing creatively. _____

Revised drafts substantially. _____

Given helpful workshop responses. _____

Written perceptive self-evaluations. _____

Edited and proofread carefully. _____

Used the journal productively. _____

Participated in class discussions. _____

These areas need special attention in the remainder of the course:

MIDTERM GRADE: _____

STUDENT RECORD FORM

Course _____

Section _____

Student _____

Midterm Grade _____ Final Grade _____

Assignment	Topic	Invention	Drafts	Critical Comments by	Revision Plan	Revision	Self-Evaluation

FINAL COURSE REPORT

Student _____   Course _____

Instructor _____   Section _____

Date _____   Term _____

Remarks on FINAL ESSAY _____

_____

_____

_____

_____

_____

_____

_____

_____

Remarks on WHOLE COURSE _____

_____

_____

_____

_____

_____

_____

_____

_____

_____

_____

FINAL GRADE: _____

Section **V**
A SELECTED BIBLIOGRAPHY IN RHETORIC AND COMPOSITION

BIBLIOGRAPHIES

Bizell, Patricia, and Bruce Herzberg. *The Bedford Bibliography for Teachers of Writing.* New York: St. Martin's, 1991.

Hillocks, George, Jr. *Research on Written Communication.* Urbana, IL: NCTE, 1986.

Moran, Michael G., and Ronald F. Lunsford, eds. *Research in Composition and Rhetoric: A Bibliographic Sourcebook.* Westport, CT: Greenwood, 1984.

North, Stephen M. *The Making of Knowledge in Composition: Portrait of an Emerging Field.* Portsmouth, NH: Heinemann, Boynton/Cook, 1987.

Tate, Gary, ed. *Teaching Composition: Twelve Bibliographic Essays.* Fort Worth: Texas Christian UP, 1987.

HISTORIES OF RHETORIC AND THE TEACHING OF WRITING

Applebee, Arthur N. *Tradition and Reform in the Teaching of English: A History.* Urbana, IL: NCTE, 1974.

Bender, John, and David E. Wellbery. *The Ends of Rhetoric: History, Theory, Practice.* Stanford: Stanford UP, 1990.

Berlin, James A. *Rhetoric and Reality: Writing Instruction in American Colleges, 1900–1985.* Carbondale: Southern Illinois UP, 1987.

———. *Writing Instruction in Nineteenth Century American Colleges.* Carbondale: Southern Illinois UP, 1984.

Brereton, John, ed. *Traditions of Inquiry.* New York: Oxford UP, 1985.

Connors, Robert J. "The Rise and Fall of the Modes of Discourse." *CCC* 32 (Dec. 1981): 444–63.

Connors, Robert J., Lisa S. Ede, and Andrea Lunsford, eds. *Essays on Classical Rhetoric and Modern Discourse.* Carbondale: Southern Illinois UP, 1984.

Corbett, Edward P. J., James L. Golden, and Goodwin F. Berquist, eds. *Essays on the Rhetoric of the Western World.* Dubuque, IA: Kendall/Hunt, 1990.

Covino, William A. *The Art of Wondering: A Revisionist Return to the History of Rhetoric.* Portsmouth, NH: Heinemann, Boynton/Cook, 1988.

Crowley, Sharon. *The Methodical Memory: Invention in Current-Traditional Rhetoric.* Carbondale: Southern Illinois UP, 1990.

Halloran, S. Michael. "Rhetoric in the American College Curriculum: The Decline of Public Discourse." *PRE/TEXT,* 3 (Fall 1983).

Horner, Winifred Bryan, ed. *The Present State of Scholarship in Historical and Contemporary Rhetoric.* Columbia: U of Missouri P, 1983.

Jarratt, Susan. *The Return of the Sophists: Classical Rhetoric Refigured.* Carbondale: Southern Illinois UP, 1991.

Johnson, Nan. *Nineteenth-Century Rhetoric: Theory and Practice in North America*. Carbondale: Southern Illinois UP, 1991.

Kennedy, George A. *Classical Rhetoric and Its Christian and Secular Tradition from Ancient to Modern Times*. Chapel Hill: U of North Carolina P, 1980.

Knoblauch, C. H., and Lil Brannon. *Rhetorical Traditions and the Teaching of Writing*. Portsmouth, NH: Heinemann, Boynton/Cook, 1983.

Murphy, James J., ed. *The Rhetorical Tradition and Modern Writing*. New York: MLA, 1982.

———. *A Short History of Writing Instruction from Ancient Greece to Twentieth Century America*. Davis, CA: Hermagoras, 1990.

Neel, Jasper. *Plato, Derrida, and Writing*. Carbondale: Southern Illinois UP, 1988.

Phelps, Louise Wetherbee. *Composition as a Human Science: Contribution to the Self-Understanding of a Discipline*. New York: Oxford UP, 1988.

Royster, Jacqueline Jones. "Perspectives on the Intellectual Tradition of Black Women Writers." *The Right to Literacy*. Ed. Andrea Lunsford et al. New York: MLA 1990.

Swearington, C. Jan. *Rhetoric and Irony: Western Literacy and Western Lies*. New York: Oxford UP, 1991.

Welch, Kathleen E. *The Contemporary Reception of Classical Rhetoric: Appropriations of Ancient Discourse*. Hillsdale, NJ: Erlbaum, 1990.

MODERN AND POSTMODERN RHETORIC AND DISCOURSE THEORY

Aronowitz, Stanley, and Henry A. Giroux. *Postmodern Education: Politics, Culture, and Social Criticism*. Minneapolis: U of Minnesota P, 1991.

Atkins, C. Douglas, and Michael L. Johnson, eds. *Writing and Reading Differently: Deconstruction and the Teaching of Composition and Literature*. Lawrence: UP of Kansas, 1985.

Beale, Walter H., *A Pragmatic Theory of Rhetoric*. Carbondale: Southern Illinois UP, 1987.

Belanoff, Pat, Peter Elbow, and Sheryl I. Fontaine, eds. *Nothing Begins with N: New Investigations of Freewriting*. Carbondale: Southern Illinois UP, 1991.

Berthoff, Ann. *The Making of Meaning: Metaphors, Models, and Maxims for Writing Teachers*. Portsmouth, NH: Heinemann, Boynton/Cook, 1981.

Bitzer, Lloyd F. "The Rhetorical Situation." *Philosophy and Rhetoric* 1 (Winter 1968): 1–14.

Bizzell, Patricia. *Academic Discourse and Critical Consciousness*. Pittsburgh: U of Pittsburgh P, 1992.

Bridges, Charles W., ed. *Training the New Teacher of College Composition*. Urbana, IL: NCTE, 1986.

Britton, James, et al. *The Development of Writing Abilities (11–18)*. London: Macmillan, 1975.

Bullock, Richard, and John Trimbur, eds. *The Politics of Writing Instruction: Postsecondary*. Portsmouth, NH: Heinemann, Boynton/Cook, 1991.

Clark, Gregory. *Dialogue, Dialectic, and Conversation: A Social Perspective on the Function of Writing*. Carbondale: Southern Illinois UP, 1990.

Crusius, Timothy W. *Discourse: A Critique and Synthesis of Major Theories*. New York: MLA, 1989.

Donovan, Timothy R., and Ben W. McClelland. *Eight Approaches to Teaching Composition*. Urbana, IL: NCTE 1980.

Elbow, Peter. *Embracing Contraries: Explorations in Learning and Teaching*. New York: Oxford UP, 1986.

———. *What is English?* New York: MLA, 1990.

Emig, Janet. *The Web of Meaning: Essays on Writing, Teaching, Learning, and Thinking*. Ed.

Dixie Goswami and Maureen Butler. Portsmouth, NH: Heinemann, Boynton/Cook, 1983.

Faigley, Lester. *Fragments of Rationality: Postmodernity and the Subject of Composition.* Pittsburgh: U of Pittsburgh P, 1992.

Foucault, Michel. "The Discourse on Language." *The Archaeology of Knowledge.* Trans. A. M. Sheridan Smith. New York: Pantheon, 1972.

———. *The History of Sexuality.* Vol. 1. *The Will to Know.* Trans. Robert Hurley. New York: Vintage, 1980.

Freedman, Aviva, and Ian Pringle, eds. *Reinventing the Rhetorical Tradition.* Urbana, IL: NCTE, 1980.

Giroux, Henry A. *Postmodernism, Feminism, and Cultural Politics: Redrawing Educational Boundaries.* Albany: SUNY P, 1991.

Kinneavy, James L. *A Theory of Discourse.* New York: Norton, 1980.

Lindemann, Erika. *A Rhetoric for Writing Teachers.* New York: Oxford UP, 1987.

Lindemann, Erika, and Gary Tate, eds. *An Introduction to Composition Studies.* New York: Oxford UP, 1991.

McClelland, Ben W., and Timothy R. Donovan, eds. *Perspectives on Research and Scholarship in Composition.* New York: MLA, 1985.

Macdonell, Diane. *Theories of Discourse: An Introduction.* Oxford: Basil Blackwell, 1986.

Miller, Susan. *Rescuing the Subject: A Critical Introduction to Rhetoric and the Writer.* Carbondale: Southern Illinois UP, 1989.

———. *Textual Carnivals: The Politics of Composition.* Carbondale: Southern Illinois UP, 1991.

Moffett, James. *Teaching the Universe of Discourse.* Boston: Houghton Mifflin, 1968.

Perelman, Chaim. *The Realm of Rhetoric.* Trans. William Kluback. Notre Dame, IN: U of Notre Dame P, 1977.

Schilb, John, and Patricia Harkin, eds. *Contending with Words: Composition and Rhetoric in a Postmodern Age.* New York: MLA, 1991.

Secor, Marie, and Davida Charney, eds. *Constructing Rhetorical Education.* Carbondale: Southern Illinois UP, 1992.

Tate, Gary, and Edward P. J. Corbett, eds. *The Writing Teacher's Sourcebook.* New York: Oxford UP, 1981.

Toulmin, Stephen. *The Uses of Argument.* New York: Cambridge UP, 1964.

WRITING AS A PROCESS

Cooper, Charles R., and Lee Odell, eds. *Research on Composing: Points of Departure.* Urbana, IL: NCTE, 1978.

Emig, Janet. *The Composing Processes of Twelfth Graders.* Urbana, IL: NCTE 1971.

Faigley, Lester. "Competing Theories of Process: A Critique and a Proposal." *CE* 48 (Oct. 1986): 527–42.

Flower, Linda, et al. "Detection, Diagnosis, and the Strategies of Revision." *CCC* 37 (1986): 16–55.

Flower, Linda, and John R. Hayes. "Problem-Solving Strategies and the Writing Process." *CE* 49 (1977): 19–37

Gregg, L. W., and E. R. Steinberg, eds. *Cognitive Processes in Writing.* Hillsdale, NJ: Erlbaum, 1980.

LeFevre, Karen Burke. *Invention as a Social Act.* Carbondale: Southern Illinois UP, 1987.

Murray, Donald M. "Writing as Process: How Writing Finds Its Own Meaning." *Eight Approaches to Teaching Composition.* Ed. Timothy R. Donovan and Ben W. McClelland. Urbana, IL: NCTE, 1980.

Nystrand, Martin, ed. *What Writers Know: The Language, Process, and Structure of Written Discourse.* New York: Academic P, 1982.

Perl, Sondra. "The Composing Processes of Unskilled College Writers." *RTE* 13 (1978): 317–36.

———. "Understanding Composing." *CCC* 31 (Dec. 1980): 363–69.

Pianko, Sharon. "A Description of the Composing Processes of College Freshman Writers." *RTE* 13 (1979): 5–22.

Rose, Mike, ed. *When a Writer Can't Write: Studies in Writer's Block and Other Composing-Process Problems.* New York: Guilford P, 1985.

Sommers, Nancy. "Revision Strategies of Student Writers and Experienced Adult Writers." *CCC* 31 (1980): 378–88.

Sudol, Ronald A., ed. *Revising.* Urbana, IL: NCTE, 1982.

COLLABORATIVE LEARNING

Brooke, Robert E. *Writing and Sense of Self: Identity Negotiation in Writing Workshops.* Urbana, IL: NCTE, 1991.

Bruffee, Kenneth A. "Collaborative Learning and the 'Conversation of Mankind.'" *CE* 46 (Nov. 1984): 635–52.

Dyson, Anne Haas, ed. *Collaboration through Writing and Reading: Exploring Possibilities.* Urbana, IL: NCTE, 1989.

Gere, Ann. *Writing Groups: History, Theory, and Implications.* Carbondale: Southern Illinois UP, 1987.

Golub, Jeff, ed. *Focus on Collaborative Learning.* Urbana, IL: NCTE, 1988.

Lunsford, Andrea, and Lisa Ede. *Singular Texts/Plural Authors: Perspectives on Collaborative Writing.* Carbondale: Southern Illinois UP, 1990.

Weiner, Harvey S. "Collaborative Learning in the Classroom: A Guide to Evaluation." *CE* 48 (Jan. 1986): 52–61.

METACOGNITION, READING, AND GENRE THEORY

Bereiter, Carl, and Marlene Scardamalia. *Psychology of Written Composition.* Hillsdale, NJ: Erlbaum, 1987.

Brown, Ann L. "Metacognitive Development and Reading." *Theoretical Issues in Reading Comprehension.* Ed. Bertram Bruce, et al. Hillsdale, NJ: Erlbaum, 1980.

Cope, Bill, and Mary Kalantzis, eds. *The Powers of Literacy: A Genre Approach to Teaching Writing.* Pittsburgh: U of Pittsburgh P, 1993.

Dillon, George L. *Constructing Texts.* Bloomington: Indiana UP, 1981.

Freedman, Aviva. "Show and Tell? The Role of Explicit Teaching in the Learning of New Genres." *RTE* 27.3 (Oct. 1993): 222–51.

———. "Situating Genre: A Rejoinder." *RTE* 27:3 (Oct. 1993), 272–81.

Halliday, M. A. K., and Ruqaiya Hasan. *Cohesion in English.* London: Longman, 1976.

Kinsch, Walter. "The Role of Strategies in Reading and Writing." *Forum* III 67 (1982).

Kress, Gunther. "Genre as Social Process." *The Powers of Literacy: A Genre Approach to Teaching Writing.* Ed. Bill Cope and Mary Kalantzis. Pittsburgh: U of Pittsburgh P, 1993.

Meyer, Bonnie J. F. *Research on Prose Comprehension: Applications for Composition Teachers.* Tempe: Arizona State U Prose Learning Series Research Report, 1979.

Miller, Carolyn. "Genre as Social Action." *Quarterly Journal of Speech* 70 (1984): 151–67.

Newkirk, Thomas, ed. *Only Connect: Uniting Reading and Writing.* Portsmouth, NH: Heinemann, Boynton/Cook, 1986.

Petersen, Bruce T., ed. *Convergences: Transactions in Reading and Writing.* Urbana, IL: NCTE, 1986.

Pianko, Sharon, "Reflection: A Critical Component of the Composing Process." *CCC* 30 (1979): 275–85.

Schank, R., and Abelson, R. *Scripts, Plans, Goals, and Understanding.* Hillsdale, NJ: Erlbaum, 1977.

Slevin, James F. "Interpreting and Composing: The Many Resources of Kind." *The Writer's Mind.* Ed. Janice Hays et al., Urbana, IL: NCTE, 1983.

Williams, Joseph M., and Gregory G. Colomb. "The Case for Explicit Teaching: Why What You Don't Know Won't Help You." *RTE* 27.3 (Oct. 1993): 252–64.

WRITING IN THE DISCIPLINES

Bartholomae, David. "Inventing the University." *When a Writer Can't Write.* Ed. Mike Rose. New York: Guilford P, 1985.

Bazerman, Charles. *Shaping Written Knowledge.* Madison: U of Wisconsin P, 1988.

Bazerman, Charles, and James Paradis. *Textual Dynamics of the Professions: Historical and Contemporary Studies of Writing in Professional Communities.* Madison: U of Wisconsin P, 1991.

Bullock, Richard. *The St. Martin's Guide to Teaching Writing in the Disciplines.* New York: St. Martin's, 1994.

Fulwiler, Toby, and Al Young, eds. *Programs That Work: Writing across the Curriculum.* Portsmouth, NH: Heinemann, Boynton/Cook, 1990.

Gere, Anne Ruggles, ed. *Roots in the Sawdust: Writing to Learn in the Disciplines.* Urbana, IL: NCTE, 1985.

Herrington, Anne. "Writing to Learn: Writing across the Disciplines." *CE* 43 (1981): 379–87.

Maimon, Elaine P. "Collaborative Learning and Writing across the Curriculum." *WPA* 9 (1986): 9–15.

Russell, David R. *Writing in the Academic Disciplines, 1870–1990.* Carbondale: Southern Illinois UP, 1991.

Walvoord, Barbara, and Lucille McCarthy, eds. *Thinking and Writing in College.* Urbana, IL: NCTE, 1990.

GENDER, CLASS, ETHNICITY

Annas, Pamela J. "Style as Politics: A Feminist Approach to Teaching of Writing." *CE* 47 (Apr. 1985): 369–71.

Ashton-Jones, Evelyn, and D. Thomas. "Composition, Collaboration, and Women's Ways of Knowing." *Journal of Advanced Composition* 10 (1990): 275–92.

Belenky, Mary Field, et al. *Women's Ways of Knowing: The Development of Self, Voice, and Mind.* New York: Basic Books, 1986.

Caywood, Cynthia L., and Gillian R. Overing. *Teaching Writing: Pedagogy, Gender, and Equity.* Albany: SUNY P, 1987.

Eichhorn, Jill, et al. "A Symposium on Feminist Experiences in the Composition Classroom." *CCC* 43 (Oct. 1992): 297–322.

Flynn, Elizabeth A., and Patrocinio Schwickart, eds. *Gender and Reading: Essays on Readers, Texts and Contexts.* Baltimore: Johns Hopkins UP, 1986.

Fontaine, Sheryl, and Susan Hunter, eds. *Writing Ourselves into the Story: Unheard Voices from Composition Studies.* Carbondale: Southern Illinois UP, 1993.

Heath, Shirley Brice. *Ways with Words: Language, Life, and Work in Communities and Classrooms.* Cambridge: Cambridge UP, 1983.

Hill, Carolyn Eriksen. *Writing from the Margins: Power and Pedagogy for Teachers of Composition.* New York: Oxford UP, 1990.

Johnson, D. M., and Duane Roen, eds. *Richness in Writing: Empowering ESL Students.* New York: Longmann, 1989.

Langer, Judith A., ed. *Language, Literacy, and Culture: Issues of Society and Schooling.* Norwood, NJ: Ablex Publishing, 1987.

McCracken, Nancy Mellin, and Bruce C. Appleby. *Gender Issues in the Teaching of English.* Portsmouth, NH: Heinemann, Boynton/Cook, 1992.

McQuade, Donald A., ed. *The Territory of Language: Linguistics, Stylistics, and the Teaching of Composition.* Carbondale: Southern Illinois UP, 1986.

Rose, Mike. *Lives on the Boundary: The Struggles and Achievements of America's Underprepared.* London: Collier-Macmillan, 1989.

Shaughnessy, Mina. *Errors and Expectations.* New York: Oxford UP, 1977.

Smitherman-Donaldson, Ginevra, and Teun A. van Dijk, eds. *Discourse and Discrimination.* Detroit: Wayne State UP, 1988.

Tate, ed. *Black Women Writers at Work.* New York: Continuum, 1985.

Tedesco, J. "Women's Ways of Knowing/Women's Ways of Composing." *Rhetoric Review* 9.2: 246–56.

RESPONDING TO AND EVALUATING STUDENT WRITING

Anson, Cris M. *Writing and Response: Theory, Practice, and Research.* Urbana, IL: NCTE, 1989.

Belanoff, Pat, and Marcia Dickson. *Portfolios: Process and Product.* Portsmouth, NH: Heinemann, Boynton/Cook, 1991.

Cooper, Charles, and Lee Odell, eds. *Evaluating Writing.* Urbana, IL: NCTE, 1977.

Faigley, Lester, et al. *Assessing Writer's Knowledge and Processes of Composing.* Norwood, NJ: Ablex, 1985.

Freedman, Sarah W. *Response to Student Writing.* Urbana, IL: NCTE Research Report No. 23, 1987.

Gorman, T. P., et al., eds. *The IEA Study of Written Compositional Writing Tasks and Scoring Scales.* New York: Pergamon, 1988.

Greenberg, K. L., et al., eds. *Writing Assessment: Issues and Strategies.* New York: Longman, 1986.

Horvath, Brooke K. "The Components of Written Response: A Practical Synthesis of Current Views." *Rhetoric Review* 2 (Jan. 1985): 136–56.

White, Edward M. *Teaching and Assessing Writing.* San Francisco: Jossey, 1985.

Williams, Joseph M. "The Phenomenology of Error." *CCC* 32 (May 1991): 152–68.

Witte, Stephen P., and Lester Faigley. *Evaluating College Writing Programs.* Carbondale: Southern Illinois UP, 1983.

St. Martin's